VIPERS
IN THE
STORM
DIARY OF A GULF WAR
FIGHTER PILOT

VIPERS
IN THE
STORM
DIARY OF A GULF WAR
FIGHTER PILOT

KEITH ROSENKRANZ

McGraw-Hill

New York   San Francisco   Washington, D.C.   Auckland   Bogotá
Caracas   Lisbon   London   Madrid   Mexico City   Milan
Montreal   New Delhi   San Juan   Singapore
Sydney   Tokyo   Toronto

Library of Congress Cataloging-in-Publication Data

Rosenkranz, Keith.
Vipers in the storm: diary of a gulf war fighter pilot/ Keith
Rosenkranz—1st ed.
   p.   cm.
ISBN 0-07-134670-8
1. Rosenkranz, Keith. 2. Persian Gulf War, 1991—Personal narra-
tives, American. 3. Persian Gulf War, 1991—Aerial operations,
American. 4. Fighter pilots—United States—Biography. I. Title
DS79.74.R67 1997
956.7044′248′092—dc21
[B]

97-14209
CIP

McGraw-Hill

A Division of The McGraw-Hill Companies

   3 4 5 6 7 8 9 0 AGM/AGM 9 0 4 3 2 1 0 9

ISBN 0-07-134670-8

Printed and bound by Quebecor/Martinsburg.

The editor for this book was Shelley Carr.

This book is printed on recycled, acid-free paper containing a
minimum of 50% recycled, de-inked paper.

To Colette, Candice, and Kristen

My heart . . . My strength . . . My inspiration

CONTENTS

FOREWORD

Keith Rosenkranz's *Vipers in the Storm* is a remarkable account by one of our outstanding pilots of what it was like to fly an F-16 jet fighter plane in Desert Shield and Desert Storm. His story, based on thirty combat missions over Iraq and Kuwait, is an excellent portrayal of the tremendous skill and dedication of the men and women of today's U.S. Air Force. It also shows the human side of battle from a serviceman's point of view.

One of my most memorable moments of Desert Storm was an afternoon that General Colin Powell and I spent in Saudi Arabia with a group of our pilots, who had been flying missions over Kuwait and Iraq during the air war, prior to the beginning of the ground campaign. It was an unforgettable event because of the immediacy of their combat experiences, and because they were able to give us firsthand accounts of the effectiveness of American air power.

I also remember the day we welcomed home the troops of Desert Storm with a parade down Constitution Avenue in Washington, D.C. It was a grand and glorious occasion, as a grateful nation expressed its thanks to the thousands of servicemen and women who brought us one of the most decisive victories in military history. But before the parade, there was a memorial service at Arlington National Cemetery for those who had paid the ultimate price for that victory. At the end of the service, a group of aircraft passed over Arlington in the "missing man" formation. I will never forget the tragic, stricken faces of the families of those who were killed in action. Reading Capt. Rosenkranz's account of his experiences rekindled all of those memories for me—the pride we all felt in the accomplishments of our armed forces, and the sense of despair over the loss of those who sacrificed everything for our victory.

"Rosey" (Keith's call sign) goes beyond his personal experiences and gives us a first-rate account of the performance of the F-16, and of the grueling and demanding training missions that convert young civilians into the world's finest pilots. His story will have readers "in the cockpit" as he recounts the procedures and the performance of the combat systems of the F-16.

Capt. Rosenkranz also captures the personal costs involved in military service. He relates the frustration that goes with the endless days of waiting for something decisive to happen. He describes the debilitating impact on morale of not knowing what the future may hold, and the fears that are a natural part of contemplating combat for the first time.

Vipers in the Storm accurately reflects the decisive role that the United States Air Force played in defeating Saddam Hussein's military and liberating Kuwait. It is a superb account of modern air warfare. Most of all, it is a reminder of how enormously fortunate we are that there are young Americans like Keith Rosenkranz able and willing to defend the nation.

—Dick Cheney

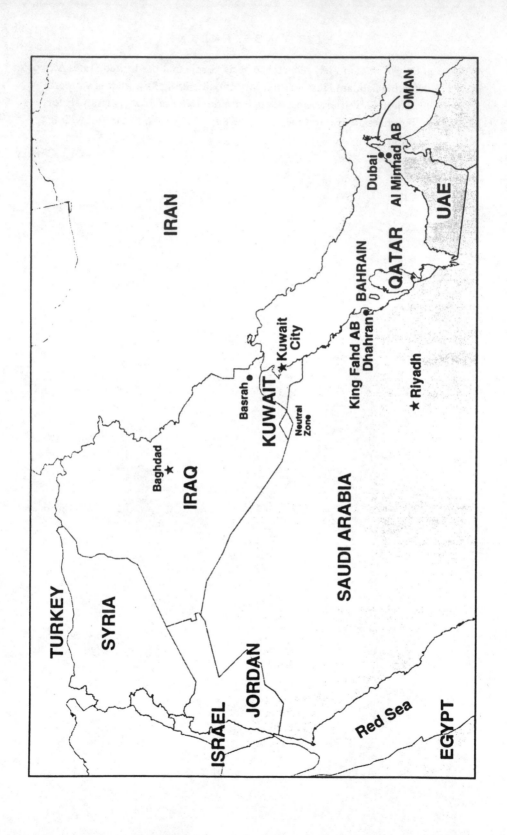

1.
GREEN FLAG

Fuujin 24, disconnect!" As I make the radio call, I nudge my throttle back and watch the refueling boom drift past my canopy. My airspeed is 310 knots, and I'm level at 21,000 feet, slightly below the tail section of a KC-135 Stratotanker. My F-16 is the last of four to refuel in the cloudless sky. Once I clear the tanker I make a gradual descent, float to the right of my element lead, Fuujin 23, and close my air-refueling door. The boom operator retracts the refueling boom, and the tanker begins a lumbering turn to the north. Fuujin 21 and 22, the two other F-16s in our flight, head west, and we follow ten seconds later. I continue to fly fingertip formation off Fuujin 23's right wing. As soon as we pick up the 270-degree heading, my flight lead, Capt. Tim "Bopper" Bopp, porpoises his jet, signaling me to tactical formation. I push my throttle up to military power and position my F-16 about 9,000 feet away and 1,000 feet above his right side. Fuujin 21 and 22 are flying a similar formation three miles ahead of us.

It's a clear July day. The visibility is well over fifty miles. The sun bakes the desert floor below us in triple-digit temperatures. But, for the moment, I'm comfortable in my air-conditioned cockpit. That will all change soon, though. Our four-ship box formation is less than ten minutes from the forward edge of the battle area, what tacticians refer to as the FEBA. A small ridge line ahead marks our descent point. As we approach it, I concentrate on clearing for our formation. We accelerate to 400 knots at an altitude of 20,000 feet.

"Fuujin 21: Go victor 11, fence in!"

"Two!" "Three!" "Four!"

I switch my VHF radio to channel 11 and make one last check of my systems as we prepare to cross the "fence" into enemy territory. I set the range of my radar to forty-mile scope with a search altitude of 20,000 feet and above. I arm my chaff and flare systems, activate my electronic countermeasures pod, adjust the volume on my radar threat warning receiver, and make one last check of my fuel quantity. With these checks complete, I continue to scan the skies for enemy fighters as I wait for our four-ship flight lead, Capt. Scobey "Sudds" Suddreth, to check us in.

"Fuujin 21 check!"

"Two!" "Three!" "Four!"

"Fuujin 21 ops check. One is twenty-seven, thirty-one, eleven-four . . . tanks feeding."

Lt. Bruce "Rip" Stinar, flying in the number two position, responds, "Fuujin 22 is twenty-seven, thirty-one, eleven-three . . . tanks feeding."

Bopper follows with his call, "Fuujin 23 is twenty-seven, thirty-one, eleven-five . . . tanks feeding."

Finally, me, "Rosey": "Fuujin 24 is twenty-seven, thirty-one, eleven-five . . . tanks feeding." Our fuel is good. We're ready for battle.

As we approach the ridge line, Sudds initiates a combat descent for his two-ship element. I watch the two F-16s plummet toward the ground, anxiously waiting for Bopper to follow. When he does, I roll inverted with him and pull the nose of my F-16 down until it is pointed at the desert floor. My aircraft accelerates rapidly as I rocket toward the sand below. I roll upright again—still flying my tactical spread to the right of Bopper—and decrease my descent. In less than a minute, our four-ship descends from 20,000 feet to 300 feet above the ground while accelerating to 480 knots. We're inside enemy territory.

Our low-level ingress takes us across miles of rugged, barren desert. Our plan is to terrain-mask behind a southern ridge line opposite a number of enemy radar installations. Keeping the mountains between our four-ship and our adversary's early-warning radar allows us to fly undetected deep into the enemy's domain. The key to our mission is the element of surprise.

Our target is an SA-8 Gecko missile site situated one mile east of an airfield approximately 200 miles beyond the FEBA. The airfield is a MiG-29 fighter base. Three of our unit's aircraft have already been knocked out by this particular surface-to-air missile (SAM) system over the last four days. The base is heavily defended, and we're expecting resistance from the MiGs. B-52s are scheduled to bomb the enemy base twenty minutes after we depart the area, so it's imperative that our mission be successful.

Destroying the SA-8 site will require superior airmanship from each pilot in our four-ship. The Gecko is a low-altitude surface-to-air missile, 10.5 feet long. It has an effective range of approximately 6.5 nautical miles and can reach speeds up to Mach 2.5 (two-and-a-half times the speed of sound). Its command guidance system can track targets both optically and with radar. Even more impressive, it can intercept aircraft flying as low as 150 feet above the ground. We are expected to destroy the entire SAM site, which includes a radar installation encircled by four missile batteries. Fuujin 21 and 23 will target the radar van, while Fuujin 22 and I attempt to knock out as many of the missile batteries as possible. The four of us are carrying two MK-84 (pronounced *Mark-84*) general purpose bombs that weigh 2,000 pounds apiece. These generate craters fifty feet deep and destroy just about anything within a 1,000-foot radius.

Everything is running smoothly as we approach our first checkpoint on the low-level. I'm still about 9,000 feet from Bopper, and we're flying three miles behind Fuujin 21's element. Since I'm flying in the number four position, I have the added responsibility of checking the four-ship's backside, or six o'clock position, which is the most vulnerable to enemy fighters. I'm also responsible for clearing the area between the elements in case someone tries to jump Sudds and Rip.

2

I incorporate the radar into my cross-check, searching 20,000 feet and above while Bopper searches from the surface up. Reaching the target area undetected is extremely important. The last thing we want to do is encounter a MiG. Even though my radar scope is clear, my head swivels as if it's on a spring, checking left, right, forward, rear, high, low. These simple motions are not so simple while flying a few hundred feet above the ground at 480 knots. Screaming across the desert floor, it seems like I'm spending more time looking to the rear than out front. The slightest trace of complacency or the smallest miscalculation of rising terrain while twisting my body and head could prove fatal. And I'd never even know it.

As we pass over the first checkpoint, Bopper executes a hard turn, 45 degrees to the right. I bank slightly to the left and watch him cross behind me while I check his six. As soon as he passes I go into a hard right turn, timing it to roll out on the opposite side of him in a line-abreast position. We pick up our new heading and begin a shallow climb to crest a fast-approaching hill.

Suddenly Sudds calls out, "Fuujin 21 has two contacts, twenty right for thirty miles, high aspect!"

Bopper replies, "Fuujin 23, same!"

Sudds has to make a quick decision. He calls out again, "Fuujin 21 flight, check twenty left—now!"

There's no reason to answer on the radios. Each of us makes an immediate hard turn, 20 degrees to the left. We don't want to engage the fighters. Instead, we stiff-arm them to the right and remain undetected. The turn puts me slightly ahead of Bopper, so I pull my throttle back to allow him to catch up.

Once we're clear of the fighters, Sudds checks us back on course. We're roughly eight minutes from the initial point (IP), our last checkpoint before the target. My radar warning receiver, or RWR (pronounced *raw*), is quiet. But the silence doesn't mean enemy fighters haven't seen us. I continue clearing, and I make one last check of my air-to-ground systems. We have one more ridge line to cross before the terrain flattens out for good. If enemy radar has not detected us by now, it surely will when we cross that last mountain peak. Once they know the direction from which we are ingressing, it won't take them long to prepare their defenses for our attack.

I check our timing in the bottom-right corner of my head-up display (HUD). We're right on schedule. As we approach the IP, I get a burst of adrenaline. My heart pounds, and my breathing rate increases as I continue to scan the skies for enemy aircraft. I feel like a lone antelope roaming across the plains of Africa while hungry lions lurk behind nearby bushes.

"Fuujin 21, check cameras on HUD, master arm on!" Sudds radios.

"Two!" "Three!" "Four!"

I flip the master arm switch from Simulate to Arm, and then I reach down to turn on my camera. The switch activates an internal VCR that can record the HUD or either one of two multifunction displays (MFDs) that are located on the instrument panel. The videotapes are used to review and critique missions.

Fuujin 21 and 22 accelerate to 540 knots to prepare for the attack. We're on a 140-degree heading, seconds from the IP, which is an intersection of a small service road and a highway that leads into the base. I glance outside and spot the highway below my right wing. The features match my map perfectly. I cross-check my HUD to make sure the diamond symbol of my inertial navigation system (INS) is superimposed over the highway intersection. When I see that the diamond is left of the intersection, I use the cursor/enable switch on my throttle to reposition it to the correct spot. The adjustment updates my IP and target location as well.

Bopper pushes up his power and accelerates to 540 knots. He crosses right over the road intersection and turns 20 degrees to the right, which puts him on our run-in heading to the target. I continue to check our six o'clock while calling up my air-to-ground radar system. I maneuver my F-16 to within 6,000 feet of Bopper and cross over to his right.

Suddenly Sudds's voice erupts over the radio: "Fuujin 21, SA-8 raw . . . left ten o'clock!"

Our formation has been detected. It's up to Sudds's element to take out the radar van before the missile operators have enough time to launch their SAMs. Bopper and I are only thirty seconds behind the lead element. I scan the skies one last time while cross-checking my HUD as the distance measuring equipment (DME) counts down. Only three more miles to the action point!

"Fuujin 21 is in!" Sudds calls out.

At the same time, my RWR lights up, indicating the SAM site's radar has acquired my aircraft. The symbology on the RWR scope and a distinctive chirping noise in my headset let me know that the SA-8 site is still operational.

Rip follows Sudds down the chute and calls out, "Fuujin 22 is in!"

My eyes focus on Bopper as we approach the action point. Our F-16s hug the terrain as we make our final preparations for the attack. At 4.5 DME, Bopper and I snap into a hard right turn. Bopper will attack using the 10-degree low-angle, low-drag method. My attack is called a "20 high."

We use dissimilar attacks for a couple of reasons. The first has to do with the bomb itself. When a MK-84 explodes, blast fragments can fly up to 3,000 feet in all directions. They can take up to thirty seconds to fall. Flying a different attack pattern keeps the second plane away from the fragmentation of the bombs from the first aircraft. The overall strategy is called "deconfliction." Our two-aircraft element is deconflicted from Fuujin 21 and 22 by virtue of the distance we're flying behind them. I'll deconflict from Bopper by dropping my bombs from a higher altitude, thus staying above the fragmentation of his weapons.

The second reason for varying our attacks is to confuse the enemy. We don't want to make it easy for someone on the ground to shoot us down. If each F-16 attacked from the same piece of sky, we would be too predictable. As the last pilot rolling in on the target, I would be the most vulnerable to such an approach.

As soon as we action to the right, I pull the nose of my F-16 up to a climb angle of 30 degrees. During the ascent, I use my left hand to hit the chaff dispense switch, sending multiple bundles of shredded aluminum into the air. The F-16 chaff dispenser diverts radars from antiaircraft artillery (AAA, pronounced triple-A), SAMs, and air-interceptor command guidance systems.

I look to my left and see Bopper slightly below me in a similar climb. The target is at our left ten o'clock, and he will be rolling in any second. I cross-check my HUD for my pull-down altitude of 4,900 feet. My heart is in my throat as I shoot toward the sky. Passing through 3,000 feet, I spot the smoke from the bombs that were dropped by Fuujin 21 and 22. The smoke makes the target easy to identify. It also leaves me with an optimistic feeling that the radar van has been destroyed.

Bopper rolls in and radios, "Fuujin 23 is in!"

As soon as his finger comes off the mike button, Sudds calls out, "Fuujin 21 and 22 are off, egressing south!"

Shortly thereafter, I see 4,900 feet in my HUD, roll into 120 degrees of bank, and make a five-G turn toward the target. I click the mike and make my call: "Fuujin 24 is in!"

Once I'm aligned with the target area, I roll back to wings level. I'm pointed 20 degrees nose low, and I only have a few seconds of track time to acquire the target visually. The radar van is billowing in flames, and just to the right, I see two embankments of dirt built up around the remainder of the SA-8 missile battery. I push the missile step button on the stick, which in the air-to-ground mode calls up the CCIP (continuously computed impact point) pipper and the bomb fall/steering line. While continuing my descent, I make a quick correction to the right, so I can place the bomb fall/steering line over the target. Within two seconds, my pipper reaches the embankment. I press the pickle button, and my F-16 shudders slightly as the two MK-84s fall from my wings. I make an immediate five-G pull toward the sky. As soon as the nose of my F-16 reaches the horizon, I turn hard toward my egress heading. I perform a series of jinking maneuvers to throw off enemy gunners and expend chaff to confuse their radar.

My next priority is to get back down to 300 feet above ground level (AGL) while attempting to locate my element lead. I make my "off target" radio call while descending, and roll out on our egress heading of 180 degrees. I spot Fuujin 23 at my right one o'clock and call for a weave. Bopper acknowledges the call with a shallow turn to his left. Within thirty seconds, I'm abeam him and back in tactical position.

My thumb flips the dogfight/missile override switch on the throttle to the missile override position, which instantly calls up the range-while-search mode of my air-to-air radar. Once again, I'm searching for enemy fighters. Two returns pop up on the scope at my twelve o'clock for ten miles. The returns are Fuujin 21 and 22. Bopper and I keep our speed up as we close the distance between the two elements. All of a sudden, the radio erupts.

"Fuujin 21 is tally-ho bandit . . . twenty left, four miles. Fuujin 21 is engaged!"

"Fuujin 22 supporting!" Rip answers.

Adrenaline shoots through my body as I continue to check our six o'clock. I'm beginning to feel like the antelope again. But still, no MiGs are in sight. A quick check of the radar shows nothing at high altitude. I frantically search the skies and finally spot the engagement a few miles in front of me.

"Fuujin 21, fox two!" Sudds radios. "Fox two" is a standard call made when a pilot launches a heat-seeking missile. After a slight pause, Sudds calls out again, "Fuujin 21, kill the bandit in a right-hand turn at eight thousand feet."

As our element approaches the frenzy, Bopper spots another aircraft attempting to roll in behind Rip. Bopper interjects, "Fuujin 22, break left, break left! Bandit your left seven . . . flare . . . Fuujin 23's engaged!"

Fuujin 22 snaps into a hard left turn and dispenses two flares. Intel briefed that the MiG-29s would likely be armed with AA-8 Aphid infrared heat-seeking missiles. Just over seven feet in length, the Aphid carries a thirteen-pound warhead and can reach speeds in excess of Mach 2. The MiG caught Rip by surprise. If the enemy fires a heatseeking missile, Rip has to hope his flares will lure it away. If the flares don't work, he'll have to rely on the turning capability of his F-16. There's a good chance the missile will overshoot if Rip can turn hard enough and create sufficient angles between the two jets. While he's doing that, Bopper and I will try to enter the fight and shoot down the MiG before he can shoot down Rip.

I rejoin to a fighting wing position and support Bopper while continuing my search for trailing bogeys. Rip's hard turn puts the enemy warplane about two miles in front of Bopper, who hits the pickle button and calls out, "Fuujin 23, fox two!" It's a quick and easy kill.

Sudds calls for an egress heading of 210 degrees. Soon our entire four-ship is back in box formation. Our airspeed approaches 550 knots as we hug the desert floor, speeding toward the FEBA and safe territory.

As soon as we cross the FEBA, Sudds terminates the low-level and then radios, "Fuujin 21 flight, knock it off!" The rest of us respond in order:

"Fuujin 22, knock it off!"

"Fuujin 23, knock it off!"

"Fuujin 24, knock it off!"

We start to climb, and Sudds calls out again, "Fuujin 21 flight, fence out . . . rejoin . . . standby fuel check." I safe up my chaff, flare, and master arm switches, and turn off my camera and countermeasures pod. My fuel checks good, and I quickly rejoin on the right wing of Fuujin 23 as we join the lead element.

Our training mission is over.

We're one hundred miles north of Nellis Air Force Base, just outside of Las Vegas, Nevada. Drenched with sweat, I complete a battle-damage check on the other F-16s and then assume a loose route position for the flight back. It appears that our mission has been a success. I'm anxious to see the results.

After landing, the four of us walked back to the squadron and reviewed our film. Everyone dropped good bombs and both of the missile shots were legitimate as well. After we reviewed the film, we grabbed sodas and filed into the mass-briefing room. About fifty other pilots representing the six different squadrons participating in the exercise filed in as well. Every unit flew a different type of aircraft and played a specific role, but as a group we had one thing in common: We were USAF pilots training for a desert war.

The exercise was called "Green Flag." I was a member of the 4th Tactical Fighter Squadron's Fightin' Fuujins, representing the 388th Tactical Fighter Wing from Hill AFB, Utah. We'd been in Las Vegas for nearly two weeks, flying missions similar to the one just completed. The other pilots participating in the exercise had come from as far away as Europe to take part in the mock battle.

Our mission was considered successful because we destroyed our target and returned home safely to talk about it. Actually, this was only the third time in seven that I'd survived without being shot down by an enemy fighter or ground defense system. Taking part in a Green Flag exercise is as close to war as one can get without actually fighting. The flying is extremely demanding.

At the conclusion of the briefing, the Green Flag commander congratulated us on a good day of flying and turned the debrief over to a pair of officers from the Nellis AFB intel division. Each wing has an intel branch with representatives working in each squadron. Their job is to help educate the pilots on the military systems of other countries and to keep the unit updated on world events. They usually focus on the Soviet Union, but this afternoon's intel briefing covered a different area of the world: the Middle East.

The young air force major approached the microphone and announced the shocking news: "Iraqi forces have invaded the tiny country of Kuwait."

Earlier in the week, during a routine briefing, we were informed of an Iraqi troop presence on Kuwait's northern border. American warships were put on an increased state of alert. But, according to intelligence sources, the Iraqi buildup was considered to be nothing more than an act of intimidation on the part of Saddam Hussein.

"It's still too early to speculate," the officer said. "We'll know more in twenty-four hours, and as soon as we have any details to pass along, you'll be notified."

The briefing concluded, and everyone in the hall was dismissed. As we gravitated toward the exits, the topic of discussion was the invasion. Many of us wondered aloud what would happen if Kuwait sought America's assistance. We were all keenly aware of the Persian Gulf's strategic importance to the United States and its allies. The security of the region was vital, and the only question was how far America would go to protect it.

2.
OIL AND WAR

After planning the next day's mission, we returned to our hotel just outside the main gate at Nellis. After a quick shower, I relaxed in front of the television and watched the unfolding news of Iraq's invasion of Kuwait. The Middle East was rocked by shock waves at the thought of one Arab country having invaded another. But instability has plagued this region for years. The main ingredient, of course, is oil—the lifeblood of the world's economy.

The United States has always played an active role in the Middle East. In the early 1970s, our staunchest ally in the region was Iran, who, at the time, was the second largest exporter of oil to the world. The United States depended on Iranian oil; and the ruler of Iran, Shah Mohammed Reza Pahlavi, depended heavily on U.S. military arms and advisors. This relationship started to deteriorate in late 1978 when religious factions began to challenge the shah's rule. Americans and other foreigners began to flee, and on 16 January 1979, the shah himself left the country never to return.

Our other ally in the region was Saudi Arabia, the most powerful member of the Organization of Petroleum Exporting Countries (OPEC). But Saudi Arabia's confidence in America was shaken by the turmoil in Iran and by Soviet gains in Ethiopia, Afghanistan, and Yemen. The Saudis had witnessed the collapse of Iran's government, and many officials viewed the United States as both unable and unwilling to do anything about it.

On 22 September 1980, Iraq, led by Saddam Hussein, commenced an eight-year war with Iran. Fielding a powerful army, Saddam's socialist Baath Party made no secret of its desire to replace both Iran as the premier military power in the region, and Egypt as leader of the Arab world. Iraq's invasion of Iran stemmed from ancient hatreds, territorial claims, and religious tensions. What Saddam Hussein wanted most of all, though, was the strategic Shatt al-Arab waterway, where the Tigris and Euphrates rivers merge to form part of the border between the two nations. The narrow 120-mile waterway flows into the Persian Gulf; and to expand his oil revenue, Saddam needed the outlet so he could build a major shipping port and gain access to the Gulf. But the Iranian oil cities of Khorramshahr and Abadan also relied on the Shatt al-Arab waterway, and Iran's Shiite religious leader Ayatollah Ruhollah Khomeini had no intention of relinquishing it to Saddam Hussein.

The United States considered an Iranian victory over Iraq a significant threat to the Middle East, both politically and militarily. After Khomeini's forces achieved a significant military victory at the Faw peninsula in early 1986, America had no choice but to support

Iraq. But when Saddam's troops gained an upper hand in the fighting, Saudi Arabia and other Gulf states became disturbed over the influence that a victorious Iraq would have on oil policies and Gulf security. The fighting halted shipments of almost three million barrels of oil a day to the rest of the world. The hostilities, combined with the shortage of oil, brought the United States and Saudi Arabia closer together; and the Saudi military, which was no match for Iraq's or Iran's, finally requested military backing in case things got out of hand. The United States sent E-3A Airborne Warning and Control System (AWACS) aircraft to the area to bolster Saudi Arabia's air defenses, and began stocking Saudi bases with fuel, parts, and munitions. Egypt asked the United States to intervene in the region as well, and Oman made its bases available to U.S. jets for refueling.

By 1987, the two countries were still at war and casualties had reached nearly one million. Each side accused the other of smuggling arms into the Gulf, and threatened to attack ships transiting Persian Gulf waters. American warships patrolled the region, searching for mines and letting their presence be felt by both Iran and Iraq. Still, many countries feared that the fighting would soon spill over into their territory. One of these nations was Kuwait, which was closer to the action than any other.

Kuwait, slightly smaller than the state of New Jersey, is situated on Iraq's southern border at the western edge of the Persian Gulf. Though tiny, the country possesses more crude oil per square mile than any other nation on earth; however, its small military was no match for either Iraq or Iran. Even though the two countries were not the best of friends, Kuwait sided with Iraq for ethnic and religious reasons. Most of Kuwait's citizens were Sunni Muslims, who feared Iran's militant Shiites. Kuwait allowed Iraqi war planes to overfly its airspace to attack Iranian-bound tankers, and the emir of Kuwait supplied Saddam Hussein with billions of dollars to bolster Iraq's war-torn economy.

Fearing Iranian attacks against its own tankers and supply ships, Kuwait sought protection from the United States, requesting American warships to escort its tankers in and out of the Gulf. Congress feared that escorting Kuwaiti tankers under the auspices of the American flag—"reflagged"—might draw American servicemen even deeper into the conflict. Once Congress found out the Soviet Union had been given the same offer, though, it decided to step in.

On 17 May 1987, an Iraqi jet fired a French-built Exocet missile at the USS *Stark*, killing thirty-seven American sailors. The Iraqi government claimed the attack was an accident and sent an official apology to the United States. They also agreed to compensate the sailors' families and pay reparations for the ship. Another incident occurred on 24 July 1987, when the reflagged tanker *Bridgeton* hit a mine near Iran's Farsi island. It was the fifth vessel damaged since mid-May.

Iran's attacks on shipping escalated until July 1988, when the USS *Vincennes*, patrolling waters northwest of Oman and fifty miles south of Iran, responded to gunfire against one of its helicopters. In the ensuing battle, the *Vincennes* and a companion ship destroyed two Iranian gunboats and damaged a third. During the skirmish, Iran Air Flight 655, a civilian airliner, was mistaken for a hostile military aircraft and shot down, killing its 290 passengers. The unfortunate incident turned out to be a turning point in the war. On 20 August 1988, Iran and Iraq agreed unconditionally to accept a United Nations cease-fire resolution.

The prolonged war left Iraq's economy in shambles. The quickest way for Saddam Hussein to revitalize his country was to expand his oil exports. Iraqi production peaked at three million barrels per day, but even this was not enough to help Saddam bail out a swamped economy and pay the massive war debt, most of which was owed to Kuwait. Saddam needed access to the Persian Gulf, and since the eight-year war with Iran did not win the strategic Shatt al-Arab waterway, he decided to turn his attention to Kuwait.

A large estuary lies near Kuwait's northeast border, just south of Basrah and west of the Shatt al-Arab waterway. The Iraqi shoreline in this area is no more than twenty miles long. Facing the entrance to the estuary are Warba and Bubiyan, two uninhabited islands belonging to Kuwait. As an alternative to the Shatt al-Arab, Saddam Hussein sought access to the Gulf by widening and extending this estuary until it reached Basrah. To complete the task, he would need to control Warba and Bubiyan, which guard the entrance to the city of Umm Qasr, Iraq's only functioning port on the Gulf.

In September 1989, the emir of Kuwait, Sheikh Jaber al-Ahmad al-Sabah, made his first trip to Iraq in more than a decade to receive Iraq's highest honor, the Rafadin Medal. Kuwait had loaned more money to Iraq than any other country and had remained a staunch supporter of Saddam Hussein during the war. But the friendship didn't last long. The emir refused to lease the strategic islands to Saddam and sent hopeful Kuwaiti officials to Baghdad to negotiate a nonaggression pact. Saddam Hussein not only refused to sign, he reiterated his demands for the disputed islands, and then informed the Kuwaiti officials that he had no intention of paying back the billions of dollars their country had loaned him. The emir had badly miscalculated when he assumed that his loans to Saddam Hussein would buy his country peace.

In early 1990, the price of oil began to drop steadily. At the Arab League summit meeting in May, Saddam Hussein accused Kuwait and the United Arab Emirates (UAE) of exceeding their OPEC production quotas, driving down prices. The Iraqi leader said his country was losing $1 billion per year in revenue for every one-dollar drop in oil prices, and on 17 July 1990, he called the overproduction "an act of war." Saddam said that the UAE and Kuwait were part of "an imperialist-Zionist plot against the Arab nation," and force might be required to stop them from strangling his economy. One week later, just before OPEC's midyear meeting in Geneva, Saddam Hussein placed a division of Iraq's elite Republican Guard on Kuwait's northern border. Kuwait and the UAE gave in to Saddam's threats and agreed to OPEC's first price hike in four years, from eighteen to twenty-one dollars per barrel.

Saddam Hussein used the minor victory to portray Iraq as the new superpower in the Middle East, but instead of withdrawing his forces, he claimed to have evidence that Kuwait intended to renege on the agreement at Jidda within two months and shift back to its old policy. He sent 70,000 more troops to the border and demanded that all of

Iraq's war debt be forgiven. He also demanded the strategic islands of Warba and Bubiyan, and insisted that Kuwait, along with the Saudis, give financial assistance for the rebuilding of Iraq. Saddam claimed that Iraqi soldiers had fought against Iran on behalf of all Arabs, and that the two countries should consider the loans they made to him as payment for victory and stability in the region. He also accused Kuwait of expanding its border 2.5 miles to the north, into Iraq, so it could pump oil from the rich Rumaila oil field. Saddam's foreign minister, Tariq Aziz, said this was "tantamount to an act of war." Saddam wanted the border "reinstated" and he demanded $2.4 billion in compensation for the oil he claimed belonged to Iraq.

Tensions in the Middle East increased to their highest level since the Iran-Iraq War. The United States became concerned because much of its oil is imported from the Middle East, and rising prices could send its already weak economy into a recession. The UAE became concerned as well and asked Washington to conduct joint maneuvers. The United States agreed, sending a number of combat ships and air force refueling planes to the area.

On 25 July 1990, April Glaspie, America's ambassador in Baghdad, met with Saddam Hussein. According to an Iraqi transcript of the meeting, Glaspie told Saddam Hussein that she admired the effort he was making to rebuild his country. "I have lived here for years," she said. "I know you need funds. We understand that, and our opinion is that you should have the opportunity to rebuild your country. But we have no opinion on the Arab-Arab conflicts, like your border disagreement with Kuwait."

"We want to find a just solution which will give us our rights, but not deprive others of their rights," Saddam Hussein replied. "I told the Arab kings and presidents that some brothers are fighting an economic war against us. And that not all wars use weapons, and we regard this kind of war as a military action against us."

Saddam went on to say that he had spoken with Egyptian president Hosni Mubarak, and that the Kuwaitis had agreed to a meeting which would involve their prime minister and Iraq's deputy chairman of the Revolutionary Command Council. The meetings would be held in Saudi Arabia, then shift to Baghdad for deeper discussions.

President Mubarak told Saddam that the Kuwaitis feared the troop concentrations; to which he replied: "Regardless of what is there, whether they are police, border guards, or army, and regardless of how many are there, and what they are doing, assure the Kuwaitis and give them our word that we are not going to do anything until we meet with them. When we meet and when we see that there is hope, then nothing will happen. But if we are unable to find a solution, then it will be natural that Iraq will not accept death, even though wisdom is above everything else."

By 30 July, eight Iraqi divisions and 350 tanks were poised on the Kuwaiti border. Kuwait's crown prince, Sheikh Saad al-Sabah, and the vice chairman of Iraq's Revolutionary Command Council, Izzat Ibrahim, met on 1 August in Jidda. Kuwait said it would pay Iraq a sizable price in exchange for peace, but talks between the two countries broke down. In the early morning hours of 2 August 1990, more than 100,000

Iraqi soldiers stormed into Kuwait. Iraqi commando units were also involved, assaulting Kuwait by both sea and air. Iraqi troops advanced to the south, and artillery units attacked Kuwait's northernmost base at Ali Al-Salim. The airfield was quickly captured, but not before fifteen Kuwaiti Mirage F-1s escaped to Saudi Arabia and Bahrain. For a short time, Kuwaiti defense units held their ground with American-built Hawk SAMs, which destroyed twenty-three Iraqi aircraft. But the Iraqis had overwhelming firepower. When the Kuwaiti defenses exhausted their supply of Hawk missiles, they were overrun.

As fighting continued, Iraqi armored divisions advanced toward Kuwait City along a modern highway that had been built between the two countries as a symbol of friendship. The Kuwaitis put up little resistance along the road, and it took only a few hours for Iraqi troops to reach the Kuwaiti capital. Hundreds of tanks roamed through the city while fifty more surrounded both the emir's palace and the U.S. embassy. Panicked residents, fleeing their homes to escape to Saudi Arabia, were dragged from their cars and beaten. A two-hour battle for the palace took place and, once again, the Kuwaiti army succumbed. The emir and his family escaped by helicopter to Saudi Arabia, where they quickly established a government in exile.

In less than one day, Iraqi forces had seized Kuwait, placing roughly 20 percent of the world's oil reserves in the hands of Saddam Hussein. He instantly became the strongest leader in the Arab world, and declared that oil should be used as a weapon against the United States and Israel. Iraq now ranked second to Saudi Arabia as the world's largest oil power.

One day after Iraq's invasion, I flew my last Green Flag training sortie. The attack against Kuwait was a hot topic. We couldn't help but wonder if the United States might become involved militarily. Iraq's assault added realism to our final training scenario: an all-out attack against an enemy airfield. The large force employment consisted of more than eighty aircraft, and, once again, the 4th TFS Fightin' Fuujins performed extremely well. The majority of our squadron's F-16s successfully destroyed their assigned targets. Unfortunately, I learned during the debrief that I was one of three aircraft shot down by an SA-6 missile system during egress.

Later that night, my friends and I ventured downtown to Caesar's Palace, hoping to take a few extra dollars back home to Utah. We befriended a blackjack dealer named Roberta who asked us the question we were all asking ourselves: Would our unit be sent to the Middle East?

Nobody knew. But our experiences in the Green Flag exercises had given us confidence. We joked among ourselves about the coincidence of flying F-16s in a desert warfare exercise and the possibility of doing it for real if the United States became involved in the dispute between Iraq and Kuwait.

3.
VIPER

Two days after Iraqi troops invaded Kuwait, with many of us still wondering what America's response would be, we prepared to return to Hill AFB in Utah. A third of the squadron flew from Nellis at 09:00, and the rest of us assembled in front of the hotel to take a bus. The trip would be a long one. It was already 93 degrees outside, and the temperature would hit 110 by early afternoon. Riding on a hot bus through the Nevada desert in the middle of summer is not the way to return from a successful training deployment. Given a choice, I'd have preferred to fly home in an air-conditioned F-16. But the squadron had more pilots than aircraft.

Interstate 15 isn't far from the hotel, and as we proceeded north, the Las Vegas skyline was visible off the right side of the bus. Some of the guys were still talking about all the money they had won at Caesar's Palace the night before. "That blackjack dealer, Roberta, was awesome last night," Jeff "Ark" Arkell blurted out. "I couldn't lose!"

"Let's plan a trip with the wives," I replied. "We'll get a few couples together and come down for a weekend."

"I'm game."

"Count me in too," said Phil "Opie" Oppenheimer.

We all had a great time. The deployment gave everyone an opportunity to get to know one another, and I made some good friends. Our squadron had great leadership, and I could tell the next few years were going to be very enjoyable for me and my wife, Colette.

By midafternoon, our bus had crossed the Nevada border into southern Utah. There wasn't a cloud in the sky, and the heat was blistering. Every window on the bus was open, but none of it was enough to keep us from baking. Some guys passed the time playing cards, while others slept or talked. I stared out at the mountains, thinking about Colette and our twin girls, Candice and Kristen. I pictured the two of them playing in our backyard or chasing our cat, Gizmo, around the house.

Finally, a security guard waved our bus through the southern gate of Hill AFB, one of the most beautiful bases in the U.S. Air Force. Thirty miles north of Salt Lake City, the base sits on a plateau at the foot of the Wasatch Range. In the winter, the mountains are covered with snow, but that day they were lush with vegetation.

There are two fighter wings at Hill: the 419th Tactical Fighter Wing (an air force reserve unit) and the 388th Tactical Fighter Wing, which consists of three operational fighter squadrons—the 4th TFS Fightin' Fuujins, the 421st TFS Black Widows, and the 34th TFS Rams.

During the Vietnam War, the U.S. Air Force and the pilots of the 388th relied heavily upon the F-105 Thunderchief and the F-4 Phantom II. The F-105, nicknamed the "Thud," was designed as a supersonic fighter-bomber that traded maneuverability for speed and bomb capacity. The F-4 Phantom II, primarily designed as an air-superiority fighter, weighed close to 60,000 pounds and flew escort missions for the F-105. The multirole F-4 dropped tons of bombs and racked up 107 MiG kills, more than any other aircraft during the war. During the Vietnam era, the air force increasingly relied on heavier aircraft that could fly long distances and strike targets deep inside enemy territory. Aircraft like the F-4 could carry a heavy payload as well as an ample supply of long-range air-to-air missiles. When missiles like the AIM-7 Sparrow were developed, many air force leaders felt that close-in aerial dogfighting would be de-emphasized. Unfortunately, American pilots fighting in Vietnam had to follow strict rules of engagement that required them to visually identify North Vietnamese aircraft before firing their missiles. The result was more aerial dogfighting against an arsenal of Soviet fighters that were specifically built to outmaneuver the heavy U.S. fighter-bombers in a close-in fight.

In the late 1960s, air force planners began to develop an air-superiority fighter they felt would eventually replace the F-4 Phantom II. The concept they came up with was called the "Fighter Experimental," or FX. The FX's primary mission was going to be air superiority with a secondary mission of air-to-ground. In September 1968, the FX became the F-15, and McDonnell Douglas was awarded a contract to build the new fighter. The YF-15 Eagle finally made its first flight in July 1972. Capable of exceeding Mach 2 and armed with heat-seeking and radar missiles, the F-15 was supposed to be the USAF answer to the Soviet Union's increasing stockpile of fighter aircraft. But some saw the twin-engine F-15 as too heavy and too expensive to meet the Soviet threat.

While the FX program was taking shape, a small group of men began to promote the concept of a less expensive lightweight fighter that could more flexibly challenge Soviet aircraft. One of this group was an air force officer named John Boyd, a fighter pilot who flew F-86s during the Korean War, then served as an instructor at the U.S. Air Force's Fighter Weapons School, Nellis AFB. He taught other pilots his air combat strategies and published a number of articles during his tour, including a catalog of tactics and maneuvers entitled "Aerial Attack Study." Boyd felt strongly that the air force should turn its attention to aircraft that could strike quickly and outmaneuver enemy fighters during one-on-one dogfights.

In late 1966, Boyd was transferred to the Pentagon, where he joined forces with Pierre Sprey, a weapons and systems analyst who worked in the Office of the Secretary of Defense (OSD). Sprey studied the development of various fighter aircraft, including the F-15. Like Boyd, he also concluded that the military was making a mistake by developing sophisticated aircraft that were large and expensive. In 1967, Boyd and Sprey began to advocate a fighter that would be inexpensive to produce, weigh only about 25,000 pounds, and outperform any other aircraft in a close-in battle.

Two years later, Boyd and Sprey joined forces with Col. Everest E. Riccioni, who believed that the navy was secretly working on the development of a lightweight air-superiority aircraft. The navy had already imposed two of its aircraft designs on the air force, the McDonnell Douglas F-4 Phantom II and the LTV A-7 Corsair. Riccioni was determined not to let that happen again. Yet air force brass saw the trio as conspirators looking to kill the F-15—they were dubbed the "Lightweight Fighter Mafia."

Toward the end of the Vietnam War, the Nixon administration began to take a hard look at the increasing cost of military weapon systems. Two systems in particular, the F-14 Tomcat and the F-15 Eagle, drew criticism from several senators and congressmen. Many of them felt the new weapon systems would cost several times more than the aircraft they were supposed to replace. If Congress decided not to fund the F-14, and if the F-15's high-cost components didn't develop properly, the navy would be in a good position to promote its new lightweight fighter. Once again, the air force would be forced to take on another navy-designed aircraft. In March 1970, Col. Riccioni expressed his concerns in a memorandum written to Lt. Gen. Otto Glasser, Deputy Chief of Staff for Research and Development. Lt. Gen. Glasser, an advocate of an air force lightweight fighter, encouraged Col. Riccioni to continue with his research. By 1970, Sprey's concepts and Boyd's philosophy concerning combat tactics had finally caught the attention of air force planners, but when Gen. John C. Meyer, Vice Chief of Staff, got wind of what was going on, he told Lt. Gen. Glasser that he wanted Riccioni out of the Pentagon. In March 1971, Riccioni was relieved of his job as Chief of Development, Plans and Analysis, and was assigned to Korea. In the months preceding his departure, Riccioni teamed with Boyd and Sprey and prepared a presentation called "The Falcon Brief," and Sprey was given an opportunity to testify before the Senate Armed Services Committee. Shortly thereafter, the Pentagon finally decided to go forward with a lightweight fighter development program. Requests for proposals (RFPs) were sent to the aerospace industry on 6 January 1972, and five companies responded: General Dynamics, Northrop, Boeing, Lockheed, and LTV. Emerging as the two finalists were General Dynamics, which proposed a single-engine fighter called the YF-16, and Northrop, which proposed a twin-engine prototype designated the YF-17. On 13 April 1972, both companies were awarded development contracts worth nearly $38 million dollars apiece.

Twenty-one months after the contracts were awarded, General Dynamics became the first to unveil its new prototype. The sleek new fighter, painted red, white, and blue, was armed with Sidewinder heat-seeking missiles and a twenty-millimeter multibarrel rotary cannon capable of firing 6,000 rounds per minute. The YF-16's fly-by-wire control system replaced heavy cables, pulleys, pushrods, and mechanical linkages. This dramatic decrease in weight allowed the aircraft to carry 15,000 pounds of bombs and equipment. The YF-16 weighed 22,800 pounds and measured forty-seven feet in length.

It was supposed to exceed Mach 2 and fly more than 2,000 miles without refueling. It had a bubble-shaped canopy, the first of its kind, which provided more visibility than any other fighter. Cockpit controls were within easy reach, and the aircraft was equipped with a side-stick controller that operated the flight controls electronically when the pilot applied pressure. Seats in normal fighters are tilted back approximately 13 degrees, but the seat in the YF-16 was tilted back 30 degrees to increase the pilot's G tolerance and rearward visibility.

The YF-16 was the first of the two prototypes to make it into the air. In January 1974, a General Dynamics test pilot named Philip Oestricher was performing a high-speed taxi test. During the test, he discovered a problem with the horizontal stabilizer, which caused the aircraft to inadvertently lift off the ground. Instead of risking a high-speed abort, Oestricher allowed the aircraft to fly and was airborne for approximately six minutes before safely landing. A month later, on 2 February 1974, the YF-16 finally made its first official flight. The YF-17 didn't fly until 9 June. By then, the YF-16 was well into its flight-test program.

The air force decided to stage a fly-off between the two prototypes. Over the next eleven months, two YF-16s and two YF-17s were put through a series of comprehensive tests at Edwards AFB. The competition was fierce and the stakes got higher when officials from General Dynamics and Northrop learned that several NATO allies were also interested in replacing their aging fleet of aircraft. Denmark, Belgium, the Netherlands, and Norway formed a consortium and let it be known that they would negotiate for 350 new aircraft to replace their Lockheed F-104 Starfighters. Their choice would come down to France's Mirage F-1, Sweden's Viggen, or the winner of the fly-off between General Dynamics and Northrop.

The European consortium was in a hurry to make a decision, and Secretary of Defense James R. Schlesinger promised them that the winning prototype would be announced by January 1975. A month before the scheduled announcement, air force officials conducted their evaluations of all the flight-test data. Each prototype had flown more than 300 hours, and many predicted the General Dynamics YF-16 would emerge as the winner of the competition. As it turned out, the predictions were right on. The YF-16 was clearly the superior aircraft. It outperformed the YF-17 in both the transonic and supersonic portions of the air combat flight routine. The YF-16 was more maneuverable and could fly farther and faster than the YF-17. Its single-engine design was also much more fuel-efficient than its twin-engine competitor.

Air Force Secretary John L. McLucas received a final briefing on 7 January 1975, and six days later he announced that General Dynamics had won the lucrative air force contract. He said the U.S. Air Force would buy 650 F-16s at a cost of $4.3 billion. In July, the European consortium announced they had also chosen the General Dynamics F-16 as the replacement for the F-104. Denmark announced they would purchase 58 F-16s, Norway wanted 72, the Netherlands 102, and Belgium 116. The 348 aircraft would cost approximately $6 million apiece, for a total cost of about $2.2 billion.

Shortly after the European announcement, a co-production agreement between the United States and the four NATO countries was signed. The new agreement became the largest international military co-production program in history. Full-scale production of the F-16 began at the General Dynamics plant in Fort Worth, Texas, and involved fifty-five major U.S. subcontractors and approximately 4,000 other firms. The European-built F-16s were assembled in the Netherlands by Fokker Aircraft and in Belgium by SONACA/SABCA. Production of the European F-16s involved sixty-three U.S. subcontractors and twenty-nine European manufacturers.

In November 1978, the first F-16 maintenance hands-on trainer was delivered to the 388th TFW at Hill AFB, Utah. The following month the 388th received its first F-16B, a two-seat version of the F-16 that would be used to train new pilots. The initial cadre of pilots, including one Royal Netherlands pilot, completed their F-16 training on 18 December 1978. They were subsequently assigned to the 16th Tactical Fighter Training Squadron (TFTS), which was officially activated on 1 January 1979. The 16th TFTS became the first F-16 replacement training unit (RTU), and the squadron's first class consisted of pilots from the 34th TFS at Hill. The 34th TFS Rams became the second squadron, and first operational fighter squadron, to start flying the F-16.

By the end of 1979, the U.S. Air Force had accepted delivery of sixty-five F-16s. That same year, Belgium accepted delivery of fourteen, and seven more were sent to the Netherlands. The remaining two members of the European consortium, Denmark and Norway, began receiving aircraft the following year.

In March 1980, pilots from the 4th TFS at Hill began transitioning from the F-4D Phantom II to the F-16A. The conversion was complete by the end of the year and the 4th TFS Fightin' Fuujins became the first F-16 squadron to attain C-1 status, a combat rating that requires a minimum number of aircraft and crews to be ready in the event of war.

The 421st TFS Black Widows received its first F-16 in June 1980; they were the last of the four squadrons at Hill to start flying the new fighter, which still didn't have an official name. In 1977, General Dynamics proposed the name "Falcon" for the F-16. But the Dassault Fan Jet Falcon already carried that name, so Falcon couldn't be used. Over the next three years, names like "Persuader," "Eaglet," and "Condor" were considered. Condor almost made it, but like the others, it too was eventually discarded. Fighter pilots flying the F-16 started referring to the aircraft as the "Viper." The name was extremely popular—even today, most fighter pilots still call it that—but that name was also rejected. Three years after General Dynamics first proposed the name "Falcon," the word "Fighting" was added to the front, and the F-16 finally had its name. On 21 July 1980, during a ceremony at Hill AFB, the 388th TFW commander's aircraft was christened the "Fighting Falcon."

It didn't take long for other foreign nations to realize that the F-16 would evolve into one of the world's top fighters. Israel ordered seventy-five F-16s from General Dynamics, and the first was delivered in July 1980. Eleven months later, the F-16 engaged in combat duty for the first time. On 7 June 1981, Israeli fighter pilots used eight of them to attack Iraq's Osirak nuclear power plant. The mission was a complete success.

In July 1981, the 8th TFW at Kunsan AB, Korea, became the first unit of the Pacific Air Forces (PACAF) to fly the Fighting Falcon. Six months later, the 50th TFW at Hahn AB, Germany, became the first unit of the U.S. Air Forces in Europe (USAFE) to start flying the F-16. By the end of the year, the air force had accepted delivery of 351 aircraft. General Dynamics also received orders from Egypt and Pakistan. These two nations would start receiving their aircraft in 1982.

During the first two years of production, F-16As coming off the assembly line were equipped with Block 10 avionics. But by the end of 1981, significant technological improvements were being made by engineers at General Dynamics, and the models sent to the 50th TFW at Hahn AB, Germany, were the first equipped with Block 15 avionics. Throughout the rest of 1982, Block 15 aircraft were delivered to air force units at Kunsan AB, Korea, Shaw AFB, South Carolina, and Hill AFB, Utah. The USAF Thunderbirds aerial demonstration team, which had been flying the T-38, also accepted delivery of the newest version of the F-16.

On 25 March 1983, the 16th TFTS at Hill AFB graduated its last class of RTU students. Over 1,000 F-16s were being flown by more than a dozen units in the United States and overseas. To handle the large influx of new training, F-16 RTUs were established at MacDill AFB in Tampa, Florida, and at Luke AFB in Phoenix, Arizona.

Over four years, the 16th TFTS had trained approximately 240 pilots for worldwide assignments in the F-16. On 1 April 1983, a week after the last class graduated, the 16th TFTS became the fourth operational fighter squadron at Hill AFB. At that point, the 388th TFW was out of the training business. The following January, the 419th TFW (air force reserve) was activated at Hill, and the total number of tactical fighter squadrons on base increased to five.

In 1984, the first F-16C developed under the F-16 Multinational Staged Improvement Program (MSIP) rolled off the assembly line at General Dynamics' Fort Worth division. The new aircraft, equipped with Block 25 avionics, included a new Westinghouse APG-68 multimode radar; two MFDs to control options for stores, sensors, radar, and other avionic systems; a larger head-up display; an up-front control system; and many other improvements. The first wing to accept delivery of the new aircraft was the 58th TFTW at Luke AFB. The first jets arrived in October 1984, and a few months later, fighter pilots from Shaw AFB in South Carolina arrived to begin their transition training from the F-16A to the F-16C. In April 1985, the 363rd TFW at Shaw AFB became the first operational fighter wing to start flying the new F-16C. Every F-16 manufactured up until this point had been fitted with the Pratt & Whitney F-100-PW-200 engine, which produces 25,000 pounds of thrust and yields a 1.1 to 1 thrust-to-weight ratio. In October 1986, the first Block 30 aircraft, equipped with an engine even more powerful than the Pratt & Whitney, was delivered to Ramstein AB, Germany. The newest F-16C was fitted with the

General Electric F110-GE-100 engine, providing 27,000 pounds of thrust—2,000 pounds more than the PW-200. Because of the increased thrust, these aircraft had larger intakes, called "big mouths."

By the end of 1986, 1,680 F-16s had been produced and sold to ten different countries, including the United States. The U.S. Air Force purchased 1,073 of the aircraft—785 F-16A/Bs and 288 F-16C/Ds. The remaining 607 jets were purchased by Israel, Egypt, Pakistan, Venezuela, Korea, and the four NATO countries in Europe—Denmark, Belgium, the Netherlands, and Norway.

On 28 June 1986, the 16th TFS at Hill AFB was deactivated, leaving the 388th TFW with three operational fighter squadrons. All three squadrons continued to fly the F-16A until July 1989, when the 388th became the first wing to receive new F-16Cs with Block 40 avionics. The aircraft were equipped with GE F110 engines, and the Block 40 upgrade introduced low-altitude navigation and targeting infrared for night (LANTIRN) to the fighter community. An upgraded avionic system and a larger head-up display were added to facilitate use of the new forward-looking infrared (FLIR) system, which allowed pilots to attack targets at night using tactics similar to those employed in daylight.

All three squadrons at Hill completed their transition to the F-16C Block 40 by the beginning of 1990. By June, pilots from the 34th TFS Rams were receiving LANTIRN training at Luke AFB; the Rams were scheduled to become the first operational LANTIRN squadron in the United States.

I completed my tour at Kunsan AB in February 1990 and attended Squadron Officer School at Maxwell AFB, Alabama, during March and April. I began LANTIRN training in May and arrived at Hill AFB on 1 June as the wing's first LANTIRN-qualified pilot. But instead of becoming a member of the Rams, I was assigned to the 4th TFS Fightin' Fuujins.

As of 2 August 1990, the day Iraq invaded Kuwait, 2,683 F-16s had been produced. Thirty-nine U.S. Air Force bases, including guard, reserve, overseas, test, and training, were equipped with the F-16. F-16Ns were being flown by pilots at three different navy bases, and fifteen foreign nations were also flying the F-16. The airplane's versatility made it the premier multirole fighter in the world. It started out as nothing more than a test bed for emerging aircraft technologies, but today, the F-16 is the world's most sought-after fighter.

F-16 COCKPIT ARRANGEMENT

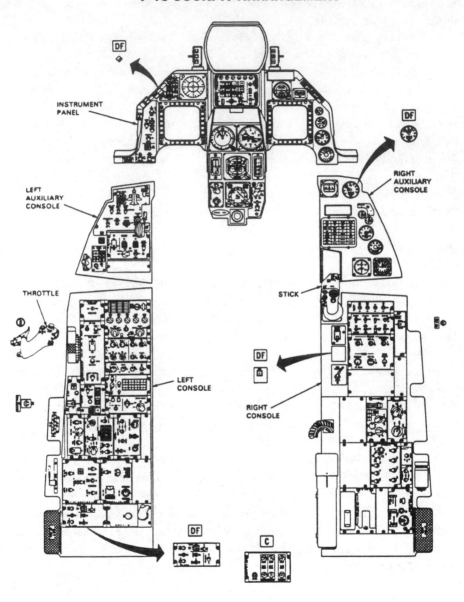

INSTRUMENT PANEL

LEFT AUXILIARY CONSOLE

RIGHT AUXILIARY CONSOLE

THROTTLE

STICK

LEFT CONSOLE

RIGHT CONSOLE

DF

DF

DF

DF

C

LEFT CONSOLE

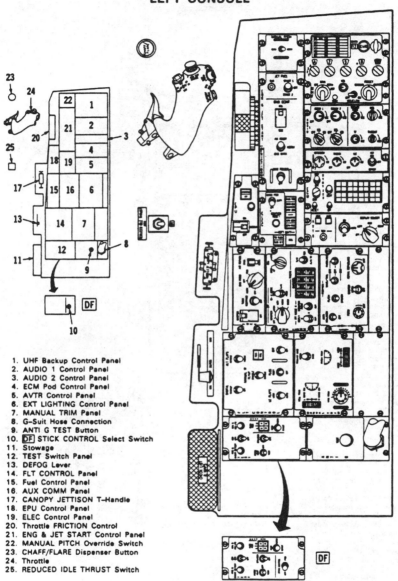

1. UHF Backup Control Panel
2. AUDIO 1 Control Panel
3. AUDIO 2 Control Panel
4. ECM Pod Control Panel
5. AVTR Control Panel
6. EXT LIGHTING Control Panel
7. MANUAL TRIM Panel
8. G–Suit Hose Connection
9. ANTI G TEST Button
10. DF STICK CONTROL Select Switch
11. Stowage
12. TEST Switch Panel
13. DEFOG Lever
14. FLT CONTROL Panel
15. Fuel Control Panel
16. AUX COMM Panel
17. CANOPY JETTISON T–Handle
18. EPU Control Panel
19. ELEC Control Panel
20. Throttle FRICTION Control
21. ENG & JET START Control Panel
22. MANUAL PITCH Override Switch
23. CHAFF/FLARE Dispenser Button
24. Throttle
25. REDUCED IDLE THRUST Switch

21

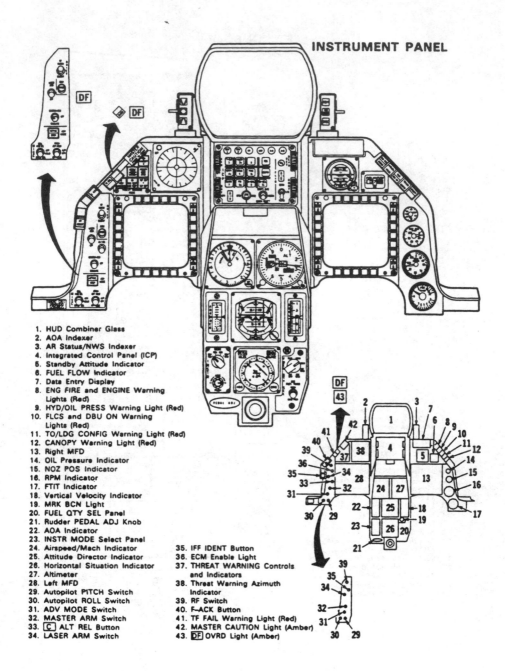

INSTRUMENT PANEL

1. HUD Combiner Glass
2. AOA Indexer
3. AR Status/NWS Indexer
4. Integrated Control Panel (ICP)
5. Standby Attitude Indicator
6. FUEL FLOW Indicator
7. Data Entry Display
8. ENG FIRE and ENGINE Warning Lights (Red)
9. HYD/OIL PRESS Warning Light (Red)
10. FLCS and DBU ON Warning Lights (Red)
11. TO/LDG CONFIG Warning Light (Red)
12. CANOPY Warning Light (Red)
13. Right MFD
14. OIL Pressure Indicator
15. NOZ POS Indicator
16. RPM Indicator
17. FTIT Indicator
18. Vertical Velocity Indicator
19. MRK BCN Light
20. FUEL QTY SEL Panel
21. Rudder PEDAL ADJ Knob
22. AOA Indicator
23. INSTR MODE Select Panel
24. Airspeed/Mach Indicator
25. Attitude Director Indicator
26. Horizontal Situation Indicator
27. Altimeter
28. Left MFD
29. Autopilot PITCH Switch
30. Autopilot ROLL Switch
31. ADV MODE Switch
32. MASTER ARM Switch
33. C ALT REL Button
34. LASER ARM Switch

35. IFF IDENT Button
36. ECM Enable Light
37. THREAT WARNING Controls and Indicators
38. Threat Warning Azimuth Indicator
39. RF Switch
40. F-ACK Button
41. TF FAIL Warning Light (Red)
42. MASTER CAUTION Light (Amber)
43. DF OVRD Light (Amber)

RIGHT CONSOLE

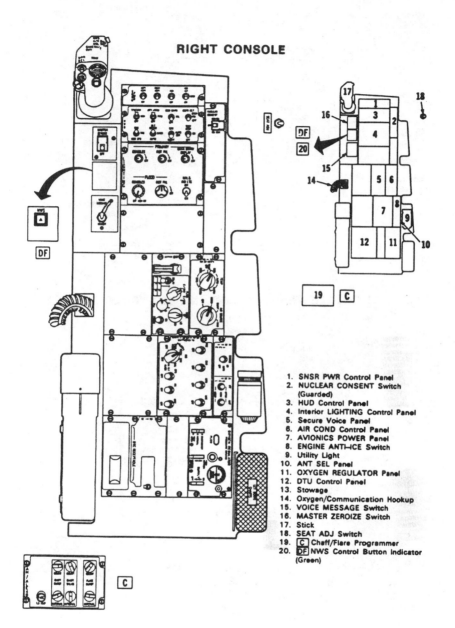

1. SNSR PWR Control Panel
2. NUCLEAR CONSENT Switch (Guarded)
3. HUD Control Panel
4. Interior LIGHTING Control Panel
5. Secure Voice Panel
6. AIR COND Control Panel
7. AVIONICS POWER Panel
8. ENGINE ANTI-ICE Switch
9. Utility Light
10. ANT SEL Panel
11. OXYGEN REGULATOR Panel
12. DTU Control Panel
13. Stowage
14. Oxygen/Communication Hookup
15. VOICE MESSAGE Switch
16. MASTER ZEROIZE Switch
17. Stick
18. SEAT ADJ Switch
19. C Chaff/Flare Programmer
20. DF NWS Control Button Indicator (Green)

AIR-TO-GROUND HEAD-UP (HUD) DISPLAY

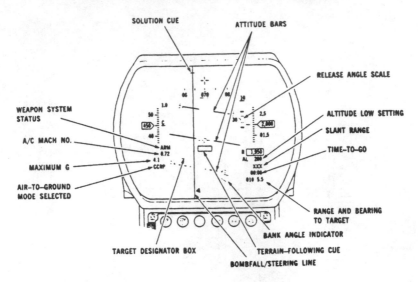

SOLUTION CUE

ATTITUDE BARS

RELEASE ANGLE SCALE

WEAPON SYSTEM STATUS

ALTITUDE LOW SETTING

A/C MACH NO.

SLANT RANGE

MAXIMUM G

TIME-TO-GO

AIR-TO-GROUND MODE SELECTED

RANGE AND BEARING TO TARGET

BANK ANGLE INDICATOR

TARGET DESIGNATOR BOX

TERRAIN-FOLLOWING CUE

BOMBFALL/STEERING LINE

THROTTLE WEAPONS SYSTEMS CONTROLS

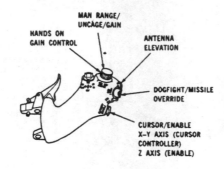

MAN RANGE/ UNCAGE/GAIN

HANDS ON GAIN CONTROL

ANTENNA ELEVATION

DOGFIGHT/MISSILE OVERRIDE

CURSOR/ENABLE X–Y AXIS (CURSOR CONTROLLER) Z AXIS (ENABLE)

STICK CONTROLS

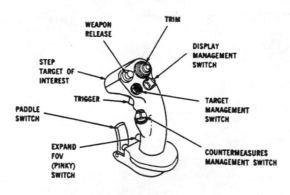

TRIM

WEAPON RELEASE

DISPLAY MANAGEMENT SWITCH

STEP TARGET OF INTEREST

TRIGGER

TARGET MANAGEMENT SWITCH

PADDLE SWITCH

EXPAND FOV (PINKY) SWITCH

COUNTERMEASURES MANAGEMENT SWITCH

4.
THE STORM GATHERS

To understand the history of the Middle East, one has to look back as far as the beginning of mankind itself—to the evolution of an area the ancient Greeks once called Mesopotamia. Civilization thrived in the lands between the Tigris and Euphrates rivers. To this day, many Iraqis believe that the town of Qurna, where the two rivers meet, is the original site of the Garden of Eden. Other countries in the region have made similar claims, but no one can dispute the fact that Mesopotamia is where mankind first began to flourish.

During the eighteenth century, British imperialism began to spread throughout the Middle East. The British set up a number of trading posts along the coastal route to India, and one of those posts was established in the territory now known as Kuwait. The Ottoman Turks controlled the domain, but they allowed it to be governed by the al-Sabah royal family, who had established the tiny sheikdom in 1756. The British were seeking greater control in the region, and when they found out the Turks had allied themselves with Germany at the onset of World War I, they sent forces from India into southern Iraq and drove the Turks from Arab land. The British and French subsequently took control of the region, and by the end of the war, the British occupied a large portion of Iraq, including Baghdad, and the French occupied Syria and Lebanon.

In 1922, the modern borders of Kuwait, Iraq, and Saudi Arabia were drawn, and ruling families loyal to Great Britain and France were given control. Sir Percy Cox, a high commissioner from Great Britain, met with a junior cabinet member representing Iraq, a British political agent representing Kuwait, and with Sheikh Abdul-Aziz ibn Saud, who would soon become the ruler of what is now Saudi Arabia. The meeting lasted seven days. When the parties could not reach a compromise on where to draw the borders, Cox dictated where the lines would be drawn. Afterwards, representatives of Iraq—the most sophisticated of the three nations—were extremely bitter, because the new borders denied their country any access to the Persian Gulf.

In 1932, Iraq finally gained its independence and was accepted into the League of Nations. One year later, Iraq's King Faisal died and the throne passed on to his son Ghazi. King Ghazi despised Great Britain's presence in the Gulf and its influence over his country. He considered Kuwait to be part of the Basrah province, and in 1937 called upon his southern neighbor to rebel against the British and become part of Iraq. This was Iraq's first attempt to gain control of Kuwait.

Two years later, King Ghazi was killed in a car accident. He was succeeded by his son,

Faisal II, who remained in power until July 1958, when he was overthrown by a group of military officers led by Brig. Gen. Abd al-Karim Qassim. When Kuwait gained independence three years later, British forces began to withdraw from the region. Qassim's troops tried to take advantage of the situation by invading Kuwaiti border posts, but British political and military pressure forced them to withdraw.

During the presidency of Gen. Qassim, the Baath Party began to seek power. Their goal was to rid the area of both the British and the French, and to revitalize Arab culture. When party members succeeded in overthrowing Gen. Qassim in February 1963, they agreed to recognize Kuwait's independence. In return for this recognition, Iraq received a loan of $85 million. But the Baath Party was unable to remain in control, and, nine months later, they, too, were overthrown. The party resurfaced again in July 1968, during a military coup organized by two non-Baathist army officers: Col. Abdel-Razzaq Nayif and Col. Ibrahim al-Daud. The officers carried out the coup under the leadership of Maj. Gen. Ahmad Hasan al-Bakr.

In order for the Baath Party to be in complete control, Gen. al-Bakr and his staff decided to rid themselves of Col. Nayif, the newly appointed prime minister, and Col. al-Daud, the party's new defense minister. Since both were non-Baathists, they were seen as obstacles to the new regime. One of Gen. al-Bakr's aides—a rising star in the Baath Party named Saddam Hussein—was put in charge of their disposal. Gen. al-Bakr appointed himself president, commander-in-chief, chairman of the ruling Revolutionary Command Council, and secretary-general of the Baath Party—positions he held until 16 July 1979, when Saddam Hussein took over as Iraq's new president.

After Iraq invaded Kuwait, it was still too early to say what role, if any, the United States military would play in the crisis. At the height of the Iran-Iraq War, Kuwait and Saudi Arabia had questioned America's commitment to the Middle East. Both countries needed a strong ally in the region, but they were unsure of the United States' willingness to help. When the Reagan administration finally agreed to offer military assistance, the United States gained the leverage it needed to increase its political influence in the region. More importantly, it kept the Soviets out and proved to Kuwait and Saudi Arabia that our nation could be relied upon.

The Cold War ended in the late 1980s with the reunification of Germany and the breakup of the Soviet Union, signaling a new beginning for nations seeking peace. President Bush called it "the new world order," but the invasion of Kuwait was a serious blow to this concept. "What is at stake is far more than a matter of economics or oil," Bush declared after the invasion. "What is at stake is whether the nations of the world can take a common stand against aggression . . . whether we live in a world governed by the rule of law or by the law of the jungle."

When asked by reporters about the invasion, President Bush condemned the attack as an act of violence. He called for Saddam Hussein to withdraw his troops, and he began campaigning for other Arab leaders to denounce the invasion. But the Arabs were slow to respond. Many resented the wealth and the country-club lifestyle of Kuwait. To them, the small nation was nothing more than a rich oil power that refused to share its wealth. Others were afraid of saying anything for fear of upsetting Saddam Hussein further. Arab leaders concluded that it was in their best interest to resolve the crisis peacefully.

Shortly after the invasion, King Hussein of Jordan met with Egyptian president Hosni Mubarak. The two leaders prevented the Arab League from condemning the invasion, and they asked President Bush to hold back until they could devise an Arab solution. King Hussein and Mubarak arranged for a mini-Arab summit at Jidda and invited Saddam Hussein to attend, but when they asked Saddam to withdraw from Kuwait and restore the al-Sabah family, he refused. They next offered Saddam a portion of Kuwait that would provide him the access to the Gulf he desired, but President Bush stepped in to kill the plan. King Hussein was distressed because he supported Saddam, but President Bush was able to convince Mubarak and King Fahd of Saudi Arabia that Iraqi aggression could not be left to stand.

The following day, Iraq announced that it had entered Kuwait at the invitation of young radicals who had overthrown the emir and were attempting to establish a new government. Baghdad claimed that the revolutionaries had installed a new regime led by nine Kuwaiti military officers. They also announced formation of a new Kuwaiti army, which was to be supported by more than 100,000 Iraqi soldiers who "volunteered" to "assist" their southern neighbor. Saddam Hussein then promised to withdraw his troops as long as no other nation interfered. To ensure he would be taken seriously, Baghdad radio announced, "We will make Kuwait a graveyard for those who launch any aggression."

The United Nations Security Council passed Resolution 660, demanding that Iraq withdraw, immediately and unconditionally, all its forces to the positions of 1 August 1990. The council threatened to impose economic sanctions if Iraq refused to abide by the ruling. While this was going on, the United States, Britain, and France froze Iraqi and Kuwaiti assets and imposed a boycott of Iraqi oil. The European community quickly followed suit, banning all arms sales to Iraq.

After speaking with Soviet president Mikhail Gorbachev, President Bush dispatched Secretary of State James Baker to the Soviet Union to meet with foreign minister Eduard Shevardnadze. The Soviet Union, one of Iraq's strongest allies, was the main supplier of Iraq's arsenal of weapons, and some diplomats feared the Soviets would side with their ally to gain political influence in the region. But when Baker and Schevardnadze emerged from their meeting, they were armed with a shocking blow to Saddam Hussein. The Soviet Union, together with the United States, denounced Iraq's attack as "brutal and illegal," and called on other nations of the world to join in economic sanctions. The unity between the United States and the Soviet Union was unprecedented, and as soon as other nations saw the superpowers condemning Iraq's aggression, they fell into agreement and pledged their support.

On 4 August, President Bush met with his advisors at Camp David. There was deep concern among the group because satellite photos revealed six Republican Guard divisions moving south toward the Saudi-Kuwaiti border. President Bush knew that the rich oil reserves of Saudi Arabia were vital to America's economy, and to the economies of Japan and Western Europe. He also knew that Iraq's Republican Guard would meet little resistance if Saddam ordered them south, down the Saudi coastal road that runs through Ras al-Mish'ab, Al-Jubayl, and Al-Dammam. If Saddam were to invade Saudi Arabia and capture the strategic oil fields along the eastern coast, he would have control of more than half the world's oil supplies. He would be able to manipulate oil prices and redefine the region's power structure.

Saddam Hussein declared he had no plans to invade the Saudi kingdom, but he had told Egyptian president Hosni Mubarak the same thing about Kuwait shortly before he invaded that country. Realizing what was at stake, President Bush ordered the aircraft carrier USS *Independence* from the Arabian Sea to the Gulf of Oman, and the carrier USS *Eisenhower* from the Mediterranean Sea to the Red Sea. He also dispatched Secretary of Defense Dick Cheney to Saudi Arabia to meet with King Fahd.

On 6 August, the United Nations Security Council passed Resolution 661, ordering a worldwide trade embargo against Iraq. Even though an oil embargo had already begun, pipelines in Turkey and Saudi Arabia needed to be shut down. To garner support, Secretary of State James Baker traveled to Turkey, where he met President Turgut Ozal. The Turkish leader was hesitant to interrupt the flow of more than $300 million a year that Turkey earned in oil pipeline fees. But when Baker persuaded the emir of Kuwait to compensate the Turks for their loss in revenue, President Ozal agreed to join the coalition. He also granted permission for American fighter planes to use his bases.

President Bush's next challenge was to convince Saudi Arabia's King Fahd that he should shut down Iraq's southern pipeline and accept America's help. When Secretary of Defense Cheney arrived in Saudi Arabia, he told the Saudi ruler that America was prepared to send forces to defend his kingdom. King Fahd realized his military was no match for Saddam's, but he too was hesitant to cut off the flow of Iraqi oil. To ensure that the king and his advisors understood the gravity of the situation, Cheney showed them the satellite photos depicting the massive buildup along their northern border. After a short debate, King Fahd turned to Cheney and said, "Okay, you can come." The following day, American forces began a massive deployment to the Saudi kingdom. Twenty-four F-15C fighters from the 1st TFW at Langley AFB departed Virginia for Dhahran, Saudi Arabia. Five E-3A AWACS aircraft joined the F-15s, and, one day later, C-5 and C-141 transport aircraft delivered troops from the army's 82nd Airborne Division. The aircraft carrier *Saratoga* and the battleship *Wisconsin* left port for the Persian Gulf, and fifty B-52s were put on alert at Diego Garcia in the Indian Ocean. A squadron of F-111 fighter-bombers, already stationed in Turkey, was put on alert as well.

During the 1980s, Saudi Arabia, fearing an expansion of the Iran-Iraq War, had allowed the U.S. Army Corps of Engineers to build military facilities throughout their country, at Khamis Mushayat, Tabuk, and King Khalid Military City. In addition, port facilities had been constructed at Ras al-Mish'ab, Jidda, and Al-Jubayl. Headquarters complexes, military schools, and support facilities for F-16 and F-15 fighter aircraft had all been built to be used by U.S. forces during a time of crisis.

On 8 August 1990, after Iraq announced it had annexed Kuwait as its "nineteenth province," President Bush addressed our nation. His speech marked the beginning of Operation Desert Shield.

5.
WAITING FOR SADDAM

G reen Flag could not have come at a better time for the 4th TFS Fightin' Fuujins. Pilot turnover had been high, and the experience level of our squadron had dropped considerably. The deployment to Nellis AFB provided invaluable training, and it gave the new guys a chance to get to know one another. It takes time for a flight lead to develop confidence in his wingman, and the Green Flag exercise gave everyone a solid foundation to build on. If the crisis in the Middle East escalated, we'd be ready to fight.

On Monday, 6 August, I pulled into the 4th TFS parking lot behind the 388th TFW headquarters building. Lt. Col. Scott scheduled a pilot meeting for 08:00, and I had a pretty good idea what the meeting would be about. As soon as everyone took their seats in the squadron briefing room, a member of wing intel stepped up to the podium and updated us on the situation in Kuwait. It became apparent rather quickly that Saddam Hussein had no intention of pulling back. His army was more than one million strong and was well armed with the latest Soviet equipment. According to intel, the Iraqis fielded the fourth largest army in the world, equipped with more than 5,500 tanks and an air force of approximately 635 combat aircraft.

"If Saddam is going to attack Saudi Arabia," the officer told us, "he will have to act soon. If he waits too long, U.S. forces will have time to establish themselves in the region to defend the Saudi kingdom and its oil wealth."

Shortly after the start of the meeting, our wing commander, Col. Michael Navarro, and director of operations, Col. William Huddle, walked into the briefing room. Someone near the door barked out "Room, ten *hut!*" Everyone snapped to attention. As the commanders took their seats, I wondered if they'd come to announce that the 4th TFS would be deploying to the Middle East. Everyone present was a warrior who had spent his air force career training for a moment like this. None of us craved war. But if one started, we all wanted the chance to put our training to the test.

When intel finished, Col. Navarro faced the group.

"Two F-16 squadrons from Shaw AFB took off this morning for a base in the Middle East. At the moment, there are no plans to send any of the three squadrons assigned to the 388th, but that doesn't mean we aren't going to be prepared to go. I spoke with Gen. Horner this morning, and the next few days are going to be critical."

He continued, "I'm canceling all leaves, except for those who remain in the local area. We're going to do a lot of flying this week, so take advantage of every sortie you get. I spoke with Lt. Col. Scott earlier this morning, and he told me your Green Flag exercise was a success. Congratulations. That training may come in handy during the next few weeks."

As soon as Col. Navarro concluded his speech, everyone in the room snapped to attention, and he departed with Col. Huddle. As the door closed, Lt. Col. Scott stepped up to the podium and told us to take our seats. Scotty, as he is known, is a fighter pilot's fighter pilot—highly respected as a commander. If I was going to fight in a battle, I wanted to be flying on his wing. I'm sure the rest of the pilots felt the same way. The room fell silent, waiting for Lt. Col. Scott to speak.

"Gentlemen! Most of you are aware that only a short time ago, I led this squadron on a deployment to Panama in support of Operation Just Cause. I'm here to tell you that I've seen a number of things take place over the past few days that remind me of the weeks preceding that deployment. I can't tell you we are going to go to the Middle East, but I can guarantee you that we will be prepared to go. When the wing commander decides which squadron he will send first, I don't want him to think twice about sending the Fightin' Fuujins!"

He continued, "If we have to leave tomorrow, I know we'll be ready. But like Col. Navarro said, let's take advantage of every sortie we can get. You guys are the best fighter pilots in the world. Remember one thing, though. There's always room for improvement. If there are no questions, let's go fly!"

The meeting broke up and most of the pilots left to prepare for their sorties. I was keyed up about going to the Middle East, but since I was not on that day's schedule, I spent a couple of hours studying in the weapons shop before heading home to be with Colette, Candice, and Kristen.

As soon as I walked in the door, I sensed that Colette was upset. "So when are you leaving?" she said sarcastically.

I knew she was scared, and I tried to calm her fears. Part of me wanted to go, to take on the Iraqis. The thought of remaining at home while friends in other units fought the war was something I couldn't stomach. But I felt my obligations to Colette and the girls just as powerfully. I had recently returned from a remote tour in Korea, and a day didn't go by without my dreaming of being with them. Now that I was back, it was hard to justify leaving again. But, then, neither of us would have a choice in the matter. I had to go wherever the air force sent me.

Colette and I had discussed potential sacrifices at length before I joined the service. She was only twenty-one when we were married, and the thought of being a military wife scared her, but she knew it was my dream to become an air force pilot. We decided to make the commitment to each other, and as soon as I was commissioned as a second lieutenant, we committed to the air force as well.

I took Colette in my arms and told her it was still too early to say whether or not our squadron would be needed in the Gulf.

Later that evening, Colette looked at me.

"You wish you were going too, don't you?"

"If Iraq were to attack Saudi Arabia, we will defeat them easily. I know you don't want me to leave, but I don't want to be stuck at home while my friends are fighting a war."

I was, in fact, willing to put my life on the line. But I was also terrified of the thought of going to the Middle East and never coming back. The year I spent in Korea was hard on both Colette and me, but I knew, to the day, when I was going to come home. This time, there was no telling when anyone would return.

On 9 August, the U.N. Security Council responded to Iraq's annexation of Kuwait by passing Resolution 662: "Annexation of Kuwait by Iraq under any form and whatever pretext has no legal validity, and is considered null and void." This was the third resolution passed by the Security Council since the invasion. The following day, Arab leaders met in Cairo where twelve out of twenty-one Arab League members voted to honor the United Nations trade embargo—to support Saudi Arabia's decision to bring in American forces, and to commit troops to an all-Arab military force that would join in the defense of Saudi Arabia.

As the American buildup continued, the Bush administration held out hope that U.S. forces could be in position before Saddam Hussein decided to attack Saudi Arabia. President Bush warned the Iraqi dictator that the United States would not tolerate any further aggression. Saddam Hussein did not back down. What President Bush needed most was time. In order to increase America's presence in the Gulf, a massive airlift campaign had to begin. Many of us believed our wing would be part of the campaign. Rumors of a deployment were soon rampant, and it was hard not to notice that the air-logistics center was working twenty-four hours a day. On my way back from the commissary one evening, I noticed dozens of pallets heaped with equipment sitting in front of the loading dock. The girls were in the back seat of our car, and when I looked into Kristen's eyes, I realized that I would soon be leaving her.

We approached each training mission as though it were our last sortie before war. Nearly all of the training scenarios focused on desert warfare, and we squeezed the most out of every flight. Intel was great about keeping us updated on the situation in Kuwait. They incorporated Iraqi aircraft and SAM defense systems into their briefings and tested us daily on aircraft recognition. We scrutinized the strengths and weaknesses of every weapon in the Iraqi arsenal, and we also studied Iraqi fighter tactics.

Squadron life-support personnel reviewed desert survival and evasion techniques. We also held "battle week" exercises covering the use of our chemical-warfare equipment. Nobody liked to wear the cumbersome gear—especially in the heat of summer—but we knew Saddam Hussein had chemical weapons and was capable of using them.

We updated our search-and-rescue cards, which include each pilot's name, rank, social security number, and fingerprints. The cards contain four statements and a four-digit number—information used by SAR forces to identify pilots behind enemy lines. A typical statement might be, "My first job was as a box boy at a grocery store in Los Angeles, California." To verify they are rescuing the correct person, underground operatives working with the SAR teams ask you questions pertaining to your statements. Another form of verification might include a question pertaining to your number, such as, "What is the sum of the first and last digits?"

Least favorite preparation is receiving immunization shots. Early one Saturday morning, all the pilots came in to receive immune serum globulin and meningitis vaccines. We felt lousy for the rest of the weekend, but by Monday, we were ready to fly again.

My duty title in the squadron was assistant chief of weapons, and I worked for Capt. Scobey "Sudds" Suddreth and Capt. Kevin "Duck" Perry, squadron weapons officers, whose job was to ensure that each pilot knew everything he could about F-16 weapon systems and tactics. Both graduated from the air force's prestigious Fighter Weapons School at Nellis AFB in Nevada, and both were outstanding instructor pilots with over 2,000 hours of F-16 fighter time between them. I helped them with their daily briefings and kept track of the squadron's supply of bombs and ammunition. We also had two other pilots working in the weapons shop, Lt. Doug "Yogi" Podkin and Lt. Mike "Chins" Chinburg. The five of us worked together to make sure that each F-16 pilot received the best training possible.

I put in long hours at the squadron, but when I was off, I spent all my time with Colette, Candice, and Kristen. Even though she didn't want to hear it, I told Colette what I expected of her if I were shot down and killed. I wanted her to know my feelings and what I wanted for her and the girls. I held her tightly and told her that I wanted her to live a happy life, even if I wouldn't be there to share it with her.

Nearly two weeks had passed since Iraqi troops entered Kuwait. In an attempt to divert global media attention away from the invasion, Saddam Hussein announced that captured Western hostages would be placed at strategic sites to deter an attack. Saddam argued that the hostages would help bring about a peaceful end to the crisis. In response, the U.N. Security Council passed its fourth resolution, adopted unanimously on 18 August, calling for the immediate release of all foreigners in Iraq and Kuwait. Now, as Saddam Hussein realized that the Arab world was quickly turning against him, he offered a peace initiative linking his withdrawal from Kuwait to Israeli withdrawal from the occupied territories and a Syrian pullout from Lebanon. President Bush rejected the offer and, once again, called on Iraq to withdraw unconditionally. Bush warned that he would not rule out the use of force. He ordered more troops to the Gulf.

The members of the 388th could do nothing but prepare and wait for orders to the Gulf. We continued to train hard, improving on the techniques learned during the Green Flag exercise. We practiced low-level bombing, air-to-air intercepts, and both offensive and defensive basic fighter maneuvers. We also practiced night intercepts and air-to-air refueling. Everyone had become familiar with the Soviet-style tactics taught to the Iraqi pilots, and we had our own pilots simulate these tactics during our training missions.

The training gave us confidence in our aircraft and in our abilities as pilots.

From a maintenance standpoint, the F-16 had a sterling record, but over the previous months, problems with fuel lines/controls and pressure surges had surfaced in a section of the GE-100 engine. As a result, the use of afterburner was now restricted in all F-16s equipped with the GE-100. Until the engines were fixed, pilots would be limited to military power only. General Electric engineers, aware of the problem, developed a kit to fix it, but only a limited number of these kits were available. When we learned that all available kits were being diverted to Hill, we began to feel certain that we would go to the Gulf.

Then we learned that our radar threat-warning receivers were being reprogrammed with new software, upgraded from version 7 to version 8, which would include the most recent radar frequency updates. The program wasn't supposed to be available for another year or two, but by the third week of August, every one of our F-16s was reprogrammed with it.

Of all the Block 40 upgrades, the most significant was the addition of the Navstar Global Positioning System, or GPS, an all-weather, jam-resistant navigation system that receives signals from satellites circling the earth in a twelve-hour orbit. Each satellite contains precision atomic clocks and transmits signals to a GPS antenna on top of the F-16 fuselage. The receiver tracks four satellites simultaneously, and the navigational messages furnished by each satellite are used to update the F-16's inertial navigation system. A good INS is a bomber pilot's best friend and is often the determining factor in successful target acquisition. But a typical INS has a drift (error) rate of approximately fifty feet per minute. To overcome this drift, pilots try to pick coordinates that coincide with identifiable landmarks, such as road intersections, mountain peaks, dams, and bridges. Once an F-16 pilot takes off and begins his low-level, he uses his map to cross-check the different steerpoints programmed into his INS. If everything is correct, a diamond appears in the head-up display directly over the landmark. If the INS has drifted, however, the pilot can update it by performing a fix or by slewing the diamond back over the landmark with the cursor/enable switch on his throttle. This exercise is repeated at each steerpoint until the pilot reaches the target. GPS eliminates the need for this corrective work. The signals transmitted by orbiting satellites update an aircraft's INS every two seconds, ensuring that the diamond in the head-up display will be directly over each steerpoint and, most important, over the target.

The air force planned to eventually have twenty-four GPS satellites orbiting the earth to provide worldwide coverage for both civilian and military aircraft, but barely half the satellites were in orbit during the Iraq crisis. Furthermore, we knew that the military keys needed to receive and decode the incoming signals had not yet been installed in our F-16s.

Then we learned that each of our jets was being loaded with the keys, and even though not all the GPS satellites were in orbit, we were given the green light to use the system. During the 1970s, I wrote a college term paper on the Navstar Global

Positioning System and what it would do for aviation. I even got a close-up look at the first satellite during a field trip to the Rockwell plant near my school. Now, a decade later, I would be among the first to benefit from the new technology.

On 21 August, Secretary of Defense Dick Cheney announced that sufficient forces were in place to defend Saudi Arabia. In addition to the F-15Cs from Langley and the F-16Cs from Shaw, the air force deployed another squadron of F-15Cs from Eglin AFB in Florida; F-15E Strike Eagle aircraft from Seymour-Johnson AFB in North Carolina; F-4G Wild Weasels from George AFB in California; F-117A stealth fighters from Tonopah, Nevada; and A-10s from Myrtle Beach AFB in South Carolina. The air force also provided more E-3A AWACS aircraft, RC-135 reconnaissance aircraft, and both KC-135 and KC-10 tanker aircraft for aerial refueling. The army's 11th Air Defense Artillery Brigade, equipped with Patriot and Stinger surface-to-air missiles, was deployed to the region as well.

In a pilot meeting the following day, Lt. Col. Scott told us to pack for a "ninety-day deployment" and to stop by the supply depot before the end of the day to pick up two large duffel bags and an extra set of combat boots. He reminded us that anything pertaining to the possible deployment was highly classified and we were to divulge nothing.

After the meeting, I completed my local-area checkout, and I was certified as a two-ship flight lead. I had accumulated more than 450 hours in the Viper, and I felt very comfortable with the weapon system. I now looked forward to putting my training to the test. Returning home that afternoon, I told Colette that I was ordered to pack for a ninety-day trip. We spent the rest of the evening playing with the girls, trying to put the thought of being separated out of our minds. That night I rocked my girls to sleep.

The following day, Colette and I kept an appointment at the base legal office to update our wills and fill out forms giving Colette power of attorney in my absence. We had lunch together, and then I stopped by the dentist to have my teeth cleaned. Later that night, I flew a local-area sortie. We practiced night intercepts and air-to-air refueling. I was home by midnight. I fell asleep in Colette's arms.

On 24 August, the crisis took a turn for the worse when Iraqi troops surrounded the embassies of several Western countries in Kuwait City, cutting off water and electricity. President Bush warned that Saddam was responsible for their safety. He vowed retribution if any embassy personnel were harmed. Another U.N. Security Council resolution was passed on the twenty-fifth, giving Western navies the authority to stop any ship entering and exiting the Gulf and to ensure that these ships complied with the economic embargo. That same afternoon, the news we had all been waiting for was finally delivered. The 4th TFS Fightin' Fuujins would deploy within the next seventy-two hours, and the 421st TFS Black Widows would follow a day or two later.

Colette accepted the fact that I had to go, and she knew too that it was something I wanted to do. My best friend, Phil Cott, called later that evening to see how things were going. He asked if my squadron was going to be sent to the Middle East. I've known Phil since he coached me in Little League, and the two of us were roommates when I was in college. Because of the secrecy of the deployment, I couldn't tell him we were leaving, but I did let him know that he might not hear from me for a while. He understood. "I'll keep in touch with Colette," he promised.

I arrived at the squadron early the next morning to attend the deployment briefing. Lt. Col. Scott informed us that we would fly to Shaw AFB and spend the night there before making the final journey to the Middle East. Our destination would be Al Minhad Air Base, United Arab Emirates. Twenty-four of our F-16s were slated to make the nonstop flight. Lt. Col. Scott announced the lineup of those who would fly F-16s and those who would fly over on one of the transports. I was thrilled when I saw my name in the number six position of the second six-ship package.

Since it was Sunday, no training flights were scheduled, but maintenance wanted us to fly a local-area confidence flight to make sure the external fuel tanks and the rest of the avionics were in perfect working order. They had spent the previous night loading up the extra fuel tanks, and this was our last opportunity to make sure they were feeding properly. At the end of the two-hour flight, we went to the supply squadron for our chemical-warfare gear and an advance on our temporary duty pay.

We took the rest of the afternoon off, and the only thing scheduled the following day was a 10:00 pilot meeting and a final update from intel. After that meeting, Colette and I took the girls to McDonald's for lunch and then to the park to feed the ducks. I told Colette that ninety days wasn't that long, after all, and that I would be as careful as I possibly could. We talked about all the things we would do when I returned. Later that evening, I made a videotape for the girls, then told Colette to play it for them every day I was gone. I knew they wouldn't understand my leaving, and I didn't want them to forget me. I kissed them goodnight and watched them fall asleep.

Colette and I watched TV for a while and then went to bed. The deployment briefing was set for 05:30, with the first takeoff scheduled for 09:00. Colette and I held each other while talking about the past and dreaming of the future. As I held her, I visualized myself flying in battle in my F-16. I was excited and scared at the same time. Would I have to take the life of another human being? Would I lose my own life?

6.
FIRST LEG

A larm clock. It was still dark. Colette and I held each other tightly. Neither one of us wanted to get out of bed. After making sure the girls were still tucked in, I took a shower and finished packing some last-minute items. Colette cooked me a nice breakfast, and we talked. I saw the sadness in her eyes, and, in many ways, I was sad myself. What could I say to her, but that I loved her. I asked her to bring the girls by the squadron on her way to the day-care center so I could tell them goodbye.

The first sign of daylight crept over the Wasatch mountain range. The day was beautiful. The temperature, perfect. A light breeze swept across the base. I stepped into the backyard to take in one last view of the Great Salt Lake. Breathtaking.

I arrived at the squadron fifteen minutes before brief time. Everyone was in an upbeat mood, and some of the wives were there to lend their support and to wish the rest of us luck. A few of the pilots were disappointed that they weren't flying an F-16 to the UAE, but having more pilots than aircraft meant that some would have to ride on the KC-10s that were going to escort us. Most disappointed of all was Mike "Chins" Chinburg, who was scheduled to get married in a little over a week. He was hoping the deployment would be held off until after his wedding. Chins had talked with Lt. Col. Scott about going with the squadron, but the families had so much invested in the wedding that Scott told him to go ahead with the ceremony. He promised to bring Chins over in a couple of weeks.

We walked into the briefing room a few minutes before 05:30 and sat in the same order as our formation would fly—a standard procedure for large-force employments. I took the number six seat in the second row. Lt. Col. Scott would lead the package, so he took charge of the briefing, beginning with roll call and then a time hack. The first person to speak was an officer from the base weather shop, who gave us an overview of the weather between Utah and Shaw AFB in South Carolina: scattered thunderstorms, isolated; they wouldn't pose a problem for us. The weather outlook at Shaw was standard for this time of year: clear skies, temperatures in the nineties, humid.

Next up, intel. They told us Iraqi forces were still within striking distance of the Saudi border and that Saddam Hussein appeared to be adding reinforcements, despite claims that he was pulling forces back. A rumor that the Iraqis had captured some of our Hawk surface-to-air missiles from Kuwaiti forces remained unverified. The intel officer said information was still being gathered and he hoped to give us a definite answer about the Hawk missiles before we launched from Shaw the following afternoon.

When intel finished, Lt. Col. Scott began his brief, his eyes confident. He was obviously proud to be leading the twenty-four F-16s into what might be battle. The plan was to launch four elements, each consisting of six aircraft. Each element would be escorted by its own KC-10 Extender, responsible both for air-to-air refueling and the transportation of personnel and equipment. Three aircraft would fly on each wing of the KC-10, with thirty minutes separating each of the six-ship packages. The element flight lead for the second six-ship package was our squadron operations officer, Lt. Col. Tom "T-Rack" Rackley, second in command of the squadron and very popular among the pilots. He was somewhat soft spoken, but his experience in the F-16 commanded tremendous respect.

Flying in the number two position would be Capt. John "Spanky" Sepanski, followed by Capt. Scobey "Sudds" Suddreth, Capt. Bill "Senseless" Sensinig, Capt. Syd "Vicious" Oliver, and finally me—Capt. Keith "Rosey" Rosenkranz—number six. Lt. Col. Scott planned to have Vicious and me start with the first group, in case any of the first six aircraft had to fall out because of maintenance problems. If that happened, those aircraft would flow to the back of the package, allowing them time to be fixed. Vicious and I would then take their places, and members of the third formation would fill in accordingly. The start, taxi, and takeoff times were briefed. Each of us copied the pertinent information onto his lineup card, and Lt. Col. Scott covered the departure from Hill AFB, the en route flight plan, and the arrival into Shaw. He also covered contingency plans in case anyone had to divert to a different base. This flight was a dress rehearsal for the longer flight to the Middle East. Our goal: to get all twenty-four F-16s off the ground and to Shaw AFB safely. Scotty concluded the meeting with a pep talk, assuring us that our families would be well taken care of in our absence.

After the briefing broke up, we had a little more than an hour before the first group would step to the aircraft. The rest of the wives had arrived and took advantage of the extra time by spending it with their husbands. Colette showed up with Candice and Kristen, who were thinking it was time to play. Colette and I walked the girls out to the parking lot to spend a few more private moments together. Colette planned on dropping the twins off at the base day-care center so she could join the rest of the wives at the departure end of the runway to watch us take off. When we arrived at the car, I played with the girls and made them laugh. We'd become very close in the past few weeks. I gave each a kiss and helped Colette place them in their car seats. After closing the door, I turned to Colette, kissed her, and wiped the tears from her face. We had been together for thirteen years, and I had kissed her a thousand times before. But this time it was different. I told her how much I loved her and promised to call her when we arrived at Shaw. As she drove away, I stood in the parking lot and watched Candice and Kristen blow kisses as their little hands waved goodbye.

I walked back into the squadron and into the life-support shop to put on my flying gear. As I put on my G-suit, our wing commander entered the room. Col. Navarro would be flying on the wing of Lt. Col. Scott in the first six-ship. As he gathered his flying gear, I asked if he thought LANTIRN would be used in the event of war. I knew that navigation pods were going to be taken to the Gulf, but Duck and I were the only pilots in the 4th who were qualified to use them. While zipping up his G-suit, he looked up and said, "You'll get your chance, Rosey."

I smiled and continued getting dressed.

I took off my patches and scarf and placed them in my flight-suit pocket. I cleaned off my helmet visor, checked the oxygen mask, and tested the microphone. Everything worked perfectly. The rest of the pilots from the first element were also getting dressed. Within a few minutes, all of us were in the crew van heading for the flight line. It was a short drive from the squadron to where the jets were parked. Our driver stopped in front of each pilot's F-16, and, one by one, we jumped out. As I walked toward my airplane, I was met by my crew chief, who stood at attention and gave me a crisp salute. I returned it and shook his hand. "How's it going?" he asked, and began loading my gear into the travel pod mounted under the aircraft's left wing. He was young and a little nervous. I tried to project a calm and confident attitude.

"The jet is all ready to go, sir," he said.

I climbed up the aircraft ladder and placed my helmet on the canopy rail. We still had thirty minutes before engine start—plenty of time to check the aircraft forms and complete my walkaround. I looked over the jet and couldn't believe how much we were carrying.

"Hey, chief, what do you think of this configuration?" I asked.

He laughed: "This thing is so heavy, it might not be able to take off."

Every F-16 on the ramp was loaded with three external fuel tanks, four live AIM-9 Sidewinder missiles, an ALQ-131 electronic countermeasures pod, and a travel pod for each pilot's gear. Our maintenance team had done an outstanding job preparing the jets for the deployment.

Less than ten minutes to go before engine start. My stomach is in knots. I always have a few jitters before a sortie, but it's never been this bad before. Once I'm airborne, I know it will all go away. I put my gloves on, connect my parachute harness, and climb into the cockpit. My crew chief follows me up the ladder and helps me strap in. He wishes me luck, shakes my hand, and says he will see me on the ground once we arrive in the UAE. As he removes the ladder from the side of the aircraft, I put on my helmet, connect my microphone, and plug in my G-suit. I adjust the rudder pedals and then strap my checklist and lineup card to my legs. After completing my before-start checklist, I take a few deep breaths and stare at the Wasatch mountains. The scent of JP-4 fills the air.

I check my watch. One minute before engine start, I turn on the aircraft battery and I motor down the canopy. My crew chief is already standing by on the headset.

"Your intake is clear, sir, and the fireguard is posted," he tells me.

"Thanks, chief; we'll start in twenty seconds," I reply.

I take one last look around the flight line. The other seven pilots are patiently sitting in their cockpits, ready to go. I stare at my watch, counting down the last few seconds before engine start.

"Let's go start one, chief!"

I switch the jet-fuel starter to Start One, and my engine turns. As soon as the RPM reaches 20 percent, I place my throttle in the idle position. The airframe vibrates as the powerful GE engine roars to life. Within a minute, the piercing noise of all eight F-16s fills the flight line. After closing and locking my canopy, I reach down and turn the air conditioner to full cold. I spend the next twenty minutes completing my checklist items, and then I stand by, waiting for Lt. Col. Scott and the others to taxi. As soon as Scotty's crew chief removes the chocks from beneath his aircraft, I signal my crew chief to do the same.

Everything is off to a smooth start, and nobody appears to have any problems with his aircraft. Like ducklings on a pond, each F-16 falls in line behind Scotty as he taxies away from the ramp. As soon as Vicious passes in front of me, I release my brakes and begin to roll forward. My crew chief motions me out from my spot, salutes, and waves good-bye. I return a sharp salute and follow it with a thumbs-up. All of this takes place without a single radio transmission. The deployment is highly classified, and Lt. Col. Scott has instructed us to use "comm-out" procedures. He has coordinated our taxi and take-off times with the air traffic control tower in advance, so they have made sure the air-field is clear for us.

Scotty falls in line behind the lead KC-10 as it taxies toward the departure end of the runway. With perfect spacing behind one another, we follow him to the aircraft arming area. As we approach the north end of the airfield, I notice members of the 419th F-16 reserve squadron lining both sides of the taxiway in a show of support. They hold up signs that read "Good Luck" and "Drop One on Saddam for Us." I get a chill down my spine, proud to be a member of the U.S. Air Force. As they wave and cheer I hold my arms in the air with both fists clenched.

When we reach the arming area, I spot the contingent of squadron wives. Col. Pete Fox, the 388th vice wing commander, has arranged for them to be on the flight line, and I salute him as I taxi past his car. He and his wife, Debi, are neighbors, and their daughter, Leigh-Alyson, often takes care of Candice and Kristen. I feel a lot better knowing they'll be looking after Colette and the girls while I'm gone. Once I reach the arming area, I park my F-16 alongside the other seven jets and wave to Colette. She knows my tail number and waves back as I patiently wait for the arming crews to finish their final inspections. If the first six-ship takes off as planned, I will have thirty more minutes to spend in the arming area until it's time for my element to leave.

A brisk morning wind whips across the airfield as the wives huddle together. Colette is with her friend Ann Marie, who is standing alongside her husband, Lt. Rod "Kid" Gard, one of the young lieutenants in the squadron, who earned his call sign because he looks like he's still in high school. He brought a pair of binoculars out to the flight line, and he passes them back and forth to Colette and Ann Marie. I hold up against the canopy a little sign that reads "I love you, Colette." Colette sees it and blows me a kiss. I raise my visor, drop my oxygen mask, and return one to her. After that, I hold up one of the "piddle packs" we use for bladder relief while airborne. Colette has a puzzled look on her face, and she passes Kid the binoculars. He turns his head to speak to her, and she laughs.

A few more minutes pass, and, finally, the KC-10 takes off. Scotty begins to taxi, and the other five aircraft in his element follow him onto the runway. Vicious and I remain in the arming area. As soon as all six aircraft are in place, they run up their engines for one last check. Within seconds, Scotty releases his brakes and starts his takeoff roll. The ground shakes as his afterburner ignites and propels him down the runway. Each F-16 follows at twenty-second intervals. Before long, all six aircraft are safely airborne. Since Vicious and I don't have to fill in for any of the aircraft, I have thirty more minutes to spend with Colette. We wave and stare at each other as time goes by. We can't say anything, but we both know what the other is thinking.

Time passes quickly, and before long, I notice the next KC-10 taxiing toward the arming area. Lt. Col. Rackley and the second element are right behind. Twenty minutes have passed since the first element departed. The giant KC-10 takes the runway and, five minutes later, takes off. Finally, it's our turn to leave. Lt. Col. Rackley leads our formation onto the runway. As soon as we're in place, he gives us the engine run-up signal. With my feet planted firmly on the brakes, I push up the throttle. At 80 percent RPM, I make one last check of my engine instruments. Everything looks good. I give Vicious a big head-nod, and a few seconds later, T-Rack begins to roll. One after another, the Vipers take off. As soon as Vicious releases his brakes, I begin the twenty-second countdown. With ten seconds to go, I run up my engine. A lump in my throat, I look over at Colette. We wave. I release my brakes, start to roll down the runway, accelerate rapidly, and am airborne within four thousand feet. I raise my landing gear, and, as I pass by the control tower, I rock my wings in salute. We are on our way.

I accelerate to 350 knots and rejoin Vicious as we pass over the Wasatch Range. All tension has evaporated. I relax and concentrate on flying. It's a gorgeous day, and we level off at 25,000 feet. No other experience in the world can match the thrill of piloting an F-16. The cockpit wraps around me like a blanket, and I feel at home with the controls. What I enjoy most of all is the peacefulness of being by myself—though I think about Colette, Candice, and Kristen as we cruise toward the East Coast, altitude 25,000 feet, three F-16s positioned on each wing of the KC-10.

We refuel three times during the four-hour flight. Everyone's systems seem to be functioning properly, and time passes quickly. Before long we are setting up for our approach into Shaw AFB. Each aircraft takes spacing during the descent and flies a straight-in approach. I'm the last to touch down. Once I slow to taxi speed, I clear the runway. I follow the rest of the flight to the de-arm area, where crew chiefs from Shaw check over our jets and safe our missiles. When they're finished, we taxi to our parking spots on the ramp and shut down our engines.

Waiting there to greet me was my old friend Capt. Brian "Lassie" Bishop. Both of us were instructor pilots in the Air Training Command, and we went through initial F-16 training together in 1988. After that, we spent a year in the 80th TFS at Kunsan Air Base in Korea. He was now stationed at Shaw and was a member of the 19th TFS. As soon as I raised my canopy, he reached up and shook my hand. He helped me unload my gear and gave me a ride to his squadron, where we would store our equipment. Lassie was excited to see me, but extremely disappointed that his squadron was not deploying to the Gulf. His unit was one of three at Shaw. The other two had been in the Middle East for almost three weeks.

With the first leg of our journey complete, Lt. Col. Rackley gathered the flight for a quick debrief and then cleared us off. The squadron was scheduled to meet in the officer's club for dinner at 17:30. Until then, we were free to do whatever we wanted on base. Lassie gave me a ride over to the officer's club and, after a couple of beers, wished me luck and headed home.

Members of the third element arrived a few minutes later, and a few of us went over to the base exchange to pick up some items to take with us the following day. I bought a bag of candy corn to munch on during the flight and a few packs of gum as well. I also picked up a Steely Dan tape. It was against the rules to have cassette players in the cockpit, but most of us brought them along so we'd have something to listen to during the long flight. The tape was *Aja*, one of my favorites, because it reminded me of the summer of 1977, when I first met Colette.

After we finished shopping, we joined the rest of the squadron for dinner. None of us was sure what kind of food we'd be eating in the Gulf, so everyone splurged. I ordered the largest cut of prime rib on the menu, and, for dessert, a large ice cream sundae. After dinner, we were taken to a hotel in downtown Sumter, where we were booked for the night. As soon as I'd checked into my room, I called Colette, then watched television while skimming the newspaper. We weren't due to take off until 16:00 the following afternoon, so I wanted to stay up late and sleep in as long as possible. But, in fact, I tossed and turned all night—and by 08:00 the following morning I was wide awake. I picked up the bus at 10:00 to the base mess hall.

After lunch, I started preparing for the flight. The briefing was scheduled for 12:30, and the usual preflight jitters came on. Everyone was in their seats a few minutes before brief time. We all had classified folders on our desks, containing our route of flight and all the appropriate maps for the journey. The computer-generated flight plan showed the flight time as over fifteen hours with a total distance of 7,163 nautical miles. The estimated fuel burn: greater than 68,000 pounds. Each F-16 would have to refuel at least ten times during the flight. Including ground time, I would be strapped into my F-16 for nearly seventeen hours.

Right before the briefing started, our squadron flight surgeon, Capt. Tim "Doc"

Hursh, passed out packets containing seven pills—amphetamines designed to keep us alert throughout the long flight. Doc instructed us to take our first one after the briefing. The pilots refer to the drugs as "go pills," and Doc said we should take one every two hours. None of us could afford to get drowsy on this flight. The first half of the mission would be flown in the middle of the night over the Atlantic. Since each pilot would be alone in his F-16, it was imperative that we remain alert.

The briefing started right at 12:30 with a time hack. The first person to speak was Lt. Col. Terry "Zappo" Adams, the 388th's chief of standardization and evaluation (stan/eval). It was his office that prepared the mission flight plan. Vicious and I would start and taxi with the first six-ship and be prepared to go in case maintenance problems forced anyone to abort. I wasn't sure how the rest of the guys felt, but my plane would have to be on fire before I aborted. Nothing was going to keep me from making this flight.

Zappo reviewed the entire flight plan with us to make sure we understood it. He pointed out each divert base and the distance, heading, and fuel burn required to get to each. He also briefed the tanker data, showing call signs and the type of aircraft that would refuel us at the ten refueling points.

"Once you take off," he continued, "you'll proceed to the northeast over North Carolina and Virginia before heading out over the Atlantic. As each F-16 cell becomes airborne, a KC-10 Extender filled with supplies and equipment from back home will depart Seymour-Johnson and escort your formation to the Middle East. The KC-10s will also ferry our extra pilots and maintenance personnel. It's likely that the personnel at our new base have never seen an F-16 before, so we want to make sure they stay away from the jets after we land. The KC-10 will land first and the rested maintenance crews will park the F-16s and start preparing them for combat. It's possible that Iraq might decide to kick this thing off and launch an attack into Saudi Arabia while you're airborne. Maintenance plans to reconfigure each jet as quickly as possible, and the pilots flying over on the KC-10s will go on standby alert."

When Zappo finished, we received our weather briefing for the sortie. We were happy to learn that no weather problems were anticipated during the flight. Since we would be taking off to the east, the sun would set quickly, and our first glimpse of the sunrise would not come until we reached the Mediterranean early the next morning. A satellite photo of the Middle East was shown to us, which revealed nothing more than scattered clouds. Our arrival-time forecast likewise called for clear skies, but, we were warned it was going to be hot: "Temperatures this time of year are consistently above a hundred degrees along the Gulf coast," the meteorologist said, eliciting a collective sigh.

As the sigh and buzz that followed died down, Lt. Col. Scott stepped up to the podium, laughed, and said: "Don't forget your water bottle."

The mood became serious again as Scotty began his brief, covering the start, taxi, and takeoff plan, and reviewing procedures for filling in the formation in case someone had to abort and fall to the back. After that, he covered contingency plans, divert procedures, and the comm-out procedures we would use during the mission. The majority of the flight would be long and tedious, but that would change once we crossed the Red Sea and entered Saudi Arabian airspace. At that point, our attention had to turn toward Iraq.

Saddam Hussein's window for attacking the Saudi kingdom was rapidly closing, and each of us knew the war could very well be in progress by the time we arrived in Saudi airspace. The last thing any of us wanted was an air-to-air engagement thirteen hours into the mission. But since that possibility existed, Scotty discussed our tactics and how we would defend the KC-10s escorting each cell. We wouldn't be carrying bombs, but we certainly had enough weaponry to defend ourselves. In addition to the four Sidewinder missiles, each of our F-16s was equipped with an M61A1-20mm gun, loaded with more than 500 high-explosive incendiary rounds.

The final portion of the briefing covered our arrival in the Middle East. After fifteen hours of flying, we would land at Al Minhad AB. The location was highly classified, and most of us didn't know about the base until just before the deployment. At this point, we had no idea what to expect there. Lt. Col. Scott remarked that the pilots in the first element might have to stay in their jets a while with the engines running until the crew chiefs were ready for them to shut down.

"I'm not even sure where we're supposed to park," he said.

After Scotty completed his brief, Col. Navarro stepped forward to give us some final thoughts.

"I can't emphasize enough how important it is to the defense of Saudi Arabia that our wing get all twenty-four aircraft into the Middle East as quickly and as safely as possible. Our deployment will draw national attention, and the flight will be something all of you will remember for the rest of your lives. You're the best fighter pilots in the world, representing the greatest country. I'm proud of every one of you, and I look forward to seeing you on the ground at Al Minhad."

7.
INCREDIBLE JOURNEY

I was born on 7 June 1959 in Los Angeles. I vividly remember the Vietnam War, wearing POW/MIA bracelets, collecting bumper stickers that read "Don't forget our POWs and MIAs," sixties music, and watching Walter Cronkite on the evening news. Everyone seemed to know someone who was fighting in Vietnam. Our neighborhood wasn't any different. I was too young to understand the reasons behind the war, but I knew many people were against it and that thousands of American young men were dying for a cause they may or may not have believed in.

I learned about communism, the Cold War, and freedom. It was us against the Russians. Good versus evil. The Reds versus the red, white, and blue. We didn't have a bomb shelter in our yard, but I often felt as though I would live to see the end of the world. I was once told that freedom isn't free, and every generation has to fight for it.

I guess my turn had come.

Col. Navarro completed his speech, and Lt. Col. Scott called the room to attention. Morale was sky high. We knew what was at stake, where we were going, and what our role was. This was a very proud moment for all of us. We exchanged high fives and shook hands, then went off to brief individual items within our flights. Members of our formation followed Lt. Col. Rackley into one of the squadron briefing rooms. He reviewed a few more details and made sure all of our questions were answered. I was excited about flying in T-Rack's six-ship package. Most of the guys felt that flying in the lead element with the wing commander would be formal and restrictive, while being in the second element would allow us to relax somewhat. In any case, we all had complete faith in T-Rack, and would follow him anywhere.

As soon as T-Rack dismissed us, I made one last trip to the rest room, then joined Vicious and the other members of the first element in the life-support shop. Step time was 14:30, so now it was time to get dressed. I removed my scarf and patches and placed them with my cap in my flight-suit pocket. I walked over to the counter, loaded my .38 revolver, and secured it in the holster attached to my survival vest. Extra rounds went into my vest pocket. I cleaned the dust off the dark visor on my helmet and made sure the clear one in my helmet bag was clean. I checked my oxygen mask one last time. I put on my G-suit and parachute harness while life-support personnel loaded our gear into the crew van. When it was time to leave, I retrieved my water bottle out of the refrigerator and placed it in the lower left pocket of my G-suit, grabbed my flight kit, helmet bag, and the two box lunches provided by the base mess hall. Each box contained strips of ham, an apple, two pints of chocolate milk, a candy bar, and extra water. I also made sure not to short myself on piddle packs, stashing seven in my helmet bag.

I arrive at my jet about twenty minutes prior to engine start. That gives me time to relax as I pack my gear and stow my things in the cockpit. The heat is unbearable. It shouldn't be much different when I climb out of the jet seventeen hours from now. I've been a nervous wreck for hours. I can't wait to strap in, start the engine, and *go*. Our maintenance crews have again done an outstanding job getting the aircraft ready. A couple of the F-16s had minor discrepancies from the previous day's mission, but the maintenance team from Shaw AFB pitched in and made sure every jet was prepared to go.

After completing my aircraft preflight, I take a good, long drink of water and climb into the jet. My crew chief is right behind me and, once I'm seated, connects my shoulder harnesses.

"I'll be on the headset in a minute, sir," he says. "Have a great flight."

"Thanks, chief," I reply. "We're not going to taxi until thirty minutes after engine start. When my checks are done, I'll clear you off, and you can sit in the shade under the wing. Make sure you get some water. If I need you, I'll run the engine up. When you see the other crew chiefs pulling chocks, you can do the same."

We shake hands, and then he climbs down the ladder and removes it from the jet. I check my watch as I put on my gloves. Only ten minutes to go before engine start. My goal on every flight is to be strapped in with every item in its place, my checklist items complete, and time left over to clear my mind. I hate being rushed. Flying an F-16 can be very complex. Meeting the challenge requires each pilot to be fully prepared both mentally and physically. Rushing to get things done causes mistakes.

I take a few minutes to organize the cockpit, placing my extra items on the floorboard and on each console. I load the first of my two data-transfer cartridges (DTCs) into its receptacle in the right console. Each DTC holds twenty-five steerpoints. This flight is so long, though, it requires two. After strapping on my checklist, I place my flight kit in the far back corner of the left console. One box lunch goes in the back corner of the right console and the other goes on the floorboard with the chemical-warfare kit each of us has been issued. The kit contains a cape, booties, gloves, chemical-warfare medications, injectors, and a CRU-80 filter attachment used to connect the aircraft oxygen hose to a special mask. The chances of having to use the kit seem slim, but we have to be prepared for the worst. It's tight, but everything seems to fit.

The F-16 interior isn't big, so cockpit management is a must. Fortunately, the cockpit is designed with the pilot in mind. (See cockpit arrangement illustrations at the end of Chapter 3.) Every switch and dial is within easy reach. In fact, a number of tasks can be carried out without ever taking your hands off the stick and throttle. The left and right MFDs, which provide a vast amount of information, sit directly in front of the pilot on the forward panel. A larger Block 40 head-up display is also close for easy viewing, and the up-front control panel sits just below it.

46

After getting everything in place, I check my watch. Only three more minutes to engine start. My crew chief is standing by on the radio headset, and the fireguard is at his post by the extinguisher. I glance to my left and notice the other pilots are either finishing up their checklist items or relaxing like me. Vicious is parked to my left. He looks over and yells out, "Can you believe we're actually going to do this?"

I shake my head no and yell back, "Only seventeen more hours, and we'll be there!"

With one minute to go, I motor down the canopy and turn on the aircraft battery.

"How do you read me, sir?" my crew chief asks.

"Loud and clear, chief. Let's plan on using start one. I'll be ready in thirty seconds."

"Roger!"

I stare at my watch, counting down the last few seconds. At exactly 15:00:00 I switch on the jet fuel starter. The big fan engine begins to wind up. As the RPM increases, I place the throttle in the idle position, which adds fuel to the ignitors. The powerful engine lights off. The jet vibrates as the RPM increases to idle speed in unison with the other Vipers on the ramp. I lock my canopy, reach up, and hold my oxygen mask against my mouth.

"Stand by for EPU check," I tell my crew chief.

"Roger, sir. You're clear in back."

I run my engine up to 80 percent RPM and check my emergency power unit. As soon as that's complete, I switch my pri/sec switch to Secondary, which closes down my engine nozzle. I push the throttle quickly to military power, and, as soon as the RPM reaches 80 percent, I snap it back to idle. The engine checks good, and I switch back to Primary. I complete my flight control and brake checks, then begin aligning my inertial navigation system. I punch the coordinates into my up-front control for my parking spot on the ramp: N3358.8 and W8028.2, with a field elevation of 265 feet.

"You're cleared off now, chief. Relax under the wing and be ready to pull the chocks in about twenty minutes."

"Okay, sir," he replies. "Have a great flight."

While the INS is aligning, I load the mission information from my DTC into the aircraft's onboard computers. Every sortie in the F-16 requires extensive planning, and most of it is accomplished on the mission support system computer located in each squadron. The MSS computer, as it's called, allows one person to program fire control–radar system data, which stores inventory, navigation steerpoints, weapon parameters and profile data, GPS data, and up to forty different preset communication frequencies. In the old A-model F-16, pilots had to type everything in manually. With the MSS, the same information is loaded into a pilot's DTC during mission planning. All he has to do is plug the DTC into the jet. When the aircraft generator comes on line, he simply pushes a few buttons on the left MFD, and, like magic, the entire weapon and navigational system is loaded and ready to go.

While waiting for my INS to align, I load my Have Quick radio frequencies for today's date and ensure that my secure radio is operating properly. Have Quick is a jam-resistant radio system that consists of different uniform frequencies, which skip through a number of preset channels. Each day of the month requires a different set of frequencies, and everyone's radios have to be synchronized by receipt of a time-of-day, or TOD, signal from the lead F-16. The "Secure Voice" system allows pilots to communicate without fear of being overheard. The system enciphers voice messages before they are transmitted and deciphers them when they are received. It can be used in conjunction with either the UHF or VHF radio.

When I finish loading the frequencies, I call up the INS page on my up-front control to see if the initial alignment is complete. We always strive for a sixteen-minute alignment with eight minutes being the minimum. A quick check shows I have about three minutes to go. I scan my cockpit once more to make sure every switch is in the right position. Once that's complete, I go back to the INS page on the up-front control. Sixteen minutes have passed, and I reach down and rotate the INS function knob from Norm to Nav. I'm ready to go.

Normally, we taxi twenty minutes after engine start, but for today's flight, we will wait until thirty minutes to make sure everyone has ample time to finish their checks. At 15:25, I run my engine up a little and my crew chief appears from under my left wing. I give him the chocks-out signal, and, after he removes them, he stands at attention in front of my jet. I glance down the flight line. By now, the rest of the crew chiefs are also standing at attention in front of their aircraft. Standing by on victor 6 and uniform 1, I wait for Scotty to check us in. At exactly 15:30:00, his voice rings out: "Burn 11, check!"

"Burn 12, loud and clear!"

"Burn 13, loud and clear!"

"Burn 14, loud and clear!"

"Burn 15, loud and clear!"

"Burn 16, loud and clear!"

The two spare aircraft answer next: "Burn 17, loud and clear!"

"Burn 18, loud and clear!"

Vicious and I follow, "Burn 25, loud and clear!"

"Burn 26, loud and clear!"

Lt. Col. Scott plans for Vicious and me to taxi with the first group just as we had at Hill AFB the day before. If anyone has a problem with his jet, that person and his flight lead or wingman will fall out, let maintenance fix the problem, then join the last element. Then Vicious and I will take their places and the other aircraft will move up accordingly. As far as the two spare aircraft are concerned, they will take off with the first element and proceed to the first refueling point. If everyone completes the first refueling without any problems, the two spares will return to Shaw AFB. One way or another, twenty-four F-16s have to make it over to the Middle East.

We complete both Have Quick and Secure Voice radio checks and then taxi to the arming area, where we wait for final inspection from the arming crews. They remove the pins from our missiles and check each aircraft for leaks and loose panels. This is the last chance for maintenance to correct any problem. I sit patiently at the end of the line while they perform their inspections. When they finish with my jet, the arming crew supervisor gives me a salute and a final thumbs-up. It is a relief.

Less than ten minutes before takeoff, I'm anxious to get in the air. I have a feeling I'm going to be sitting here for forty more minutes. I glance back toward the flight line. The second six-ship has already started their F-16s. The third element will be stepping soon. I think about Colette and the girls and wonder what they're doing. I already miss them, but there's no turning back. I check my cockpit again, take a few deep breaths, and settle back in my seat. At 15:55, Lt. Col. Scott leads his six-ship and the two spares onto the runway. The first four taxi 1,000 feet down the runway, and the second four taxi into position at the departure end. With thirty seconds to go, the eight jets perform their engine run-up. Each pilot glances toward his instrument panel, then gives a big head-nod, signaling that they are ready. At exactly 16:00:00, Scotty releases his brakes and begins his takeoff roll. Every twenty seconds, another F-16 follows. One by one, the afterburners ignite. A plume of orange fire shoots out the tail end and propels each fighter down the runway. Even from where I am sitting, I can feel the ground shake. I watch the last aircraft become airborne and follow it until it disappears in the afternoon haze. The first element is on its way. I've got thirty more minutes to wait.

A few minutes pass before the second formation approaches the arming area. Vicious gives me a visual signal to go to channel 7, our assigned victor frequency. We sit and wait for the arming crews to finish checking the second element, and I pray that nothing will go wrong with my jet. It seems like an eternity, but 16:25 finally comes, and T-Rack leads our element onto the runway. I line up next to Vicious; the two spares are to my immediate right. Thirty seconds prior to takeoff, we run our engines up. The exhaust from the four aircraft 1,000 feet in front of us shakes my jet. I scan my panel; everything checks good. I get head-nods from the pilots to my right, and as soon as Vicious looks back at me, I give him one too. I pull the throttle back to idle and wait for the aircraft in front of me to take off. Lt. Col. Rackley releases his brakes right at 16:30, and I watch his engine nozzle expand as his afterburner lights. Heat waves roll across the runway. In a matter of seconds, his jet lifts off. He is followed by Burn 22 and, twenty seconds after that, Burn 23. When Burn 24 releases his brakes, Vicious runs up his engine. He looks over at me one last time, salutes, then releases his brakes.

With my feet pressed against the rudder pedals, I push up my throttle. The nosewheel compresses as the engine winds up. My eyes peer at the clock on my up-front control display. I count down twenty seconds, and, finally, the moment I have been waiting for arrives. I push the throttle up to mil power, then smoothly select afterburner. Once it ignites, I accelerate rapidly. As my airspeed increases, I rotate and quickly become airborne. I raise my gear and immediately lock up Vicious with my air-to-air radar.

Finally in the air, for the first time in hours, I feel at ease. I keep my power up and rejoin with the rest of the formation, maneuvering into position off the right wing of Vicious as we proceed to steerpoint number one. The first of ten air-to-air refuelings won't occur until steerpoint number three. We continue our climb to 25,000 feet. Soon we pass over the North Carolina border.

The radios are quiet until I hear the voice of Kevin "Duck" Perry, flight lead of the two spare aircraft that took off with the first element. Scotty's formation must have completed its first refueling uneventfully. Duck passes our six-ship on his way back to Shaw and, unfortunately, makes the mistake of talking on his victor radio.

"Burn 17 has contact . . . twenty left . . . thirty miles, high aspect!"

Duck's wingman responds: "Burn 18, same."

As soon as T-Rack hears the call, he barks out, "Who's talking on the radios?"

I can't help but chuckle to myself. At least Duck is smart enough not to answer.

We reach our first refueling point about ten minutes into the flight. We're over Raleigh-Durham, North Carolina, and I spot the tanker on radar, forty miles off my nose. Tan 62 is a KC-135 Stratotanker from Plattsburg AFB in New York, and he's right on time. Without a word on the radios, the aircraft makes a smooth turn to the northeast. Our package is two miles in trail with fifty knots of overtake. The timing is perfect. Burn 21, 22, and 25 join on the Stratotanker's left wing, while Burn 23, 24, and myself join on the right. The refueling order alternates from each wing, beginning with Burn 21. Once we're established on each side of the KC-135, the boom operator lowers the refueling boom, and T-Rack drops down into position.

Air-to-air refueling is a procedure we normally practice once every six months. It requires patience and steady hands. There's no way around it: flying within a few feet of a tanker loaded with over 100,000 pounds of fuel is dangerous. Everyone involved must pay close attention to what he is doing. T-Rack has no problems at all, and he's on and off the boom in a matter of minutes. Capt. John "Spanky" Sepanski is next. I continue to maintain my position off the right wing of the KC-135. As soon as each pilot completes his turn on the boom, they flow to the outside of the formation. Each F-16 takes on fuel at a rate of 1,000 pounds per minute. It isn't long before Vicious drops down to take his turn. I watch the state of North Carolina pass under me as Vicious refuels. When he disconnects, he drops back and flies back to his position on the tanker's left wing.

As soon as the precontact position is clear, I pull my throttle back and drop down behind the tanker. I add a little power to stop my backward momentum, and then I look up and see the boom operator, who is positioned in the lower portion of the tanker's aft fuselage. Our entire package is cruising at 310 knots at an altitude of 25,000 feet. As soon as I stabilize, I give the boomer a thumbs-up to signal that I'm ready to proceed forward. As soon as he lowers the boom, I notch my throttle up. The refueling technique I like best is to fly directly at the boom and then let the boomer fly the probe around my canopy and into position. I try to be as smooth as possible while the boom passes just a few feet to the right of my head. The boom has small wings on it, and the boomer uses a control stick to fly the refueling probe to the refueling port, located just aft of my canopy on the upper side of the fuselage. As soon as the boomer plugs the refueling probe into the open port, I get a green "connect" light on my nosewheel steering gauge, signaling that the boom is latched in place. My objective at this point is to not fall out of position. The rest of the guys are watching, and if I accidentally disconnect, I owe a round of drinks at the club—if the place we're going to has one. To maintain my position, I follow light signals located on the underside of the KC-135. The director lights are activated as soon as the refueling probe is in place. The lights indicate up, down, forward, and aft. If a pilot is out of position, flashing arrows signal that he's strayed too far.

It takes a lot of concentration to stay on the boom, and I'm totally focused on the director lights. To relax, I wiggle my toes. After 5,000 pounds are transferred, I'm topped off. I hit the disconnect button on the side of my control stick and ease my aircraft back. As soon as I'm clear of the boom, I return to my position on the outside of the right wing. T-Rack clears the two spare F-16s off and they return to Shaw AFB. I feel bad, because I know how much they want to make the journey with us.

Approximately thirty-five minutes into the flight, we overfly Norfolk, Virginia, leaving Tan 62 behind. The summer night is beautiful. As the sun sets, we proceed out over the Atlantic Ocean, navigating toward the northeast. Our escort KC-10 from Seymour-Johnson AFB joins the formation, and we rejoin to our briefed positions. The pilots flying the KC-10 will handle all of the radio calls required en route, while our element maintains radio silence. We want to give the impression that only one aircraft is airborne instead of seven. This precaution will be especially important when we fly north of Libya and, eventually, to the south of Iraq.

Aside from an occasional fuel check and to make sure we are feeling okay, the only planned communication will occur when it's time to take our go pills. Maj. Scott "Foot" Goodfellow, the 388th wing weapons officer, is on board the KC-10. He's our element supervisor of flying (SOF), and he will remind us to take our pills every two hours. Foot will also coordinate diverts and help with any other emergencies that might occur.

We reach steerpoint eight approximately two hours into the flight. The location marks the beginning of our second refueling track. Yellow 63, a KC-135 from Robins AFB in Georgia, is orbiting at the steerpoint when we arrive. We aren't low on fuel, but our plan is to keep our tanks topped off. Once we get out over the Atlantic, our divert options decrease significantly. The fuel capacity of our F-16s is approximately 13,000 pounds—6,200 of which is carried in three external fuel tanks. A fuel-system malfunction over the middle of the Atlantic could prove disastrous. The fact that our tankers may have mechanical problems also weighs into Lt. Col. Scott's refueling calculations.

Nighttime falls upon us as we enter the refueling track, so it's in our best interest to be a little more conservative when rejoining and refueling off the tanker. The last thing any of us can afford is a midair collision, so we take our time and make sure everything goes smoothly. Each pilot cycles on and off the KC-135 without any problem. As soon as I'm back in position, T-Rack checks in the flight for the first time on victor 7. He calls for a fuel check and takes a few seconds to converse with each of us to make sure we're feeling okay. I'm still full of adrenaline, even though I've been strapped in my jet for three hours. My longest mission before this one was a seven-hour flight from Kunsan AB in

South Korea to Singapore for a Cope West exercise. That trip was pretty easy, though I made the mistake of not packing enough piddle packs. I filled up four and that was all I had. I thought I was going to explode by the time I got to Singapore. I wasn't going to make the same mistake twice. This time, I brought seven.

The flight across the Atlantic goes very smoothly. We fly an easterly heading that takes us just north of the Azores, a group of Portuguese islands in the North Atlantic. By this point, we've been airborne nearly six hours and have air-refueled five times. We settle into a comfortable routine, with T-Rack checking in on us after every refueling. We also hear from Foot every two hours when it's time to take another go pill. I've taken three so far, and I'm amazed at how well the medication is working. I've been awake for more than twelve hours, but feel extremely alert.

When we aren't on the tanker's wing, we spread out 3,000 feet from each other, so everyone can engage autopilots and relax a little. Flying close formation and refueling at night can be mentally taxing. While on autopilot, I loosen my lap belt and stretch as best I can. Sitting in the same position for hours on end is uncomfortable. The cockpit is tight to begin with, so I twist and turn to exercise different muscles.

We don't refuel for another twenty minutes, so it's a good time to go to the bathroom. I make a quick call to T-Rack so someone will keep an eye on me. It's easy to become preoccupied and drift from the group. Urinating while flying an F-16 in the middle of the night isn't easy. If things don't work just right, a pilot can count on being moist for a couple of hours. My technique is to pull the rudder pedals all the way out and use them to prop myself up to get a downhill flow. Positioning the piddle pack is critical. The plastic pouch has a three-inch opening at the top and a highly absorbent sponge inside. I stand on the rudder pedals with my head shoved up against the canopy and pray that it all ends up in the plastic pack, and that I don't need more than one. At the same time, I keep one eye on the formation and the other on my autopilot to make sure I'm not drifting. I don't need to get lost over the ocean in the middle of the night.

As we continue toward the west coast of Europe, we approach our sixth refueling point. This will be our second and last hookup with a KC-10, which has taken off from Lajes in the Azores. His call sign is Amber 65. Since it's a KC-10, the boom operator has a "hot mike" to the pilot of the aircraft taking on fuel.

T-Rack flashes his position lights, signaling us to re-form. While flying my F-16 into position, I reach down to my left console and open my air-refueling door. I want to get the door open early enough so the tanks have time to depressurize. If they don't, they won't accept the full complement of fuel. All I've heard for the last seven hours, other than an occasional radio call, is the constant hum of my engine. Flying comm-out gets boring after a while, so I'm looking forward to having a conversation with the boomer.

Each pilot spends a few minutes on the boom and finally it's my turn. I drop down into position—a little slower since it's nighttime. As soon as I hook up, I'm greeted by the boomer.

"Contact," he says.

"Hey, how's it going?" I ask. "Are we almost there yet?"

"Only nine more hours to go, sir. How are you holding up?"

"I feel pretty good. I wish I could walk around and stretch my legs, though."

"I hear ya, sir. That cockpit of yours looks mighty small from here. Where do you put all of your stuff?"

"I've got my flight kit and one box lunch on the left console. I put the other box lunch on the right side, and I keep my chem-warfare kit on the floorboard."

"What do you do with the used piddle packs?

"They go on the floorboard too. They leak once in a while, so I need to make sure I keep them away from my box lunches. Know what I mean?"

"Copy *that*, sir. Those sandwiches don't taste too good when they get soggy."

Both of us laugh.

I cross-check my fuel tanks, and they're just about topped off. I'll be disconnecting any moment.

"Tell the guys I appreciate the fuel. Have a safe trip back to wherever you're going."

"Thanks, sir. Take care of those Iraqis for us."

The boom disconnects. I ease my throttle back and drop down away from the massive tanker. As soon as I'm clear, I transition back into position on Vicious's right wing. I close my air-refueling door, then check my fuel levels to make sure I have a full load.

By 23:00 East Coast time, we're about 350 miles off the coast of Portugal. The skies are clear, and the brilliance of millions of stars light up the night. Without a full moon and city smog, I can distinctly see a number of constellations. The Big Dipper was off my left wing earlier in the evening. Now it's right in front of me. Flying at night is so peaceful, and I'm captivated by the beauty of the stars. I wish Colette could see this with me.

The flight has almost reached the halfway point. We've been airborne for seven hours, and we've traveled over 3,400 miles. I check my map, noting that we're approximately 250 miles from the Strait of Gibraltar, which separates Morocco from the southern tip of Spain. It's still dark, and I can see the lights of Portugal's southern coast off my left. Sudds and I talked before the flight about seeing the Rock of Gibraltar as we flew over the entrance to the Mediterranean Sea. We both hoped it would be light enough for us to see it, but it looks as though the sun won't rise until we're near Italy. It's close to midnight on the East Coast of the United States, which makes it 06:00 in Spain.

By the time we finish our seventh refueling, the early morning sun has begun to creep above the horizon. We're off the southern coast of Italy and the deep blue Mediterranean sits below us. I had never been to this part of the world before, and seeing it for the first time from 25,000 feet at sunrise is a sight to behold. I can see the coast of North Africa off my right wing. Below and to my left is the island of Sicily, perched off Italy's southern coast.

Rarely has a word been spoken over the past eight hours. I'm getting tired of staring at everyone without being able to say anything. I think T-Rack feels the same way, because he finally breaks radio silence and makes conversation with each of us. Everyone is feeling good, and he asks if anyone has any jokes. Spanky tells a terrible one, and then Senseless fesses up to having brought along some Trivial Pursuit cards. He asks if we want to play. T-Rack is all for it. Deploying halfway around the world, possibly to fight a war, 25,000 feet over the Mediterranean Sea, we play Trivial Pursuit. A minute passes, and Senseless asks the first question: "Where would you find the medulla oblongata?"

The radios fall silent—just as they have been for the last eight hours. No one has a clue to the answer. The silence continues. Suddenly Sudds radios: "I know the answer to that question! Standby one!" I laugh to myself, wondering what Sudds is up to.

A few seconds pass and the radios erupt with James Brown screaming, "*I feel good! I knew that I would.*" Sudds has had enough of Trivial Pursuit. Instead of answering the question, he plays the sound track from *Good Morning, Vietnam.* We listen for about twenty minutes. When the tape ends, T-Rack asks if anyone has any more music.

"I've got some Robert Palmer!" I reply.

T-Rack tells me to go for it, so I start out with "Some Like It Hot." Since my microphone is in my oxygen mask, I have to hold the tiny earpiece in my mouth so the music will project over the radios. I play a few songs until the guys get tired of hearing me breathe along with the music.

We begin our ninth refueling fifty miles west of Cairo. Black 61, another KC-10, will take our formation the rest of the way. By the time we complete our refueling, we're directly over top of the Nile River. The amount of vegetation that lines both sides of the river is amazing. We continue along the Nile for another 150 miles until we pass over Luxor. At that point, we turn east toward the Red Sea. Airborne nearly thirteen hours, we are just now crossing into Saudi Arabia's airspace. I always thought the Red Sea was a lot smaller. I'm astounded at how long it takes to fly over it. Sudds teases Senseless and asks him if his Trivial Pursuit cards could tell us the point where Moses and the Hebrew slaves crossed. We all have a good laugh.

As we enter Saudi airspace, Foot comes on the radios and tells us it's time to take another go pill. I take my sixth one and then eat my second box lunch. While I eat, I enjoy the view of the Saudi desert below: an endless sea of sand dunes. We have one more refueling and then we will make our closest pass by Iraq. We aren't sure what to expect, but we're going to be ready in case the Iraqis try anything. As soon as T-Rack drops behind the tanker, Vicious and I drop back a couple of miles in trail and begin searching the skies south of Iraq with our radars. While the rest of the flight completes their last refueling, Vicious and I concentrate on traffic approaching from the north—the direction from which Iraqi fighters will attack if they are airborne.

I can't believe how many contacts I'm picking up on my radar scope. I lock up one aircraft after another and try to determine if they are friendly or hostile. All of the contacts are flying as single-ship aircraft, which contradicts normal fighter tactics. As each aircraft comes into visual range, I recognize that they belong to the United States Air Force. They are all transport aircraft—mainly C-5s and C-141s. Vicious and I relay the information back and forth, and I know the rest of the element is relieved when they hear us call out each contact as friendly.

As we continue through Saudi Arabia, it becomes evident that Iraq has not launched any sort of attack. We start to pick up normal radio transmissions between air-traffic controllers and other airliners, as well as the large contingent of military transports. We still remain vigilant with our radar work, though, but, as before, when a contact comes into view, it's usually a C-5 or a C-141. It's incredible how many transports are flying out of the theater. President Bush wasn't kidding when he promised to help Saudi Arabia. One of the largest airlifts in military history is well under way.

We pass over Riyadh at the fourteen-hour point, and I begin to realize why Saudi Arabia is the world's largest producer of oil. The eastern part of the country is one continuous oil refinery. Oil storage tanks linked by hundreds of miles of interconnecting pipeline crisscross the terrain below. If Saddam Hussein wants to exert his power by affecting the world's oil supplies, a precision attack on this section of the country will certainly be the place to make his point.

Thirty minutes pass and, finally, the Persian Gulf comes into view. We pass just to the south of Bahrain and over the southern portion of Qatar. The Gulf waters are a beautiful deep blue, a contrast to the parched Saudi deserts. As we continue to the east, I call up my ground-map radar and slew my navigation cursors onto the southern tip of an island called Dalma, an ideal update point for my INS, which has drifted miles off course. I complete my fix and then call up steerpoint eighteen, which is the emirate of Abu Dhabi in the UAE. Shortly thereafter, Lt. Col. Scott comes up on our victor radio.

"Burn 21, this is Burn 11, how copy?" he says.

Lt. Col. Rackley responds, "Burn 21 reads you loud and clear. Go ahead."

"Copy. Burn 11 will be landing shortly. Be advised that steerpoint nineteen is not our final destination. Those coordinates are for Dubai International Airport. When you get in range, contact Dubai approach control on 124.9 and they will give you vectors to final. Tower frequency is 118.55. How copy?"

"Burn 21 copies all," replies T-Rack. "We're about forty minutes out. See you on the ground in a little bit."

During our descent, T-Rack sends us over to Dubai approach control's frequency. The UAE coastline begins to appear. Just in time. I've hit a brick wall. As tired as I feel, I know I'm going to have to put this thing on the ground, and soon.

T-Rack calls Dubai approach control, which is ready for us.

"Burn 21, squawk 2135 and ident," the controller says.

He gives us a moment to comply with his instructions and then he calls out, "Burn 21, radar contact. Fly heading zero-eight-zero. Descend and maintain five thousand feet."

Once we reach 5,000 feet, T-Rack splits the formation into three two-ships. Approach control gives each two-ship their own transponder code and verifies their call signs. This will facilitate our approach and landing into Al Minhad. As we continue our approach, Scotty comes up on the radios again and informs us that the first element has landed. Over the secure radio, he also passes along coordinates for the airfield, and I punch them into my up-front control. After entering them, I call up the new steerpoint and receive bearing and distance information in my HUD.

About fifteen miles southwest of the airfield, Vicious and I are cleared off, and we fly a heading away from the formation to increase our spacing between the other two elements. I fly a comfortable fighting wing position as Vicious leads me toward the airfield and onto final approach. As we get closer to the base, approach control hands us off to Al Minhad tower.

"Burn 25, go 118.55!" Vicious radios.

"Two!"

I switch frequencies and wait for Vicious to check me in.

"Burn 25, check!"

"Two!"

Vicious gives me the gear-down signal, and I match his configuration. He looks my jet over and I do the same for him. Each of us gives the other a thumbs-up, signaling that our gear is safely down and locked. After that, he gives me the signal to drag. I put my speed brakes out and fall back in trail of his jet. The skies are hazy, but I can detect a long strip of runway off my nose. I'm flying over nothing but desert. Below, a herd of camels walks near a dirt road.

Vicious makes his gear-down call to the tower. After I make one last check of my configuration, I key my mike and say, "Burn 26, gear down full stop."

Once my wheels touch down, I aerobrake to slow the aircraft down. At the end of the runway, I make a left turn and proceed toward the ramp. After seventeen long hours in an F-16, I've finally reached my destination. I relax a little and look around at what will be my new home for the next few weeks. Two KC-10s are parked at the approach end of the runway. I fall in line on the taxiway with the rest of my element who are getting pinned by some of the crew chiefs who flew in on the lead KC-10. Once they finish, I taxi my F-16 to the ramp and park my jet next to the rest of the formation. As I come to a stop, my crew chief plugs in his radio and asks, "How do you feel, sir?"

"I'm beat, chief!" I reply. "It's a good thing we've finally landed. I'm not sure how much longer I could have gone on."

"Do you have any write-ups, sir?"

"This jet is code one, chief. All it needs is some more fuel and a fresh pilot, and I'm sure it'll go another seventeen hours."

While waiting for my crew chief to finish his checks, I notice a group of men in flight suits standing near the hangar. They wave at me as if I were a relative they haven't seen in years. I wave back as I lift my visor.

"Everything looks good," my crew chief tells me. "You're cleared to shut down."

I put the throttle into the cutoff position, and the GE engine winds down. I raise my canopy and begin to unstrap.

8.
IN COUNTRY

A s soon as the canopy opened, I was greeted by a blast of desert heat. I took a few deep breaths of the hot, humid air and gazed across the ramp at the arid landscape. I could have been sitting in an oven. My crew chief put the ladder on the side of my jet and stepped up to the cockpit to help me with my gear. My F-16 was the last to shut down, so it was fairly quiet on the ramp when I took off my helmet and put it in my helmet bag along with my DTCs.

"How are you feeling, sir?" my crew chief asked.

"I'm pretty tired, chief. Everything's happening in slow motion. Maybe it's this heat."

I handed him my helmet bag, which he placed at the foot of the ladder. After climbing out of the cockpit and stepping down onto the tarmac, I realized my legs were extremely stiff—and I was a little dizzy, having sat so long in the same position. My crew chief helped me with the rest of my gear, recommending that I relax until a crew van could pick me up. He passed me a water bottle and I took refuge under the shade of my wing. Vicious, sitting under the jet parked next to me, raised his water bottle: "Welcome to Al Minhad!" After acknowledging the toast, I replied, "I'm ready to go home."

Our new base, surrounded by nothing but sand, was roughly twenty miles inland from the Persian Gulf. Our F-16s were parked in front of a large hangar on the east side of the airfield next to ten small jets that looked like British Hawks. The aircraft bore a desert camouflage paint scheme along with the UAE flag. A large building adjacent to the hangar appeared to be the headquarters for the fighter squadron. The base had only one runway. Several helicopters were parked on another ramp on the west end of the field. Both ramps were separated by desert. The air-traffic control tower sat between the two ramps and was surrounded by a few more buildings.

When the crew van arrived, Sudds and I loaded our things in the back. The driver had already picked up the gear of the other members of our element. He told us everything would be dropped off at our new quarters. Once our gear was loaded, we started walking toward the hangar. We spotted Scotty and some of the other pilots from the first element, who were talking with a group of men in flight suits. As we approached the group, Scotty introduced us to the two UAE squadron commanders, who were accompanied by a small cadre of men from both the fighter and helicopter squadrons. We shook hands with all of them, and they welcomed us to Al Minhad. They were very friendly and extremely happy to see us.

"This is the first time I have ever seen an F-16 in person," one of the men said. "It's a fine-looking jet! How do you like flying it?"

His English was very good.

"There's no other aircraft in the world like it," I replied. We made small talk for a few minutes before one of the squadron commanders announced that we would be guests of the base commander that evening for a dinner party at the officer's club. We would be driven to our quarters, where we could shower and rest before dinner. That sounded great.

We left the hangar and turned onto a long two-lane road that led to the west. Sudds drove our truck, following the pilot to the opposite end of the base. Senseless joined Sudds up front while Spanky, Vicious, and I sat in the back. The heat was like a sauna, but a canvas tarp stretched over us kept out the sweltering sun. Along the way, we passed a few buildings separated by more of the sandy desert. There was a mosque on the left, and, farther down the road, on our right, we passed by the control tower. As we continued west, we passed another large hangar filled with helicopters. A two-story building sat adjacent to the hangar, and, across the street, there was a small hospital clinic with a helicopter landing site in front of it.

When we reached the perimeter of the airfield, we turned left and proceeded toward two buildings. Sudds followed the UAE pilot into a small parking area. After he stopped, we all got out of the truck. Our host pointed to the buildings; "Here are your quarters."

"Are they air-conditioned?" Spanky asked.

"Yes," the pilot replied. "You will be very comfortable here."

Vicious and Senseless began to unload our gear while Sudds and I checked out one of the rooms. The cool air was a welcome relief from the heat. The living room was pretty big, and it had a couch and three beds. A small kitchen was near the front door, and the bedroom was next to the living room. Three more beds were set up in the bedroom, and a five-drawer dresser sat next to a doorway leading to a bathroom and shower. Lt. Col. Scott showed up a few minutes later with Col. Huddle, and the two of them inspected the room.

"It's going to be a couple of days before we get the living arrangements ironed out," Scotty said. "We can probably start out with six in each room. Find a place you're comfortable with, and we'll see you at the officer's club at 17:45."

Sudds and I agreed to room together, and we planned to save a bunk for Kevin "Duck" Perry when he arrived. Since the three of us worked together in the weapons shop, the idea of being roommates made sense. When all the gear was unloaded, Sudds and I grabbed our bags and took them into the bedroom of our new residence. Lt. Rob "RC" Craig and Capt. Orlando "Big O" Cisneros followed us in and decided to settle in the living room, saving the third bed for Lt. Michael "Mick" McGuire.

I volunteered to test the shower first and was relieved to find plenty of hot water, with adequate pressure. When I finished, I put on a fresh flight suit and placed other things in one of the dresser drawers. The rest of my clothes and supplies were in two large green canvas deployment bags. The only place to put them was at the foot of my bed.

Big O took his turn in the shower while Sudds, RC, and I sat in the living room swapping stories. All of us agreed that the flight was the greatest we had ever been on, but that it was one we didn't want to repeat any time soon.

At 17:40, everyone headed over to the officer's club, anxious to meet our new hosts. Before departing Hill AFB, we had received a number of briefings describing the cultural differences between Americans and Arabs. We learned that the Arab people are very sensitive about the basing of foreign troops on their soil. If the issue came up in conversation, we were supposed to stress the defensive and *temporary* nature of our mission. We were also told to emphasize that we would stay only as long as our host nation wanted us.

We also received a number of guidelines regarding Arab customs, courtesies, and gestures. We learned that shaking hands with an Arab is proper and should be done when greeting and leaving him. We were also taught that Arabs tend to stand closer in conversation than Americans might be comfortable with; we were instructed not to back away. It was okay to strike up conversation, but we were cautioned to avoid asking personal questions or questions about the women of an Arab family. When sitting with an Arab, one had to be careful not to expose the sole of one's shoe or the bottom of one's feet; to do so is regarded as an insult. We learned that it is impolite to criticize an Arab's work or ideas in public. Moreover, an Arab's ideas or suggestions should always be acknowledged, and contradiction should be avoided if the person has status or is superior in rank or age. Americans tend to be frank, but this might well be misinterpreted as criticism.

Many of us brought our cameras along, but we were told not to photograph people, especially women, at close range. Staring at or striking up a conversation with an Arab woman was also forbidden. If offered food or drink, we were told to accept it whether we wanted it or not—but alcohol was prohibited by the muslim religion, as are pornography and sexually explicit material. Touching and holding hands with members of the same sex in public was acceptable among Arabs as a demonstration of friendship, but contact with a member of the opposite sex in public was considered obscene.

Certain gestures common to Americans had to be avoided. The "A-okay" hand signal is a sign of the evil eye for an Arab, and is used when placing a curse on someone. Hitting the right fist onto the open palm of the left hand indicates contempt and is often interpreted as an obscenity. Biting the right forefinger, while placed sideways in the mouth, is another expression of contempt or threat.

A bit uneasy, then, we entered the o'club through large glass doors leading into a marble entryway. One area was set up with about twenty long tables. Adjacent to this dining hall was a large lounge, furnished with leather couches, chairs, and a few coffee tables. Adjoining the lounge area was a game room equipped with a pool table and a Ping-Pong table. On the other side of the lounge, near the club entrance, was another room with more couches and a television.

Everyone was starving, and the assortment of seafood trays and selected cuts of meat looked delicious. The table was lined with hors d'oeuvres, and one long table was full of nothing but desserts. Everyone mingled, and we talked freely with the UAE pilots until the commanders arrived.

The UAE base commander addressed the group: "I would like to welcome the 4th Fightin' Fuujins to Al Minhad Air Base and the United Arab Emirates. This is your home now, and we will do everything possible to make you feel comfortable."

After thanking the commander, Col. Navarro added: "I want to congratulate all of you on a very successful deployment, and I would also like to thank the UAE government for opening their base to us. This is the farthest an F-16 unit has ever deployed, and each of you accomplished the feat safely and professionally. I know you are hungry and tired, but I want to take a moment to remind you that a tremendous amount of work will have to be done in the coming days to prepare this base for the possibility of war. Personnel and equipment will continue to arrive daily, and time is of the essence. I spoke with Gen. Horner a few minutes ago, and I informed him that all twenty-four of our aircraft arrived safely. I let him know that our pilots are on alert and ready to go if called upon."

As soon as Col. Navarro finished, the UAE commander motioned for us to begin eating. Our mouths watering, we politely waited for the UAE pilots to step up to the table first. But they backed away, motioning for us to begin. After an awkward moment, the UAE commander reiterated that since we were the guests, we should begin first, and we then scrambled to get in line. The meal was excellent, a hopeful indication that we would enjoy our stay here.

After dinner, many of us conversed with the UAE pilots, who expressed shock that Saddam Hussein would attack the country of an Arab brother. They considered Saddam a tyrant for what he had done, and they feared he would soon attack Saudi Arabia and possibly even the UAE. They expressed relief and gratitude that we had come to their country in defense of the region, but also assured us that Saddam Hussein had made a terrible miscalculation and would soon realize his error and withdraw his forces.

"How long do you think it will take?" I asked.

"You will see," one pilot responded. "Saddam will back down. In two or three weeks, this will all be over."

After a couple of games of pool, I went back to my room to finally get some sleep. I'd been awake for more than twenty-four hours, and the effects of my last go pill had already worn off. When I walked into the room, I was surprised to find three new roommates, Capt. Jeff "Ark" Arkell, Capt. Mike "Redman" O'Grady, and our squadron flight surgeon, Capt. Tim "Doc" Hursh. The three beds in our bedroom had been replaced by three bunk beds.

Ark and I were good buddies, so I was happy to have him as a roommate. Doc and Redman were welcome additions as well, but the fact was that we now had eight pilots sharing the same room. With only one shower, a few of us volunteered to take our showers at night. As we prepared to go to sleep, Doc passed out "no-go" pills to help make us drowsy. Just before we were ready to turn out the lights, Lt. Col. Scott dropped by to see if we were doing okay.

"Have you heard any news concerning Saddam Hussein and Iraq?" Big O asked.

"All we know right now," Scotty replied, "is that Iraqi forces have not crossed the border into Saudi Arabia. Anything can happen over the next few days, so make sure you get plenty of rest and drink lots of water. It's going to take a while to set up all the communication equipment in the command post. Until then, stand by to standby."

I fell asleep thinking of my family, thinking of Colette. Sometime during the night, I was awakened by a flashlight shining in my face. The intruder was our wing director of operations, Col. Bill Huddle. As I shielded my eyes from the light, he said, "You're not Doc Hursh."

"You're not my wife, sir, but"—Sudds and Ark erupted with laughter—"Doc is over here, sir."

Col. Huddle woke Doc up and informed him that one of the crew chiefs was ill. All of us were able to go back to sleep—for a time. I woke up again a few hours later, picked my watch up off the floor, and saw it was only 03:15. I'd been in bed for six hours. I tried to go back to sleep, but it was no use. My body clock was still on Mountain time.

Tossing and turning, my thoughts were of Colette, Candice, and Kristen. It was almost dinnertime in Utah, and I wondered what the three of them were doing. The more I thought about them, the more I wished I were at home. The more I thought about being home, the more depressed I got.

During my first month at Kunsan, I experienced the same depression and anxiety, and often questioned whether I had made the right choice in becoming a fighter pilot. But this was worse. At Kunsan, I knew the exact day I would return home. It was the light at the end of the tunnel. But at that moment, while staring into the darkness, I realized that we could be in the Middle East for months, or, even worse, many of us could lose our lives. With everyone else asleep, I took out my flashlight, pen, and paper, and wrote a letter to Colette—hoping it would make me feel better.

30 August 1990

Dear Colette,

Hi, honey. Well, I'm here. I don't know what day it is for you or how long it took for this letter to reach you, so I'll start at the beginning. First of all, I love you very much and I wish I were home with you and the girls. Yeah, I know what you're thinking. I was all psyched up to come over here and fly my F-16 into battle. Well, it's five o'clock in the morning and the realization is beginning to set in. God, what am I doing here?

Sitting in the arming area at Hill was real emotional for me and I was glad you were there to see me off. The flight to Shaw went well and I got a good night's sleep. The flight to the UAE turned out to be the most incredible experience I have ever been involved with. There is so much to tell and I will go over the whole mission with you when we talk on the phone.

Once I landed, I could barely climb out of the jet. I was mentally and physically exhausted and the temperature had to have been over 100 degrees with 90-percent humidity. Our base is in the middle of nowhere and we're surrounded by sand and desert. What I wouldn't give for a nice winter breeze. The good news is that our quarters are air-conditioned. The bad news is that there are eight of us living in the same room. Our room is about the same size as our living room and dining room. Did I mention we have only one bathroom? I guess we'll find a way to make it work.

The other good news is that the o'club will feed us three meals a day. Our first dinner was outstanding. It's not as good as your cooking, but it's ten times better than what we expected. Right now we have about 300 people on base, but the wing commander expects 1,300–2,000 by next week. So far, the people of the UAE seem happy that we're here. The Sheikh told Col. Navarro that money was no object and that he could do whatever he wanted to prepare the base for war. The Sheikh gave Col. Navarro and Col. Huddle new cars to drive around base, and the maintenance guys have brand new Land Rovers to drive.

I know this is tough on you, especially when both of us thought we would finally be together for good. Now I'm remote again and I wish I were home with you and the girls. I miss you so much, and all I can say is I hope this ends quickly. Thank you so much for the card you put in my bag! That really made my day, and the other guys in the room were jealous when they heard me say I found a card from you. I can already tell that they miss their families a tremendous amount as well.

As soon as you find out what our address is, please send me the following things: *USA Today* sports pages, a large bottle of shampoo, my *Sports Illustrated* magazines, a month's supply of gum with different varieties, and some of your homemade chocolate chip cookies. Make sure you wrap them individually or they'll end up in crumbs like the ones you sent me when I was in Korea.

How are my little babes doing? I want to kiss their soft little necks so bad. I wish they could stay the same until I come home. I've missed so much already, and those times can never be replaced. Tell everyone I'm all right and ask them to send letters. I'm sure I'll have plenty of time on my hands and it will be nice to hear from friends and family. I hope you write a lot also, and I promise I'll write every other day. I'll call every Sunday once we find out how the phone system works here.

That's about it for now. I'll write again soon and I'll number each letter so you can read them in order. I'm okay. I just want you to know how much I love you and the girls. I can't wait for the day when I fly home and hold you in my arms. Make sure you show Candice and Kristen my tape so they don't forget who I am. Tell them their daddy loves them very much. I love you too!

Keith

9.
UNEXPECTED TRANSFER

wo days after our arrival in the UAE, we were briefed that the Iraqis had nearly 200,000 men and 20 percent of their 5,500 tanks stationed on the northern border of Saudi Arabia. The Iraqis were well equipped with Soviet-made T-72 and T-62 tanks, and they had been taught Soviet tactics over the past few years by military advisors. We felt confident that we could handle their air force, but it was a tense time in the region. If Saddam Hussein wanted the eastern province of Saudi Arabia, it would be easy for him to take it. The only thing standing between the Iraqi leader and his control of more than 50 percent of the world's oil supplies was approximately 100,000 marines and troops from the U.S. Army's 82nd Airborne Division.

A military strike across the border appeared imminent, and it was what the U.S. leadership feared most. The massive deployment of American troops had barely begun. At this point, an Iraqi attack would be a cakewalk for Saddam Hussein. Iraq had long-range Scud missiles, which could reach targets up to 550 miles away. They also had French-made Exocet missiles, which could be launched from Mirage fighters or from attack helicopters. The Exocet has a range over 45 miles and, like the Scud, can deliver chemical weapons. The elite American forces are the best-trained in the world, but most of them had been in theater for only a short time. If the Iraqis decided to attack, these men would be confronted with an environment even the staunchest soldier would find difficult to survive. Desert temperatures hovered around 110 degrees during the day. Wearing chemical gear would add another 20 degrees on top of that. Drinking water through a gas mask in an air-conditioned classroom is difficult. Doing it on a desert battlefield while being fired upon is unimaginable.

Our country needed time. Fortunately, Saddam Hussein was giving it to us. Giant C-5 and C-141 transport planes, along with a large contingent of civilian aircraft from the nation's airline industry, continued to transport troops and supplies into the Middle East theater. In addition to Saudi Arabia, base agreements were being negotiated with the United Arab Emirates, Oman, Bahrain, and Qatar. The U.S. Air Force had already proven it could deploy squadrons of fighter aircraft quickly and efficiently, but bringing in army and marine divisions would take much longer. Most of their heavy equipment would have to be transported by ship, which takes weeks, if not months. But with each passing day, America's presence in the region grew stronger.

While Iraq tightened its grip on Kuwait, we continued to settle into our new base in the

UAE. Our accommodations were adequate, and rooming with seven other guys wasn't all that bad. We kept each other company and sat around telling stories like kids at summer camp. The only disagreement we had was over the temperature of the room. During the night, someone would always get up and start adjusting the thermostat. I'd go to sleep feeling comfortable and, a few hours later, wake up in a sweat. Before long, someone would walk by my bunk and the air conditioner would kick in. I'd get back to sleep, only to wake up shivering. Ultimately, we compromised on a temperature, and posted the thermostat off-limits.

No complaints about the spacious officer's club. We'd go there to relax and, most important, to get three hot meals per day. The food was good, although a few dishes were tough to identify. They were a far cry, though, from the cold MREs (meals ready to eat) everyone thought we'd be eating. Nevertheless, after a few days, the variety paled. The meat was greasy, and the rice was mixed with nuts or bones hard enough to crack teeth. It became a standing joke that whenever someone asked, "what's for dinner," the answer was, "bones and rice." Then, after three days on base, word spread that people were starting to get sick. Capt. Scott "Rounder" Rounds was the first pilot to come down with the mysterious bug. A bad case of diarrhea left him severely dehydrated, and he had to be hospitalized for a couple days. Col. Bill Huddle got the bug shortly after Rounder, and so did my roommate, Capt. Tim "Doc" Hursh. After some tests, the flight surgeons diagnosed amoebic dysentery. After further investigation, we found out that the locals used human feces to fertilize the fields where lettuce and some of our vegetables were grown. The wing commander directed some of our own enlisted personnel to help sanitize the officer's club kitchen and to help the staff prepare our meals. We were then cautioned to avoid eating lettuce and anything else that hadn't been cooked.

The other problem we encountered was dehydration. The extreme heat and humidity quickly took a toll on everyone. Lt. Col. Scott ordered us to wear our canteen belts whenever we were outside and to always carry a full canteen of water. Fortunately, the water supply on base was not a problem. The water came from the Persian Gulf and was processed through desalinization plants, the only means of supplying fresh water to the local population.

We would spend most of our free time at the officer's club, usually going into the lounge to play cards, shoot pool, play Ping-Pong, and read books. The television carried just one station, and the only show in English was the news at 22:00 each night. For the first few nights, the room was jammed with people trying to find out more information about Saddam Hussein and his forces. Each night, we hoped to hear Saddam Hussein announce an Iraqi withdrawal from Kuwait. But that news never came. The situation seemed only to get worse. After a few nights, most of us stopped watching.

The o'club had two telephones that were constantly used by pilots and other officers trying to reach loved ones back home. During my first phone call to Colette, I let her know that I was doing okay and that I missed her terribly. I promised to call her twice a week and write as often as possible. She replied that she would write to me every day, and that she would keep showing my videotape to the girls.

The population of the base almost doubled with the arrival of the 421st Black Widows on 1 September, adding twenty-three more F-16s to the base. Most of the Fightin' Fuujins were there to greet them as they taxied their jets onto the helicopter ramp. The guys were really beat, and I realized what I must have looked like right after I landed. One of my squadron mates from Korea, Capt. John "Jabba" Columbo, was a member of the 421st and flew an F-16 over on the deployment. As soon as Jabba shut down his engine, raised his canopy, and removed his helmet, I approached the aircraft, reached up, and handed him a cold bottle of water.

"Wow!" he said. "Who turned on the heat?"

With the addition of the 421st, Al Minhad quickly turned into an American fighter base. C-141 transports continued to arrive every few hours, bringing in more personnel and equipment from Hill AFB. The 421st set up shop in the helicopter squadron, while the 4th continued to work out of the fighter squadron. The ramp was crowded with aircraft, and the maintenance units took over the two large hangars adjoining each of the squadron buildings.

The next day, a vendor began delivering local newspapers to the club. Two big stacks appeared in the lounge, and most of them vanished by dinner time. The *Gulf News* and the *Khaleej Times*, printed in Dubai, were dominated by the plight of Kuwait. Clearly, the UAE government and the local media were outraged that Saddam Hussein would invade the homeland of an Arab brother, and momentum was building for the United States and the international coalition. Many of the writers expected a war to start soon. Yet none of us knew what would happen. War could start tomorrow or never at all. All I did know was that the NFL football season had begun, and for the second year in a row, I was missing it. I was also missing the baseball pennant drive. Maybe this would end soon so we could make it home for the World Series.

At this point, intel repeated that it would be a few more days before their communication network was fully operational. In the meantime, bad news arrived by way of a C-141 transport. A four-day-old *USA Today*, circulating around the club, quoted several U.S. congressmen as saying, "Economic sanctions should be given a year to work!" A cautious attitude seemed to be forming, and words like "negotiation" and "patience" were being used. Some of us saw the conflict as another Vietnam, and there was a fear that scores of American soldiers would be killed if war broke out. Suddenly it dawned on me. This deployment was nothing more than a show of force. We would not be here for ninety days. It would be more like a year. Others had the same thought. Morale suddenly plummeted.

On Monday, 3 September, Lt. Col. Scott leads the local-area orientation flight, which turns out to be a lot of fun. We take off in groups of four and depart to the west toward the Persian Gulf. After leveling off at 5,000 feet, we make a left turn and proceed south along the UAE coastline. It takes about ten minutes for the formation to reach Abu Dhabi, sixty miles south of Al Minhad. Along the way, we pass over a huge oil refinery and dozens of oil storage tanks. The hazy sky limits our visibility, but the crystal blue water of the Persian Gulf and the beach resorts we fly over quickly catch our attention.

We reach the sprawling city of Abu Dhabi, which this tiny emirate, one of the richest states in the world, has spared no expense in building. Once we pass over the area, we make a turn toward the east and fly over Al Dhafra Air Base, the new home of the F-16s from Shaw AFB. Staying above the traffic pattern, we veer north and fly over a vast stretch of desert before turning back toward the coastline and north to Dubai. As we approach the city, we spot two beautiful palaces situated on the beach. Both are surrounded by large walls and appear to be the homes of the wealthy oil sheikhs who govern the country. The palaces have large pools, helicopter landing pads, and even surface-to-air missile batteries to defend against air attacks.

We remain a mile off the coast as we fly past Dubai, then we turn back to the east and fly along the southern border of Oman, which abuts the UAE to the north near the Strait of Hormuz. The strait marks the opening to the Persian Gulf and is over 500 miles from Kuwait and southern Iraq. Most of the UAE countryside is nothing more than a vast desert, except for a large mountain range that stretches from north to south along the country's eastern border. Flying along the western ridgeline, we proceed south toward miles of sand dunes, many of which are hundreds of feet high. We drop down to 500 feet and transition to an offset box formation with three-mile spacing between the elements. The haze is worse inland, and the glare off the sand makes the low-level even more difficult. I've flown dozens of low-levels over mountainous terrain, but I never imagined I would be terrain-masking behind sand dunes that reach as high as 800 feet. We spend about five minutes at low altitude and buzz a few oil facilities scattered throughout the countryside. We even come across a Bedouin tribe tending their herds of goats and camels. I laugh when I see a fleet of Range Rovers parked alongside their tents.

It doesn't take long to see the country, and once we return to Al Minhad, we fly a few patterns for practice. This is the first time the aircraft have flown since the deployment, but thanks to our squadron maintenance, the jets perform flawlessly. Yet the heat and sand are likely to cause problems, and we will probably see component breakdowns until the jets adjust to the environment. Maintenance will have their hands full.

After we landed, we went back to the squadron to debrief the sortie. While dropping off our equipment in the life-support shop, Lt. Dan "Pigpen" Swayne commented on how isolated the base was. We couldn't help but notice that Al Minhad was surrounded by miles of open desert and the city of Dubai was a good distance away. There was soon talk of going downtown or maybe to one of the beach resorts. But I reminded everyone that we were in a part of the world that didn't hold Americans in the highest regard. I conveyed a story about two crew chiefs who were assigned to my squadron in Korea and how, seven months earlier, they were gunned down outside the gates of Clark Air Base while our unit took part in a Cope Thunder exercise.

"We'll have a tough time blending in with the locals if we go into Dubai to party or shop," I told the others. "We're on the brink of war, and the last thing any of us need is a knife in our back from a group of religious fundamentalists that sympathize with Saddam Hussein."

After lunch, we went back to the squadron, where the first order of business was to break out the dreaded chemical gear. Nearly all of our supplies had arrived now via C-141 transport, and all of us were given new outfits to store in our rooms. We received a briefing from squadron life-support, which demonstrated the proper way to wear the gas mask and the chemical-warfare suit. All of us have been trained with the equipment before, but we still practiced a few drills to see how quickly we could put on our masks. Extra filters were passed out, and "Doc" Hursh gave us our atropine, 2-PAM (pralidoxime) chloride, and Valium-injector cartridges, which are used to combat the effects of poison gas.

The masks are extremely uncomfortable. Wearing them reminded me of the chemical-warfare exercises we practiced in Korea. Our squadron conducted the exercises every six weeks, and everyone dreaded them. They were especially difficult to take in the summer, when the days were hot and humid. The worst part was trying to fly while wearing a chemical mask. During simulated chemical attacks, we would have to depart the squadron with our masks and helmets already on. Most of the time we would take off, engage the autopilot, then take the masks off. Before landing, we would put the masks back on again. Once on the ground, we would taxi our aircraft back to the parking area. Before we were allowed to open the canopy, though, we would have to put on our chemical outfits. The charcoal-lined ensemble fits over our regular flight suits. A small plastic poncho goes over the helmet and drapes over the shoulder area to protect the neck. After we'd get the outfits on, we would put on a pair of white cotton gloves, followed by a pair of black rubber ones. When it was time to climb out of the cockpit, crew chiefs were standing by at the bottom of the ladder. The first thing they did was place rubber booties over our combat boots. Then, to make sure we were completely protected, they would place giant plastic bags over us.

On one particular day, the temperature was over 90 degrees. By the time the crew van picked each of us up, we were drenched. Like astronauts in space suits, we lumbered into the back of the crew van. It's almost impossible to communicate with all the gear on. Nothing needed to be said, though. Everyone knew what the other person was thinking. It was one of those moments where we just sat there and said to ourselves, "What the hell are we doing here!"

At Kunsan, it was just an exercise. But we knew that Iraq had a large stockpile of chemical weapons and Saddam Hussein had already proven he was not afraid to use them. Another concern was whether Iraqi aircraft had the capability of reaching our base. During the break, we looked at a map and measured the distance from Kuwait to Al Minhad. We were 497 miles from Kuwait's southern tip, and Iraq was even farther away—well out of the range of Iraq's Scud missiles. The likelihood of an Iraqi jet getting this far was remote at best. We could feel pretty confident, then, that chemical weapons wouldn't be a factor for us at Al Minhad. But Lt. Col. Scott decided we should still fly with our gas masks in case we were shot down in an area that had suffered a chemical attack.

As the briefing concluded, Scotty stepped to the front of the classroom. "All right guys, listen up. A lot of people will be arriving on base in the next few weeks, and we have a great deal of work to do to fortify the base against an Iraqi air attack. I can't tell you anything new about the situation in Kuwait or the political scene back home, because I really don't know. Besides, it's not our job to worry about what the politicians are doing. Our biggest concern is to get this base ready. Portable buildings will be set up in the coming days, and every one of them will need to be fortified with sandbags. Gen. Horner will probably pay us a visit soon, and he'll expect us to be ready."

Someone in the back of the room cracked, "Do you think we'll have enough sand to fill up the bags, sir?"

Everyone laughed.

Scotty continued, "Col. Navarro is in constant touch with Gen. Horner and his staff. He told me this morning that if this thing kicks off, the general will have our wing conduct operations during the day and at night. Col. Navarro said the 421st would function as the night squadron, and our squadron would fly during the day. We'll continue to maintain six aircraft on standby alert, so check the schedule daily to see if your name is on it."

He continued, "I know you're anxious to drop some bombs. We're working with the locals to secure range space. We'll also try to arrange airspace, so we can fly air-to-air. That's all I've got. Any questions?"

"Any news about phones or mail, sir?" Opie asked.

"We're supposed to get an address sometime in the next few days," Scotty replied. "When we do, you can be sure the wives will be told what it is. I'm also looking into how we'll get mail out of here."

"What about stamps, sir?" Sudds interjected. "All of mine are stuck together because of the heat and humidity."

"Same with us, sir," some of the other guys mumbled.

"I'll check into it. Oh, and don't forget to drink plenty of water and stay away from the lettuce at the club."

As we began to file out of the room, Lt. Col. Scott asked Vicious and me to meet him in his office. We walked in, and he asked me to close the door.

"Rosey, I've got some bad news for you. Col. Navarro and Col. Huddle told me this morning that you and Kevin Perry are going to be transferred over to the 421st. As I mentioned in the meeting, the Black Widows are going to become the dedicated night squadron. Since you and Duck are LANTIRN-qualified, both of you will be needed in the unit."

I was shocked by the announcement.

"Is it permanent?" I asked.

"The D.O. hasn't given me a date yet. I won't bring the subject up. So until you hear differently, keep flying with us."

"I thought Duck and Rosey were supposed to take over the weapons shop when Sudds moves to flight commander," Vicious asked. "Can't you convince the D.O. that they're more valuable in the 4th, sir?"

"I'll try. But I can't promise anything."

I took one of the shuttle buses back to the o'club. I felt like I'd just been traded from the 1927 world champion New York Yankees to the 1962 expansion New York Mets. The 4th was the best squadron I'd ever been in, and the leadership was tremendous. The guys in the 421st were good guys, but their morale was extremely low, and the leadership had been poor. Over the next few days, the subject of the transfer didn't come up. I decided to keep a low profile, hoping the wing commander and the D.O. might forget about the idea.

With our first week at Al Minhad behind us, I already had three sorties under my belt. On a day off, I called Colette to tell her about my possible transfer. She quickly sensed the depression in my voice and did her best to cheer me up. Everything seemed to be going well back home. Colette had enrolled at Weber State University in Ogden, planning to take two classes in child development during the fall semester. The girls were enjoying our new home, and Colette had planned a little party for their second birthday, less than a week away. I told her I loved her, and I promised I'd call if things changed.

After hanging up, I joined Ark and Redman in the dining hall for dinner. Chicken and potatoes were being served, and the line to the buffet formed quickly. While eating, we talked about our families and planned what we'd do when we got back home. Ark wanted to go back to Caesar's Palace again, only this time with the wives.

After dinner, it was Ping-Pong and pool. By nine o'clock, back at the room, I wrote a birthday letter to my two precious girls. I couldn't believe they were going to be two years old already. For the second year in a row, I was stuck on the other side of the world.

With each passing day, the realization set in deeper: we would be stuck in the desert for some time to come. Everyone was getting bored, and morale continued to deteriorate. The information pipeline was as dry as the desert, and, aside from flying, there wasn't much else to do. I spent most of my time writing letters, listening to music, and thinking about Colette, Candice, and Kristen. My favorite tape was *Faith* by George Michael. The music reminded me of when Colette came to visit me in Korea. I listened to the tape every night before going to bed. It ensured that Colette was the last thing on my mind before I fell asleep.

◆ ◆ ◆

My next flight was with Capt. Scott "Rounder" Rounds, who had finally recovered from his bout with amoebic dysentery. He had lost a lot of weight, but he said he felt good and was anxious to get back in the air. I led him on his local area–orientation flight, and we had a good time touring the countryside. While flying along the coastline, I pointed out the palaces and the numerous beach resorts along the edge of the Persian Gulf. He had heard about the enormous sand dunes to the south of the airfield, so we also made a point to fly a low-level leg among the scorching mountains of sand.

After the sortie, Lt. Col. Scott, spotting me in the hall, asked me to come into his office. I knew what was coming, and my heart sank.

"Rosey, I know you were hoping this day wouldn't come. Effective tomorrow, you belong to the 421st. I hate to lose you, and I tried to convince the D.O. that you're more valuable to the wing as a member of the 4th. Unfortunately, though, LANTIRN is going to play a significant role if war breaks out, and your skills are going to be needed in the 421st. If this ends in the next few weeks, we'll all go home, and you'll come back to the 4th. In the meantime, I want you to go over to the 421st and give them your best effort. They have some problems over there, and you're the type of person that can help turn things around for them."

Scotty went on, "As far as Colette is concerned, she'll continue to be a member of the Fuujin family. When I talk to Susan, I'll have her call Colette and tell her that she will remain a part of the squadron."

I was enough of a military man to know that there was nothing I could do or say to change what happened. I used to wonder why some professional athletes got so upset about being traded from one team to another. Now I knew why.

It took a couple of trips, but I finally dropped all of my gear off at the 421st life-support trailer. Afterward, I walked over to the helicopter squadron where the Black Widows had set up shop. The first person I ran into was Capt. Tom "Badger" Schmidt. Badger and I had first met at Luke AFB when I was going through the LANTIRN course. He was a member of the 34th at the time, and the Rams were in the process of converting to LANTIRN.

"Welcome to hell," he said. "We heard you and Duck were coming over. You're not going to like it over here!"

It wasn't exactly the welcome I was hoping for.

I asked why he felt the way he did.

"A couple days before the 421st left Hill, we found out they were going to be the designated night squadron. They took six of us out of the 34th and put us in the 421st. Everyone in the squadron was upset, because they felt our squadron should have been the one to deploy. Most of the pilots in the 421st don't know us, and they're pissed because they have no idea what their role is supposed to be. The morale is extremely low in the squadron, and none of the 34th pilots have really been accepted. The unit doesn't have a single LANTIRN pilot, except for Lt. Col. Nall. Lt. Col. Cottingham is the squadron commander—and he isn't even LANTIRN-qualified!"

"You're singing to the choir," I told him. "I'm just as disappointed as you are. The 4th is a great squadron, and everyone loves working for Scotty. I was just beginning to make a lot of friends in the unit. But Duck and I are LANTIRN-qualified, so here we are."

I walked down to the commander's office to reintroduce myself to Lt. Col. Cottingham. The only person around, though, was the operations officer, Lt. Col. Tim Nall. Former chief of wing stan/eval, Nall had been given the 421st operations-officer job just before the unit deployed. I knocked on the door and he welcomed me into his office, shaking my hand. He asked if I was ready to start flying LANTIRN sorties.

"I haven't flown a LANTIRN sortie since I completed the course at Luke last May," I replied.

"Don't worry. Everyone's going to fly two day-sorties with a chase plane before we start flying at night."

Over the next few days, I completed my LANTIRN checkout, and on 11 September, I flew my first night LANTIRN sortie out of Al Minhad. Duck arrived the following afternoon, and, just as I had predicted, he was disappointed about being transferred. The two of us made one last attempt to convince Lt. Col. Scott and Lt. Col. Rackley that the 4th would be better off if we remained in the squadron. But it was too late. We were now members of the 421st Black Widows.

10.
GROUNDED

My daughters' second birthday was 13 September 1990. I looked at their picture. What in the world was I thinking about three weeks ago, when I told Colette I wanted to come to the Middle East? I wrote her about my transfer to the 421st, and I told her how bad I felt about missing the girls' birthday. I knew she was thousands of miles away, but Colette was the only one I could vent my frustrations to. Things wouldn't be so bad if we could just fight the war and come home. But as each day passed, the possibility of a quick war seemed more and more remote.

Just as I finished the letter, Orlando "Big O" Cisneros came in and asked if I wanted to go running with him and Rounder. As we passed by the 421st, I began to feel sick. My stomach cramped up, and I quickly realized I couldn't continue. Telling Big O and Rounder to go on without me, I turned around and walked back to my room. On the way, I broke out in a cold sweat. It was over 100 degrees outside, so I knew something was wrong. By the time I got back to my room, I could barely stand up. While taking a shower, I got dizzy and queasy. Afterward, I tried to take a nap, but several trips back and forth to the bathroom told me I'd caught the bug. When Doc Hursh came by and I described my symptoms, he looked at me: "I hate to tell you this, Rosey, but it sounds like you've got amoebic dysentery." This news wasn't good. I would be grounded for a minimum of seven days.

The next few days turned out to be the most depressing of my life. I was sick, thousands of miles from home, I couldn't see my family, and I was confined to an area surrounded by untold miles of scorching desert. The living quarters were not much different from prison cells, with eight pilots stuffed into every room, no privacy, and only one bathroom. The situation wouldn't have been quite so bad if I had known what was happening, but our wing leadership didn't say a word about what was going on in the outside world. Thank God I'd get to fly. That was the only thing that kept me motivated. But it was something I wouldn't be doing for at least a week.

Over the next few days, I spent most of my time on the couch in our living room. When I wasn't there, I was in the bathroom. The dysentery left me extremely weak, but I tried to make it over to the club for at least one meal a day. Not that I had much of an appetite, and the walk often left me feeling dizzy and nauseated. Each day crawled by. If I wasn't sleeping, I was listening to music, reading, or writing a letter to Colette. We finally had an address, and the good news was that we didn't have to use stamps on outgoing mail. I also spent a lot of time thinking about the events that led me here, about how I was a child when I first decided to be a pilot.

My mother was nineteen years old when I was born, and my father left us three months later. I didn't see him again until I was six years old. I could remember, as if it were yesterday, answering the door one night when he showed up at our apartment. He was living in Phoenix at the time, and he decided he wanted to be a part of my life. After that, each summer I would go to Phoenix to spend time with him. I loved the flight between Los Angeles and Phoenix, and was fascinated by big jets. The first takeoff and landing I experienced was the biggest thrill of my life.

My enthusiasm for flying stayed with me as I got older. A man my mother dated owned an airplane, and he took me flying occasionally. My mother remarried when I was eight: we moved into a neighborhood near the Santa Monica Airport—and air shows became an annual event.

In 1973, I began attending St. Bernard High School in Playa Del Rey, California. The school is located next to the north runway at Los Angeles International Airport. At any given time, I could look across an open field and see a 747 take off or land. On rainy days, I would spend my lunch hour staring out a second-story window on the south side of the school, watching the planes come in over the ocean. I'd dream of sitting in the cockpit behind the controls. Sometimes I'd go over to the airport just to talk to pilots from different airlines. To get inside the different cockpits, I would tell the stewardesses that my uncle had just gotten off the plane. Then I would ask if I could go on board to visit with the pilots in the cockpit. These were the days before terrorists and metal detectors. The pilots always said yes and were happy to answer my questions.

The summer before my senior year in high school, my parents moved with my younger sister and brother to Idaho. I was playing baseball at the time, and, like most young athletes, I hoped that one day I could play professionally. As far as I was concerned, the road to the big leagues did not go through Idaho. So instead of moving, I stayed with my grandparents while finishing my senior year of school. In the evenings and on weekends, I worked as a box boy at a local Safeway supermarket. As soon as I graduated, I moved into an apartment. From that point on, I was on my own.

I enrolled at Long Beach State University in January 1978, supporting myself with my grocery job and some construction work. A friend's father owned a construction company and recommended I get a degree in construction management. The industrial technology department at Long Beach State offered this major, and I figured I could graduate and become a project manager for a construction company. True, I was still interested in flying and playing baseball, but neither of these required me to major in anything specific. Then, in the fall of 1978, I made the Long Beach State baseball team. I looked forward to playing over the next four years, and I hoped I would be good enough to continue playing professionally afterward. A month before the season started, an old shoulder injury flared up. I had surgery in December, but my arm was never the same again.

Disappointed? Yes. But, deep down, I knew I wasn't really good enough to play professional baseball. I put the game behind me and concentrated on getting my degree. Then, when the spring semester ended in 1980, I decided to get a private pilot's license. I went to Santa Monica Airport, took my first lesson in a Cessna 152 on 23 May 1980, and, after one flight, I was hooked. During the summer, I continued to work at the market, spending any extra money I earned on flying lessons. My instructor was a former U.S. Air Force C-130 pilot named Drew Riolo. Like me, he also dreamed of one day becoming an airline pilot, but, with the country in a recession, none of the airlines was hiring. To stay current and build flying time, Riolo gave flying lessons. He was an outstanding instructor who donated a lot of time helping me map out my own strategy to become a commercial pilot. The best way to achieve my goal, he insisted, was to join the air force.

I respected Drew's opinion, but I wasn't sure I was ready to commit seven years of my life to the military. I wrestled with the idea all summer long and started school again in September. While walking on campus one day, I saw a KC-10 making its final approach to the airport in Long Beach. Suddenly I decided to pay a visit to the local air force recruiter. I told him I wanted to fly, and he explained what the qualifications were to become an air force pilot. Since I was already in school, he said the easiest way would be to enroll in the Air Force Reserve Officer Training Corps program. Classes were offered at Loyola Marymount University, not far from where I lived, so I could continue at Long Beach State and take the AFROTC classes at Loyola Marymount on Saturday mornings. As soon as I left the recruiter, I went to the school, stopped by the AFROTC office, and spoke with the detachment commander. He signed me up for the courses.

The following Saturday, I attended my first class as a new cadet. My schedule was full: I attended school at Long Beach State Monday through Friday, took AFROTC classes at Loyola Marymount every Saturday, and spent the rest of the weekend working at the market—three p.m. to midnight on Saturdays and noon to ten p.m. on Sundays. I had to take both freshman and sophomore AFROTC classes to make up for what I missed the previous year. Not that the AFROTC program guaranteed me a pilot slot. The program had far more students than slots, and the competition was fierce. The previous year, fifty applicants competed for only two pilot training slots. This year, only fifteen were competing for six slots.

Soon after the semester started, I took the Air Force Officer Qualifying Test (AFOQT), as well as pilot and navigator aptitude tests. My scores were above average, but still not high enough to guarantee me a pilot slot. High school and college grade-point averages were important, as were interviews conducted by officers on the AFROTC staff. There was also the stringent air force physical.

During the school year, I was so busy working and studying that I rarely had a chance to fly. I'd been dating Colette for a couple of years, and the time we could spend together was also limited. We saw each other during the week when I got home from school. Big dates were usually reserved for Friday nights. On Saturdays, the two of us would go to my grandparents' house to eat during my lunch hour. Colette and I also got together after I got off work; at the stroke of midnight, I would clock out and rush over to her house to catch the last hour of *Saturday Night Live.*

After church on Sunday mornings, I went to my grandparents' house, mowed the lawn, and ate a good home-cooked breakfast. I spent the rest of the afternoon and evening at the market. By now I was night manager, responsible for all the bookkeeping. Eight hours on Saturday and nine hours at time-and-a-half on Sunday gave me about twenty-two hours of pay each week. Fortunately, tuition at Long Beach State was only $115 each semester. My books cost about fifty dollars, and my rent wasn't very high. Colette's parents and my grandparents fed me well. Then, in the spring of 1981, my grandfather passed away. He had been a strong influence in my life, and losing him was hard on me. When I needed guidance, he was always there for me. It was tough, the thought of going through the rest of my life without him. I moved in with my grandmother. Being with her helped both of us heal.

One day in May, Lt. Col. Delford Britton, our AFROTC commander, called me into his office after class. He told me I had been awarded one of the six pilot-training slots.

I thought of my grandfather, and wished he could be there with me.

In June, I spent a month in AFROTC summer camp at McClellan AFB in Sacramento, California. The training was fun, and every cadet got a ride in a T-37 Tweet, a twin-engine jet built by Cessna, with a top speed of 350 miles per hour. It is the primary jet trainer for the initial phase of undergraduate pilot training. I felt a little queasy during the flight, but I got a good taste of what pilot training was going to be like. When school started in the fall, I committed to the air force and began receiving checks for $100 a month—not a lot of money, but it paid for the rest of my college education.

Colette and I were married in June 1982. We honeymooned in Hawaii. The two of us had been dating for five years, and we were excited about our future together. We moved into a small apartment in Culver City, California. Colette worked while I finished my last semester of school. I graduated in December, and the two of us celebrated with a trip to San Francisco. In January 1983, I took the air force oath and received my commission as a second lieutenant.

I learned a short time later that I would begin pilot training as a member of class 84-04 at Reese AFB in Lubbock, Texas, with a report date no later than 21 April 1983. I spent the next three months sleeping in, playing golf, and flying. Colette and I stopped working at the end of March and devoted our last three weeks in Los Angeles to visiting with friends and relatives. My last flight at Santa Monica Airport came on 15 April. I passed my FAA check ride and received my private pilot's license.

Lubbock was a three-day drive. As we approached the outskirts of the city, I spotted a formation of T-38s flying toward Reese Air Force Base. The aircraft passed directly over us at no more than 2,000 feet. I could barely keep the car on the road as we watched them pass by. We arrived at the main gate of Reese an hour later and stopped at the guard shack to ask for directions. When the young airman saw my orders and recognized that I was a second lieutenant, he snapped to attention and gave me a crisp salute—my first official salute as an air force officer. I returned the salute and gave the airman a silver dollar.

Lubbock was a culture shock. The city, perched on a flat, wide plateau—the High South Plains of Texas—was home to Texas Tech University, Buddy Holly, and Mac Davis. Colette and I spent our first few nights at a Ramada Inn not too far from the base. We didn't care. This was going to be our home for the next year, and we were willing to put up with anything.

Undergraduate Pilot Training (UPT) began on 23 April 1983 and lasted an entire year. We rented a cozy apartment about six miles from the base. Colette went to work as a secretary for a local insurance investigator. I spent the first month of UPT in the class-room, preparing for T-37 training. Before the year was over, I had received more than 350 hours of academic training and had taken thirteen exams. The minimum passing score for each test was 85. Every night Colette quizzed me on procedures. Thanks to her, I never failed a single exam.

Competition within the class was intense. Graduating was everyone's goal, but finish-ing in the top 10 percent was also important, since doing so meant a first choice of follow-on assignment. Near the end of the first month, we began training in the T-37 simulator, an exact replica of the T-37 aircraft. I flew my first simulator with my assigned instructor pilot (IP), Lt. Jerry Corbett, who had graduated from the Air Force Academy a few years earlier. I wanted to make a good impression during our first sim together, but I was so nervous that soon after the sim started, I began to hyperventilate. I wasn't used to wearing a helmet and oxygen mask, and in my anxiety to do well, I got a little too excited. Jerry put the sim on pause and gave me a quick pep talk to relax me. Everything was okay after that.

I flew my first sortie in the T-37 on 27 May 1983. Jerry helped me through the takeoff, and then we flew out to one of the military operating areas (MOAs) to practice turns, climbs, stalls, and basic precision flying. The T-37 is a fully aerobatic twin-engine jet, accommodating instructor and student side by side. The T-37 phase of training lasts four months, with each student receiving about seventy-five hours of flying. That first flight went well until we began doing aerobatics. After aileron rolls and loops, I quickly unhooked my oxygen mask, buried my face in a small plastic bag, and "gave it up." I couldn't even finish the flight. Jerry flew the rest of the way home. He did everything he could to boost my confidence, but I was in no mood for accolades. All I wanted to do was go to sleep. When we finally landed and shut down the engines, it took every bit of my feeble remaining strength to climb out of the jet and walk back to the squadron. I thought I was going to die.

At the squadron, I fell into a couch and closed my eyes. It wasn't enough to stop the room from spinning. By and by, my class commander, Capt. Ron Ashley, came by to see how I was doing.

"I understand you had an interesting first flight, Lt. Rosenkranz. How are you feeling?"

"Are all the flights going to be like this?" I replied.

"Don't worry," he said. "A lot of the guys get sick on their first flight. Before you know it, you'll be used to it."

In my case, it took exactly four more flights. It was messy at times, but after the fifth flight I never got sick again. I was lucky. Some of my classmates never got over airsickness, and washed out of the program because of it.

My classmates and I spent the rest of the summer flying the Tweet and working in the classroom. We developed a lot of camaraderie, and our class goal was to make sure everyone graduated. My last flight in the T-37 was on 7 September 1983. I flew an instrument check ride and passed with flying colors. Within days, the rest of the guys completed their check rides, and then the squadron held a small graduation ceremony for us. I was confident that I could fly the aircraft solo to any airport in the country in any type of weather; the challenge in the months ahead would be to apply the things I had learned to a faster aircraft, the T-38 Talon.

The Northrop Talon, better known as the White Rocket, is a twin-engine supersonic jet with a top speed of 800 miles per hour and a ceiling of 60,000 feet. Unlike the T-37, students and instructors in the T-38 sit in tandem, each occupying his own separate cockpit. During this phase of training, we received 105 more hours of flight training— all of it absolutely necessary, for many pilots consider the T-38 to be one of the hardest air force aircraft to land. A few of my classmates had difficulty in this phase and were washed out of the program. The formation phase was equally challenging, and a number of students washed out during this phase as well. Fortunately, I had a great instructor, Capt. David Cohn, who was able to guide me through the program without much trouble. Flying the T-38 helped me develop a great deal of confidence in myself as a pilot.

Assignment night came a month before graduation and was held at the Reese AFB officer's club. Our wives, instructor pilots, and students from other classes gathered at the club to watch us receive our assignments. Some of the guys wanted to fly fighters, while others hoped for transports and bombers. My first choice was a KC-10 to March AFB in Southern California. I had no ambition to fly a fighter, and flying a KC-10 in my home town would be a dream come true. But there were no KC-10 assignments in our block. Instead, I was selected to remain at Reese AFB as a T-38 instructor pilot. Colette and I weren't exactly thrilled about staying in Lubbock for three more years, but I liked the T-38 and being an instructor would give me a chance to hone my piloting skills.

On 6 April 1984, after a year of intense training, fifty-two pilots representing class 84-04 received their air force wings. My family was in attendance, and it was a special moment for all of us when Colette pinned the wings on my uniform. In the weeks that followed, I was sent to Randolph AFB in San Antonio, Texas, for T-38 Pilot Instructor Training. At the end of the two-month course, I was honored as the top graduate, and in September, I completed air force land- and water-survival training. One month later, I was back at Reese as a brand-new instructor pilot in the 54th Flying Training Squadron. Colette and I purchased our first home, and the next four years turned out to be great for both of us.

Being an instructor pilot was extremely challenging. We graduated a class every six months. I often worked twelve hours a day, flying as often as three times a day. When the weather was good, I could count on fifty hours of flying per month, most of which was local, but, on occasion, we took a group of T-38s cross-country on weekend training missions. Flying the T-38 is like driving a fine sports car, and there's no better way to see the country.

I was promoted to first lieutenant in April 1985 and then to captain two years later. Up for reassignment in September 1987, I still wanted to fly the KC-10. Most of my friends had said I would be happier if I asked for a fighter. Flying a fighter would, no doubt, be glamorous, I thought, but I just couldn't picture myself as a fighter pilot. Then I took a ride in the KC-10. The flight was part of a "buddy wing" program that allowed pilots to trade places with pilots from other wings for a few days. I traveled to Barksdale AFB in Shreveport, Louisiana, and sat in a KC-10 cockpit during a four-hour air-refueling sortie, experiencing firsthand the mission of a KC-10 pilot. I spoke to the pilots about the decision I was faced with, and even *they* suggested I ask for a fighter. They loved flying the KC-10, they said, but hours were hard to come by, and some of the long-haul missions were not as challenging as they would have liked. When I returned home, I described the KC-10 flight to Colette, told her what the tanker pilots had said, and she agreed that I would probably be happier if I flew a fighter. The next day, I filled out a new "dream sheet" and sent it off to the Manpower Personnel Center. Number one on my list was the F-16 Fighting Falcon. A week after my assignment board met, my boss, Maj. Mark Rogers, called me into his office and told me I had received my first choice.

I would begin lead-in fighter training at Holloman AFB in Alamogordo, New Mexico, in February 1988. Training in the F-16 would begin in May at Luke AFB in Phoenix, Arizona. The remaining months at Reese passed quickly for Colette and me. In my assignment as a T-38 instructor I had accumulated over 1,200 hours. I learned a tremendous amount from my fellow instructors, and I believe I was able to instill that knowledge into the hearts of the students I flew with. I was especially proud that more than half of my students were also chosen to remain at Reese as instructors. But Colette and I were excited about our new assignment—and we were even more excited when we found out we were expecting twins. We had been trying to have children for more than two years, and, at long last, our prayers were answered.

On 25 February 1988, I flew my T-38 "fini-flight" with Capt. Mark Miller. The two of us flew in formation with friends Capt. Tammy Rank and Capt. Mike Zimmering. After the flight, I was hosed down by my fellow instructors and given a bottle of champagne. It was a great way to end my assignment. The next day, Colette and I departed Lubbock for Holloman AFB in Alamogordo, New Mexico, where we moved into a small one-bedroom apartment. I began the Lead-In Fighter Training (LIFT) program a few days later while Colette battled a bad case of morning sickness. I was eager to begin training in the AT-38, a beefed-up version of the T-38. Before the program started, I set two goals for myself. I wanted to be the top graduate in my LIFT class and the top graduate/top gun in my F-16 class. Capt. Dion Thorpe, a good friend who was also a former T-38 instructor at Reese, had received an F-16 a couple of years earlier. After he left, word got back to the squadron that he had earned the top graduate award during F-16 training. All of the instructors who knew him were extremely proud of his accomplishment. Dion had always been somewhat of a role model for me, so I wanted to follow in his footsteps and receive the same recognition.

I was in a class of twenty-one students assigned to the 433rd TFTS Satan's Angels. We began in academics, including course work in basic fighter maneuvers (BFM) taught by retired fighter pilots. Once we started flying, I found that flying the jet was simple—but learning how to apply the BFM was very demanding. Fortunately, the 433rd had an awesome group of instructors, most of whom had years of fighter experience. Some of the veteran pilots had been flying fighters since the Vietnam War.

The LIFT syllabus consisted of thirteen BFM sorties and seven surface-attack sorties. The BFM flights focused on both offensive and defensive maneuvers. By the time the two-month course ended, I had learned a tremendous amount and had built a solid foundation leading into F-16 training. When our class graduated on 20 April 1988, Lt. Col. T. J. McGrath, the 433rd TFTS Squadron Commander, announced that I was the recipient of the class Top Graduate award. The instruction I received from the IPs in the 433rd was second to none, but it was Colette who helped me the most. Her encouragement and support gave me the energy I needed to achieve my goal. It was a proud and happy moment for both of us.

The next day, we left Holloman and drove to Phoenix. Colette was four months pregnant, and I couldn't wait to get to Luke AFB to begin training in the F-16. Luke AFB is located about thirty minutes west of downtown Phoenix. The base had four F-16 training squadrons. I was in a class of twelve pilots assigned to the 310th TFTS Top Hats. The squadron flew A-model F-16s, with Block 10 avionics. Among the unit's jets were tail numbers 001 and 002—the very first F-16s produced by General Dynamics. The first few weeks of training were spent in the classroom, undergoing a grueling regimen. Absorbing all the information was like drinking from a fire hose. We took five tests in the first month alone. I knew that competition within the class would be tough; many of the students I was competing against had graduated at or near the top of their pilot-training classes. Others came from a tactical background, having flown the T-33, OA-37, and OV-10. A few of the guys had gone through the LIFT program with me. They let me know right away that they were going to be gunning for me. We laughed about it in class, but I knew they were serious. The challenge made me even more determined.

Our class finally hit the flight line the first week of July. I couldn't wait to get my hands on the controls of the F-16. Climbing into the cockpit for the first time was like slipping on a glove. The fit was perfect. When I closed the canopy, I felt as though I were sitting on the end of a pencil. The visibility was incredible. Taking off was just as impressive, especially when the afterburner kicked in. The powerful engine threw me back in my seat and lifted me off the runway just as quickly. The aircraft was easy to fly; using the small side-stick controller didn't take long to get used to. As each week passed, I became more and more comfortable in the jet. Not that the program was easy. The most demanding sorties took place in the air-to-air arena, where I flew a number of offensive and defensive BFM sorties. The F-16 maneuvers were similar to those flown in the AT-38, but the high performance of the F-16 put a tremendous amount of physical stress on me. The Fighting Falcon is the most maneuverable fighter ever built. Its power and turning capability allow it to accelerate from one to nine Gs in a matter of seconds. At nine times the normal weight of gravity, maintaining blood pressure to the brain becomes extremely difficult. It's even more difficult when you're trying to turn your head around to keep sight of a bandit who is doing everything he can to kill you.

To help fight the effects of high G-forces, fighter pilots wear G-suits, which wrap around the legs and abdomen. A hose plugs into a valve located inside the cockpit. While pulling Gs, internal bladders in the suit inflate, squeezing the legs and abdomen, forcing blood upward. A pilot must also perform a "straining maneuver," tightening his muscles and controlling the rate at which he breathes. The combination of the straining maneuver and the G-suit helps stop the blood from pooling in the lower extremities. If a pilot fails to perform the straining maneuver properly, the decrease in blood pressure to the brain will likely result in a loss of consciousness.

While flying defensive BFM sorties, there were occasions when I got behind the power curve and experienced grayouts. Keeping up with the power of the F-16 was difficult for me. Fortunately, I was always able to recognize when I was having trouble. To keep from passing out, I had to ease up on the Gs until my vision returned. When moments like this occurred, flying the jet and maintaining sight of the bandit became impossible. As a result, I would turn into what the IPs referred to as a "duck." While I waffled in the air, struggling to stay awake, the instructors would maneuver their aircraft into position for an easy kill.

I hated defensive BFM sorties.

Halfway through the six-month program, our class began flying air-to-air combat sorties against dissimilar aircraft, F-15s from the four F-15 Eagle training squadrons based at Luke. Flying adversarial sorties against them was extremely educational. An F-15 is much bigger than an F-16, and it can be spotted from a great distance. The F-15 does have one big advantage, though. The Eagle is equipped with a powerful radar system, and also carries long-range radar missiles. The key to winning an engagement against an F-15 is to avoid getting shot with a radar missile. If you can do that, you stand a good chance of being able to outmaneuver the aircraft in a close-in fight.

On 13 September, the day after my last air-to-air sortie, I was in the squadron preparing for my first surface-attack mission when I received a phone call from the base hospital. Colette had been admitted a few days earlier so the doctors could monitor her and keep her from going into labor; the babies weren't due for another month. The nurse said I should come over right away. When I arrived at the hospital, the doctors were preparing to transfer Colette to Phoenix General Hospital, which has better facilities to handle premature births. They wanted to transport her by helicopter, but she refused. She left by ambulance instead, while I rushed home to pick up her things. I arrived at the hospital around four P.M., and at ten, Candice Leigh was born. She was followed a minute later by her sister, Kristen Alayna.

The girls were beautiful. I brought the three of them home three days later, and my squadron commander, Lt. Col. John Chambers, gave me a week off from flying so I could help out while Colette recuperated. The girls were inundated with gifts, and someone from the squadron delivered dinner every night for a week. Nevertheless, Colette and I had our hands full.

Once I started flying again, it was time to start dropping bombs. The Arizona desert is the ideal place for air-to-ground training in the F-16. Four conventional ranges and a number of tactical ranges are located just a short distance from Luke AFB. Our sorties usually began with a thirty-minute low-level to one of the conventional ranges, always flying in four-ship formations. Each pilot practiced various degrees of dive bombing as well as loft bombing. We were given six bombs to drop and one hundred rounds to shoot in the strafing pit. The standing bet among pilots in the fighter community is a quarter per bomb and a nickel for every round registered as a hit. The competition was keen, since every score was registered for the class Top Gun award. Once we became proficient on the conventional range, we started attacking targets on the tactical ranges, bombing airfields, SAM sites, tank columns, and AAA batteries. The instructors integrated tactics into many of the flights, and, every once in a while, enemy fighters would try to sabotage our missions by intercepting us prior to the target.

Strange as it sounds to say it, the most enjoyable part of training was the nuclear phase, in which we simulated carrying a nuclear weapon that was to be delivered at a specific time over target (TOT). Scoring a direct hit is difficult. Having the bomb hit the target at the exact second is even harder and takes a great deal of planning. A little luck doesn't hurt either. If you get jumped somewhere along the low-level by an enemy fighter, your timing is shot. We flew six sorties in this phase. When they were over, we were ready to graduate.

Graduation night was 1 December; I received the class Top Graduate and Top Gun awards and just missed winning the Academic Ace award too, which was captured by my classmate, Capt. Bob Sweeney. After the graduation, Colette and I packed up our things and left for California, where Colette and the girls would spend the coming year. My first assignment in the F-16 would be a one-year remote tour to Kunsan Air Base in the Republic of Korea. Colette and I had hoped for an assignment to Germany, but none was available. After the Christmas holidays, I went back to Luke AFB and completed a five-ride C-model conversion course, which was mandatory, since the wing at Kunsan AB flies C-model F-16s. As soon as I finished, I drove back to California to spend January with Colette, Candice, and Kristen. On the night of 10 February 1989, I boarded a Northwest Airlines 747 charter at Oakland International Airport. Saying goodbye was very painful; flying the F-16 can be dangerous. As I looked into Colette's eyes, part of me wondered if I would ever see her again. We kissed goodbye, I walked down the jetway, and I looked back. Colette stood near the doorway, alone. It was a sight that would remain etched in my mind.

Nearly four hundred service men and women crammed into the 747 to Korea. It was a cattle car. At Kunsan AB, I was welcomed by a group of pilots from the 80th TFS. Pilots in this unit are commonly referred to as Juvats, or Headhunters. The other squadron in the wing is the 35th TFS Pantons, or Panthers. Both squadrons are units of the 8th TFW Wolf Pack.

The first few weeks in country were tough. I was homesick despite the camaraderie. Many lonely nights got me wondering whether I had made the right assignment decision. But flying F-16s as a member of the 80th TFS was the most challenging assignment I had ever had. Starting out as a wingman, I learned from the best fighter pilots in the world. Flying the F-16 isn't all that difficult, but some of the more experienced pilots in the unit told me it would take twelve to eighteen months before I would be able to master the aircraft's complicated weapon system. Kunsan provided the perfect learning environment.

I returned to the United States on 11 February 1990. The year in Korea seemed like a lifetime, but I was a much better pilot for the experience. I got to spend three weeks in the Philippines participating in a Cope Thunder exercise, and two weeks in Singapore flying air-to-air combat against the Singapore air force. I also flew to Japan and spent a few days in Okinawa.

Two weeks after my return to the states, I was off to Maxwell AFB, Alabama, for eight weeks of Squadron Officer School. After graduating, I flew back to California, picked up Colette and the girls, and drove to Luke AFB for six weeks of F-16 LANTIRN training. By the summer of 1990, the 388th TFW was ready to become the first operational wing in the United States to fly LANTIRN-equipped F-16s. Since I was already C-model–qualified and scheduled to go to Hill, I was given a training slot in one of the initial LANTIRN classes. The course consisted of a week of academics, five simulator flights, and eight aircraft sorties.

When I wasn't flying, I spent time getting reacquainted with Colette and the girls. Being together again was a dream come true, and we couldn't wait to settle into our new home at Hill AFB, Utah. We departed Phoenix on 1 June and drove through the main gate at Hill the following day. The afternoon of our arrival was gorgeous. Colette and I were captivated by the beauty of the Wasatch mountains and the view of the Great Salt

Lake. We were happy also to be settled at last and looked forward to spending the next few years together at Hill.

I spent the rest of June and early July 1990 completing the local area checkout program, and then deployed with the squadron to Nellis AFB for the Green Flag exercise. Six weeks later, I was halfway around the world, preparing to do battle. Many pilots would envy the air force career I've had. I've traveled everywhere, and I fly the best fighter that technology has to offer.

While at Al Minhad, I was miserable. I missed my family and was so sick, I could barely make it to the bathroom. I used to think I could handle anything, but during that third week of September 1990, I learned that I might not be quite the person I thought I was. I was afraid of dying alone in the desert. I was afraid of never again seeing Colette, Candice, and Kristen.

11.
BLACK WIDOW

Thirty-five days after Operation Desert Shield began, 675 U.S. Air Force aircraft were already deployed to the Middle East, nearly two-thirds of them fighters poised to defend the Saudi kingdom. While F-15 Eagles flew combat air patrols, E-3 AWACS surveillance aircraft orbited along Saudi Arabia's northern border, searching deep inside Iraqi airspace. Other fighters included dual-role F-15E Strike Eagles, F-4G Wild Weasels, F-111 Aardvarks, A-10 Thunderbolts, F-117 Nighthawks, and F-16 Fighting Falcons. Each of these was on standby alert and could be airborne within minutes if needed.

In the meantime, the biggest airlift since Vietnam was operating at full force. Military Airlift Command (MAC) C-5, C-141, and C-130 aircraft traveled back and forth between the United States and the Middle East, delivering troops and supplies. In August alone, these aircraft flew more than 2,000 missions, hauling 72,000 troops and 106 million pounds of cargo to dozens of bases in the region.

Details of Iraq's buildup had been tough to come by during our first week at Al Minhad, but now, with wing intel having set up its communication network, a steady flow of information arrived daily from U.S. Central Command (CENTCOM) headquarters. The latest report confirmed that ten Iraqi divisions consisting of approximately 150,000 troops were situated in Kuwait. Twelve more divisions were entrenched in southern Iraq, along Kuwait's northern border. Iraq's army had 5,700 tanks, 5,000 armored vehicles, and more than 5,000 support vehicles. They also had 3,700 artillery pieces and an air-defense system equipped with more than 16,000 SAMs and 7,000 AAA pieces. Offensively, the Iraqi stockpile included more than 1,000 Scud missiles. One version, the Al Hussein, had expanded fuel tanks and could deliver a 350-pound conventional or chemical warhead. It could be launched from anywhere inside Iraq, and with a range of nearly 400 miles, it could reach key cities in Saudi Arabia and Israel.

But Iraq's biggest threat was its air force of approximately 635 attack aircraft, operating from twenty-four bases and thirty dispersal fields. Most of the planes had been purchased from the Soviet Union years ago, but others, like France's Mirage F-1 and the Soviet MiG-29, were quite modern and capable of putting up a good fight. Chances of an Iraqi bomber reaching UAE airspace were slim, however. Al Minhad is more than 600 miles from southern Iraq, and Iraqi aircraft would have had to penetrate a formidable defense of American fighters to make it that far. Yet if Saddam Hussein did decide to attack, our wing was prepared. Shortly after our arrival, civil engineering teams began

building underground bunkers, and portable trailers were brought in to provide additional office space. Each trailer was covered with camouflage netting; sandbags were
stacked against the outer walls for additional protection. Enlisted personnel had been
working sandbag detail day and night; the wing goal: fill 250,000 of them. Security was
extremely tight on base, and even though we were guests of the UAE government, we
did not let up our guard against terrorism.

For three weeks, the population at Al Minhad had grown from a few hundred to more
than 3,000. Military transports and civilian airliners arrived daily, bringing in more
troops and cargo. At this point, eight major commands and thirty-seven bases were represented by troops supporting the 388th mission. Officers stayed in hard billets, while
enlisted personnel lived in a tent city dubbed "Camp Camel-Lot."

Adjusting to life in the desert wasn't easy. We could call home as much as we wanted,
and outgoing mail was delivered for free. Going out to dinner, seeing a movie, or just
relaxing in front of the television was not possible, however. Alcohol was forbidden.
One of our biggest gripes was the laundry system. Little by little, everyone's clothes were
disappearing. We tried writing our social security numbers on each piece of clothing,
but it didn't help. With the tight security, boredom, and, finally, our social security
numbers etched across our backs, we began to feel as if we were in prison. Some of the
guys started referring to our wing commander as "The Warden."

A week had passed since my last sortie, and I finished the medicine designed to kill off
the amoebic dysentery. But another stool sample revealed I was still infected. I felt better, though, and I reported to the squadron to begin my new job as assistant chief of
weapons. Duck took over the weapons shop when the two of us transferred from the
4th, and Lt. Col. Nall made me his assistant. I was excited about the position, because it
was an opportunity to learn more about F-16 weapons and tactics.

On Saturday, 22 September, Badger and I spent the afternoon building a LANTIRN
low-level map. Col. Navarro told us that LANTIRN was the wing's highest priority.
Yet 75 percent of the squadron's pilots were as yet unqualified to perform it. At the
moment, the only Black Widows qualified to use LANTIRN were Lt. Col. Tim Nall,
Capt. Lonnie "Weasel" Sanford, Capt. Mark "Skippy" Lankford, Capt. Robin "Batman"
Adam, Capt. John "Tater" Specht, Capt. Tom "Badger" Schmidt, Capt. George "Harpo"
Stillman, Capt. Kevin "Duck" Perry, and me. Gen. Horner and his staff may have
believed the 421st was ready to take on the Iraqis, but, honestly speaking, the Black
Widows were nowhere close to being ready for war.

After Badger and I finished the map, Lt. Col. Nall called me into his office to discuss
morale.

"If this war ever starts," Nall said to me, "the success of the 388th may well depend on
what we accomplish with LANTIRN. I know you and Duck would rather have stayed in
the 4th, and I don't blame you. But the fact is, you're a Black Widow now, Rosey. I want
you to move out of the room you've been staying in and into a room with other members of the squadron. It will be good for you, and it will be good for the unit. I also need

you to get healthy again, so we can get you back in the air. We're going to be doing a lot of night flying soon, and your experience is sorely needed."

"Are anymore LANTIRN pilots coming over?"

"Ten pilots are due to complete their training at Luke by the middle of October. As soon as they finish, they'll join our squadron and replace pilots in the 421st who aren't LANTIRN-qualified. I know you're coming off of a remote tour and would like to go home, but we need all the LANTIRN pilots we can get right now."

After Nall finished, I saluted smartly and headed back to my room to begin packing, more depressed than ever. Ark and Redman were sympathetic and both tried to cheer me up, but each of us realized my days as a Fightin' Fuujin were in the past. I gathered my things, said goodbye to the guys, then walked to the east end of the compound where pilots from the 421st were being housed.

Most of my new roommates I'd met before, and two were old friends: Capt. Steve "Mac" McElhannon, who was in my pilot training class at Reese AFB, and Capt. John "Jabba" Colombo, a fellow Juvat from the 80th TFS at Kunsan. Mac invited me in, pointing out an empty bunk next to his in the back bedroom. Space was limited, so both of my duffel bags ended up on the floor at the foot of my bed. Three days later, the 836th Fightin' Medics Air-Transportable Hospital team arrived from Davis-Monthan AFB, Tucson, Arizona. The squadron's fifty officers needed a place to stay. Three of the officers—a doctor and two physician's assistants—ended up in our room. Seven men in one room was ridiculous. Now we had ten.

By midweek, I finished my medication and received a clean bill of health from Capt. Michael "Doc" McGunigal, the 421st flight surgeon. I hadn't realized how much I would miss flying, and I couldn't wait to get my hands on the controls of an F-16 again. As soon as I left the flight surgeon's office, I ran across the street to the squadron to tell Lt. Col. Nall the good news. Congratulating me, he asked if I'd like to fly that afternoon. He didn't have to ask twice. He threw me in the number two slot of a four-ship led by Badger. Capt. Mark "Skippy" Lankford was scheduled to fly the number three jet, and his wingman was Capt. George "Harpo" Stillman. Brief time was set at 13:00. Our task was to test the new LANTIRN low-level map that Badger and I had built over the weekend.

Once intel was finished briefing, the four of us met in the weapons shop, where Badger conducted the flight briefing. After passing out lineup cards and copies of the new map, Badger gave us a time hack and reviewed the objectives of the flight.

"When we built this low-level, we had two major concerns: How will the terrain-following radar [TFR] perform over water? And will the system be able to handle the monster sand dunes that reach as high as eight hundred feet in some areas of the desert? Today we're going to find out. But before I go any further, Rosey has a few things to cover."

"When I was at Kunsan," I began, "my squadron commander was Lt. Col. Ron Wilke, and my flight commander was Maj. Dave Martin. Dave graduated from test pilot school at Edwards AFB and flew most of the initial LANTIRN test flights with Lt. Col. Wilke when they were assigned to AFOTEC [Air Force Operational Test and Evaluation Command]. We discussed LANTIRN quite a bit, especially when I found out I was coming to Hill. Each spoke highly of the system. But both experienced a few close calls during the testing. In certain instances, the TFR failed to recognize the terrain and provide fly-up protection. I distinctly remember Dave telling me the incidents happened when they were flying over sand or water. So pay close attention to your TFR when we fly over the Gulf of Oman and the sand dunes in eastern Saudi."

"As you can see by looking at your maps," Badger resumed, "the second leg of the low-level is over water and should last about seven minutes. If your jet descends below your set clearance plane, there's a good chance the radar isn't recognizing the water. If that happens, let me know about it, and make sure you write it up so maintenance can take a look at it. The same is true for leg four, when we fly over the big sand dunes. The visibility isn't all that great and the sand may tend to blend in with the horizon. Keep an eye on the TFR display in your right MFD. If you see a sand dune and the radar doesn't, go manual and climb. The last thing we need is an accident."

The four of us taxi into the arming area at 16:10. After the arming crews complete their checks, I adjust my FLIR picture and check my systems one last time. Three minutes prior to takeoff, Badger holds up three fingers beside his helmet, signaling the formation to switch over to uniform channel three. After passing the signal to Skippy, I tune in the tower frequency. As Badger taxies toward the runway, he barks out: "Spider 31, check."

"Two!" "Three!" "Four!"

"Tower, Spider 31 is ready for takeoff."

"Roger, Spider 31. Winds are calm, you're cleared for takeoff."

"Spider 31 cleared for takeoff, go channel four."

"Two!" "Three!" "Four!"

I switch over to channel four, and as soon as we're in position, Badger flashes the run-up signal. With my feet firmly on the brakes, I push my throttle up to 80 percent RPM. After scanning my instrument panel, I look for a head nod from Skippy and Harpo. As soon as they acknowledge, I turn to Badger and nod my head, signaling that the three of us are ready.

"Spider 31 check."

"Two!" "Three!" "Four!"

Badger releases his brakes. Within seconds, his afterburner ignites and propels him down the runway. I keep an eye on my clock and twenty seconds later, I begin my take-off roll. Once I'm airborne, I retract my gear and accelerate to 350 knots. I quickly spot Badger at my ten o'clock in a left hand turn toward the east. Passing 800 feet, I bank to the left and fall in behind him. Once established on the departure, I complete my LAN-TIRN checks and accelerate to 480 knots.

Each aircraft is eight miles in trail of the other, and the four of us are proceeding direct to steerpoint number one, which is located 20 miles east of the airfield. Less than a minute before the low-level begins, Badger checks us in.

"Spider 31 ops check. One is twenty-seven, thirty-one, ten-five . . . tanks feeding."

"Spider 32 is twenty-seven, thirty-one, ten-four . . . tanks feeding."

"Spider 33 is twenty-seven, thirty-one, ten-four . . . tanks feeding."

"Spider 34 is twenty-seven, thirty-one, ten-two . . . tanks feeding."

We begin the low-level on time, and as soon as I engage the automatic terrain-following (TF) system, my aircraft descends to 500 feet. The first leg is planned over flat terrain to give everyone a chance to warm up. The second leg is where the fun begins. Rugged mountains that separate Oman from the UAE are just a short distance away, and it doesn't take long to reach them. As we proceed toward steerpoint two, most of my energy is focused on the FLIR display in my HUD. I check my spacing behind Badger and keep a close eye on my right MFD, which provides TFR returns 36,000 feet ahead of my aircraft. My life depends on the TFR, which recognizes rising terrain and keeps me at my programmed set clearance plane (SCP).

The east coast of Oman is only minutes away and my F-16 is performing flawlessly. It feels great to be in the air again. While the LANTIRN system helps me stay on course, I glance down at my map and do a quick study of the third leg. Once I reach the port city of Fujayrah, I'll be making a right turn to the south towards a small town called Liwa. My new heading will be 160 degrees, and I'll be flying over the water for roughly eight minutes.

A quick check of my radar shows Badger in a right turn over the steerpoint. My spacing and timing look good. Less than a minute later, I pass over Fujayrah. I look out both sides of my canopy to catch a glimpse of the small city. The locals have probably never seen an F-16 before. I hope they don't think they're being attacked.

"Spider 32, take a look at all these ships out here," Badger radios. "It's incredible!"

Dozens of tankers begin to emerge through the afternoon haze. I'm only a mile off shore, and I haven't seen this many ships since I was in Singapore, one of the largest ports in the world. I try to count them, but at the speed I'm flying it's impossible. There can't be any less than one hundred, though.

"Spider 32 copies," I reply. "They're probably not allowed to enter the Persian Gulf because they're destined for Iraq."

"It's nice to know the embargo is working," Badger radios.

As I buzz past the ships, I spot several crew members waving from their decks. I rock my wings to acknowledge them. Since the TFR has no trouble recognizing the water, I decide to experiment a little. I reprogram my SCP for 1,000 feet, and the auto TF mode climbs me right up. After leveling off, I program 500 feet again. Without hesitation, the aircraft descends and levels off at the correct altitude. The final test comes when I push forward on the stick. As I pass through 400 feet, the TFR recognizes the error. I quickly get a break *X* in the HUD, followed by a fly-up. I try the experiment in manual, and the results are the same. The LANTIRN system works like a champ.

A few minutes later, I pass over steerpoint three. I turn to my next heading of 285 degrees, which takes me over mountainous terrain and back into UAE airspace. Minutes after crossing a large highway, I fly directly over an oasis filled with trees and vegetation. Twenty miles later, towering sand dunes begin to appear. My cross-check alternates between the sand dunes in front of me and the TFR returns on my right MFD. Once again, the system performs like it's supposed to. The auto TF climbs and descends me like a roller coaster, keeping my F-16 at the programmed SCP. Our two biggest concerns going into the flight were water and sand. The nav pod has handled both with ease.

As soon as I pass over the next steerpoint, I turn north and proceed towards Al Minhad. The terrain begins to flatten out, which gives me a chance to relax a little. The last point on the low-level is a bombing range twenty miles south of the air base, and each of us will execute a 10-degree attack when we get there. I pick up a heading of 355 degrees and accelerate to 540 knots.

"Spider 31, check cameras on."

"Two!" "Three!" "Four!"

I reach down to my left console, turn on my videotape recorder, and select HUD. Afterward, I check my pop numbers and switch from auto TF to manual TF so I don't get a fly-up during the attack. Ten miles from the target, I cross-check my airspeed and the DME readout in the lower right corner of my HUD. When the DME reads 4.7, I pull back on my stick and establish a climb angle of fifteen degrees.

"Spider 32's up."

My jet climbs rapidly, and at 2,500 feet I roll inverted. While upside down, I pull on the stick until the nose of my jet is five degrees below the horizon line. At that point, I roll upright again. I'm ten degrees nose low and I have five seconds to find my target. My diamond is right where I expect it to be. As I scream towards the desert floor, I push the missile step button on my stick, which brings up the CCIP pipper. I cross-check my altitude and airspeed, and make a small correction to the left, which puts my bomb fall line directly over the diamond. The pipper approaches the target as I descend through 1,800 feet. My planned release point is 1,400 feet, with a minimum release of 1,200. If I pickle below that, the bombs won't have time to arm.

My thumb rests gently on top of the pickle button. As soon as the pipper is over the diamond, I release my weapons. I begin an immediate five-G pull away from the ground, and execute a hard right turn toward my egress heading of 90 degrees. Once established, I reengage the auto TF. The system kicks in immediately and descends me to 500 feet.

"Spider 32 is off, egressing east."

When Skippy and Harpo complete their attacks, Badger calls for a knock-it-off. Minutes later, the four of us are on final for runway 27 at Al Minhad AB. We fly a few patterns, then full stop and taxi back to the ramp in front of the 421st headquarters.

After debriefing maintenance, the four of us reunited in the life-support trailer to congratulate one another on a good mission. We walked back to the weapons shop to debrief.

"How did everything go?" Lt. Col. Nall asked.

"It went great, sir," Badger replied. "The LANTIRN system worked perfectly. Flying over water was not a problem, and the TFR handled the sand dunes just as easily."

Nall watched each of our attacks and complimented us on the success of the mission. Then Col. Huddle walked into the room.

"I hope I'm not interrupting anything important."

"Not at all, sir," replied Nall.

"Good. I've got something I want all of you to see."

He opened up a brown folder, pulled out a satellite photo, and set it on the table in front of us.

"In case any of you are wondering, that's a picture of Saddam Hussein's presidential palace in Baghdad." We were speechless. The picture looked like it was taken from a helicopter hovering a few hundred feet above the palace. The detail was intense.

"I know our reconnaissance satellites are powerful," Skippy remarked, "but I've never seen a photo like this before."

"Col. Navarro and I want you to plan a night attack using LANTIRN. I'll leave the photo with you along with the palace coordinates. Can you have it done by tomorrow?"

"No problem, sir," replied Nall.

"Keep the photo in the safe, and I'll stop by tomorrow afternoon to see what you've come up with."

We could do nothing more than look at each other. Did Col. Navarro want to see what we could do with LANTIRN, or had CENTCOM issued a secret tasking order sending us to Baghdad to attack Saddam Hussein in his own palace?

12.
LANTIRN

The concept of low-altitude navigation and targeting infrared for night (LANTIRN) originated from lessons learned during the Vietnam War. At the height of the conflict, North Vietnam possessed over 5,000 AAA pieces, mostly medium-range 37-millimeter and 57-millimeter guns with optical sights. Accurate and deadly, they could shoot down aircraft flying as high as 18,000 feet. Vietnam's long-range 85-millimeter and 100-millimeter guns were even deadlier, and used radar to track targets even above 40,000 feet. AAA flak accounted for 80 percent of the combat losses during "Rolling Thunder," the series of bombing missions flown over North Vietnam.

In addition to the big guns, North Vietnamese soldiers were equipped with a deadly stockpile of Soviet SAMs, one of the most effective of which was the SA-2 Guideline. Thirty-five feet in length and armed with 400 pounds of explosives, the SA-2 could reach as high as 60,000 feet and travel at speeds approaching Mach 3.5. Pilots flying combat missions north of the DMZ often referred to these SAMs as "flying telephone poles."

As the war dragged on, penetrating North Vietnamese air defenses at high altitude became increasingly difficult for American fighter pilots. Losses mounted, and pilots began flying high-speed, low-level bombing strikes, masking themselves behind mountainous terrain. Shortly before reaching their targets, the aviators would pop up, pickle their bombs, then drop back down to low altitude for the egress. These tactics were effective during the day, but performing them at night was next to impossible. Realizing this, North Vietnamese supply trucks began traveling along the Ho Chi Minh Trail at night. F-4 Phantoms tried using flares to illuminate the trails, but this method of attack was difficult and ineffective. What the air force really needed was an aircraft with a terrain-following radar that would permit it to fly at low altitude during the night. That plane turned out to be the General Dynamics F-111 Aardvark.

In March 1968, under the code name Combat Lancer, the F-111 entered operational service in Southeast Asia. The fighter-bomber could carry a 25,000-pound payload nearly 3,000 miles without taking on fuel. Unfortunately, problems with the TFR resulted in numerous aircraft losses, and the F-111 was taken out of service, not to be redeployed until 1972.

After the Vietnam War ended, air force officials began to prepare for what many believed would be the next great battle: war against the Soviet Union. To defeat the Soviets, American fighter pilots would need the ability to attack at night. Otherwise, Soviet tanks in eastern Europe would have a strong advantage over U.S. and NATO troops. The aircraft best suited for this role was, again, the F-111. TFR problems that hampered flying at the tail end of the Vietnam War were corrected, and the fighter-bomber proved it could handle the deep-interdiction, low-altitude night-attack mission.

By the 1980s, the F-111 was showing its age. Faced with an impending shortage of all-weather strike aircraft, the air force decided it was time to find a replacement. Requests for proposals were sent to defense contractors, and the Pentagon focused on two aircraft: a two-seat version of the F-15B, designed by McDonnell Douglas; and the F-16XL, a derivative of the General Dynamics F-16. To convert the F-15B into a ground-attack aircraft, McDonnell Douglas strengthened the airframe and added extra pylons to stiffen the wings, so the fighter could carry bombs. Similar modifications were made to the F-16XL to increase its range, speed, and payload. Impressed with both aircraft, the air force decided to conduct a fly-off. Both fighters performed extraordinarily well during the competition, but the F-15B had greater endurance and could carry a larger payload than the F-16XL. Officials decided to go with the F-15B. In 1984, McDonnell Douglas was awarded a contract to begin full-scale development of the next-generation deep-interdiction strike aircraft: the F-15E Strike Eagle. After full-scale production began, the air force announced an initial purchase of 392 aircraft. The Strike Eagle's first flight was planned for late 1986, with initial deliveries expected by 1988. To enhance the aircraft's night-strike capability, McDonnell Douglas planned to outfit the Strike Eagle with the AAQ-13/14 LANTIRN system. A $2.9-billion-dollar contract was awarded to Martin Marietta, which began production of 561 LANTIRN navigation pods and 506 targeting pods.

Even though the F-16XL had lost the competition with the F-15E, General Dynamics engineers were convinced the F-16 could handle the LANTIRN mission as well as—maybe even better than—the Strike Eagle. The F-16 cost considerably less than the Strike Eagle, and the Viper had already proven itself as a daytime ground-attack aircraft. It was up to GD to convince the Pentagon that the plane could handle the mission at night. At length, air force leaders agreed. In 1985, a year before the Strike Eagle's first flight, F-16 LANTIRN developmental testing and evaluation began at Edwards AFB, California. It didn't take long for the Viper to establish itself as the new test bed for LANTIRN technology. However, problems with the navigation pod caused system production to fall behind schedule, and two years passed before Tactical Air Command (TAC) fighter pilots were allowed to begin their own LANTIRN operational testing and evaluation. In the meantime, F-16 Block 40/42 aircraft designed to carry the AAQ-13 navigation pod were rolling off the assembly line. (Block 40 aircraft are powered by the General Electric F110-GE-100 engine, while Block 42 models are equipped with the Pratt & Whitney F100-PW-220.) In January 1989, one month after I graduated from F-16 training, the 310th TFTS at Luke AFB received its first F-16 Block 42 aircraft. Under normal circumstances, the 422nd Test and Evaluation Squadron (TES) at Nellis AFB, Nevada, would have performed LANTIRN operational testing before the 310th TFTS would be allowed to fly with it, but Martin Marietta was plagued with delays, and the company fell behind on its deliveries. By the time the pods were ready, the air force was set to begin training at the operational level. As a result, the 422nd TES was bypassed; the pods were delivered directly to the 310th.

Top Hat instructors spent most of 1989 and the early part of 1990 training in their new F-16 Block 42 aircraft. Once the first shipment of LANTIRN pods arrived, the unit developed a curriculum that could be used to teach pilots who were about to begin training in the air force's newest version of the F-16. Classes began in early 1990 and the first operational wing in the United States to begin training was the one I was about to join; the 388th TFW from Hill AFB. After completing a tour in Korea and two months of squadron officer school, I arrived at Luke for the six-week LANTIRN course, completing my training on 31 May 1990, and reporting to Hill the following afternoon as the wing's first LANTIRN-qualified pilot.

LANTIRN was developed for one simple reason: so a pilot flying at night could navigate and deliver weapons as if he were flying during the day. Each AAQ-13 navigation pod weighs 442.5 pounds and is mounted on the left side of the F-16 intake. The pod uses a forward-looking infrared sensor that displays an infrared picture to the pilot via the wide-field-of-view HUD and/or either one of the two MFDs located on the forward panel. The FLIR imagery is displayed in shades of green and gray, which represent differences in temperature between an object and its background. In addition to the FLIR, LANTIRN incorporates a TFR system linked directly to the F-16's autopilot. The system uses airspeed, aircraft angle of attack, radar altimeter altitude, and data from its own signal return to ensure that the aircraft flies at the proper altitude.

Several limits, warnings, and cautions are presented in the HUD to protect and advise pilots who approach the edge of the LANTIRN envelope. If a pilot inadvertently exceeds bank angle, turn rate, airspeed, or pitch limits, the aircraft will automatically climb away from the terrain. This event is called a "fly-up." Fly-ups also occur when pilots try to descend too far below their selected set clearance plane, or if they attempt to turn in the direction of terrain without climbing.

Ingressing into and egressing out of enemy territory is difficult and challenging, but the most demanding aspect of night flying is weapons delivery. During the day, F-16s can drop bombs from virtually any altitude or dive angle. After sunset, though, the only way a pilot can visually acquire his target is with the aid of a FLIR. Since the FLIR picture is projected onto the pilot's head-up display, a straight-ahead pop or direct attack must be performed to keep the target in the HUD field of view—a 30-by-20-degree cone immediately in front of the aircraft.

The attack phase begins at the IP when a pilot accelerates from 480 to 540 knots. Approximately ten miles from the target, the air-to-ground system is called up, and a switch is made from auto TF to manual TF to prevent uncommanded fly-ups during the roll-in. As soon as the aircraft is 4.7 miles from the target, a straight-ahead pop is initiated. The pilot climbs at an angle of fifteen degrees until the pull-down altitude is reached. When that occurs, he rolls inverted, pulls toward the ground until he's five degrees nose low, then rolls upright again. Once he rolls out, he should be in a ten-degree dive with the target in the HUD field of view. If the coordinates programmed into the F-16's fire-control computer are correct, a diamond symbol will be superimposed over the target to aid acquisition.

Once the pilot rolls out, he has approximately five seconds of track time to acquire the target and drop his bombs. After the weapons are released, a five-G vertical pull is initiated to climb away from the ground. When the nose of the aircraft reaches the horizon, a turn to the egress heading can be safely accomplished. After the turn is complete, the auto TF should be activated, so the aircraft can drop back down to low altitude. The entire attack lasts less than a minute. If four aircraft strike the same target, the effects can be devastating.

As Operation Desert Shield neared the end of its first month, life at Al Minhad was difficult for many of us. Frustration levels were high, and we often asked ourselves if being here was right for America. As air force officers, though, we knew that our job was to defend the United States and its allies. Many of us also felt a bond with President Bush, a fellow fighter pilot who served in the Navy during World War II. I knew he resented the political intervention that handcuffed our military in Vietnam, and there was no doubt in any of our minds that he would let *this* military handle the crisis if war came to pass. None of us wanted war, but we admired President Bush for taking an immediate stand in the face of aggression. We were prepared to do whatever he asked of us.

In late September, rumors began to surface that Saddam Hussein might be willing to withdraw his forces in exchange for the rights to Bubiyan and Warba, and for a settlement to Iraqi claims regarding oil rights in the Rumaila oil field. In an attempt to find a peaceful solution to the crisis, U.N. Secretary General Javier Perez de Cuellar flew to Jordan, where he met with Iraqi foreign minister Tariq Aziz. The session ended in disappointment. During a press conference after the meeting, President Bush was asked if he would support a negotiated settlement: "The things Saddam wants can be negotiated with Kuwait after he withdraws his forces."

The following day, Saddam Hussein formally designated Kuwait as Iraq's "nineteenth province" and proclaimed that there would be no withdrawal. He threatened to destroy oil fields within the region and announced preparations to launch an attack against Israel. Iraq's Revolutionary Command Council vowed that there would be no retreat from Kuwait. The "mother of all battles" was inevitable.

Following the announcement, news reports indicated that Iraqi soldiers had instituted a systematic campaign to loot Kuwait. Homes were being burned to the ground; soldiers stole treasures from the Kuwait National Museum and shipped them back to Baghdad. More than 300,000 Kuwaiti citizens fled to Saudi Arabia. Citizens who remained in Kuwait were forced to obtain Iraqi identity papers, use Iraqi currency, and even replace Kuwaiti auto tags with Iraqi ones. Computer files containing financial, land, and citizenship records were demolished, and Iraq went so far as to make new maps excluding Kuwait entirely. Kuwait City was renamed Kathima, and statues of Saddam Hussein were erected throughout the city. Citizens were raped, arrested, tortured, and executed. Reports were also received that Iraqi soldiers were stealing hospital equipment, including incubators, leaving the babies on the floor to die. These reports drew outrage from President Bush, who declared, "Saddam Hussein will be held responsible for his actions and the atrocities that have been committed against the citizens of Kuwait."

While Iraqi soldiers pillaged Kuwait City, President Bush and Secretary of State James Baker continued their campaign to build a coalition, which included not only European and Asian allies, but also Bahrain, Kuwait, Oman, Saudi Arabia, Qatar, and the UAE. The U.S. Navy stationed carrier task forces in the Red Sea and the Gulf of Oman, while the air force spread itself across more than two dozen bases in Saudi Arabia, Oman, the UAE, Qatar, Bahrain, Egypt, Diego Garcia, Turkey, and Spain. It was hard to imagine so much firepower in one area.

One nation that would have liked to have seen the buildup slow down was the Soviet Union, a major ally of Iraq and the supplier of nearly all of that nation's arms. President Bush flew to Helsinki to meet with Soviet President Mikhail Gorbachev. As a result, Moscow agreed to cut off arms sales to Saddam, and Gorbachev vowed to support the worldwide economic embargo against Iraq. According to wing intel, that embargo, seven weeks old, was beginning to take hold. Long lines for bread and food were becoming commonplace, and Saddam Hussein announced a food-rationing program. Yet, declaring that Iraqi children were starving, he went on to call for a jihad, or holy war, against the coalition. This was echoed by Iran's Ayatullah Ali Khamenei. "Anyone who fights America's aggression has engaged in a holy war in the cause of Allah," he declared, "and anyone who is killed on that path is a martyr." Yet, when pressed, Iranian officials pledged to continue to abide by the economic sanctions in place.

According to intel, coalition air forces now outnumbered Iraq's by three to one. More than seven hundred sorties a day were being flown, and Iraqi forces no longer seemed poised to attack. Republican Guard units pulled back into defensive positions, and infantry troops appeared to be digging in for the long haul.

Changes continued at Al Minhad as well. On the last day of September, workers delivered a big-screen television and a VCR to the officer's club lounge. Some of the pilots had brought movies with them, and Lt. Col. Scott said MWR (morale, welfare, and recreation) was making arrangements with a video store downtown to get more. Everyone was ecstatic about the new TV, but getting a major shipment of mail was even better. I received three letters from Colette and a CARE package from my mother-in-law, Lucile. It felt like Christmas, and seeing everyone in a good mood was refreshing. It was movie night at the o'club and the lounge was packed. *Caddyshack* was playing, and for two hours, the thought of war was far from my mind.

13.
TACTICS AND MORALE

The arrival of October gave us our first break from the brutal summer heat. Both the 4th and the 421st continued to fly heavy training schedules. The Fightin' Fuujins flew two periods per day; the Black Widows flew twice also, once in the afternoon and a period at night for LANTIRN training. Intel briefed us twice a day, and pilot meetings were held three times a week. Pilots also took turns pulling twenty-four-hour alert duty. Six F-16s from each squadron were configured with four CBU-87 cluster bombs, and, if necessary, pilots could be airborne within thirty minutes.

Alert duty began each morning at 04:00, when crews reported to the squadron for a briefing from army Capt. Rob "Glo" Lytle, who provided ground intelligence for the wing. "Glo" stood for Ground Liaison Officer, and every morning, Capt. Lytle spent an hour updating pilots on the position of Iraq's army. He also provided detailed analysis of their arms, as well as their strengths and weaknesses. I pulled alert duty once a week, arriving at the squadron tired and groggy. By the time I would leave Glo's briefing, I'd feel as if the Iraqis were about to invade.

During a pilot meeting on Tuesday, 2 October, Lt. Col. Cottingham announced that ten pilots from the unit would rotate home and be replaced by LANTIRN pilots who had just completed training at Luke.

"We'll take volunteers first," Cotto said. "If there aren't enough, a group will be chosen."

I leaned over to Capt. Kevin "Cuda" Lingle: "I don't think they'll have any problem getting volunteers."

"No kidding," he replied.

At the end of the meeting, most of the guys had approached their flight commanders to ask that their names be added to the volunteer list. I know Col. Navarro wanted to fill our squadron with LANTIRN pilots, but that didn't stop me from trying to go home.

Two days later, the names of the ten pilots rotating home were placed on the squadron bulletin board. I knew Colette would be upset when she found out I was not on the list.

I was scheduled to fly four times that particular week, with three sorties at night. The day sortie would be the biggest challenge, however, since dissimilar aircraft would be incorporated into the schedule. The experience of working together with other units would be vital should war break out.

In this war, no aircraft would be relied upon more than the KC-135 Stratotanker and the KC-10 Extender. Since Iraq and Kuwait were quite a distance from many of the bases in theater, every combat aircraft could count on air refueling at least once per sortie. Tanker tracks were set up at strategic points throughout the region, and fuel would be available twenty-four hours a day. Each element was assigned a particular track, so they could top off their tanks before crossing the FEBA or on their way home. KC-135s, carrying approximately 120,000 pounds of fuel, could remain on station for hours. The bigger KC-10s could orbit even longer, off-loading as much as 170,000 pounds.

Another important aircraft was the E-3A Sentry, which provided airborne warning and control systems services. The E-3A AWACS is a modified Boeing 707 equipped with sophisticated communication, computer, radar, and navigation gear. A large Westinghouse radar dish sits on top of the fuselage and provides a look-down capability, giving sixteen AWACS mission specialists the ability to track multiple targets. The E-3A operated out of Riyadh and started patrolling the skies over Saudi Arabia once the invasion began. As soon as we started flying into Saudi Arabia, flight leads were required to check in and out of the area with AWACS controllers. Mission specialists controlled access to the tanker tracks, provided updated target information, obtained bomb-damage assessment, and provided radar coverage of Iraqi airspace. If Iraqi fighters got airborne, AWACS controllers were among the first to know.

On 6 October, I arrived at the squadron early. The 421st was scheduled to launch a package of twelve F-16s, and I was flying the number three aircraft in the second four-ship. Our mission was to bomb a target in central Saudi Arabia. After takeoff, we were to rejoin and proceed west toward the Saudi desert; we would spend nearly an hour in the tanker track, and once our fuel tanks were topped off, we were to proceed toward our target, an oil-storage facility located near Abu Qabr. Four F-15 Eagles were to act as "red air," setting up a combat air patrol (CAP) to defend the airspace above the target area. As we were to approach our IP, the AWACS controller assigned to the F-15 unit would identify us and alert the Eagles. A controller would be assigned to our package as well; he'd let us know when the Eagles were ready to attack.

Capt. Lenny "Tiny" Dick would lead our formation, and my wingman was Skippy. Since this was to be our first large-force employment (LFE), I expected to learn a great deal. Working with AWACS would be a challenge, as would getting all twelve F-16s in and out of the target area successfully.

Engine start occurs at 14:10, and Lt. Col. Nall checks the formation in at precisely 14:30. Twenty minutes later, the arming crews complete their final inspections. It takes four minutes for the twelve of us to get airborne, and before long, the entire package is cruising southwest at 23,000 feet. When we arrive at our tanker track, three KC-135s are orbiting with 1,000 feet of separation between each jet. Some of us haven't refueled in a while, and a couple of guys fall off the boom. They get right back on, though, and shortly thereafter, the package heads toward enemy territory.

As we approach the IP, I begin to get nervous. I haven't flown in a strike package this large since I was in Korea. It doesn't take long to realize that my situational awareness isn't what it should be. Fortunately, Tiny gets us to the target area, and everyone in our formation is able to roll in and put their bombs on target. As soon as we come off, I check my radar and quickly spot Tiny's element a few miles in front of me. Skippy is in perfect position off my right wing. As soon as the two of us are established on our egress heading, the fun begins.

"Widow 21, bandit three-two-zero for twenty-five, high aspect," our controller calls out. Realizing the Eagles are close, I feel the hair stand up on the back of my neck. I quickly check my radar as Tiny replies, "Widow 21 has contact . . . single bandit . . . twenty left . . . eighteen miles . . . high altitude."

I tilt my radar up and, after a sweep or two, the contact appears. I key my mike: "Widow 23, same."

At this point, I just want to maintain position and not allow the Eagle to roll in behind Tiny and his wingman, Jabba. Our four-ship is currently cruising at 14,000 feet; our airspeed is 470 knots. The sun is at my left nine o'clock, and spotting the F-15 is difficult. I cross-check the bandit's position on my radar and continue to search the skies so I can pick up a visual. Suddenly the radios erupt; Skippy calls out: "Widow 24 has tally, left ten o'clock high. Request permission to engage."

"Widow 24, you're cleared to engage," I reply. "Widow 23 will support." As Skippy pulls to his left, I spot the F-15 in a descending turn with his belly up to us. The Eagle driver has his fangs out, preparing to take a missile shot on Jabba.

"Widow 22, break left ... break left!" I radio. "Bandit, your left eight o'clock . . . flare!"

Jabba goes into a hard turn, and two flares pop out the back of his jet. Unfortunately for the Eagle driver, he doesn't realize he's descending right in the middle of our four-ship. It's an easy shot for Skippy who calls out, "Widow 24, kill the bandit in a left-hand turn at eighteen thousand feet."

Our controller gives us credit for the kill and the Eagle rocks his wings to acknowledge the call. Tiny calls out a reference heading. Within minutes, our four-ship is back together heading toward friendly territory.

Training missions like this provided necessary experience for everyone involved, but they didn't come free. The day after our LFE, an F-15E Strike Eagle crashed on a low-level training mission, killing both crew members. A few days later, two F-111 Aardvarks skimmed off the sand during separate low-level training missions. The fact that the crews survived amazed everyone. On 9 October, an RF-4 crashed, killing both crew members. The following afternoon, an F-111 hit the ground—the third fatal accident in a week.

Gen. Horner and his staff decided they'd seen enough. A three-day stand-down was ordered. We had been working nonstop since our arrival, and, clearly, had approached the edge of the envelope. A few days of rest and relaxation now would pay dividends later on.

Flying resumed on Saturday, 13 October, but Gen. Horner now restricted all aircraft in theater from going below 1,000 feet. I understood the rationale behind Gen. Horner's decision, but to train properly with LANTIRN and to continue developing sound night tactics, we needed to get down at least to 500 feet. Lt. Col. Nall tried to convince Col. Navarro of our need to fly lower, but the commander replied that his hands were tied.

Later that night, I was scheduled to fly a four-ship LANTIRN sortie with Duck, Skippy, and Badger. During mission planning, Duck and Badger recommended experimenting with high-altitude attacks.

"Terrain masking in the desert is going to be virtually impossible," Duck pointed out, "but if we can attack targets from medium or high altitude, we'll stay out of the SAM envelope and above the barrage of small arms fire that would normally be used against us down low."

Everyone agreed, so we decided to give it a try. By 21:00, the four of us were proceeding to a tanker track located out over the Gulf. After everyone refueled, Duck led us back to an area fifty miles south of the air base. Our plan was to work between two steerpoints located thirty miles apart. The target steerpoint was a pumping station located in the open desert. The IP was just an imaginary point that allowed us to set up on our run-in heading.

Duck wanted us to fly a trail formation with eight miles of spacing between each aircraft. This range was effective because it gave everyone the freedom to fly his own jet without sacrificing mutual support. Each pilot could keep track of other aircraft in the formation using radar, the FLIR, or the air-to-air TACAN (tactical air navigation). Radar allowed a pilot flying in the aft part of the formation to see other aircraft in front of him. An altitude readout for those aircraft was also provided. The FLIR system recognized the hot exhaust from the F-16's tail section, the infrared signature of the aircraft displayed as a bright spot in the HUD, making it easy to stay in position. As a last resort, pilots could use their air-to-air TACAN, which provided a distance readout between two aircraft.

While en route to the IP, the four of us climbed to 25,000 feet. The plan called for us to execute six attacks: two each from 25,000, 20,000, and 15,000 feet. Each attack would be flown at 400 knots and commence seven miles from the target. The first attack would occur from a shallow dive. At the action point, each of us planned to lower the nose of our aircraft until the dive angle reached twenty degrees. As soon as the pipper—the aiming indicator—reached the target, we would pickle our bombs, then climb back up to the run-in altitude and turn back toward the IP to prepare for the next attack.

The second attack was going to be more aggressive. At the action point, we would roll inverted, and pull the nose of our aircraft down until we reached a forty-five-degree dive angle, as in a combat descent. The third attack was going to be a standard level delivery.

The first attack worked well, but starting the high-altitude dive bomb seven miles from the target was too far away. As Duck came off target, he keyed his mike and instructed the rest of us to move the action point in to five DME. Once I reached the new action point, I pushed forward on the stick and descended toward the target. Retarding my throttle to idle to avoid going supersonic, I called up the CCIP pipper. The FLIR gave me a good infrared picture of the desert floor, and the pumping station was clearly visible. My pipper reached the target as I passed through 14,000 feet, and as soon as I hit the pickle button, I started a five-G pull back toward the horizon.

The rest of the attacks went well. During the debrief, the four of us concluded that the best altitude to attack from was 25,000 feet. This elevation gave us more of a buffer against the SAM and AAA threat. We also concluded that a forty-five-degree dive bomb worked better than a twenty-degree, and an action point of 4.5 DME was better than 7.0 DME. Rolling in closer to the target reduced exposure to enemy ground fire and provided a better FLIR picture. The twenty seconds of track time was another luxury everyone enjoyed because target acquisition became easier when you had more time to search.

After the debrief, Duck asked Lt. Col. Nall to come in and take a look at our film. After viewing the attacks, Nall complimented us and told us to continue refining the attacks from high altitude. "Col. Navarro is scheduled to fly with us later in the week," he said. "This is something he'll probably be interested in."

The next set of LANTIRN pilots arrived during the second week of October, bringing the squadron total to sixteen. One of the new guys, Capt. Stan "Biff" Colgate, moved into our room. Jabba asked how he was picked.

"Lt. Col. Kohler had a pilot meeting and asked for ten volunteers. You should have seen the look on his face when no one raised their hands."

"How come no one wanted to come over?" Jabba asked.

"Are you kidding?" Biff erupted. "We see your wives at the club every Friday night, and they've been telling us how much you guys hate it here. Kohler finally had to pick ten of us himself."

True enough, the overcrowding and the restriction to base ate at everyone. Morale dropped even lower when the nurses living across the courtyard complained that they couldn't sleep when pilots played volleyball outside. Col. Navarro now ordered volleyball to end by 17:00. No one was happy with "The Warden's" decision. We'd been here a hell of a lot longer than the nurses, and when the war started, it would be our lives on the line. Volleyball was one of the few activities available to us. But all was forgiven two days later, after Lt. Col. Nall announced permission from Gen. Horner to open a beer tent on base.

When we first arrived in the UAE, we were told that alcohol consumption was strictly forbidden. However, the Al Minhad commander said the rules in the UAE were not as strict as in Saudi Arabia, and Col. Navarro convinced Gen. Horner that a couple of beers per night would be okay. Local workers put up a temporary building across the street from the club, and, within a week, the beer tent was open for business from 19:00 to midnight. Ration cards allowed each pilot two beers per night. A couple of pilots tried to take advantage of the system by making copies of the ration cards to claim more than their share, but the scheme fell apart when they decided to roof stomp the nurses in retaliation for the volleyball incident. A fire extinguisher was also emptied during the melee. The following morning, everyone was called into the squadron for a special pilot meeting.

"Let me have everyone's attention, please," Lt. Col. Nall announced. "Some of you may not be aware, but an incident occurred last night that needs to be discussed. Some of the pilots in the squadron had a little more to drink than they should have, and they decided to pay a visit to the nurses' quarters. They woke everyone up with a roof stomp and set off a fire extinguisher as well. When Col. Navarro found out about the incident this morning, he announced he was relieving Lt. Col. Cottingham of his command. I'm extremely disappointed in you guys. I'm sure Lt. Col. Cottingham is disappointed as well. Unfortunately, the damage has been done."

Everyone in the room was silent.

"The name of our new commander will be announced later today. You are dismissed."

All the pilots snapped to attention as Nall left the room. Some were shocked by the news, while others quietly agreed that a change needed to take place. The previous night's incident was not Cotto's fault, but squadron morale had been extremely poor of late, and cliques in the pilot group had torpedoed the unit's cohesiveness. LANTIRN pilots from the 34th TFS continued to feel their squadron should have been chosen to deploy. Duck and I didn't have the greatest of attitudes either. We did not want to leave the 4th, and we did everything we could to remain there. LANTIRN might turn out to be extremely important to the 388th TFW, but at that point, it seemed to have driven a wedge between the pilots in the 421st.

14.
T-RACK STEPS IN

Rumors immediately began to circulate as to who might become the next commander of the 421st Black Widows. Duck and I pulled for Lt. Col. Tom Rackley, the 4th TFS operations officer. T-Rack would be perfect for the job, a commander who could light a fire under the troops and provide both discipline and direction.

Another name mentioned was Lt. Col. Jeff Kohler, commander of the 34th TFS Rams. His squadron had been the first to convert to LANTIRN, and the pilots who transferred over from his unit wanted to see him get the job. Being LANTIRN-qualified was certainly an advantage for Kohler. Another plus was the fact that many of his pilots were almost finished with LANTIRN school and would be coming over soon to replace a handful of pilots in the 421st. Col. Navarro had a tough decision to make, but either way, he couldn't lose. Both men were outstanding leaders. And besides, the squadron had only one way to go—up!

Two days passed. On Thursday morning, 18 October, all of the Black Widows were called in to the squadron for a special meeting.

"Let me have everyone's attention," Nall began. "Col. Navarro announced this morning that Lt. Col. Tom Rackley will take over as the new squadron commander of the 421st, effective tomorrow."

Nall continued, "The events that took place last night are not indicative of the personnel in this squadron. It's unfortunate for Lt. Col. Cottingham that things turned out the way they did, but this is a damn good unit, and I'm confident Lt. Col. Rackley will recognize that as soon as he takes over. I realize many of you are under a lot of stress. Heck, all of us are. No one knows if there's going to be a war, and given the choice, we'd all prefer to be at home with our families. But we're here to do a job, and if we're going to be successful, we're going to have to come together as a group."

Nall went on, "Is there a problem within the squadron right now? Yes, I think there is. The unit is taking on a new role and many of you feel upset and left out. I also realize that some of you are new to the squadron, and, given the choice, you would have probably preferred to remain with your old unit. Well, you're Black Widows now, and I don't want to hear any more griping. As for the beer-card incident, Lt. Col. Rackley and I will be meeting this afternoon to decide if those involved will be sent home. What happened last night was unprofessional, and if the privilege of drinking beer is abused again, it will be taken away from everyone."

He concluded, "That's about all I have to say. This meeting will end in a few minutes, and when we walk out of here, I want all of our problems behind us. If anyone has something to say, now's the time to do it."

A few guys stared at the floor, while others looked around to see if anyone had the courage to say something. I wanted to raise my hand. One of the factors contributing to the unit's morale problem has been the lack of communication. For example, Duck and I had been conducting academic training for weapons and tactics (ATWATS) sessions, so everyone could learn about the new tactics we'd been developing for LANTIRN and for large-force employments. We encouraged discussion, but on many occasions, Lt. Col. Nall interrupted the discussions and told everyone to just shut up and listen. Pilots became afraid to speak out or ask questions.

I found myself speaking: "I've got something, sir."

"Go ahead, Rosey."

"I haven't been in the squadron too long, sir, but one thing I've noticed during ATWATS training is that every time a pilot has a comment or a question, they're cut off at the knees. Nobody wants to be stuck here in the desert. But if we're going to fight a war against Iraq, then I think it's important that everyone have a chance to ask questions and express viewpoints."

Everyone knew my comment was barbed toward Lt. Col. Nall. A few of my friends glared in my direction with you-sure-have-done-it-now looks on their faces. The room was quiet.

"That's a good point, Rosey," Nall answered. "From now on, our meetings will be run a little different."

Following this, other pilots raised their hands and offered additional suggestions on morale. Topics included living conditions, lack of communication from the wing leadership, lack of activities on base, and off-base privileges. When the meeting was over, everyone felt better. It was a turning point for the unit and a new beginning for the Black Widows.

Lt. Col. Nall and I shook hands after the meeting. He said nothing about my comment, but I could tell by the look in his eye that he respected me for speaking out and, perhaps, for showing him a way to become a more effective leader. I began to feel good about the unit, and I was certainly excited about T-Rack being named the new commander. For the first time, I started to think that being a member of the 421st might not be so bad after all.

Our first pilot meeting with T-Rack came in the o'club game room right after dinner. Duck and I were happy to see him wearing a Black Widow patch and scarf. Approachable and a good motivator, he was also a great pilot. I'd been in a few squadrons commanded by pilots who couldn't fly a kite, but T-Rack was capable of leading the unit on the ground and in the air.

Rackley briefed everyone about his background and set goals and expectations for the unit. He announced that the pilot responsible for the forged beer cards would be sent home first thing in the morning. Talking about living conditions on base, he promised to purchase a washer and dryer for the squadron in the coming week. Best of all, he told us we'd be allowed to go off base. Col. Navarro had worked out a deal that allowed us to use one of the beach resorts along the Persian Gulf. They were normally occupied by rich European tourists at that time of year, but tensions in the Middle East resulted in massive cancellations.

Monday did not come soon enough. Half of the pilots in the 421st and half of those in the 4th signed up for rooms at the Metropolitan Beach Club. The rest would get to go downtown later in the week. By 10:00, about forty of us gathered in front of the officer's club, where buses were waiting to take us downtown. Because of the terrorist threat, I'd been leery about going off base. But seven weeks of life at Al Minhad made terrorism the least of my concerns. Maj. Mike "Grumpy" Daniels, the squadron's assistant operations officer, warned us, however, to "travel in groups and don't highlight yourselves. Stay away from side streets. If anyone asks why you're here, tell them you're tourists. Don't bring up the fact that we're American fighter pilots, and don't mention anything about the base."

We spent about twenty minutes on the highway before reaching the outskirts of Dubai, a very beautiful city with streets bustling with traffic. A Safeway supermarket gave me a twinge of nostalgia for my box-boy days in L.A. Before long, we came upon a string of residential neighborhoods. The homes were nice, but they were nothing compared to the large palaces that soon appeared off to the right. The mansions were surrounded by large stone walls and lush, green grass. Two SAM batteries were parked between the estates, the missiles aimed toward the Persian Gulf. I wondered how long it would be before they were used.

At the Metropolitan Beach Club, we stood in line to check in, gazing through a large plate-glass window overlooking the pool.

"Check out the size of this pool," Tater barked out. "It has a fountain in the middle of it, and it looks like it has a built-in bar you can swim up to."

"I'll be there in ten minutes," replied Skippy. "Order me a club sandwich and a couple of beers."

Soon, at poolside, weeks of stress evaporated. Some of the pilots swam while others played volleyball on the beach. Later in the evening, a group of us went downtown and ate dinner at, of all places, a Mexican restaurant, then hit a large shopping mall, no different from what we had back home. We were amazed, too, to come across a 31 Flavors ice cream shop, and everyone splurged on dessert.

The following morning, I walked in solitude along the shores of the Persian Gulf, my thoughts with Colette, Candice, and Kristen. I collected some colorful shells for the girls, then sat beneath a palm tree to write to Colette, my letter beginning, "I feel guilty telling you this, but I'm sitting on the beach looking out at the crystal blue water of the Persian Gulf." I continued: "As each day passes, I grow more confident that the crisis will be resolved peacefully. Everyone wants the sanctions to work. And from what I've read, they seem to be having an effect on the Iraqi people. . . . President Bush and the American people don't want to see casualties during the Thanksgiving and Christmas holidays, so I think it's safe to say that there won't be a war any time soon."

Our bus passed through the main gate right before sunset, dropping everyone off in front of the o'club. Being back at the "prison" was hard to take, but as soon as I walked into the marble entryway, I noticed a stack of mail on the floor. Sifting through dozens of packages, I found two with my name on them: one from Colette and another from my good friend Phil Cott. Phil's parcel included packages of granola, dried fruit, and peanut-butter pretzels, as well as an envelope containing thirty letters written by students in a fifth-grade class at Webster Elementary, Malibu, California. I was touched that a group of kids who didn't know me would take the time to write. For the next hour, I sat in the club and read each of the letters. The kids wrote about their school and the different activities they were interested in. Of course, everyone wanted to know what it was like to fly an F-16 and whether or not there would be a war. Most of the boys said they wanted to be pilots some day, and many of them drew pictures of the different jets they wanted to fly. After finishing the last letter, I decided to write a personal note to every child.

Back in my room, I opened the package Colette sent me. It contained candy, gum, a new toothbrush, laundry detergent, shaving cream, razors, six *Sports Illustrated* magazines, and two beautiful letters with pictures of her and the girls. The photos of Candice and Kristen were taken just before I left for the Gulf. Each girl took turns wearing my flight cap and Fuujin scarf while standing in my combat boots. They were so excited to dress up like their daddy. I stared at the pictures, wishing I could relive the moment again.

Over the next six days, I flew four LANTIRN sorties focused on low-altitude tactics. Everyone was now comfortable with the medium- and high-altitude attacks, but a few kinks still had to be worked out down low. One of the sorties, involving eight aircraft, ended up a nightmare. Radio discipline was poor, getting all eight aircraft on and off the tanker took too long, and the attack was poorly executed. Duck lashed out at a few of us during the debrief. We deserved it. Had we been dropping real bombs, at least two aircraft would have been fragged.

We concluded that the maximum number of aircraft in any given formation could not exceed four. If the air-tasking order (ATO) called for a larger package, then additional elements would execute their attacks from parallel routes. We also decided that attacks would have to come from different directions, so trailing F-16s would not be subjected to an inordinate amount of enemy ground fire. Shooting us down in the middle of the night would be hard for the Iraqi gunners, but if everyone rolled in out of the same piece of sky, the odds of being hit would increase dramatically, especially for tail-end charlie. The key to survival is to be unpredictable. Our goal was to come up with tactics that allowed each pilot to roll in on a target from a different direction than the aircraft preceding him. Through trial and error, we came up with a blueprint for the low-altitude tactics we planned to use. Every pilot would play an integral part in the formation, regardless of specific position.

The four-ship flight lead is normally the most experienced member of the flight, responsible for coordination, navigation, and threat avoidance. If he spots enemy ground fire, his job is to steer the formation around it. If he's confronted with AAA or a SAM launch, then he must jink to avoid the artillery or execute a break-turn to defeat the missile. When this occurs, number two will break with him so he can offer support if additional missiles are fired. If one and two fall out of formation, number three—who trails the lead by one minute—will take over responsibility for leading the group to the target. If the first element successfully defeats the ground threat, they simply fall to the back of the formation and assume the positions of number three and four.

As the lead F-16 approaches the IP, he accelerates to 540 knots and flies directly toward the target. At 4.5 DME, he executes a ten-degree direct attack. To approach the target from a different direction, number two flies an offset ground track thirty degrees away from the target run-in line. At 6.0 DME, with the target at either his ten o'clock or two o'clock position, number two will turn hard to put the target on his nose, then execute his own ten-degree attack.

If ground fire isn't a factor, number three flies the same ground track as number one. The one difference is the type of attack he performs. To avoid being fragged by number two's bombs, three must deconflict by executing a twenty-degree attack. The increase in altitude will confuse the gunners and keep him above the frag pattern. By the time number four arrives, the enemy—if any of them are still alive—should be thoroughly confused as to which direction the next attack will come from. If ground fire is still a factor, four has the option of offsetting left or right. The only thing he has to avoid is an attack from the same direction as number three.

In theory, our attack plan seemed logical. Every LANTIRN pilot would have an opportunity to fly different positions and execute different attacks within each formation. Threats would be called out at various times during low-levels, so everyone would have a chance to react. Performing a break-turn 300 feet off the ground at night was risky, certainly, but practicing this type of maneuver in a controlled environment would build everyone's confidence and prepare them for combat.

By the end of October, the 421st was launching eight F-16s a night. Pilots flew a variety of low-levels throughout the UAE, Oman, and northern Saudi Arabia. Duck and I anticipated problems, which did occur quite often. One flight almost ended in disaster because everyone's clocks were not set properly. A midair collision nearly occurred on the low-level and again during the attack. We discovered that the clocks were off because two of the pilots performed their emergency power unit checks with their fire-control computers (FCC) turned on. When this is done, the clock on the up-front control freezes for the duration of the check. At the speeds we fly, ten to fifteen seconds is crucial.

Another incident involved uncommanded fly-ups in the target area. Some believed the TFR was reacting to birds, but the culprit turned out to be chaff. Dispensing these small bundles of shredded aluminum is common practice when rolling in on a target during the day. The results, however, are much different at night. The LANTIRN TFR system is extremely sensitive, and its radar was able to pick up the chaff bundles as they floated to the ground. The computer interpreted them as obstacles. The result: a fly-up.

We also discovered that chaff cartridges released at night leave a trail of light as they disintegrate in the air, actually highlighting the position of the aircraft, making it susceptible to enemy ground fire. We decided that chaff would not be used in the target area unless we were tracked by enemy radar and being fired upon.

These sorties were precisely intended to work out the bugs. Everyone made their share of mistakes, but the lessons learned were invaluable. Confidence increased. The effort was paying off.

15.
BELONGING

With the arrival of November, construction workers were busy putting the finishing touches on sixteen new port-a-cabins for additional housing. Each fifty-by-twenty-foot trailer contained two small rooms separated by a bathroom and shower. Uncarpeted, the rooms were furnished with two twin beds, a table, a dresser, and a large wooden locker. We had assumed that officers assigned to the air-transportable hospital would be moved into the port-a-cabins, but it was the pilots who had to move. Incensed, we all agreed that if Iraq were to attack and somehow make it to the UAE, the port-a-cabins would be among the first buildings destroyed. Fairness was also an issue. The pilots were the first to arrive on base, and we occupied the hard billets for nearly a month before the Fightin' Medics showed up. Unfortunately, our opinions didn't count for much, and, on Thursday, 1 November, dozens of pilots from each squadron made the transition into the port-a-cabins, four pilots assigned to each facility.

My new roommates were Capt. Roland "Rip" Wright, Capt. Bill "Sweet Pea" Craig, and Lt. Bruce "Fist" Hamilton. Rip and I agreed to share one room, while Sweet Pea and Fist took the other. Rip, also known as "Cheese," arrived at Al Minhad fresh out of LAN-TIRN school. The two of us had been Juvats in the 80th TFS at Kunsan. He was the funniest guy in the unit. Told by the squadron commander that his hair was longer than regulations permitted, he walked into the mass briefing room the next day sporting his new "'do." For some reason, Rip had decided to cut his own hair. Unfortunately, he forgot to use a mirror. It took weeks for the hatchet job to grow out, and, needless to say, it was hard to keep a straight face whenever he was around.

Our first day in the new quarters did not make us happy. The cabins sat in the middle of the desert, and dirt was tracked in constantly. A massive water leak was sprung whenever the toilet was flushed, so that the bathroom floor was always full of mud. On the plus side, I didn't have to fight nine other guys for that one leaky bathroom.

Later in the afternoon, I rode the shuttle bus to tent city for evening mass in a makeshift chapel tent located on the outskirts of "Camp Camel-Lot." Father John W. Pierson, our wing chaplain, offered Catholic services on Thursday evenings and Friday mornings. I preferred the Thursday service, and usually arrived early so I could spend some quiet time alone.

Father Pierson and I got to know each other pretty well. Extremely friendly, he loved to collect baseball cards as much as I did, and was always there when I needed someone to talk to. Our discussions usually focused on the prospects of war and what it meant to kill people. When I had decided to ask for an F-16 on my "dream sheet," what I wanted was the challenge of flying the world's best fighter. I never dreamed I would use it for its intended purpose: to kill an enemy and his resources. I was raised a Catholic, served as an altar boy, and attended parochial schools for twelve years. God was always part of my life, and I had grown even closer to Him since the crisis began. I remember being taught in elementary school that God would end the world as we know it if there was ever a third world war. I wondered then if this counted, since more than twenty nations had joined the coalition.

I sat next to Col. Navarro during Mass, and afterward he asked if I wanted to ride with him back to the officer's club. I had first met the colonel at Luke AFB the previous April, when I was going through LANTIRN training. He was the Luke AFB vice wing commander at the time, and had just been named the new wing commander of the 388th TFW. Since the wing was in the process of transitioning to LANTIRN, Col. Navarro wanted to fly a few sorties to get a feel for the new program. The two of us mission-planned and flew together on more than one occasion. In a one-on-one situation, Col. Navarro was a pleasure to be around. Personable, he had the qualities many of us look for in a leader. Yet much of that seemed to disappear after we arrived at Al Minhad. We rarely felt his presence, and, well into our deployment, he still had not addressed the pilot group. We began to wonder if we were the men he wanted to lead.

My next scheduled flight was an air-to-air sortie—my first in theater. The 388th TFW's primary mission was dropping bombs, but aerial combat is where a fighter pilot earns his reputation. No two missions are alike, and becoming a proficient dogfighter requires tremendous patience and skill. One of the wing's best was Duck, who led this particular mission. After it was over, we debriefed, then checked our mailboxes before heading to the club for dinner. I had received more letters from schoolchildren: one group from Phil's wife, Charlee, who taught third grade in Palos Verdes, California, and another from my old friend and roommate Al Friedenberg, who taught fifth grade in Thousand Oaks, California. I spent most of Sunday morning, 4 November, in the o'club lounge, answering the children's letters. A few of the kids asked tough questions about America's role in the Gulf and whether or not I would support a war. I wanted them to know that I joined the air force voluntarily, and I tried to impress upon them the importance of freedom—not just for Americans but for all people around the world.

After lunch, a few of us watched a Gene Hackman movie called *The Package*. Halfway through it, a new group of LANTIRN pilots arrived in the lounge, including Lt. Col. Mark "Boomer" Welsh, who was scheduled to take over as the new squadron commander of the 4th TFS the following week. A "fast-burner," he had been promoted early to both major and lieutenant colonel; those who knew him spoke highly of his leadership and piloting skills.

The makeup of the wing continued to change rapidly. By mid-November, each squadron had a new commander, and more than half of the Black Widows were LANTIRN-qualified.

Capt. Eric "Grinder" Pell and Capt. Donnie "Cliffy" Moore were the squadron's newest flight commanders. During dinner, I asked if either of them had heard any rotation rumors before leaving Hill.

"Secretary of State James Baker is supposed to travel to the Middle East this week," Cliffy answered. "I saw him on the news the other night, and he seemed optimistic that a peaceful settlement could be reached. I also heard a rotation schedule is in the works. When I went through the LANTIRN school, a bunch of pilots from Moody were in my class. They were under the impression that their squadron would deploy here in December to replace the 4th."

"Once they arrive and get checked out in the local area," Grinder added, "the 4th will go home. In early January, another squadron is supposed to arrive as a replacement for the 421st."

This was the best news any of us had heard in some time. If some of us could make it home by Christmas, that would be great. All I wanted was a firm date, so I could have something to look forward to.

With renewed enthusiasm, I arrived at the squadron the following day to begin work on a new project. Halfway through my tour at Kunsan, my good friend Capt. Dion "Skull" Thorpe took over as the squadron weapons officer. He had attended the air force's prestigious weapons school, and, after graduation, was sent to the "Koon," where he immediately implemented a weapon-and-fuse-of-the-week program to familiarize pilots with the large variety of guided and unguided weapons the F-16 was capable of delivering. I decided to introduce the program to Al Minhad. Our first featured weapon was the MK-82 LDGP (Mark 82 low-drag general purpose) bomb. Each weighs approximately 531 pounds and has a 2,140-foot vertical and 2,550-foot horizontal fragmentation pattern that can last as long as twenty-five seconds at sea level. MK-82s are normally targeted against bridges, refineries, soft buildings, aircraft in the open, tanks, armored personnel carriers (APCs), SAMs, or AAA. A typical configuration consists of six bombs loaded on triple ejector racks (TERs), mounted at stations three and seven under the F-16 wing. The Fighting Falcon is equipped with nine separate stations capable of carrying weapons, fuel tanks, or ECM pods. Stations one and nine are located at the end of each wingtip and carry AIM-9 Sidewinder missiles. Stations two and eight are usually empty, but if additional AIM-9s are needed to counter a heavy air threat, this is where they are loaded. There are two 370-gallon fuel tanks, one on station four, the other on station six. For extra endurance, a 300-gallon centerline tank can be mounted on station five. We used station five for the ALQ-119 ECM pod, however, and stations three and seven were reserved for weapons.

I explained the purpose of the new program during the afternoon pilot meeting, and everyone seemed receptive. Our squadron intel officer, Capt. Carla Sutherland, also wanted to be involved, and offered to display a "threat of the week." Air threats would focus on Iraq's inventory of fighters and the air-to-air missiles they were capable of carrying. Ground threats would highlight the various SAM and AAA systems the Iraqis were equipped with.

Morale in the 421st improved daily under Lt. Col. Rackley. The port-a-cabins turned out to be a lot more comfortable than anyone thought they would be. Meals at the o'club seemed to be improving, mail deliveries were steady, and our movie library was loaded with new selections. I ran every other day, went to mass once a week, and talked to Colette on Sundays and Wednesdays.

When the 4th TFS threw a surprise going-away party at one of the beach resorts for Lt. Col. Scott, some of my old friends invited me to attend. A big cookout was planned, and Scotty didn't know a thing about it.

"He thinks he's going to Al Dhafra AFB for a meeting," Vicious said to me. "But the helicopter is going to drop him off here instead."

As the sun began to set, everyone gathered near the beach, awaiting Scotty's arrival. When the helicopter finally landed, Scotty jumped out, and was completely surprised. Everyone shook his hand, eager to thank him for being such a great squadron commander. The hotel provided a delicious dinner and, afterward, gifts were handed out and toasts made. Scotty, very appreciative, made a moving speech. I had a great time. But, no longer a member of the unit, I felt out of place. Two months earlier, I had hoped and felt I would someday be a Fightin' Fuujin again. After that night, I realized the best place for me was the 421st.

16.
THANKSGIVING COMES — AND GOES

Falling out of touch with America is all too easy in the desert. World news was hard to come by, and it seemed as though our thirst for information was never slaked. Since early September, the only connection we had had to the real world was through the *Gulf News* and the *Khaleej Times*. Every once in a while, editions of *USA Today* or *Stars and Stripes* would come in on one of the transports, but the papers were usually two or three weeks old. However, on 14 November, a C-130 Hercules arrived from Saudi Arabia with three pallets of mail, including recent editions of *Time* and *USA Today*. According to the headlines, President Bush had decided to send an additional 200,000 troops to the Gulf. "From the beginning," President Bush was quoted in the article as saying, "we and our coalition partners have shared common political goals—the immediate, complete and unconditional withdrawal of Iraqi forces from Kuwait, restoration of Kuwait's legitimate government, protection of the lives of citizens held hostage by Iraq, both in Kuwait and Iraq, and restoration of security and stability in the Persian Gulf region."

The president's words were extremely motivating. I could only hope that Americans back home agreed with him, because their support would be vital to our success. In my heart, though, I knew there were many people who disagreed with the president. Some of those people were relatives of American soldiers serving in the Gulf. A few wrote letters to the editor. One I read, written back in August by Alex Molnar, a University of Wisconsin professor, stated that many of his son's friends "joined the marines as a way of earning enough money to go to college." He went on: "I intend to support my son and his fellow soldiers by doing everything I can to oppose any offensive American military action in the Persian Gulf. The troops I met deserve far better than the politicians and policies that hold them hostage. In the past you have demonstrated no enduring commitment to any principle other than the advancement of your political career. This makes me doubt that you have either the courage or the character to meet the challenge of finding a diplomatic solution to this crisis. If, as I expect, you eventually order American soldiers to attack Iraq, then it is God who will have to forgive you. I will not."

I understood this gentleman's concern for his son, but he seemed to have forgotten that ours is an all-volunteer force. His son or his son's friends may have joined the marines to pay for college, but if they thought that should have precluded their fighting, they were sadly mistaken. Yet reading Molnar's letter made me wonder how members of my own family felt. I wrote my own parents: "No matter what your feelings are, . . . never protest to the president or anyone else on behalf of me. I volunteered to join the air force and I'm proud of the fact that I'm here serving my country. I would love to be home with Colette and the girls. But if there is a war and I end up being killed in action, don't be bitter towards our government and don't let Candice and Kristen grow up that way either. I'm doing exactly what I want to do in life."

On 17 November, Lt. Col. Rackley announced that Gen. Horner would be arriving at Al Minhad later in the afternoon to meet with Col. Navarro and his staff. Word of Horner's visit spread quickly, and everyone hoped he would meet with the pilots to relay information and answer questions. We'd been here for more than ten weeks, and, so far, we'd only had one commander's call—when Col. Navarro told us we couldn't go off base. Just before dinner, a few of us ran into Lt. Col. Scott.

"Is Gen. Horner going to have a pilot meeting?" I asked.

"I'm afraid not," Scotty said dejectedly. "He's going to eat dinner here and spend the night, but he'll be leaving first thing in the morning."

"I can't believe he's not going to talk to us, sir," Opie exclaimed.

"He'll probably be in the beer tent after dinner," Scotty replied. "Maybe you can talk to him there."

As soon as dinner was over, everyone headed for the beer tent, anticipating the CENTAF (CENTCOM's air force component) commander's arrival. Some of the LAN-TIRN guys were flying, but most of the pilots from the 4th were there, along with half of the 421st. The music was loud, and everyone seemed to be in a festive mood. Opie, Ark, Senseless, and I sat at one of the tables near the bar as Gen. Horner finally arrived. Making a beeline for the bar, he bought a couple of beers, then looked around for a place to sit.

"There's a chair for you here, sir," Opie offered.

As the general approached, the rest of us stood up and introduced ourselves.

"How was dinner?" Ark asked.

"Not bad," Horner answered. "It was a lot better than some of the MREs I've been eating."

"We've been hearing rumors that Moody is going to send a couple of squadrons over to replace us soon. Is that true, sir?" Opie asked.

By now, other pilots in the room had gathered around the table, and everyone was anxious to hear Gen. Horner's response. He took a drink from his bottle, then set it on the table.

"You better enjoy your Thanksgiving and Christmas here," he replied. "You guys aren't going anywhere. Secretary Cheney just announced there will be no rotations. We tried that during Vietnam, and it just doesn't work. All forces in theater will be here for the duration. As a matter of fact, I need to bring in more fighters. You can count on another squadron joining you here at Al Minhad sometime during the next month or two."

"Do you think we're ready to fight a war, sir?" I asked.

"The air force was ready back on 13 September," Horner continued. "We couldn't do anything, though, because the army didn't have enough assets in place. It'll probably be another month or two before they have all their equipment in theater, and we have to give the troops time to train and become acclimated with the desert environment."

As soon as Gen. Horner finished his beer, he got up and walked over to visit with some of the nurses. The music continued to blare as we sat, now numb from his comments.

"I've heard enough," Ark said. "I'm outta here."

"Let's go watch a movie," I suggested.

The two of us walked outside and proceeded toward the club.

"How the fuck long is 'for the duration' supposed to be?" Ark growled.

The next morning, I got up and ran for thirty minutes. After showering, I threw on a clean flight suit and headed to the club for lunch. I joined Fist and Sweet Pea sitting at a table in the back of the mess hall. Knowing we wouldn't be home for Christmas had a devastating effect on morale. While we ate, Sweet Pea said that Oman's military had just agreed to let us use the Al Qarin bombing range on an island named Masirah, off the east coast of Oman in the Arabian Sea. According to Sweet Pea, the wing had a large supply of practice bombs, and flights were to begin as soon as he could arrange tanker support. Sweet Pea also advised us that mission planning cell (MPC) teams would start planning the wing's missions right after Thanksgiving.

"CENTAF planners in Riyadh will send us a daily air-tasking order. If we go to war, the ATO will provide a list of targets and the aircraft assigned to attack them. It will also include takeoff and landing times, assigned air-refueling tracks, fuel off-loads, and the types of munitions required on each sortie. Each squadron will have one MPC team for every day of the week."

After lunch, the three of us caught the shuttle bus to the squadron. I was scheduled to fly as number three in a LANTIRN four-ship later that night, and Col. Navarro would be flying on my wing. We hadn't flown together since we were in LANTIRN training at Luke last May. A lot had changed since then, and we had developed a great set of LANTIRN tactics. Tonight's sortie would give us a chance to show the wing commander what we had accomplished.

Lt. Col. Nall was set to lead our four-ship, with Badger as his wingman. The three of us were now extremely proficient at high altitude, and Nall believed it was time for Col. Navarro to see a high-altitude attack. Even though we were still practicing low-altitude tactics, we'd come to the conclusion that the war should be fought from medium to high altitude. Ingressing to a target down low is great if there are mountains to terrain-mask behind, but the desert was relatively flat. Hiding from enemy gunners would likely prove difficult. Attacking from high altitude would keep us above small arms fire and help us avoid the majority of Iraq's AAA.

Brief time was scheduled for 20:15, and Col. Navarro arrived thirty minutes early to look over our plan. I went over our low-level map and explained some of the low-altitude tactics we'd been working on. I wasn't sure how Navarro would react to the high-altitude stuff, so I left that for Lt. Col. Nall to discuss.

In fact, Navarro was receptive to our concerns about flying down low, and, as soon as the brief was finished, the four of us changed into our flying gear and stepped to the jets. The skies were clear and it was a beautiful night for flying. After the mission, Lt. Col. Nall went over everyone's film to review the different attacks. When he finished, he asked Col. Navarro for his impressions of the high-altitude tactics we'd developed.

"I thought the sortie went real well," Navarro replied. "But there's something each of you needs to realize. The *L-A* in LANTIRN stands for *low altitude*. So if we go to war, you will fly low."

Col. Navarro thanked us for the flight, then left.

Badger and I were pretty upset, and Nall wasn't pleased either.

"We're going to get the shit shot out of us down low," Badger observed.

"I know," Nall replied. "I'll sit down with Lt. Col. Rackley later tonight and discuss the situation. In the meantime, we'll keep on doing what we're doing."

Two days before Thanksgiving, Gen. Schwarzkopf and his staff kicked off the first combined-forces exercise in the KTO (Kuwait theater of operations). The maneuvers began when U.S. Army troops simulated a mock attack in the northern deserts of Saudi Arabia. A full-scale amphibious-assault landing, involving thousands of U.S. Marines, occurred simultaneously, and close to one thousand sorties were flown by navy and air force aircraft. The 388th TFW was scheduled to launch forty-eight F-16s, twenty-four in the morning and another twenty-four in the late afternoon. Many of us were curious about the purpose of the exercise. Were we trying to entice Iraq's forces into attacking? Or were we simply showing Saddam Hussein the massive U.S. military machine he would face, should he remain in Kuwait?

The afternoon mass briefing, held in the beer tent, began at 14:30. The 4th had launched their F-16s nearly three hours earlier, and they weren't due back until 16:00. Our first takeoff wasn't even scheduled until 17:40 local, which meant the sun would be setting long before we commenced our IP-to-target runs.

T-Rack was set to lead our squadron's package, which was broken down into six separate four-ships. I was flying in the number three position in the second element, and Cliffy was my four-ship flight lead. After intel gave us an overview of the exercise, the briefing began. T-Rack planned to have us take off and proceed across the Gulf to a tanker track just north of Qatar and Bahrain. After everyone refueled, the package was to continue east into northern Saudi Arabia. Each element would fly a fluid-four formation, with one-minute spacing between four-ships. Element flight leads would check in with AWACS as they approached Saudi airspace, and AWACS controllers would clear each element to its target. When T-Rack informed us that our target was a mere twelve miles south of Kuwait's southern border, everyone got excited. At an ingress altitude of 24,000 feet, the lights of Kuwait City would be clearly visible, but Iraqi radar would also be able to identify us.

Each F-16 carried four live AIM-9 Sidewinder missiles, and our M61A1 20mm guns were loaded with 510 high-explosive incendiary rounds. The simulated attack would occur out of a level delivery. Afterward, we'd egress south and fly back to Al Minhad.

We take off right on time. Thirty minutes later, twenty-four Vipers are cruising across the deep blue waters of the Persian Gulf. As we approach the tanker track, I look down and spot a carrier battle group and a white hospital ship with a red cross painted on it.

The sun sets as we complete our air refueling, and, a few minutes later, Cliffy is leading our four-ship toward the Saudi coastline. AWACS clears us into Saudi airspace. After a fence check, we turn north toward Kuwait. Fifty miles from the target, I can see the lights of Kuwait City glowing dimly on the horizon. I can't believe I'm this close to the enemy. My heart feels like it's going to explode, and my breathing rate has increased dramatically. I call up my air-to-air radar and switch to eighty-mile scope. I don't anticipate seeing Iraqi aircraft, but if they launch, I want to be ready.

Thirty-five miles from the target—an imaginary point near the border—I access the air-to-ground master mode and call up my ground-map radar. After I place the master arm switch in Simulate, I check the left console to ensure my VTR is on. Moments later, I call up the continuously computed release point (CCRP) bombing mode, a system designed to provide aiming symbology and attack cues for preplanned targets. An azimuth steering line appears in my HUD for lateral guidance, and a target designator (TD) box is superimposed over the target. As I continue north, I check the lower-right corner of my HUD for the distance to the target and the time to release. I plan on performing a level pass, but I also have the option of lofting the bombs out of a climbing delivery.

Inside of ten miles, the maximum-toss anticipation cue appears in my HUD. The large circle tells me I'm only two seconds away from the maximum range for weapons release. When the solution cue appears at the top of the steering line, the max-toss anticipation cue flashes for two seconds, then disappears. As I approach the target, the solution cue descends toward my flight-path marker. To drop accurate bombs, I have to keep the flight-path marker on top of the steering line. If the marker is left or right of the line when I reach the release point, the bombs will miss. While making small corrections with the control stick, I depress the pickle button with my right thumb. A few seconds later, the solution cue and flight-path marker merge and the flight-path marker begins to flash. If I were dropping real bombs, they would release at this point. As soon as I release the pickle button, I roll into 30 degrees of bank and make a 180-degree turn to the right. Halfway through the turn, I roll out for a moment to take one last look at the lights of Kuwait City. I feel comfortable and secure in my cockpit. I can't help but think of the people of Kuwait and what they must be going through. Perhaps their nightmare will end soon.

Thanksgiving day finally arrived, and the Black Widows were invited to spend the afternoon at the palace of the Sheikh of Dubai, a dinner party arranged for us by the helicopter squadron commander. While we waited for transportation downtown, Grumpy drove up to announce that we should all bring bathing suits and towels.

"The sheikh's got a pool!" Jabba exclaimed. "This is going to be *great!*"

As our bus passed through the Al Minhad main gate on our way to the palace, Rip and I speculated on what the afternoon held in store for us.

"Do you think one of the sheikh's thirty wives will rub suntan lotion on my back?" Rip joked.

Mans yelled out: "This isn't the Playboy mansion, Rip."

"It will be when *we* show up!" Rip answered.

The mood on the bus was festive. But then our driver passed the main entrance to the palace, continuing south along the coastal highway. We began to sense something wasn't right. A few minutes later, we turned down a deserted side street leading toward the beach. We came to a dead end; the bus stopped and the front door opened. Everyone remained in their seats. Finally, word began to spread that our visit to the sheikh's palace had been canceled.

"What the hell's going on?" Biff grumbled.

"I knew something wasn't right when Grumpy told us to bring trunks and a towel," Harpo said.

Grumpy instructed everyone to get off the bus. We walked toward the beach; I ran up alongside him to ask what happened.

"Some ambassador flew into Dubai last night for a special meeting with the sheikh," Grumpy replied. "The helicopter commander called T-Rack this morning and said the dinner party would have to be postponed. So instead of sitting around the base all day, we thought it would be better to have a party on the beach."

"Couldn't we do it at one of the beach clubs?" Batman asked.

"I wish we could," Grumpy replied, "but the club requires a few days' notice before they allow us to come."

"I wish someone would have told us that before we left. The o'club has a big dinner planned for tonight, and we could have stayed there."

By sunset, most of us were tired, hungry, and bored with the beach. I hadn't eaten anything since the night before, and all I could think about was the great dinner my friends in the 4th were eating back at Al Minhad. When a few of the UAE helicopter pilots arrived around 20:30 with trays of meat and bread, we descended on the food like a pack of hungry wolves. Without plates or utensils, everyone grabbed whatever they could get their hands on. The food wasn't bad, but neither was it the kind of

Thanksgiving dinner we'd expected. Our only hope was to make it back to the base in time for leftovers and dessert. After an hour, a pair of buses showed up to take us back to Al Minhad. By the time we arrived at the o'club, the mess hall had closed. We walked dejectedly into the lounge, where a bunch of pilots from the 4th were watching a movie. I spotted Ark and Vicious on one of the couches, walked over, sat down, and asked what they had eaten for dinner.

"I feel like a beached whale," Ark replied, leaning back and rubbing his stomach. "It was the best meal we've had since we got here."

"What a feast!" Vicious interjected. "They served turkey, prime rib, stuffing, mashed potatoes, vegetables, and rolls. It was awesome!"

"You should have seen the desserts, Rosey," Ark continued. "They had ice cream and *five* varieties of pie. I'm so full I probably won't have to eat again until tomorrow night."

"How was your visit to the sheikh's palace?" Vicious asked.

"We never got to the sheikh's palace," I replied angrily. "We sat on the beach all day with nothing to drink or eat. It was a joke!" Not wanting to torture myself any longer, I decided to walk back to my room and go to sleep.

On 28 November, the U.N. Security Council unanimously passed Resolution 677, condemning Iraq for attempting to alter the demographic composition of the population of Kuwait and for destroying Kuwaiti civil records. The following day, the U.N. Security Council met again and voted 12 to 2 in favor of passing Resolution 678, authorizing member states cooperating with Kuwait to use "all means necessary" to enforce previous resolutions if Iraqi forces did not withdraw by 15 January 1991. Only Cuba and Yemen voted against the resolution. China abstained.

After passage of the resolution was announced, President Bush made a formal offer to meet with Iraqi foreign minister Tariq Aziz at the White House during the week of 10 December. Other members of the coalition were also invited, including Soviet foreign minister Eduard Shevardnadze. In addition, President Bush announced his willingness to send Secretary of State James Baker to Baghdad for a meeting with Saddam sometime between 15 December and the 15 January deadline imposed by the U.N. Security Council.

The next day, Saddam Hussein announced that Iraq would never pull out of Kuwait, even as he agreed to the meetings Bush proposed.

The vote authorizing force seemed a turning point. My initial reaction was excitement, anticipation of a glimmer of light at the end of the tunnel. But what would happen if Saddam Hussein decided to pull his troops back to the Iraqi side of the border? Would President Bush keep his word and simply bring American troops home? Would the coalition break up, on the chance that Saddam Hussein would keep his word and negotiate peacefully with Kuwait? What would prevent him from withdrawing, then attacking again a few months later? Saddam Hussein, I concluded, was in a very powerful position. He wouldn't back down.

17.
CROWDED SKIES

The imposition of a deadline on Saddam Hussein and Iraq had no effect on the training schedule of the 388th TFW. Everyone hoped for a diplomatic solution, but the focus of the wing remained on war. Each squadron flew approximately twenty-four sorties per day, and individual pilots averaged four flights a week. Flying on Sundays back in the states was an extremely rare occurrence. At Al Minhad, though, we flew every day. On the first Sunday of December, I arrived at the squadron a little before noon to prepare for my sortie to the Al Qarin bombing range. My wingman was Lt. Brad "Martyr" Bartels, one of the squadron's youngest pilots. The briefing began at 13:00 and by 15:30, the two of us were taxiing toward the arming area.

As the crew chiefs prepare to inspect our jets, ground control radios, "Spider 31, contact Minhad command post on 124.7 for a message."

"Spider 31 copies," I reply.

I motion to the crew chiefs to stay back, and then I key my mike and radio: "Spider 31, go 124.7."

"Two!" Martyr answers sharply.

I reach to my up-front control and punch in the new frequency. After a slight pause, I call out again, "Spider 31, check."

"Two!"

"Minhad command post," I call out, "Spider 31 is on freq."

"Roger, Spider 31, Minhad command post has you loud and clear. Be advised that all sorties have been terminated, and you are instructed to return to the squadron. How copy?"

"Spider 31 copies. Stand by to authenticate."

I flip through the plastic pages on my left kneeboard, searching for today's authenticators. Orders from AWACS, ABCCC (Airborne Battlefield Command and Control Center), or on-base command posts must be authenticated to ensure validity.

"Spider 31 authenticate echo-delta," I radio.

After a few seconds of silence, the command post responds, "Mike-alpha."

The authentication is a match.

"Spider 31, go channel two."

"Two!"

I switch back to ground control and receive clearance to back-taxi to the 421st ramp.

A short time later, Martyr and I shut down our engines and crawl out of our cockpits.

"What's going on, chief?" I ask while stepping down off the ladder.

"Iraq fired a pair of Scud missiles," he answers.

Thinking the war might have started, Martyr and I rushed back to the squadron. Grumpy greeted us by the sign-in desk and ordered us into crew rest.

"I'm not sure if anything's going to happen," he said. "But the D.O. wants everyone in crew rest in case Iraq decides to launch an all-out offensive."

Later in the afternoon, we learned that the Scud missiles were fired from one side of Iraq to the other and not into Saudi Arabia, as we had thought. Nevertheless, flying was canceled for the next two days, all of the F-16s on base were loaded for combat, and everyone was restricted to the base, including those hoping to spend the night downtown at one of the beach clubs.

The next morning, I got up early and ran to the opposite end of the base and back. After showering, I spent an hour cleaning the bathroom while Rip swept out our half of the trailer. The two of us arrived at the o'club for lunch around 12:45, and, after eating, we left for the squadron for a pilot meeting at 15:00. As soon as everyone was assembled, Lt. Col. Rackley read a classified message sent by the staff of Gen. Horner. CENT-COM commanders had planned another exercise. This time, they wanted to test Iraq's early-warning capabilities. At midnight, every air force aircraft in theater would start their engines and proceed as if they were going to take off. Fighters and bombers would be loaded with a full complement of weapons, and all radio calls would be made in the clear. If Iraqi intelligence was sophisticated enough to detect what we were doing, they might sense an attack was imminent and launch their fleet of aircraft or, at the very least, activate all of their offensive and defensive radar systems. According to T-Rack, the 388th TFW planned on taxiing all forty-eight of its F-16s. The briefing was set for 22:00 in the beer tent, and Lt. Col. Mark "Boomer" Welsh would lead the package.

After dinner and a movie, pilots from both squadrons walked over to the beer tent. The trailer was crowded, and as soon as everyone saw which position they'd be flying in, they took their seats. I was in the number three aircraft in the second to last four-ship, so I ended up near the very back. As soon as the briefing began, Boomer displayed the aircraft lineup and went over the step, engine-start, and taxi times.

"Step time will be 22:50," Boomer briefed. "Plan on starting engines at 23:15, and our first check-in will be at 23:40 in the clear on uniform channel three. When the last pilot checks in, we'll run the drill again on victor. After that, I'll call for taxi and proceed toward the arming area. I've already coordinated with the tower, and we'll be cleared onto the runway at 23:55. At precisely midnight, I'll request clearance for takeoff, taxi down to the departure end, then return to the ramp. Each aircraft will follow using twenty seconds of spacing."

He continued, "Every jet is loaded with a pair of MK-84s, so they're going to be heavy. Watch your taxi speeds on the runway, and don't ride the brakes. As soon as you exit the runway, fire crews will be standing by to perform a hot-brake check. When the fire chief gives you a thumbs-up, taxi back to your parking spot and shut down. Any questions?"

I was a little nervous about the mission, but once I got my engine started, I began to settle down. All forty-eight aircraft checked in and taxied on time. Boomer received clearance for takeoff right at midnight, and, nearly twenty minutes later, the last F-16 taxied off the runway. As far as we were concerned, the exercise was a success. Whether or not Iraq knew what we were doing remained to be seen. We hoped to hear something by the next day when intel received a report from CENTCOM headquarters in Riyadh. Intelligence personnel at the command center would spend the next few hours analyzing data from spy satellites and air force RC-135 Rivet Joint aircraft, which were used to eavesdrop on Iraqi forces electronically. If Saddam Hussein flinched and activated SAM and AAA radar systems, intel would be able to identify the radar transmissions and pinpoint their exact locations.

The following afternoon, Capt. Carla Sutherland addressed the squadron.

"A few hours ago," she began, "I spoke with a friend at CENTCOM headquarters who told me that Iraqi forces were completely unaware of what took place last night. Radar activity inside Kuwait and Iraq was the same as any other night. Iraqi fighters flew a few sorties north of Baghdad. But in the southern half of the country, things were relatively quiet."

Three days later, Saddam Hussein surprised the world by announcing he would release all foreign hostages held since the invasion of Kuwait. The 4,000 captives, 20 percent of whom were Americans, were expected home by Christmas. The announcement came less than two weeks after President Bush said he would meet with Iraqi foreign minister Tariq Aziz, and that Secretary of State James Baker would meet with Saddam Hussein. Many perceived President Bush's offer as a last chance for peace, and my friends and I hoped Saddam Hussein's intentions were geared towards the same objective.

By Friday, 7 December, the 388th TFW was ready to start flying again. Squadron MPC teams had been planning their units' missions since Thanksgiving, but, starting that night, the teams would combine to form seven mission-planning cells—one for every day of the week. Each MPC team would be run by a weapons officer, and I'd been assigned to work with Capt. Rob "Lips" Hertberg, weapons officer of the 4th TFS. Capt. Tom "Raj" Schiess and I were the only members of the 421st assigned to team one; joining us from the 4th were Capt. Mark "Stinger" Adams and Capt. Ken "Spike" Hull. As soon as the five of us finished dinner, we left for the squadron to begin work. Lips delegated responsibilities: Stinger would serve as our tactical liaison officer, and most of his time would be spent working with CENTAF planners in Riyadh. Raj and Spike would program the two MSS computers located in the planning room, working closely with Lips and intel to design routes of flight and IP-to-target runs for each mission. They would also be responsible for building line-up cards, programming weapon loads, and loading mission data into each individual pilot's DTC. Capt. Carla Sutherland, our intel representative, would advise Raj and Spike of the location of Iraq's AAA and SAM emplacements. Her assistants, Sgt. Craig Beste and Senior Airman Reese Lee, would build maps and draw threat rings depicting SAM and AAA system ranges along each route of flight. Raj and Spike needed this information to plan ingress and egress routes to avoid highly concentrated areas.

The two squadron executive officers, Lt. Tom "TK" Kelly of the 421st and Lt. Bob "D" Diantonio of the 4th, would be responsible for building the "smart packs," which provide a tremendous amount of information. Each pilot carries one on every mission, and the packs include a week's worth of authenticators, information on different divert bases and tanker tracks, search-and-rescue (SAR) data, rules of engagement (ROE), special instructions (SPINS), Have Quick radio frequencies, and the current list of frequencies and code words used by AWACS and ABCCC controllers.

Since I was the only member of the team who was LANTIRN-qualified, Lips suggested I concentrate on the Black Widow packages. My main responsibility would be to design the attacks our squadron would use. Each pilot was to receive an attack card listing the parameters and attack numbers for his specific mission.

As MPC chief, Lips had responsibility for all aspects of mission planning. When he wasn't working with maintenance or intel, he concentrated on planning attacks to be used by members of the 4th.

While the packages were being built, ops officers from both squadrons would meet with the squadron schedulers to decide who would fly and which missions they would be assigned. When the lineup was complete, the schedulers would provide the names and flight positions to Sweet Pea, who would forward the list to the mission planners. A copy would also be given to the squadron maintenance officers, so they could schedule the aircraft and ensure that each jet was loaded with the appropriate weapons. Spare aircraft in each squadron would also be prepared, in case a pilot had a malfunction after engine start.

As soon as we finished, TK and D would deliver the mission packages, DTCs, and smart packs to their squadrons. When pilots showed up for their briefing, they would find individual lineup cards, attack cards, tanker cards, maps, target satellite photos, and a DTC printout inside each mission envelope.

The deadline for Saddam Hussein to withdraw his troops from Kuwait was only thirty-six days away when commanders at CENTCOM headquarters turned up the heat on Iraq's military. Beginning on Tuesday, 11 December, every combat unit in theater, including the 388th TFW, started flying missions along the southern border of Kuwait and Iraq. The hope was that the massive show of force would convince Saddam Hussein that the United States meant business.

The day before the flights began, Duck and I spent the afternoon in the 421st weapons shop developing tactics. CENTCOM wanted 388th TFW F-16s operating in the area a minimum of eighteen hours a day. To accomplish this, elements of two needed to take off every thirty minutes. Each two-ship had to fly across the Gulf, rendezvous with a tanker in northern Saudi Arabia, then proceed to their assigned area. Once an element was established in its airspace, it would have thirty minutes of "play time"—the amount of time allotted to deploy weapons before the next two-ship arrived.

Looking at a large-scale map of Kuwait and northern Saudi Arabia, Duck and I noticed two highways paralleling the border, one approximately twenty-five miles to the south, running from the coastal town of Ras al-Mish'ab directly west; the other only ten miles from the border, running east to west toward the neutral zone, where the borders of Iraq, Kuwait, and Saudi Arabia meet. There were also two roads running north to south, connecting with the two east-west highways. Duck and I agreed that the roads would be an ideal place to practice ground moving target (GMT) bombing.

I suggested that each two-ship fly a lead-trail formation with eight miles of spacing between aircraft. If the pilots flew at altitudes above 12,000 feet, they would have no trouble avoiding low-altitude SAMs and light AAA. MPC teams could load steerpoint coordinates for each of the four highways, and the element flight leads could choose whichever one they wanted to work. On the first pass, while flight leads searched for ground threats and enemy aircraft, wingmen would simulate dropping their bombs. Afterward, each wingman would call for an in-place 180-degree turn, which, in effect, would place his jet eight miles in front of his flight lead. At this point, their roles would reverse. In a wartime situation, the element would return to base as soon as each pilot dropped his bombs. During training, however, multiple passes could be conducted to help pilots gain proficiency.

Duck presented the plan to Lt. Col. Nall and asked if we could fly the first sortie together. Nall agreed, and the following night, Duck and I came in early to brief the mission. Once we reached the target area, our goal would be to make three passes along the southernmost highway running east to west. Afterward, we'd drop down for a ten-minute LANTIRN low-level, ending with a ten-degree attack on one of the army camps located near the FEBA. Before the briefing, Duck asked the Glo for coordinates to a few of the army camps. The troops had endured harsh conditions for months, and we figured they might enjoy knowing the air force would be there for them should war begin.

Takeoff is an hour after sunset, and the two of us proceed across the Gulf toward our assigned tanker track. As we approach the Saudi coastline, Duck checks in with AWACS and authenticates the controller. Working with AWACS is extremely important. If either of us experiences a navigation malfunction, an AWACS controller assigned to our formation will keep us from crossing into enemy territory. He or she will also alert us if Iraqi jets are in the area. The controller responds with the correct authentication for that day's date. After Duck gives him our mission number, he tells us our tanker is on station and clears us to the track. It takes about ten minutes for us to top off our tanks, and then we turn north toward the southern border of Kuwait. When we reach steer-point six, Duck radios, "Spider 21, go red one."

"Two!"

I reach toward my up-front control and switch over to AWACS strike primary. Seconds later, Duck checks me in.

"Spider 21, check."

"Two!"

"Choctaw, Spider 21."

"Choctaw reads you loud and clear, Spider 21. Picture's clear."

Our first run is to the east, and Duck is in the lead. After a fence check, I access the air-to-ground master mode and call up GMT. Programming forty-mile scope, I begin to sweep along the highway. My cursors are twenty miles in front of me, and, before long, targets begin to appear. I slew my cursors over one of the returns, then designate it with the target management switch (TMS) on my stick.

"Spider 22 has a mover locked, twenty miles on my nose," I call out.

"Spider 21 copies."

I make one last check to ensure my camera is on and my master arm switch is in Simulate. Using the missile step button on my stick, I call up the CCRP mode, and the steering line appears in the HUD. The TD box appears over the highway. The range is fourteen miles. I correct to the left a little to place my flight-path marker on the steering line. As soon as I get the max-toss cue, I depress the pickle button. The solution cue appears immediately and begins to track toward the flight-path marker. After the bombs release, I let go of the pickle button and call out, "Spider 22 bombs off . . . 180 right . . . now!"

"Spider 21," Duck replies.

I roll into thirty degrees of bank and begin a right turn back to the west. After reaching down to turn off my camera, I call up my air-to-air radar and check my fuel.

"Spider 21 reference two-eight-zero. One is twenty-seven, thirty-one, nine-five . . . tanks feeding."

"Spider 22 is twenty-seven, thirty-one, nine-four . . . tanks feeding."

As soon as I roll out on our reference heading, I begin sweeping with my air-to-air radar, and I look down at the ground to practice clearing for SAMs and AAA. I notice lights belonging to some of the army camps. I can't believe how spread out they are. With hundreds of thousands of troops in theater, I expected to see lights everywhere, as if I were looking at a big city. But the desert is big, and the camps are few and far between—like small towns out in the country.

After Duck completes his pass, we reverse rolls again and proceed back toward the east. To simulate wartime conditions, we practice the next two passes with our lights off. Keeping sight of an aircraft without its lights on can be difficult. But with radar, a FLIR, and an air-to-air TACAN, the adjustment is easy.

As soon as Duck makes his last pass, he resumes the lead and begins to descend for the low-level. I call up my LANTIRN TFR and program my SCP for 500 feet. Once we complete our LANTIRN checks, we accelerate to 540 knots and prepare for our attack. Duck, thirty seconds ahead of me, calls off target as I approach the action point. As soon as I see 4.7 DME in the HUD, I pull to fifteen degrees nose high. At 2,500 feet, I roll inverted and pull back toward the ground. When I roll upright again, I'm ten degrees nose low, staring right at the middle of an army camp. I switch to CCIP and simulate pickling my bombs on a row of tents. As soon as I pull off, I plug in the afterburner to make sure the troops know I'm overhead. After a hard turn to the south, I call out, "Spider 22 is off."

"Spider 21, knock it off," Duck radios.

"Spider 22, knock it off."

"Spider 21, reference heading zero-nine-zero . . . rejoin eight-mile trail . . . one is five thousand and climbing."

"Two is forty-nine hundred."

Another hour passed before we landed at Al Minhad. The four-hour mission complete, we debriefed, reviewed our HUD film, and talked about the tactics. Both of us were extremely pleased with the sortie, and Duck remarked that he would introduce the new tactics to the rest of the squadron during ATWATS training the following afternoon.

As soon as we finished debriefing, we headed for the beer tent to unwind over a cold one.

"The skies were crowded tonight," Duck remarked.

"I'm sure the Iraqis knew we were there," I replied. "It must have been a scary sight when they looked at their radar screens."

"It's going to be that way from now until the deadline," Duck said. "They might as well get used to it."

18.
WE OWN THE NIGHT

During a pilot meeting on 12 December, Lt. Col. Rackley announced that the 69th TFS Werewolves from Moody AFB, Valdosta, Georgia, were coming to Al Minhad AB to join the 388th TFW. Since October, pilots from both squadrons had been eagerly anticipating the arrival of another F-16 LANTIRN unit. Rotation rumors had always centered around Moody, and many of us had figured we'd get to go home as soon as they arrived. Those hopes were dashed when Defense Secretary Dick Cheney announced all units would remain in theater for the duration of the conflict. Still, we were excited to have more company.

Since I wasn't on the schedule that day, I headed back to the club to work on a few letters and read the newspaper. According to the headlines, former chairman of the Joint Chiefs of Staff, Admiral William J. Crowe, Jr., USN (retired), told the U.S. Senate Armed Services Committee: "We should give sanctions a fair chance before we discard them." But Secretary of Defense Dick Cheney said the sanctions weren't working fast enough, and Secretary of State James Baker told the U.S. Senate Foreign Relations Committee he was "very pessimistic" that sanctions alone would work. Baker cautioned that, while sanctions would have a dramatic effect on the Iraqi people, the military and the government would be the last ones to feel the pain.

With Christmas only a week away, a steady stream of cards and gifts had been arriving at the squadron. I received quite a few letters from friends and relatives, but my best Christmas present was a package from Colette, Candice, and Kristen. Inside the box was a beautiful Christmas card with a touching letter from Colette and scribbling from the girls. Gifts included new sheets for my bed, laundry detergent, batteries for my cassette tape player, and two boxes of granola bars. The following day, I received a letter from my friend Steve Oakley and a box of candy from my grandmother Nana. I also got a CARE package from Colette's parents, Ed and Lucile, and one from a young boy named Brant Myers—one of the fifth-grade students I had written to in early November. Extremely anxious to see what was inside, I grabbed a knife as soon as I got back to my room and sliced open the box. Underneath wads of newspaper were two boxes of cereal, three bags of candy, comic books, magazines, a bottle of vitamins, shampoo, toothpaste, homemade cookies—and a giant Superman poster. I couldn't believe someone I'd never even met would go to such trouble.

The next morning, I called to thank Brant personally. A local operator put the call through. The boy's mother, Kathy, answered the phone.

"I can't believe it!" she said. "It's so nice of you to call. How are you doing?"

"Considering the circumstances, I'm doing okay. I received Brant's package yesterday, and I have to tell you, it was one of the nicest things anyone has ever done for me."

"He saved his money and paid for everything himself," Kathy said. "It was something he really wanted to do."

When Brant got on the line, I thanked him and told him how much my friends and I would enjoy the snacks he sent. He seemed rather quiet, so I did most of the talking.

"How do you like being in Mr. Friedenberg's class?" I asked.

"It's okay."

"Did Mr. Friedenberg ever tell you he used to coach me in Little League?"

"He said you used to like *Gilligan's Island* and *Gomer Pyle*," Brant replied.

"Well, that's true!"

We chatted for a while, then I thanked him again for his support.

"Say hello to Mr. Friedenberg for me, and tell all of your friends I'll stop by and visit the class when I return home from the Gulf."

After a three-mile run and a quick shower, I caught the shuttle bus to the squadron, where I spent the rest of the day working in the weapons shop. My next sortie wasn't until the twenty-third, and the day's schedule was cut short so everyone in the wing could attend the 388th Christmas party. Service men and women of all ranks attended the event, which took place at a beautiful hotel in downtown Dubai. It was hard to get very excited, knowing we'd miss Christmas with our families. Fortunately, there was a lot of camaraderie in the wing, which helped ease the pain of being away from home.

That evening, I put a call in to Colette. It was early in the morning back in Utah, and hearing her voice was the best present I could ask for.

"You should see outside," she said excitedly. "It's been snowing all night."

"I'd give anything to see snow right now. I've experienced nothing but summer for the last eight months."

We spent thirty minutes on the phone, and I could barely hold back the tears when Candice and Kristen were on the line. With a little help from Colette, they told me about the snowman they'd made, and that Santa Claus would be coming to see them soon.

The following afternoon, two more pilots arrived on base: Capt. Ed "Tonto" Christian, formerly of the 34th TFS, the newest LANTIRN pilot in the 421st; and Capt. Michael "Chins" Chinburg, who was married early in September and missed the initial deployment. Scotty had promised to bring him over right away, but Chins had been reassigned to the 34th TFS and sent to LANTIRN school in October. Since Chins was LANTIRN-qualified, I assumed he'd join our squadron, but when I saw him in the club, he said he'd been assigned to the 4th.

I arrived at the squadron early in the afternoon on 23 December. A check of the week's schedule showed that I was also going to be flying on Christmas Eve and Christmas Day. I'd flown along Kuwait's southern border three times in the previous two weeks, and what was once a comprehensive mission was now routine: We'd brief, take off, fly across the Gulf, refuel in Saudi Arabia, do some area work near the Kuwaiti border, then fly home. The skies could get pretty crowded, but AWACS controllers had been doing an outstanding job coordinating airspace. A lot has to be said for the tanker crews, too. Air refueling at night is one of the most challenging events we perform in the F-16. The tanker crews made it easy for us. They were always on station when we arrived, and the boom operators performed flawlessly.

My wingman for the night's sortie was my roommate, Rip. We began our briefing at 18:00, and as soon as we finished I called a few of the army units to let them know we'd be coming over low and fast around 23:10. A short time later, Rip and I were cruising across the Gulf at 24,000 feet.

Rip maintains a trail position until we reach the tanker track in northern Saudi Arabia. Once I pick up our tanker on radar, I flash my exterior lights, a signal for Rip to rejoin to the fighting wing position.

Using my air-to-air radar, I spot the tanker at my left ten o'clock for thirty miles. I place my radar cursors over the square symbol and designate with the TMS switch to lock it up. Once the tanker is locked, information on my radar screen shows its altitude, airspeed, and aspect angle. I maneuver to keep the contact on the left side of my scope, and, at the ten-mile point, I begin a thirty-degree bank turn to the left. If everything works as planned, I'll roll out about a mile in trail with fifty knots of overtake.

Halfway through the turn, I reach down and open my air-refueling door so my tanks can depressurize and accept fuel. As I approach the aft end of the KC-135, I pull my throttle back to reduce the overtake. After I'm stabilized in the precontact position, I turn off my radar and dim my exterior lights. Rip has automatic clearance to the left wing of the tanker, where he'll remain until I complete my turn on the boom.

I push my throttle forward and ease my F-16 into the contact position. My airspeed is slightly above 310 knots and the boom is approximately twenty feet in front of me. Continuing forward, I watch as the boom operator maneuvers the fueling probe around my canopy. The roar of the tanker's inboard engines and turbulence from its wing tell me I'm a little high and tight. To correct, I pull the throttle back about a quarter of an inch and add a touch of forward pressure on the stick. The muscles in my body tighten—a midair collision at this altitude and airspeed would not be good. Finally, I settle into position, and the boom operator plugs in the probe.

A green contact light near my HUD confirms the connection. Seconds later, fuel begins to flow. Throttle and stick movements need to be extremely small, and my eyes are fixated on signal lights located underneath the Stratotanker. I dare not blink. To relax, I wiggle my toes. After my tanks are topped off, I hit the disconnect button on my control stick and ease away from the tanker. When I'm clear, I close my air-refueling door and maneuver to the KC-135's right wing.

A few minutes later, Rip completes his turn on the boom. He rejoins to my right wing.

As soon as we're heading north, I begin a climb away from the tanker. Fifteen minutes later, the two of us are working the area just south of the Kuwaiti border. We practice GMT bombing on one of the highways. After a few passes, we drop down and attack some of the army camps.

By 02:30, Rip and I were ready for a good night's sleep. My alarm awakened us at 10:30 the next morning. After lunch, we left for the squadron to prepare for another night sortie. Neither of us ever dreamed we'd be spending Christmas Eve in the cockpit of an F-16—though the only date that really meant anything to us was 15 January.

Rip and I flew the same profile as the previous night, and we were back on the ground by 22:30. As soon as we finished refueling in the hot pits, we returned to the 421st ramp and shut down our engines. Before I could climb out of the jet, Lt. Col. Nall walked up with a camera and a Santa's hat. He tossed the hat into the cockpit, telling me to put it on. After he snapped my picture, he reached up and shook my hand.

"Merry Christmas, Rosey. I know you'd rather be with your family tonight, and I wanted to come out and thank you for all the hard work you've been putting in."

"Thank you very much, sir. I appreciate your coming out."

After we shook hands, I tossed down the hat to Nall, who walked over to greet Rip. After climbing out of the jet and filling out the forms, I wished my crew chief a merry Christmas and walked over to the hangar to debrief maintenance. Rip and I were back in the life-support shop by 23:15, and we agreed to cut the debrief short so I could attend midnight Mass.

I arrived at the chapel a few minutes before midnight and picked out an empty chair in the back. Christmas carols played softly in the background. The Christmas celebration lasted about an hour. I found my thoughts focused on peace, and I prayed for a quick end to the conflict. I asked God to return me home safely, so I could be with my family again. When mass ended, I shook Father Pierson's hand and thanked him for being there when I needed someone to talk to.

Christmas day was no different from any other day of the last four months. I led Tonto on a local-area orientation sortie—his first flight in theater—and the two of us arrived at the o'club in time for Christmas dinner: chicken, lamb chops, potatoes, and rice. For dessert, the mess-hall staff served ice cream and an assortment of cookies. After eating, I poured myself a cup of hot tea and relaxed on a couch in the lounge. One of the pilots received a CARE package earlier in the week, which included a tape of *Rudolph the Red-Nosed Reindeer* and *The Grinch That Stole Christmas*—two of my all-time favorites. Christmas is all about memories, and both shows took me back to my childhood. Afterward, I grabbed some more cookies, made another cup of tea, and watched *It's a Wonderful Life*. Back in my room, I wrote to Colette:

25 December 1990

Sweet Colette:

Merry Christmas! I just came back from the club and I'm getting ready to go to bed. We watched *Rudolph the Red-Nosed Reindeer*, *The Grinch That Stole Christmas*, and *It's a Wonderful Life* tonight. The lounge was packed. I enjoyed the shows, but I wish I could have watched them with you and the girls.

I ate an MRE for dinner on Christmas Eve, then flew another mission near Kuwait. This afternoon I led Ed Christian on his local-area orientation flight. When we returned, we ate Christmas dinner at the club. They put out a nice spread for us—including ice cream for dessert. It was a lot better than the Thanksgiving debacle.

We should be close to the 15 January deadline by the time you receive this letter. Things are already starting to get tense on base. We haven't had a day off since 7 December and we found out yesterday that we're not going to be allowed off base anymore. If the deadline passes and Saddam Hussein still hasn't withdrawn, President Bush will probably decide to use force. I would expect to see something happen right away or maybe during the third week of February. The nights will be moonless during these two periods, making it the ideal time for an attack. I know you're scared, but you have to have faith in my abilities as a pilot. I'm as proficient in the .F-16 as I've ever been, and if Saddam wants a fight, we'll give him one he won't soon forget.

If the Raiders make it to the Super Bowl, be sure to tape the game for me. I doubt we'll get to see it. Think about switching our mutual funds into the money-market account. If war starts, the market will probably go down. I should know a day or two ahead of time when the war is going to start. I won't be able to tell you anything over the phone, but if I call and tell you to switch the funds, that will be your signal.

If they shut off the phones, I'll write every day. Be strong for the girls. If they see you upset, they won't understand. I love you and I promise I will be home soon.

Love, Keith

In the second half of December, Lt. Gen. Calvin A. H. Waller, CENTCOM's deputy commanding general, told the press that American ground forces would not be ready to attack Iraq until possibly mid-February. "The transportation system is overloaded," Waller said, "and additional forces assigned to the region will not arrive until late January." Some questioned the timing of Gen. Waller's comments. But the Bush administration downplayed the remarks, even though anonymous sources continued to admit an American offensive might have to wait until February. In contrast to outsiders, pilots believed that Gen. Waller's comments were designed to keep Saddam Hussein off balance. In any case, New Year's Eve was spent in the beer tent celebrating the end of our fourth month at Al Minhad. The base had made enormous strides and, thanks to Lt. Col. Rackley and a group of dedicated pilots, the 421st had evolved into a top-notch squadron. Twenty-four of the pilots in the unit were now LANTIRN-qualified, and the others were proficient enough with the FLIR to fly virtually any night mission. Fighter pilots will usually tell you they prefer flying during the day, but the Black Widows had taken the LANTIRN mission and turned it into one of the coalition's most effective weapons. Our motto: "We own the night."

19.
A NEW YEAR

New Year's Day arrived and the headline across the front page of the *Gulf News* read "Dawn of New Hope." Under normal circumstances, a statement like this might mark the beginning of any new year. For the pilots of the 388th Tactical Fighter Wing, however, the first day of 1991 was of little significance. The day could have been 7 June. No one would have known the difference. No one drank champagne on New Year's Eve; there were no party hats, streamers, or magic countdowns. The only date with meaning was 15 January, the deadline for Iraq's withdrawal from Kuwait.

I arrived at the squadron shortly after 15:00 and began to prepare for another night sortie. Duck would lead the formation, and he came with great news. The 1,000-foot floor was rescinded. Effective immediately, all units in theater were once again allowed to fly at 500 feet. Flying at medium and high altitude during the past few months gave us the opportunity to develop new tactics, but to take full advantage of LANTIRN, we needed to be down in the weeds, 500 feet and below.

Batman and Harpo, the other members of our four-ship, arrived in the weapons shop a few minutes after I did. We had to do some last-minute planning since the low-level rules had changed. Harpo jumped on the MSS computer, while Duck and I built a new low-level to take us over the giant sand dunes in northeastern Saudi Arabia. Duck suggested we practice a couple of threat reactions before executing a ten-degree direct attack on our target, a remote oil facility near the Saudi-UAE border. After we completed the attack and were established on our egress heading, Duck would terminate the low-level and lead us back to Al Minhad. The sortie would normally end at this point, but Duck got permission from T-Rack to do an airfield attack.

As soon as we finished mission planning, we walked over to one of the briefing trailers across from life-support. Duck covered the details of the flight; then we walked next door, changed into our flying gear, and stepped to the jets.

When I arrive, my crew chief hands me the aircraft forms and takes my helmet bag so he can place it in the cockpit. After I complete my walkaround, I climb into the jet and begin to strap in. My crew chief follows me up the ladder and helps me connect my G-suit and shoulder harnesses.

"Thanks a lot, chief."

"Any time, sir. Have a great flight, and I'll see you when you get back."

"I almost forgot to tell you. Make sure you and your friends are out on the ramp around 21:10. We're going to do an airfield attack, and you won't want to miss it."

"I'll spread the word, sir."

Good ground operations set the tone for every flight. Today they go exceptionally well. Everyone sounds crisp on the radios, and the four of us taxi with perfect spacing from the ramp to the arming area. After the arming crews complete their inspections, I adjust my FLIR and title my VTR tape. Five minutes before takeoff, I turn my radar on, tighten my lap belt, and check my cockpit switches one last time. I'm ready to fly.

"Widow 31, go channel three!" Duck radios.

"Two!" "Three!" "Four!"

"Widow 31, check!"

"Two!" "Three!" "Four!"

"Minhad tower, Widow 31 is ready for takeoff."

"Widow 31, winds are two-three-zero at six," the controller replies. "You're cleared for takeoff."

"Widow 31 cleared for takeoff, go channel four!"

"Two!" "Three!" "Four!"

Three minutes later, the four of us are airborne. We depart to the south and rejoin two-plus-two with three miles of spacing between elements. Duck levels off at 21,000 feet and proceeds toward the tanker track. A single KC-135 is orbiting alone when we arrive, and Duck performs the rejoin flawlessly. Once everyone's tanks are topped off, we exit the track and proceed south toward steerpoint four, the first point on our low-level. Fifty miles from the point, we execute a combat descent. Duck had briefed that we could fly at 300 feet if we felt comfortable, but I plan on leveling off at 500. It has been three months since any of us have flown down low, and I prefer to be a little more conservative.

Once I level off and complete my LANTIRN checks, I accelerate to 480 knots and call up the auto TF. The autopilot immediately descends me down to 500 feet. I hit the first point right on time. I'm a little behind on my cross-check during the first two legs, but by steerpoint number six, I'm back in the swing of things.

Halfway to steerpoint number seven, Duck calls for a threat reaction. He and Batman break hard to the right to evade an imaginary SAM. I assume the lead and continue toward the next point. As soon as Duck tells me he's saddled—a call from the wingman or element, indicating the return to briefed formation position—I wait a minute, then call for my own threat reaction.

"Widow 33, break right, break right! SAM at right five o'clock."

"Widow 34, supporting," Harpo replies.

I depress the paddle switch near the bottom of my control stick, which inhibits the TFR and allows me to perform a high-G turn without getting a fly-up. I continue the turn for 180 degrees, and then I terminate the maneuver. Using my air-to-air radar, I do a quick search for Duck's element.

"Widow 32 has buddy spike at right two o'clock, high aspect," Batman calls out.

"Widow 33, buddy lock," I reply.

Now that I have Batman locked up, I wait until he's abeam my jet, and then I execute a 180-degree right turn and fall into position behind him. As soon as I roll out, I call saddled and re-engage my auto TF.

The reactions go well, and by the time we reach the IP, everyone is in perfect position to attack. While accelerating to 540 knots, I call up my air-to-ground bombing system. I glance down at my kneeboard to review my pop numbers one last time, then switch to manual TF for the final run-in. A quick check of the GPS page on my up-front control shows the system is operating with "high" accuracy. Knowing my INS diamond will be directly on top of my target boosts my confidence.

"Widow 31, check cameras on," Duck radios.

"Two!" "Three!" "Four!"

I reach down to the left console and turn on my VTR. As I scream across the desert floor, the manual TF box has me climb and descend over sand dunes that sit between me and the target. Approaching the pop point, my eyes focus on the DME in the lower-right corner of my HUD. When I see 4.7, I aggressively pull the nose of my jet up to fifteen degrees. I cross-check my altimeter while climbing, and, within seconds, I reach my pull-down altitude of 2,500 feet. I immediately roll inverted, pull the nose back down, then roll out again. As I expected, the INS diamond is right on top of the station. I push the missile step button on the right side of my control stick, which calls up my CCIP pipper. A quick correction to the left puts my bombfall line directly over the station. As soon as the pipper reaches the southwest corner of the facility, I hit the pickle button. Without hesitation, I pull off target and perform my turning safe-escape maneuver.

In the middle of the turn, I check my altimeter to make sure I'm not sinking. Hitting the ground at over 500 knots would mean instant death. After I roll out on my egress heading, I call up the auto TF and flip my missile-override switch inboard. I check my air-to-air radar for enemy fighters and do a quick search for the lead element. Once I spot Duck and Batman, I call off target. Moments later, I'm back at low altitude, skimming across the desert floor.

As soon as Harpo calls off, Duck terminates the low-level.

"Widow 31, knock it off," he radios.

"Widow 32, knock it off."

"Widow 33, knock it off."

"Widow 34, knock it off."

The four of us climb to 2,000 feet and turn to a heading of 330 degrees. I check my fuel and reach down to turn off my VTR. As I level off, I call up steerpoint ten. Al Minhad is seventy-three miles on my nose, and the four of us are proceeding direct. I flip through the pages on my kneeboard and review my numbers for the airfield attack. Duck is targeted against the officer's club; Batman will hit the enlisted mess hall; I'm going to strike the 421st's maintenance hangar; and Harpo will hit the 4th's.

Thirty miles from the field, Duck radios, "Widow 31, push it up. Check cameras on."
"Two!" "Three!" "Four!"

I engage my auto TF and push my throttle up to mil power. The lights of the base begin to appear on the horizon, and, a few seconds later, I'm in the pop. As soon as I roll out, I spot the maintenance hangar and pickle my weapons on top of it. As I pull off target, I select afterburner with my throttle. After I cross the airfield, I pull my throttle to idle, and extend my speed brakes. Once I slow down, I throw my landing gear down and make a right turn to roll out on final.

"Widow 33, gear down full stop," I radio.

"Widow 33, winds are calm, you're cleared to land."

I touch down, and Harpo follows less than a minute later. The four of us refuel in the hot pits and, thirty minutes later, we're back on the 421st ramp, shutting down our engines.

As I raised my canopy, a few of the crew chiefs walked over to the jet.

"Were you guys outside when we flew over?" I ask.

"I thought the world was coming to an end, sir," one of them replied. "We were standing on the ramp, and it was real quiet. Then, without any warning, this F-16 comes flying over the top of our hangar with its afterburner cooking. It was the loudest thing I've ever heard."

"I don't know how low you got, sir," replied another, "but that was the greatest show I've ever seen."

"Imagine what it would be like if we were dropping real bombs," I told him.

"I'm just glad I'm not an Iraqi," he replied.

After we debriefed the mission, we took the shuttle back to the o'club. *The Sting* was the featured movie, and the lounge was full. I sat in an empty seat next to Jabba and Capt. Geoff "Grover" Cleveland, and asked if they heard us come over.

"The movie was about to start and everyone thought the roof was going to cave in," Grover replied. "Which one of you flew over the o'club?"

"That was Duck."

"After you guys came over," Jabba interjected, "Col. Navarro walked over and told T-Rack there would be no more airfield attacks. I think you guys shook him up a little."

"He deserves it after making that announcement today," Tater interrupted.

"What announcement was that?" I asked.

"I guess you haven't heard. A KC-135 guard unit from Pennsylvania is coming here, and 'The Warden' told T-Rack and Boomer that the officers are going to move into our port-a-cabins."

"He wants them to be 'comfortable,'" Jabba interjected.

"Where the hell are *we* supposed to go?" I asked, stunned.

"They're going to erect more tents behind the hard billets," Tater said. "They should be ready by this weekend."

"That's bullshit," I replied. "I'm not moving again—especially into a tent. Those guys got to spend Thanksgiving and Christmas at home. We've been here since August!"

"I've never seen a commander treat his men like Navarro treats us," Grover grumbled. "There's no excuse for it."

I went to bed angry and woke up the following afternoon even more upset. After running to burn off steam, I headed to the club for lunch, sat in the lounge, and wrote about the previous day's events. A journal of my experiences would be nice to have one day—especially if we went to war.

Editions of the *Gulf News* and the *Khaleej Times* arrived around 15:30, and, according to the Associated Press, an American soldier died after shooting himself—apparently on purpose—with his M-16 rifle. A spokesman from U.S. Central Command said the soldier was with the 4/26th supply-and-transportation battalion of the 101st airborne division. He was the sixth serviceman to die in accidents, two involving shootings, since the previous Saturday. I felt sad for both the soldier and his family. I sympathized with the depression he must have been feeling. The solitude of the desert mixed with thoughts of war can drain the hope out of you.

Other news stories suggested the possibility of a meeting between Secretary of State James Baker and Iraqi foreign minister Tariq Aziz. An American official said there were signs of flexibility on Baghdad's part, and Iraq's ambassador in Washington stated that Saddam Hussein would no longer insist on 12 January as the only date for the meeting.

After dinner, I left for the squadron. I was coming down with a cold and probably shouldn't have been flying, but I was the element lead of a two-ship scheduled to work the area near Kuwait's southern border, and my wingman for that evening's flight was our D.O., Col. William "Wild Bill" Huddle. Taking my name off the schedule wouldn't have been difficult, but I'm not one to turn down a flight. Besides, I'd never flown with Col. Huddle before, and I was anxious to show him the tactics that Duck and I had perfected over the past three weeks. I had a feeling he'd be impressed.

The sortie went extremely well, and I was pleased with my performance as a flight lead. We locked up a lot of movers with GMT, and even though he didn't fly as much as he would have liked, Col. Huddle performed well as a wingman. After we finished reviewing our HUD film, Col. Huddle told me how impressed he was with our squadron.

"It looks like this unit is ready for war. You've come a long way during the past three months."

"Lt. Col. Rackley has really turned this squadron around, sir," I replied. "The LANTIRN pilots have worked hard, and things are really starting to gel for the unit."

"Don't let up, Rosey. I have a feeling things will heat up quickly if Saddam Hussein doesn't withdraw his forces by the deadline."

We concluded the debrief around 01:00. I picked up my mail, and Col. Huddle dropped me off in front of the beer tent. The music was loud, and I was tempted to join the fun, but I had a couple of letters from Colette, and a Christmas card from Candice and Kristen. As soon as I got to my room, I changed clothes and climbed into bed. The letters were postmarked 18 December, and they included pictures of Colette and the girls. I read each one twice, and when I finished, I taped the pictures next to the others I had on the wall near the head of my bed. I wanted the three of them to be the first thing I saw when I woke up each day.

Rip and I strolled over to the club the next afternoon in time to catch a late lunch. The two of us were scheduled to drop live bombs on the Faisal range in northern Saudi Arabia. It had been quite a while since any of us had dropped live, especially at night.

We take off for the Faisal range at exactly 21:30. Both of us are carrying six MK-82s, and everything is going well until I make my initial call to AWACS. Despite repeated efforts, I'm unable to contact them. Approaching the Saudi coastline, I switch us over to our assigned tanker frequency. Once again, there is no answer. I try pink six, the tanker common frequency, and the controller tells me our assigned tanker had a maintenance problem and never took off. I ask if we can bootleg some fuel from another tanker, and he clears me to a nearby track where an orbiting KC-10 accommodates us.

With full tanks, Rip and I depart the track and proceed north toward Faisal range. I make another attempt to contact AWACS, and, when that doesn't work, I try ABCCC. We don't have to have permission to enter the airspace, but having an AWACS controller on freq would make me feel a lot more comfortable, especially if Iraqi fighters decide to cross the border.

We begin our descent fifty miles south of the range, and, by now, I'm extremely frustrated. I try to contact one of the close air support (CAS) units and two different forward air controller (FAC) units. Still no answer.

"Widow 42, this is Widow 41 on victor."

"Go ahead," Rip replies.

"I'm starting to get real annoyed with this. Unless you have a better idea, I think we should just call Faisal range and see if the range officer will let us in."

"Widow 42 agrees."

"Widow 41, go yellow one!"

"Two!"

"Widow 41, check!"

"Two!"

"Faisal range, this is Widow 41. How copy?"

"Widow 41, Faisal range has you loud and clear."

"Widow 41 is a pair of F-16s with MK-82s. Mission number is 6251 alpha and we're thirty south."

"I'm sorry, sir, but the range is closed."

"We're scheduled from 23:00 to 23:15," I plead.

"We have no F-16s on our schedule tonight."

There's no point in arguing with him. We need to get rid of these bombs, though. The last thing I want to do is land at Al Minhad with live munitions. The range controller suggests I contact one of the American army units in the area. I switch Rip over to OB-2 and make my call. An army controller answers, and I tell him I'm looking for a place to drop some live munitions. He gets real excited and says the troops would love to see a show. I ask where we can drop, and he tells me to stand by while he looks up the coordinates. He checks back in and gives me a pair of coordinates not too far from Faisal range.

"I'll call some of the units and tell them you'll be dropping in about ten minutes," the controller says.

I tell him to make sure the area is clear, and I read back the coordinates one more time to make sure there is no mistake. Rip and I program the coordinates into our F-16 computers. As soon as we finish, I call for a distance-and-bearing check. Everything checks good. I instruct Rip to take spacing while I accelerate for the run-in. I come in low and fast, so the troops on the ground can hear me coming. I pull up a few miles from the target and execute my roll-in. My INS diamond is in the middle of an empty desert, and I pickle my bombs off right on top of it. As soon as I come off, I roll to the left and see the string of six MK-82s explode across the desert floor.

"Widow 41, off south," I radio.

Thirty seconds later, Rip calls off. I check to the right about thirty degrees, just in time to see Rip's bombs explode. I make another call to OB-2 and ask if they saw the bombs.

"The guys loved it!" he says excitedly. "Come back again soon!"

Two hours later, Rip and I were in the beer tent reflecting on the mission with some of the other Black Widows. Everything that could have gone wrong went wrong, but it was the kind of sortie that everyone needs now and then to stay sharp. I was glad we had the chance to put on a good show for the army troops. I knew there were a lot of young men down there who were scared about their immediate future. Rip and I were happy to add a little excitement to their night, and help them realize the U.S. Air Force would be there for them.

Tonto woke me up at 10:00 the following morning and said we'd been cleared to go into town.

"The buses leave in an hour."

I got ready as quickly as possible and, a short time later, I was on my way over to the o'club. I ran into Yogi, Duke, and Bopper, and we agreed to ride into town together. Shortly before noon, our bus pulled into a parking lot across the street from the mall. We didn't have to be back until 16:30—more than four hours to relax and shop. The four of us ate pizza at the local Pizza Hut and did a lot of window shopping. I ended up buying a new pair of Nike running shoes.

When we returned to Al Minhad, Yogi and I walked over to the beer tent. The 147th Air Refueling Squadron (AREFS) from Pittsburgh had arrived earlier that afternoon, and six of the pilots were standing by the bar drinking beer. Some friends from the 4th and the 421st were talking with them, and we walked up to join the conversation. Ark introduced Yogi and me to Maj. Jerry "Weenie" Moore.

"He's a pilot for Delta," Ark said excitedly.

We shook hands, and I welcomed him to Al Minhad.

"When were you guys activated?" I asked.

"We've been flying support missions for Desert Shield since September," Weenie replied, "but the unit was activated for real on the twentieth of December. One week later, we were on our way to Jidda in Saudi Arabia."

"How many of you are coming here?" Yogi asked.

"Our squadron is combining with members of the Columbus Air National Guard and the Tennessee Air National Guard. Our new designation is the 1713th Air Refueling Wing (Provisional). There obviously isn't any room for our jets here at Al Minhad, so we're going to fly them out of Dubai International Airport. But all of the crews will stay here, and I'd say there's about a hundred and ten officers in the group."

"We were told you'd be moving into our port-a-cabins," Yogi remarked.

"Our commander, Col. Fred Foresster, spoke with Col. Navarro earlier this afternoon," Weenie continued, "and told him our unit would stay in the tents, so we can all be together. I'm pretty sure Navarro said okay."

That was the best news any of us had heard in a while. We celebrated in the beer tent until it closed, and then I headed back to my room to go to sleep. I woke up the following morning with renewed enthusiasm and flipped through the pages of the previous days' newspapers.

The lead story in the *Khaleej Times* reported that President Bush had outlined a proposal for Secretary of State James Baker to meet with Tariq Aziz in Switzerland on either 7, 8, or 9 January. The president called the proposal "one last attempt to go the extra mile for peace."

Later in the afternoon, I ran into Redman and Maj. Glenn "Ahkbar" Bender on the front steps of the o'club. I asked if there had been any word about President Bush's proposal. Ahkbar said a meeting between Aziz and Baker was set to take place in Geneva on Wednesday, 9 January.

Three days before this meeting, in a speech marking Army Day, Saddam Hussein declared that the Iraqi army had "unshakable faith in their mission in the struggle which will not break regardless of the sacrifices. . . . The return of Kuwait to Iraq is a fact and not a claim. It is the nineteenth province on the map of Iraq. . . . The Iraqi army will entail great sacrifices in quantity and quality." Saddam continued: "But the results will please friends and displease foes. This is a battle for the sake of Palestine. Iraq is pitted against the U.S. administration, its puppet Zionist entity, and those bad people who have allied with them."

20.
FALLEN WARRIOR

The scent of JP-4 lingered in the air as I ran past the Fuujin ramp. It was a hot winter morning and the flight line was bustling. Four Vipers had just begun to taxi. The piercing whine of their engines drowned out the morning call to prayer. Alone with my thoughts, I continued west along the dirt path, dreaming of the day I would finally get to leave the place. Passing the control tower, I gazed toward the flight line. Air force "Red Horse" construction teams had just completed work on a new ramp, and, in three hours, twenty-four F-16s from the 69th TFS at Moody AFB would be parked on it.

After showering, I walked over to the o'club to catch a bite to eat. Lt. Col. Scott was sitting by himself, and I asked if there was anything I could do to help him prepare for the Werewolves' arrival.

"The first cell is due to arrive in a couple of hours," Scotty said. "There are two cars parked near my office that need to be positioned on the ramp. One is for the Moody D.O., and the other is for the 69th squadron commander. It would be a big help if you would drive them there for me, Rosey."

"No problem, sir. A few of my friends are flying in, and I want to be there to greet them when they arrive."

After we finished eating, Lt. Col. Scott dropped me off in the 421st parking lot. As soon as I parked the first car, Scotty drove me back to pick up the second one. A short time later, the two of us were joined by more than a dozen pilots from the 4th and the 421st, who were also there to welcome the Werewolves. Morale was high, and when the first landing light appeared on final, everyone cheered. Each F-16—with "MY" painted on its tail—landed uneventfully and taxied off the runway. After the de-arming crews completed their post-flight checks, the pilots taxied to the new ramp, where crew chiefs stood by to chock the jets.

Lt. Col. Harry Davis, squadron commander of the 69th TFS, led his formation onto the ramp and, moments later, shut down his engine. As soon as he raised his canopy, Col. Navarro and Col. Huddle approached the side of his aircraft. Backed by a cheering crowd, Navarro and Huddle shook the Werewolf commander's hand, welcoming him to Al Minhad Air Base.

Jabba and I walked over to greet some of the other pilots, hoping to run into our good friend from Kunsan, Capt. Mark "Rock" Clemons. Rock lived across the hall from me when I was a member of the 80th TFS in Korea, and I was anxious to see him. A gourmet cook from Louisiana, Rock was one of the most popular pilots in our unit. On weekends, his room resembled a crowded Bourbon Street restaurant. Red beans and rice were his specialty, and the hot wings he used to make would set our mouths on fire. During exercises, some of our missions would end well after midnight. Meeting in Rock's room afterward became a ritual. We'd watch *Caddyshack* and stuff ourselves with his delicious pancakes.

Jabba and I spent the next hour welcoming the remaining members of the 69th. Seeing their reactions as they drew their first breath of hot, humid Gulf air reminded me of when I arrived on base. Before long, aircraft from the fourth and last cell began to appear on final. The first one to land was Rock, and as soon as he taxied in, Jabba and I were there to greet him with Juvat snake signals and a cold bottle of water.

"How was the flight?" Jabba asked.

"Too long," Rock replied. "I wish I would have flown on one of the KC-10s."

Rock climbed down off the ladder and turned to shake our hands.

"Is it always this hot?" he asked.

"This is nothing compared to last summer," I told him.

The three of us talked until the crew van arrived. We agreed to meet at the club for dinner. After the van left, I walked over to the 421st and spent the rest of the afternoon studying in the weapons shop. Dinner did not come soon enough. When I arrived at the club, Rock and other members of his squadron were relaxing in the lounge. I walked in and recognized some friends I hadn't seen for quite a long time. Capt. Scott "Pop" Poppleton, a fellow instructor from Reese AFB, and Lt. Dave "Crotch" Crochet, a fellow Juvat, were here now. And so was Capt. Mark "Stal" Stalnaker, a pilot I had become good friends with during LANTIRN training. Stal and Rock introduced me to some of the other pilots in the unit. During dinner, I gave everyone a rundown on what life at Al Minhad had been like during the past four months.

Exhausted from their flight, the Moody pilots retired early. Lips and I took the shuttle bus to the 421st for another night of MPC duty. The frag came in about thirty minutes earlier, and when we arrived at the squadron, other members of the team were already hard at work. Our group had been together for more than a month, and everyone seemed to be comfortable with their role. It used to take us a minimum of ten hours to complete all of the packages. Lately, we'd been finishing up around two in the morning.

Music was playing in the background, and everyone was in a great mood. The Werewolves were a welcome addition to the 388th. Seeing old friends again renewed my spirit. The 15 January U.N. deadline was only a week away, and, the next morning, talks between Secretary of State James Baker and Iraqi foreign minister Tariq Aziz would begin. Morale had taken a tremendous beating over the past few months, but now it was as high as it had ever been.

Shortly before nine o'clock, our wing weapons officer, Maj. Scott "Foot" Goodfellow, walked into the planning room. "The 4th has just lost a jet," he said.

The room fell silent. Finally, Spike asked who the pilot was and whether or not he ejected. "I don't know," Foot answered. "I'm on my way over to the command post, and as soon as I hear something, I'll come back and let all of you know."

The atmosphere in the room suddenly turned somber. I had been happy a few minutes before, but now I felt as if I'd been rolled over by a truck. We continued planning. An hour passed before Foot returned. As soon as he walked in, Stinger hung up the secure phone and Raj turned down the music. Everyone expected the worst.

"This is what I know. We received a dispatch from CENTAF headquarters about an hour ago telling us that one of our jets had gone down near the Saudi-Kuwaiti border. According to army personnel on scene, the pilot did not get out. Those who haven't checked in with the command post yet are Maj. Jay 'Momar' Lindell, Capt. Mike 'Redman' O'Grady, Capt. Scobey 'Sudds' Suddreth, and Capt. Mike 'Chins' Chinburg. I'll let you know when we hear from them."

Leaning against the table, I put my hands over my face and asked myself why this had to happen. If Foot could only walk back in and tell us he made a mistake. Aircraft accidents have claimed the lives of too many friends over the years. I've lost classmates, fellow instructors, and even one of my students. It's something you never get used to.

The four pilots Foot mentioned were all married. My closest friend in the group was Sudds, who took me under his wing when I joined the 4th. We really hit it off during the Green Flag deployment. Another good friend was Momar, a former F-111 pilot who earned his tactical call sign when he participated in Operation El Dorado Canyon, the bombing raid against Libya in April 1986. The two of us flew together on several occasions, and I always enjoyed being around him.

Redman and I became friends shortly after we arrived at Al Minhad. He had the bunk next to mine before I was transferred to the 421st. We spent a lot of time playing cards and talking about our futures. Redman knew how hard it was for me to leave the 4th, and he was very supportive throughout the ordeal. Chins, on the other hand, had only been in theater for a couple of weeks. He married his sweetheart, April, a week after we deployed, and, instead of coming over to join us, was sent to LANTIRN school at Luke AFB. Chins and I worked together in the Fuujin weapons shop before the deployment.

While Lips and I were building attack cards, Foot walked in with another update.

"Momar and Redman checked in with the command post a short time ago. They should be on the ground in twenty minutes."

That narrowed it down to Sudds and Chins.

Finally, around midnight, Col. Huddle delivered the news to us. The downed pilot was Capt. Michael "Chins" Chinburg. Col. Huddle didn't know what caused the accident. He would meet with Sudds as soon as he landed. Filled with emotion, I walked out on the squadron balcony overlooking the 421st flight line. Spike joined me a few minutes later. The two of us stared into the night.

"I hope this isn't God's way of preparing us for things to come," Spike said.

"I never understand why things like this happen," I replied. "It's hard for us to lose a friend, but the person I feel for the most is April. In an hour or two, she's going to get a knock on the door. When she opens it, she'll see Col. Fox, the chaplain, and one of the flight surgeons. All three will be in their dress blues, and before anything is said, she'll know the reason for their visit."

We left for the beer tent as soon as we finished mission planning. When we arrived, the room was crowded with pilots. Most of the guys were talking quietly among themselves, waiting for the commanders to arrive. I grabbed a soda and walked over to talk with Ark and Vicious. A short time later, Sudds and Lt. Col. Welsh walked in. Visibly shaken, Sudds went up to the bar. I just put my hand on his shoulder and told him things would be okay. Before anything else was said, Lt. Col. Welsh asked for everyone's attention.

"Listen up, men," he began somberly. "All of you are aware by now that we lost a pilot earlier this evening. Many of us have experienced this before, and I'm here to tell you that it's something you never get used to, especially when it's someone from your own squadron. All of us know that Chins is in God's hands now. He will watch over and guide all of us."

He went on, "Chins always wanted to be a warrior. He believed in what we're doing, and he will always be remembered as a true soldier. He died as a warrior, and none of us would want to die any differently."

Everyone listened intently as Boomer continued to speak. A few of us gathered around Sudds and did our best to console him.

"I'd like to propose a toast," Boomer continued.

Everyone raised their beer cans. He began: "He shall not grow old as we who are left grow old. Age shall not weary him, nor the years condemn. At the going down of the sun and in the morning, we will remember . . ."

When Boomer finished, everyone gathered around the wall with the Fuujin patch drawn on it. The pilots in the 4th signed their names on the wall right after the beer tent was built. The only member of the squadron who hadn't signed it yet was Chins. With a black marker, Sudds walked up and signed Chins right below the patch.

Sudds walked back to the bar and explained to us what happened.

"We were flying in northern Saudi Arabia near the Kuwaiti border. The weather was clear, and we set up for our first attack at twelve thousand feet. I was in the lead, and Chins was eight miles in trail. I briefed him on the setup, and I told him if he had any problems with spacing or situational awareness, we would knock it off and set it up again.

"I was in the middle of my pass, and, all of a sudden, Chins called 'knock it off.' After I acknowledged him, I called for an in-place turn to the south. As soon as I rolled out, I asked him if he was ready for the next maneuver. There was no answer. I called him again, and there was still no answer. I thought we were having radio problems. A few minutes later, an army unit came up on guard frequency and said an aircraft had gone down. I made one more call, and, when there was no reply, I knew it was him."

Though it was still too early to speculate, everyone suspected the accident was a result of spatial disorientation. Flying at night over sparsely populated areas with no discernible horizon can be difficult, especially in the F-16, with its big bubble canopy. Lights on the ground can easily be mistaken for stars in the sky. What feels like straight and level flight could just as easily be a descending left turn. If a pilot becomes disoriented at night or while flying in the weather, he must immediately transition to his instrument gauges and believe what *they're* telling him, not what his senses report. Unfortunately, a lot of pilots think they're infallible when it comes to spatial disorientation. Some will tell you it could never happen to them. But it happens. It happens more often than even the most confident pilots think. Sometimes the results are deadly.

Sudds was having a tough time. I suggested we go back to his room so he could get some rest. The two of us feasted on a salami sent by Sudds's wife, Teresa, and we talked until four in the morning. I knew the accident was not Sudds's fault, but losing a wingman is a pilot's greatest fear. It was going to take some time for him to get over it, and, I knew, he'd never get over it completely.

The next morning, I woke up at 07:30 and caught the early shuttle to the squadron. Gen. Merrill A. McPeak, Air Force Chief of Staff, was scheduled to visit the base and would be touring the 421st at approximately 08:00. Meeting the air force's highest-ranking general would be a thrill, but the person I really wanted to see was Col. Pat Gamble, Gen. McPeak's executive officer. Col. Gamble was the commander of the 8th TFW Wolf Pack during my tour at Kunsan. Pilots affectionately named him "Super Dave" because of his strong resemblance to the comic thrill-seeker Super Dave Osborne.

Col. Gamble left Kunsan in June 1990 to become executive officer for Gen. Michael J. Dugan, who had just replaced Gen. Larry Welsh as Air Force Chief of Staff. Gen. Dugan was very popular and a strong air force leader, but he made a spectacular mistake in September, 1990. While returning from a trip to Saudi Arabia, Gen. Dugan gave an interview to members of the press. "Air power is the only answer that's available to our country," he said, "and the best way to hurt Saddam Hussein is to target his family." The four-star general also freely discussed tactics and potential targets. Gen. Dugan claimed his comments were off the record. Be that as it may, they ended up on the front page of the *Washington Post.* The damage was done. During a news conference the following day, Defense Secretary Dick Cheney fired Dugan for "lack of judgment," "wide-ranging speculation," and for discussing "the substance of operational matters." Gen. McPeak, commander of PACAF, was named to replace him. He kept Col. Gamble on as his executive officer.

Duck and I were the only ones in the weapons shop when Col. Navarro and Lt. Col. Rackley escorted the chief of staff through the squadron. Col. Gamble was also present, and when the group entered the weapons shop, Duck and I snapped to attention. Lt. Col. Rackley introduced us, but McPeak didn't say a word. Cold and distant, he glanced quickly around the room, turned around, and walked out.

Col. Navarro and Lt. Col. Rackley followed the chief of staff out into the hall, but before joining them, Col. Gamble walked over and shook my hand.

"It's good to see you again, Rosey. How are things going?"

"I'm doing fine, sir. Congratulations on your new job with the general."

We talked about what each of us had done since we were at Kunsan together, and I asked him if he had heard about the accident.

"We arrived late last night and Col. Navarro told us what happened. I was real sorry to hear that, but that's the nature of this business, and you need to put it behind you as quickly as possible. Some big things are going to happen in the next few days, and you need to be mentally ready. I envy the opportunity you and your friends are going to have. You're all going to be heroes!"

After Col. Gamble left, I went back to the o'club to eat breakfast. Some of the pilots from the 69th and the 4th were gathered in the mess hall. Serving myself some eggs, I walked over to join Rock and Crotch at one of the tables. I told them I had just met Gen. McPeak and that Super Dave Gamble was there, too. I told my friends in the 4th all about Super Dave, and everyone was looking forward to hearing from the chief of staff before he left later in the morning. The day before had been hard for us, and a few words from Gen. McPeak would boost everyone's morale.

After we finished eating, I went into the lounge to watch a tape of *Married with Children* and *In Living Color*. Then Grumpy walked in and sat down next to me.

"What time is the commander's call supposed to be?" I asked.

"There isn't going to be one," he replied. "Gen. McPeak watched some of our LAN-TIRN film, and then he got on a plane and left."

"You *gotta* be shittin' me. Does he realize how long we've been here? We're on the verge of war, and he comes all the way over to the UAE, and won't even give us ten minutes? He should know how upset everyone is after last night's accident. He had a perfect opportunity to pump everyone back up again."

"I can't understand it either," said Grumpy.

"He's the Air Force Chief of Staff! The highest-ranking officer in the air force! How does a guy like that become a four-star general?"

After lunch, editions of the *Gulf News* and the *Khaleej Times* were delivered. Secretary Baker and Tariq Aziz were to meet, and I was anxious to hear the results. Both men arrived in Geneva the day before, and, according to the *Gulf News*, Aziz told reporters, "I have come in good faith. I am open-minded and I am ready to conduct positive, constructive talks with Secretary Baker."

President Bush called the meeting Iraq's last chance to accept an opportunity to withdraw peacefully from Kuwait before the 15 January deadline. "Let me be clear about the deadline," Bush was quoted as saying. "January 15 is not a date certain for the onset of armed conflict. It is a deadline for Saddam Hussein to choose—to choose peace over war."

Later in the afternoon, I left for the squadron to attend an ATWATS briefing. The subject was radar missile defense and SAM defense. Duck spent an hour discussing different tactics, and when the training session ended, Capt. Sutherland informed us that the meeting between Secretary Baker and Tariq Aziz had been in progress for more than four hours. The length of the meeting made us cautiously optimistic, since both men had stated earlier that if the other were going to issue nothing but ultimatums, the meeting would end quickly.

By 17:00, the o'club lounge was packed with pilots and other officers from around the base. The big-screen television was tuned in to the Dubai channel. During the newscast, the station unexpectedly switched to CNN for a press conference featuring Secretary of State James Baker. As he approached the podium at the Hotel Intercontinental, the room fell silent. Everyone eased forward in their seats. Grim-faced, the secretary calmly unfolded his notes. Before he began, I said a little prayer to myself.

"Regrettably, ladies and gentlemen," Baker began, "I heard nothing today that . . . suggested to me any Iraqi flexibility whatsoever on complying with the United Nations Security Council resolutions."

"Regrettably," was all I needed to hear.

We are going to war.

Everyone in the room appeared to feel the same thing. Those who had been on the edge of their seats were now slumped back.

"There have been too many miscalculations," the secretary continued. "The Iraqi government miscalculated the international response to the invasion of Kuwait, and it miscalculated that it could divide the international community and gain something thereby from its aggression."

When a reporter asked about the letter President Bush had written to Saddam Hussein, the secretary answered, "I regret to inform you that the minister chose not to receive the letter from President Bush. He read it—very slowly and very carefully—but he would not accept it."

When Baker finished, Iraqi foreign minister Tariq Aziz stepped up to the microphone to present his view of the meeting. "We have not made miscalculations," he began. "We are very well aware of the situation. We have been very well aware of the situation from the very beginning."

The foreign minister was calm, as if he expected all along that the talks would be unsuccessful.

"We know what the deployment of your forces in the region means. We know what the resolutions you imposed on the Security Council mean. And we know all the facts about the situation—the political facts, the military facts, and the other facts."

When asked why he didn't accept President Bush's letter, Aziz replied, "I told him I am sorry I cannot receive this letter, and the reason is that the language in this letter is not compatible with the language that should be used in correspondence between heads of state."

The Iraqi foreign minister's most chilling statement came when a Jewish reporter asked if Iraq would attack Israel in the event of hostilities. Looking sternly at the reporter, Aziz answered, "Yes, absolutely yes!"

I'd heard enough at that point and decided to go into the mess hall, where dinner was being served. Other friends joined me and, throughout the meal, barely a word was spoken. I thought about my family and friends back home, certain they were watching the news conference. Like me, they were probably wondering how long President Bush would wait past the deadline before he set the war machine in motion.

After dinner, I made myself a cup of tea and, with a hand full of cookies, walked back into the lounge. The news was still on. President Bush commented on the talks.

"I sent Jim Baker to Geneva, not to negotiate, but to communicate, and I wanted Iraqi leaders to know just how determined we are that the Iraqi forces leave Kuwait without condition or further delay. Secretary Baker made clear that by its full compliance with the twelve relevant United Nations Security Council resolutions, Iraq would gain the opportunity to rejoin the international community. And he also made clear . . . how much Iraq stands to lose if it does not comply."

Bush continued, "I watched much of the Aziz press conference, and there was not one single sentence that has to relate to their willingness to get out of Kuwait. This was a total stiffarm. This was a total rebuff."

Asked about Saddam Hussein, President Bush commented, "He is living under a delusion. I don't think he has felt that force would be used against him, and I think he has felt that if it were, he would prevail. He is wrong on both counts."

21.
THE INEVITABLE

When a fighter pilot dreams, he always sees a MiG at twelve, never at his six. With good energy and the sun at his back, the fighter pilot sees himself roll in for the kill. After he locks the MiG up with an AIM-9 Sidewinder, he lets the missile fly. As the Sidewinder corkscrews through the air, the pilot comes off hard-left to avoid the impending fireball. One kill is never enough, so as soon as he rolls out, he spots the helpless wingman searching frantically for his leader. Too close for a missile shot, he switches to guns, squeezes off a short burst of twenty mike-mike, then returns to base—always to a hero's welcome.

When I opened my eyes on the morning of 10 January, I realized that war with Iraq was now inevitable. I stared at the ceiling, imagining my first combat mission. What will it be like the first time I cross the border into Iraqi airspace? Will the SAM and AAA be as heavy as intel predicts? Will we engage Iraqi fighters? How many kills will I get? Will I survive?

Wiping the sleep from my eyes, I stumbled into the shower. After dressing, I sat on the edge of my bed. Still numb from the previous night's news conference and Chins's death, I laced up my boots, then headed for the o'club to call Colette. I could tell by the tone of her voice that she, too, was now convinced that America would soon be at war. We talked about the news conference, and I recounted the events of the previous night. Everyone at Hill AFB now knew about the accident.

"Debi Fox called yesterday afternoon and told me about the accident," Colette said. "I spoke with a few of the other wives last night, and everyone's in shock. We know there's going to be a war."

"Everything is going to be okay," I told her.

"What am I supposed to do if Col. Fox knocks on *my* door in the middle of the night?" she interrupted. "I don't think I can handle that, Keith."

"I'm as proficient in the F-16 as I've ever been. I know you're going to worry, but you need to have faith in me. You need to be strong, not only for yourself, but for Candice, Kristen, and the other wives in the squadron. I love you very much, and I *will* come home. I promise."

I spent the rest of the morning at the o'club working on my journal. Rip and Tonto strolled in around noon, and the three of us headed into the mess hall for lunch. Grumpy was standing in the buffet line. He informed us that CENTAF Director of Campaign Plans, Brig. Gen. Buster Glosson, was due to arrive on base within the hour.

According to Grumpy, Gen. Glosson planned to meet with the pilots at 14:00 in the beer tent. This could mean only one thing: he was coming to prepare us for war.

Everyone jumped to their feet as Gen. Glosson walked into the room. Following close behind him were Col. Navarro and Col. Huddle.

"Take your seats," the general barked out.

A big man with silver hair, Gen. Glosson looked more like my grandfather than a fighter pilot. But his swagger and booming voice quickly marked him as a leader.

"I want everyone in the room who isn't a pilot to leave," Glosson bellowed. He paused for a moment, waiting to see if anyone would walk out. Finally, he began.

"Yesterday in Geneva, Switzerland, Secretary of State James Baker met with Iraqi foreign minister Tariq Aziz for six and a half hours. Unfortunately for Iraq, the secretary was unable to convince the foreign minister that it's in his country's best interest to withdraw from Kuwait. It doesn't take a genius to figure out that Saddam Hussein made a huge mistake when he invaded his southern neighbor. He made an even bigger one yesterday when he refused to leave. Now, men, he's about to suffer the consequences."

He continued, "Iraq was given every opportunity to end this crisis peacefully, but Aziz's refusal to accept President Bush's letter to Saddam Hussein was the final slap in the face. As a result, the greatest air war in military history is about to begin. We are on the verge of decapitating every nuclear, chemical, and biological weapons plant in Iraq. We will crater each and every runway. We will hunt down each and every leader in their country—including Saddam Hussein—and we will eliminate them. We are going to wipe the Republican Guard off the face of the earth."

The room erupted with cheers and applause. The fear and anxiety we walked in with ten minutes earlier were replaced by excitement and high emotion. At that moment, we all realized we had been waiting for an announcement like this since September. At long last, the moment had arrived. When everyone quieted down, Glosson continued.

"During the last few weeks, I've had experts run different scenarios through computer models. As a result, my staff estimates the Iraqi air force will launch approximately seventy-two sorties during the first day of fighting. The United States and other members of the coalition are going to launch over 1,400. Fighting will begin under the cloak of darkness, and Iraq's radar defense system will be among the first targets destroyed. British Tornadoes will crater every Iraqi runway, and F-16 Fighting Falcons will follow up with CBU-89 Gator to prevent the Iraqis from doing any repair work."

The general went on, "F-15 Eagles will saturate the skies above Iraq and Kuwait. Air superiority is essential, and any Iraqi fighter that is lucky enough to get airborne will be shot down. The only thing you have to concern yourselves with is hauling iron. If any F-16 pilot goes trolling for a kill, and I find out about it, I'll send him home! The point I'm trying to make is this: Your job is to drop bombs—period!"

He continued, "I was at the White House in October to brief the president on the air plan. And I'll tell you something, men, we are extremely lucky to have a man like George

Bush as our president. He promised me this would not turn into another Vietnam. 'You guys fight the battle, and I'll take the heat from Congress,' he said."

The general picked up a glass of water, took a drink, then set it down on the table. The look on his face became serious.

"War is a dangerous business, and we expect to lose some brave men. The first few missions are going to be terrifying. You're going to see more SAMs and AAA than you ever thought possible. Just remember one thing: Bravery is controlling your fear and apprehensions. Stupidity is having neither of the two."

A pause. Then, "I know you have a lot of questions. The afternoon is yours, and I'll stay until all of them are answered."

Foot raised his hand first.

"We heard a rumor that the F-117s have already been to Baghdad and back. Is that true, sir?"

"Contrary to what the Iraqi government has been saying," Glosson replied, "it isn't true. To test Saddam Hussein's radar defense capabilities, I've had the F-117s fly toward Iraqi airspace, retract their radar reflecting antennas, then turn to parallel the border. The F-117s disappear from Iraq's radar screens, and every time we do it, Baghdad claims we're invading their airspace. The truth is, though, we haven't."

"Are there any 'silver bullets' in theater?" Ark asked, referring to nuclear weapons. Gen. Glosson smiled and shook his head. "That's one question I'm not going to touch."

"How do we convince the Israeli government to remain on the sidelines once the war begins?" Lt. Col. Scott asked.

"That's a very important question," Glosson answered sharply. "During the news conference yesterday, a reporter asked Tariq Aziz if Iraq would attack Israel should war begin. His answer was yes. The Israelis know Saddam Hussein has placed Scud missiles here in western Iraq." The general pointed toward a map. "Some of the missiles are on mobile launchers, and others are located at fixed sites near H-2 and H-3. I had to promise the Israelis that these bases would be bombed the minute the war began. They, in turn, promised to let us handle things as long as they saw bombs falling in western Iraq. So, guess what, guys? The ATO will have missions dedicated against H-2 and H-3 on a daily basis, even if it means dropping bombs in the open desert."

When the general finished, Lt. Col. Nall stood and introduced himself.

"Sir," he began, "how do you feel about the LANTIRN pilots flying missions at low altitude?"

"Here we go," Skippy observed. "I can't *believe* he asked that question in front of Navarro."

Duck leaned forward. "That took a lot of balls."

Col. Navarro was sitting in the front row with Col. Huddle and the three squadron commanders. We'd been trying to convince him that flying down low in the open desert would be suicidal, even at night. So far, he had refused to listen.

Now every LANTIRN pilot in the room was on the edge of his seat, waiting to hear

Gen. Glosson's response. He looked Nall directly in the eye: "You guys have been flying these jets for months. You've taken a brand-new program and developed all of the tactics. If you want to fly low, fly low. If you think it's safer to fly at medium or high altitude, do it. And Mike here,"—the general pointed toward Col. Navarro— "will support you."

Everyone in the back of the room let out a silent cheer. It took guts for Lt. Col. Nall to stand up and ask that question. A few of us almost fell out of our chairs when he did. But Col. Navarro's edict that "you will fly low" was tantamount to a death sentence. Nall stuck his neck out for us, and "The Governor" told "The Warden" he was giving us a reprieve.

When the general finished, I raised my hand.

"How long do you expect the war to last, sir, and how will we know when to end it?"

"Once the ball starts rolling downhill," Glosson began, "it's going to be awfully hard to stop it. When President Bush asked how long we thought the war would last, I predicted Saddam Hussein would surrender within seven days. My latest prediction is about three weeks. We've assembled an enormous amount of firepower here in theater, and I don't think Saddam will allow his army to be destroyed."

The general continued, "This is going to be the air force's show. We're going to fly in the neighborhood of twelve hundred to thirteen hundred sorties *per day*, which is unprecedented. I visited the A-10 wing earlier this morning. The Iraqis have three hundred sixty-nine tanks stationed near the front, and I bet the wing commander that his men couldn't knock them all out on the first day. I have a feeling I'm going to lose that bet." He chuckled.

When asked about rules of engagement, Glosson replied, "I only have three rules for you to worry about: First, bring every American home alive; second, don't kill any more Iraqi civilians than necessary to get the job done; and, third, by no means are you to let rule number two get in the way of rule number one."

He looked at us hard. "I don't care what anybody says, there is not a single target in Iraq or Kuwait worth losing one American life over. I repeat, there is not a single target in Iraq or Kuwait worth losing one American life over. If you roll in on your target, and it doesn't look right, come off, and we'll go back and hit it again the next day."

He went on, "One of our main goals is to win this war with as few casualties as possible, so don't expect to see the army or any other ground forces get involved until the air force has bombed the Iraqi military into submission. We're going to do this right the first time, so we don't have to come back here five years from now and do it again. When you guys are through, the Iraqi army will be happy to see our ground forces—so they can surrender!"

Gen. Glosson answered a few more questions. Before leaving, he made one more statement: "I want you to know that I'm extremely proud of every single pilot in this room. America is proud of you too. You've sacrificed more for your country in the past four months than most Americans do in a lifetime. I look forward to seeing you again in

Colette and I in front of a T-38 at Reese AFB, Texas, 1987.

"If you ain't a Juvat, you ain't shit!" Serving with the 80th Tactical Fighter Squadron at Kunsan AB, Republic of Korea, 1989. Officially the "Headhunters," we were usually called "Juvats," after our motto: "Audentes fortuna juvat"— Fortune favors the bold.

The first F-16 Block 40 at the General Dynamics (now Lockheed Martin) plant, Fort Worth, Texas.
The aircraft is equipped with a LANTIRN pod (to the pilot's left, below the intake)
and a Targeting pod (to the pilot's right, below the intake). A pair of Maverick missiles
and an AIM-9 Sidewinder can also be seen.

Helicopter view of the port-a-cabins at Al Minhad AB, UAE. My room is the
near side of the port-a-cabin at the top right.

Original LANTIRN cadre (from left): Skippy, Harpo, Weasel, Badger, Duck, Rosey, Damien, Tater, and Batman.

The 421st Tactical Fighter Squadron, Hill AFB (deployed). Al Minhad AB, UAE, February 1991.

At Al Minhad AB.
A Maverick missile
is under the wing,
February 1991.

I woke up to these
photos every day
at Al Minhad:
Candice, Kristen,
and Colette with
the girls.

Leaflets I "delivered" to
the Republican Guard on
25 January 1991.

A moment with Colette, a few days
before the war.

With Carlos "Jackal" Nejaime, my wingman.

Mark "Stitch" Miller in the
cockpit of his F-16 minutes before
engine start on 19 February 1991.
(Credit. Reuters/Corbis-Bettmann)

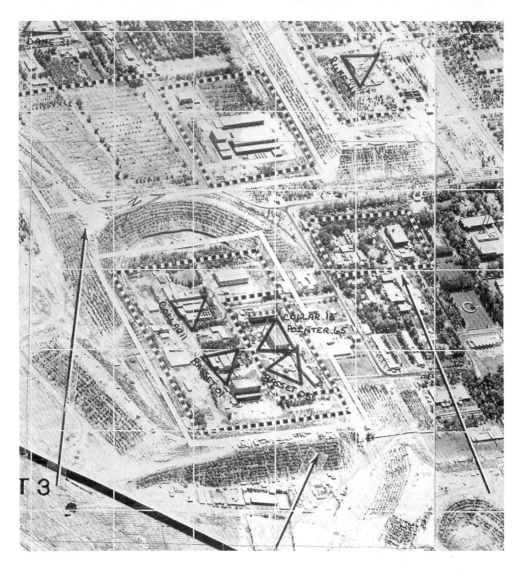

Satellite target photo of the Tawaitha nuclear research facility, Baghdad. I wore this on my kneeboard during the mission.

Message to Saddam Hussein—on a 500-pound MK-82.

Mark "Stitch" Miller
cheered on by the
crew chiefs.
(AP/Wide World Photo)

Kill-box map
I carried in the
cockpit during the
ground war.

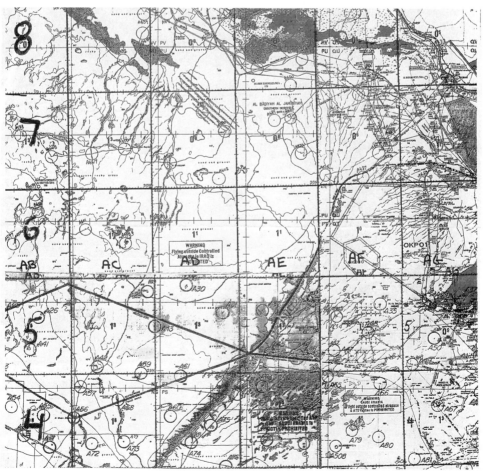

The "Highway of Death."
(AP/Wide World photo)

Heading home on a
C-5 Galaxy with
(top to bottom) Batman,
Norge, Jabba, and Raj
on 5 March 1991.

a few weeks, so I can congratulate you on our victory. Now let's go out there and end this thing as quickly as possible, so we can go home and let the Arabs enjoy their Ramadan."

After Glosson left, there wasn't a pilot in the room who was not ready to go out and win this war.

The following afternoon, pilots from all three squadrons assembled on the flight line to pay their last respects to Capt. Michael "Chins" Chinburg. The ceremony took place on the ramp behind the 4th TFS headquarters. A solitary F-16, tail number 495, sat in front of a crowd of more than two hundred. The space below the canopy bore the name of our fallen comrade, and sitting undisturbed on the canopy rail was a lone helmet. Below the left wing hung a single G-suit and a parachute harness. A podium was placed near the front of the jet. Standing to the rear was the 388th TFW color guard, each member wearing desert camouflage fatigues, a beret, and white gloves. With tears in my eyes, I stared at the American flag as it flapped gently in the breeze. A young airman, eyes focused and white-gloved hands wrapped firmly around his M-16, stood beside it.

Father Pierson began with a prayer. Afterward, Capt. Dundy "Skids" Aipoalani and Capt. Orlando "Big O" Cisneros stepped up to the podium and read separate passages from the Bible. When they finished, everyone sang "The Battle Hymn of the Republic." Lt. Col. Mark "Boomer" Welsh concluded the service with a short tribute: "Like the rest of you," Welsh began, "Mike Chinburg answered the bugle's call. But now he has a higher calling. Like so many that have gone before him, now he rides with each one of you."

"Chins," Welsh said, turning toward the jet, "the Fuujins wish you clear skies and tail-winds. We wish you a pipper jet and a ten-meter bull. We wish you a MiG at twelve and your best friend's hat on the bar. But, most of all," Welsh said, his voice cracking, "most of all, buddy, we wish you peace."

After the ceremony, I took the shuttle bus back to the 421st. Shortly after I arrived, Lt. Col. Nall walked into the weapons shop and handed me a notebook.

"This is the ATO for the first forty-eight hours of the war," he said. "I want you to go through it carefully and highlight anything that pertains to our squadron. We're going to have a pilot meeting tomorrow afternoon, and I want you to brief the wartime SPINS and the ROE."

"Is this our only copy?" I asked.

"Each squadron has their own copy," Nall answered. "It's highly classified, so make sure you put it in the weapons safe when you're through."

I could hardly believe my eyes when I saw the first page. "H-hour" marked the beginning of the war, and the first target listed in the frag was Saddam Hussein's presidential palace in Baghdad. At precisely 00:00, eight Tomahawk missiles were due to hit the palace. As if that weren't enough, a pair of F-117 stealth fighters were scheduled to hit the same facility at H-hour plus 00:08. The minute-by-minute countdown listed every target, its coordinates, the time it would be attacked, recommended ordinance, and the unit fragged against it. Radar facilities, air bases, nuclear plants, Scud missile production facilities, ammunition dumps, command and control centers, petroleum oil lubricant (POL) sites, factories for chemical and biological weapons—the list went on and on. The first two days of the war were perfectly scripted, and every allied unit in theater was scheduled to participate.

The first targets allocated to the 388th TFW were Ali Al Salim Air Base and Ahmed Al Jaber Air Base in Kuwait. Ali Al Salim AB is in central Kuwait, approximately eight miles west of Al Jahra. Ahmed Al Jaber AB is in the southern half of Kuwait, approximately twenty-five miles southwest of Kuwait City. The TOT was H-hour plus 02:00, and the frag called for eight F-16s to attack the airfields with CBU-89 Gator, a high-tech weapon consisting of seventy-two BLU-91/B antitank mines and twenty-two BLU-92/B antipersonnel mines. The BLU-91/B weighs four pounds and has a 1.3-pound bi-directional mass-focus warhead. These mines are effective against tanks or armored vehicles; they detonate when the sensor detects a target, or the mine is disturbed. They also detonate when a preset self-destruct time expires or when mine battery voltage drops below an acceptable level. The BLU-92/B antipersonnel mine is similar to the antitank mine with one exception. The BLU-92/B has a fragmenting case warhead, which weighs .905 pounds and is triggered by tripwires. Each submunition contains eight tripwires and sensors, four per side. At ground impact, the tripwires deploy to a maximum distance of forty feet. The mines detonate when a disturbance or target sensor is provoked, when low battery voltage occurs, or when the self-destruct timer expires.

The F-16 is capable of carrying four canisters of CBU-89, and the submunitions dispersed by each weapon typically cover an 800-by-1,000-foot area. After an enemy airfield is cratered, CBU-89 is usually deployed to prevent attempts at reconstruction. Antitank and antipersonnel self-destruct settings range from minutes to days, making Gator one of the air force's most effective—and nastiest—weapons.

I continued to review the ATO. The wing's first large-force employment was set to occur on day two of the war. The target was the Latifya Scud missile production facility twenty miles southwest of downtown Baghdad and three miles east of the Euphrates River. The TOT was scheduled for H-hour plus 31:00, and the frag called for forty-eight F-16s from the 388th TFW. Each aircraft would carry two MK-84s weighing 2,000 pounds apiece.

The ROE was very specific when it came to civilians. Civilian areas throughout Iraq and Kuwait were to be avoided, period. The SPINS discussed the role of AWACS, and detailed how to avoid being shot down by our own fighters. F-15 Eagles would set up combat air patrols in different corridors covering all of southern Iraq and Kuwait. CAPs would also be set up in northern Iraq to defend allied bases in Turkey, and in western Iraq to defend Israel. Aircraft egressing from their targets would be required to squawk specific transponder codes that could be interrogated by patrolling F-15 pilots. The SPINS also dictated that egressing aircraft should fly at specific altitudes along designated lines of longitude. Any aircraft that didn't meet the criteria would be shot down, no questions asked.

I woke up the next morning convinced that war with Iraq would begin sometime during the next few days. I couldn't imagine Saddam Hussein giving in at this point, so I decided to write a letter to Colette:

12 January 1991

My Dearest Colette,

Hello, my love. I just woke up a few minutes ago and I wanted to share my thoughts and feelings with you. This is a very important letter because we will likely be at war by the time you receive it. I pray that is not the case, but nothing has happened in the last few days to make me think otherwise.

I know this war will be difficult for you to handle, and I want you to know what my present state of mind is, going into the upcoming battle. Gen. Buster Glosson came to brief us a couple of days ago, and it was the greatest motivational speech I have ever heard in my life. He spent more than two hours alone with the pilots, and by the time he left, morale was as high as it has ever been here in the desert.

I realize you would prefer to have me at home in your arms. Let me assure you, there's a part of me that would like nothing more than to be there. But every one of us has a defining moment in our lives, and mine is to participate in this war. Please understand that I love you more than anything in the world. But this is a matter of good versus evil, right versus wrong. The people of the United States are depending on us, and so are the citizens of Kuwait.

I have no regrets about what I have done or what I am about to do. I would be lying if I told you I wasn't scared. I'm more afraid for you, though, because I know how helpless you must feel right now. The other pilots are just as scared as I am, but if you had to choose a war to fight in, this would be the one. Think back to World War I and II, the Korean War, and even Vietnam. Compare them to the Persian Gulf, and you will realize that America has never held a stronger advantage over its enemy.

Experts say the Iraqi army is the fourth largest in the world. Well, babe, they're about to be annihilated. Our technology and training is so superior, and I feel confident that we will win this war very easily. That's not to say we won't lose people, but the numbers should be minimal.

I want you to get together with your friends and pray not only for us, but for the people of Iraq. Set the example for the other wives. Show them what you've gone through and let them see how strong you are.

I am truly at peace with myself and with God. I'm putting myself in His hands, and I'm doing everything I can to prepare for war. My strength comes from looking at pictures of you and the girls. If you look at mine, it will give you the same strength and love that I feel.

Please don't be upset when you read this letter. Be happy for the love we had—and more importantly, the love we will have in the future. Have faith that I will return home safely to you. I love you, and I will carry your spirit with me wherever I am.

Love, Keith

I had not flown in five days and I was beginning to feel uncomfortable. I had tremendous confidence in my abilities, but Chins's accident left me somewhat shaken. Since Gen. Glosson's visit, maintenance had been removing aircraft from the flight schedule to ensure they'd be ready when the war started. With the 15 January deadline only three days away, I was desperate to get back in the air again. I didn't want my next sortie to be a combat sortie.

I spent Saturday afternoon at the squadron, reviewing local-area procedures and night tactics with the pilots from the 69th TFS. The Werewolves began flying local-area orientation sorties two days before, and half the squadron was scheduled to fly into northern Saudi Arabia later in the evening. I'd flown fifty-two training missions since arriving in theater, but those poor guys were lucky to get three or four sorties under their belts before the deadline passed.

Later in the evening, Lt. Rod "Kid" Gard and I sat on the front steps of the o'club and discussed what each of us would like for our families in case one or the other were killed in action. Ann Marie and Colette were very close, and if I got shot down, I wanted Ann Marie to be notified first, so she could be with Colette when Col. Fox came over to break the news.

"I don't want to die," I told Kid, "but I'm prepared to if that's what God has planned for me. If I'm shot down and captured as a POW, tell Colette I'm sorry and that I love her. I'm aware of everything the POWs in Vietnam went through, and I've always had great admiration for those men. We all have our breaking points, but I'll die before I betray my country or a fellow pilot. If I'm considered missing in action, all I ask is that Colette give me five years before she remarries. If I haven't been heard from by then, make sure she gets on with the rest of her life."

Kid shared his feelings as well, and we both agreed to watch over each other's families in the years to come. When we finished, we spent the rest of the evening in the lounge watching a movie called *Black Rain*.

The following night, I was scheduled to fly my first sortie in nearly a week. I knew it would be my last before the deadline, and I wanted to make the scenario as realistic as possible. My wingman was Rip, and the two of us were fragged to fly into northern Saudi Arabia. After we air refueled, we practiced a few attacks from medium altitude with our lights off. We finished up with a LANTIRN low-level, a threat reaction, and a ten-degree attack on one of the U.S. Army compounds near the Kuwaiti border. We landed an hour later, and, after the debrief, I made one last phone call to Colette. Col. Navarro was going to turn off the phones the next day.

The two of us spent more than an hour on the phone. During the conversation, Colette told me Congress voted earlier in the day to authorize the use of force to expel Iraqi forces from Kuwait. "The Senate voted 52 to 47, and the House vote was 250 to 183," she said.

"What about the talks between the U.N. secretary general and Saddam Hussein?"

"CNN said he spent three hours with Tariq Aziz and then met with Saddam Hussein for two more hours. He left Baghdad for Paris on his way to New York, where he's supposed to brief the Security Council on the results of the talks."

I told Colette to switch our mutual funds to the money-market account—our pre-arranged signal that the war was about to start. I wished I could tell her about the meeting with Gen. Glosson, but the information he presented was highly classified and couldn't be discussed over an open phone line. Realizing what would soon happen, Colette began to cry. I told her I loved her and tried to assure her that I'd be okay.

Colette put Candice and Kristen on the phone, and I told them how much I loved them. I had spent a total of four months with them over the past two years. They barely knew me, and it hurt to think I might never have the chance to watch them grow up.

During lunch on Monday, 14 January, Grumpy told me to report to the 4th TFS for a special meeting at 14:00. When I arrived at the squadron, I found out my first combat mission would occur on day two of the war. Our target was the Latifya Scud missile production facility. The large-force employment would consist of sixty-six aircraft: forty-eight F-16s, eight F-15s, eight F-4Gs, and two EF-111s. Twenty-four of the F-16s belonged to the 388th TFW. Each aircraft would be configured with two wing tanks, an ECM pod, two AIM-9 Sidewinder missiles, 510 rounds of M56 high-explosive incendiary, and a pair of 2,000-pound MK-84s.

I was scheduled to fly in the number three position of a four-ship led by Grumpy. His wingman was Wheel, and I had the honor of leading the D.O., Col. William "Wild Bill" Huddle. Col. Huddle was a combat veteran of the Vietnam War, and I looked forward to having his experience on my wing. The exact date and takeoff time for the mission were yet to be determined, but we did have satellite photos of the target area. Grumpy pointed out the target assigned to our four-ship: a large rectangular building that sat between a pair of buildings running from east to west. A large square lake a short distance from the buildings made our target easy to identify. Other targets in the facility were also easy to discern. A few, however, would require a fair amount of target study.

"The only reason you have such a big target, Rosey, is because Wild Bill is on your wing," RC laughed.

Col. Huddle walked into the room while RC was teasing me, and everyone began to laugh.

"You saved the big one for the old man, huh, RC?" Huddle quipped.

After everyone had a chance to look over their target, Maj. Dick "Marshman" Marsh, chief of wing intel, conducted a briefing on the SAM and AAA threat. The Scud facility was well protected by SA-2, SA-3, SA-6, and SA-8 surface-to-air missiles and an array of ZSU-23-4 AAA guns. He suggested we plan our IP-to-target run over the Euphrates River, heading east.

"Most of the SAMs are positioned on the northern and eastern sides of the facility," Marsh briefed. "If you attack from the west and egress south, you should have no trouble avoiding the heavier concentrations. Not all of these sites are fixed," he cautioned. "The Iraqis can reposition the SAMs anywhere they want rather quickly."

Maj. Marsh also informed us that the actual U.N. deadline for Iraq to withdraw from Kuwait was midnight Eastern Standard Time on Tuesday, 15 January. The local time in Iraq and Kuwait at the deadline would be 08:00 on 16 January—09:00 in the UAE.

After the briefing, I rode the shuttle bus back to the o'club. A dozen pilots were watching television while others read through afternoon editions of the *Gulf News* and the *Khaleej Times*. I picked up a copy of each newspaper and took a seat on one of the gray leather couches. On the front page of the *Gulf News*, Defense Secretary Cheney said the latest reports out of Baghdad indicated neither progress in talks to avert a war nor any sign of the start of an Iraqi withdrawal. Cheney declined to say if the war would start immediately after the deadline, but he did say: "There should be absolutely no doubt at this time as to the determination of the president, or the support he now has from the Congress."

Also printed in the paper was the text of President Bush's letter to Saddam Hussein:

Mr. President:

We stand today at the brink of war between Iraq and the world. This is a war that began with your invasion of Kuwait; this is a war that can be ended only by Iraq's full and unconditional compliance with U.N. Security Council Resolution 678.

I am writing you now, directly, because what is at stake demands that no opportunity be lost to avoid what would be certain calamity for the people of Iraq. I am writing, as well, because it is said by some that you do not understand just how isolated Iraq is and what Iraq faces as a result. I am not in a position to judge whether this impression is correct; what I can do, though, is try in this letter to reinforce what Secretary Baker told your foreign minister and eliminate any uncertainty or ambiguity that might exist in your mind about where we stand and what we are prepared to do.

The international community is united in its call for Iraq to leave all of Kuwait without condition and without further delay. This is not simply the policy of the United States; it is the policy of the world community as expressed in no less than twelve Security Council resolutions.

We prefer a peaceful outcome. However, anything less than full compliance with U.N. Security Council Resolution 678 and its predecessors is unacceptable. There can be no reward for aggression. Nor will there be any negotiation. Principle cannot be compromised.

However, by its full compliance, Iraq will gain the opportunity to rejoin the international community. More immediately, the Iraqi military establishment will escape destruction. But unless you withdraw from Kuwait completely and without condition, you will lose more than Kuwait. What is at issue here is not the future of Kuwait—it will be free, its government will be restored—but rather the future of Iraq. The choice is yours.

The United States will not be separated from its coalition partners. Twelve Security Council resolutions, twenty-eight countries providing military units to enforce them, more than one hundred governments complying with sanctions—all highlight the fact that it is not Iraq against the United States, but Iraq against the world. That most Arab and Muslim countries are arrayed against you as well should reinforce what I am saying. Iraq cannot and will not be able to hold on to Kuwait or exact a price for leaving.

You may be tempted to find solace in the diversity of opinion that is American democracy. You should resist any temptation. Diversity ought not to be confused with division. Nor should you underestimate, as others have before you, America's will.

Iraq is already feeling the effects of the sanctions mandated by the United Nations. Should war come, it will be a far greater tragedy for you and your country. Let me state, too, that the United States will not tolerate the use of chemical or biological weapons or the destruction of Kuwait's oil fields and installations.

Further, you will be held directly responsible for terrorist actions against any member of the coalition. The American people would demand the strongest possible response. You and your country will pay a terrible price if you order unconscionable acts of this sort.

I write this letter not to threaten, but to inform you. But I do so with no sense of satisfaction, for the people of the United States have no quarrel with the people of Iraq. Mr. President, U.N. Security Council Resolution 678 establishes the period before 15 January of this year as a "pause of good will" so that this crisis may end without further violence.

Whether this pause is used as intended, or merely becomes a prelude to further violence, is in your hands, and your hands alone. I hope you weigh your choice carefully and choose wisely, for much will depend on it.

—George Bush

22.
WAR BEGINS

A time-honored tradition among fighter pilots is the receipt of one's tactical call sign. Most call signs are simple nicknames based on a pilot's name, looks, or personality. Others are earned when a memorable event occurs—either in the air or on the ground. Some fighter jocks receive their call signs during initial training. Most pilots, however, receive their names shortly after joining their first operational fighter squadron.

I've been known as "Rosey" since pilot training. But when I arrived at the Koon, I was given the name "Moron." During my sweep, the naming committee, led by Capt. Tom "Toad" Twohig, declared: "Anyone who's a FAIP must be a *moron*." A FAIP is a first-assignment instructor pilot. When the crowd in the Long Beach Club cheered wildly, I knew the name would stick. I could have bought the naming committee a case of beer and asked for a different call sign, but there was no guarantee it would be better than the first, considering the squadron had pilots named "Smegma" and "Anus."

The 421st TFS had changed dramatically over the past four months. Many pilots were new to the squadron and a few had yet to be named. Since no one was allowed off base anymore, we decided to hand out tactical call signs in the beer tent.

By eight o'clock, the music was blasting, the beer light was on, and thirty large pizzas from Pizza Hut were waiting to be eaten. While everyone gathered around the bar, the naming committee, which consisted of all the lieutenants in the squadron, called Lt. Col. Tom Rackley to the front of the room. The lieutenants didn't care for the name "T-Rack," so they changed it to Taz—short for Tasmanian Devil. Rackley, a short, stocky man who could get wound up on occasion, raised his arms in triumph. A chorus of cheers rang out and everyone began to chant, "Taz!" "Taz!" "Taz!"

Lt. Col. Tim Nall was next in line, and shouts for "Damien" emanated from the crowd. The previous October, when Nall came down on several pilots for expressing their views during ATWATS meetings, Jabba made a passing comment: "We should call him 'Damien.' If you cross him, he'll make you disappear." The vote for Damien was unanimous, and the call-sign committee made it official.

By the end of the night, most of the new guys seemed satisfied with their call signs. Those who weren't, simply bribed the naming committee with enough beer to last the squadron a month. It was evident that the camaraderie missing a few months ago was back, and morale was extremely high. The 421st TFS had come a long way since the beginning of Desert Shield, and that night's event gave us a chance to laugh and celebrate together. Each pilot in the unit was now proud to call himself a Black Widow.

The party ended at midnight, and, on the way to my room, I ran into Father Pierson. We talked about the deadline, and he asked if I'd made a videotape for Colette yet. Two weeks earlier, Montgomery Ward had sent the wing a video camera and more than 3,000 videocassettes. The generous donation was designed to give everyone a chance to make a film for loved ones back home. I hadn't had a chance to sit in front of the camera yet, so Father Pierson suggested I get a tape and go down to the chapel office.

"The video camera is ready to go," Pierson said. "Why don't you take my keys and go make a tape for Colette. Nobody will be there this late. Stay as long as you want and put the keys inside my door when you finish."

I rushed to my room, grabbed a cassette, then left for the chapel office. For the next two hours, I sat in front of the camera and reminisced. I recounted the day Colette and I met at Foster's Freeze ice cream parlor in Culver City, California; our first date, when it took us two hours to find my car in the parking lot at Disneyland; our wedding day; and the birth of our children. We'd been through a lot during the past fourteen years, and I wanted her to know I'd cherished every moment. I finished up with a message to Candice and Kristen. If anything happened to me, they'd be able to look back, see who their father was, and know that he loved them.

16 JANUARY 1991

A knock on the trailer door awakened me from a deep sleep. I rolled over and saw Spike standing in the doorway.

"Hey, Rosey," he called out. "Time to get up and go to work. Col. Huddle wants our MPC team in the squadron ASAP!"

"I'll be ready in a few minutes."

I glanced at my watch: 09:20. The U.N. deadline for Iraq to withdraw its forces from Kuwait had passed twenty minutes earlier, and, by the looks of things, President Bush appeared ready to use force. I threw on a clean flight suit, brushed my teeth, then headed over to the o'club to catch the shuttle bus. It was a magnificent day. The previous day's rain had passed, and a cool morning breeze was blowing in from the west.

When I arrived, Spike was sitting alone on the steps.

"Well, buddy," he said with a grin, "I guess today's the day."

"It's hard to believe, isn't it?" I replied. "Seems like yesterday we were at Green Flag."

"Green Flag seems like a decade ago," Spike answered sarcastically.

When the shuttle arrived, the two of us stepped aboard. Sitting behind the wheel was a young airman. He closed the door behind us and began to pull away. "Do you guys think the war will start now that the deadline has passed?" he asked.

"I'm not sure," Spike replied. But both of us knew in our hearts that it *would* start.

A few minutes later, he dropped us off in front of the 421st and wished us luck.

Spike and I joined the other members of MPC team 1 in the planning room. Lips greeted us, and said Col. Huddle was on his way to give us instructions. We weren't anticipating a lot of mission planning. The first two days of the war had been planned months before, so all that was left to do was load DTCs and fill out lineup cards.

Col. Huddle and Lt. Col. Scott walked into the planning room shortly after 10:00, and Col. Huddle announced that H-hour was set for midnight that night, Baghdad time.

"I want every LANTIRN pilot in crew rest," Huddle continued. "That means you, Rosey. If we need you, you'll be notified."

I returned to the o'club and ran into Batman, Harpo, and Skippy.

"I just came from the squadron," I whispered. "Col. Huddle wants every LANTIRN pilot in crew rest. H-hour is set for midnight tonight, Baghdad time."

Their eyes immediately lit up. "Mister," Skippy said excitedly, "I knew we wouldn't wait that long after the deadline passed."

I spent the rest of the morning cleaning and doing laundry. I wanted all of my clothes ready and my room clean before the war started. After a short workout, I showered and walked back over to the o'club to write a few letters. On my way out the door, I ran into Col. Huddle. We exchanged salutes, and he asked if I'd seen Father Pierson. I told him no, and before he left, I asked if this was really the night.

"This is what we've been waiting for, Rosey," he replied. "We received a message a short time ago that H-hour has been pushed back to 03:00 Iraqi time—the precise time our first package is scheduled to take off." I knew that 03:00 Iraqi time was 00:00z (Zulu, or Greenwich Mean Time).

I walked away feeling numb. It was hard to believe that in fifteen hours we'd be at war with Iraq. When friends and relatives tuned in that night's evening news, the allied offensive would already be under way. If there were only a way for me to communicate to them that I'd be okay. At that point, though, there was nothing I could do.

I walked past the weight tent on my way to the o'club and noticed Ark, Rounder, and Kid inside, lifting weights. I stopped to say hello, and each of them shook my hand and wished me luck. A pair of doctors from the air-transportable hospital walked by and wished me luck too. Even though nothing had been announced, they, too, sensed something significant was about to happen.

I spent the rest of the afternoon writing letters and watching TV. I tried to take a nap, but I was too nervous to sleep. To pass the time, a few of us watched the movie *Ghost*. When it ended, I joined the squadron in the mess hall for dinner. Most of the guys sat and ate quietly. My thoughts were with Damien, Rip, Stitch, Ensign, Duck, Tater, Harpo, and Capt. Greg "Popeye" Froehle. A few hours from now, they'd take off and fly the wing's first combat mission. I'd lived and worked with these guys every day for the past four months, and I couldn't help but wonder if I'd ever see them again.

17 JANUARY 1991

Midnight had passed, and my friends left for the squadron to brief their first combat mission. Eight F-16 engines would soon come to life. In less than four hours, nearly 1.2

million troops would mass throughout the Gulf to engage in battle. Coalition forces representing Argentina, Australia, Bangladesh, Belgium, Canada, Czechoslovakia, Denmark, Egypt, France, the Gulf Cooperation Council (Bahrain, Kuwait, Oman, Qatar, Saudi Arabia, and the UAE), Great Britain, Greece, Honduras, Italy, Morocco, the Netherlands, Nigeria, Norway, Pakistan, Poland, Portugal, Senegal, Sierra Leone, the Soviet Union, Spain, Syria, and the United States had contributed aircraft, warships, and approximately 640,000 troops to the region. Of that total, the United States contributed 370,000 troops—a number that was expected to reach 430,000 by the end of January.

Coalition aircraft in the region totaled more than 2,600. Of these, 1,990 were American—1,540 land-based aircraft and 450 aboard six different carriers. American ships in the Gulf included the aircraft carrier USS *Midway*, the battleships USS *Wisconsin* and USS *Missouri*, and an array of amphibious assault vessels. Two aircraft carriers, the USS *Saratoga* and the USS *Kennedy*, were stationed in the Red Sea, along with four cruisers, one destroyer, one frigate, and eight supply ships. U.S. ground forces were equipped with more than 1,000 tanks in Saudi Arabia, including the M1 Abrams and the updated M1A1, as well as more than 2,000 armored fighting vehicles. The U.S. also had 1,500 helicopters, including the AH-1 Cobra and the AH-64 Apache.

In the meantime, intel estimated Iraq had 540,000 troops stationed in Kuwait and southern Iraq. Most of the men were veterans of the Iran-Iraq War, and nearly a quarter of the troops were members of Saddam Hussein's elite Republican Guard. Iraq's military lineup included more than 5,500 tanks, 6,000 armored personnel carriers, 3,000 artillery pieces, 7,000 antiaircraft guns, and 16,000 radar-guided and heat-seeking missiles. The Iraqi air force consisted of 360 attack fighters and 275 air-superiority fighters. Included in the inventory were a variety of Soviet-built aircraft, many of which were old and of little value. However, Iraq also had an arsenal of MiG-29 Fulcrums and French Mirage F-1s, which were modern and extremely capable.

By 02:50, pilots from all three squadrons were gathered in the beer tent, nervously awaiting the first takeoff. The 69th TFS launched twelve F-16s at approximately 02:30, but the package was destined for King Fahd AB in Saudi Arabia. The unit had only been in theater a week, and since the first two days of the war had been planned months before, there wasn't enough tanker support for them to fly directly to the war zone. Once the Werewolves landed at King Fahd AB, everyone in the package would hot-pit refuel. As soon as the jets were ready, the Werewolves would take off again and attack targets along the western border of Kuwait. After they completed their mission, the pilots would return to Al Minhad.

At precisely 03:03, Damien's F-16 screamed past the west end of the airfield. Everyone stepped outside the trailer to watch as the Viper disappeared into the night. Twenty seconds later, the ground began to shake again as Rip's jet lifted off. The sound was piercing, and as the afterburner cooked, flaming streaks of orange and blue extended from the aircraft's tail. One by one, each F-16 was swallowed by darkness. The last aircraft was airborne within three minutes, and as soon as it disappeared, the base was quiet again.

I walked back to my room and set my alarm for 05:15. I wanted to make sure I was on the flight line to greet my friends when they returned from their mission. When the alarm went off, I jumped out of bed, laced up my boots, and headed back to the o'club. Cuda and Tonto joined me, and the three of us arrived in time to hear a local radio station interrupt its program with a speech by President George Bush. Standing beneath a speaker in the marble entryway, the three of us listened as our president began: "Just two hours ago, Allied air forces began an attack on military targets in Iraq and Kuwait. These attacks continue as I speak. Ground forces are not engaged. . . ."

As I stood in the corridor and listened to the president, chills ran down my spine. I was extremely proud to be an American, and it was hard to hold back the tears, knowing Colette was sitting at home, frightened, listening to the same speech. As the president continued to speak, my thoughts turned to my friends. They should have dropped their bombs by now and, God willing, be on their way home.

Bush continued, "Our operations are designed to best protect the lives of all the coalition forces by targeting Saddam's vast military arsenal. Prior to ordering our forces into battle, I instructed our military commanders to take every necessary step to prevail as quickly as possible, and with the greatest degree of protection possible, for American and allied servicemen and women. I've told the American people before that this will not be another Vietnam, and I repeat this here tonight. Our troops will have the best possible support in the entire world, and they will not be asked to fight with one hand tied behind their back."

He went on, "No president can easily commit our sons and daughters to war. They are the nation's finest. Ours is an all-volunteer force, magnificently trained, highly motivated. The troops know why they're there."

I glanced at the others standing beside me in the corridor. They, too, looked proud, knowing that President Bush was referring to people like us.

When the president finished, Cuda, Tonto, and I took the shuttle bus to the squadron. Some of the pilots were watching CNN in the lounge, and early reports indicated we had caught the Iraqis by surprise. Other pilots began to filter in. By 06:00, half the squadron was out on the flight line, waiting for the flights, christened Rash and Chancer, to land. It was a damp, cool morning, and even though the sun hadn't risen, daybreak had arrived.

While we waited for the F-16s, Cuda and I struck up a conversation with some of the crew chiefs. They took a lot of pride in their work, and we depended on their skill and professionalism every time we climbed into a jet. We talked about President Bush's speech, and we wondered aloud what the people back home were thinking.

All of a sudden, one of the crew chiefs spotted a landing light on final approach and yelled out: "Here they come!"

We rushed to the edge of the taxiway and began counting as other lights appeared. As each aircraft touched down, another came into view. When the eighth light emerged from the morning haze, everyone began to cheer. By now, the ramp was crowded with maintenance personnel and dozens of pilots from all three squadrons.

The first aircraft to taxi onto the ramp was tail number 466. Lt. Jim "Ensign" Palmer was behind the controls, and, as soon as he shut down, everyone rushed over to congratulate him. Before long, the remaining pilots taxied in and shut down their engines. Cuda and I walked over to greet Stitch as he climbed out of his cockpit.

"How'd it go, buddy?" I yelled.

"Awesome!" Stitch replied. "We were in the weather and almost had to abort the mission, but things started to clear up right after we hit the IP."

"Did you see any SAMs or AAA?" Cuda asked.

"I saw two SA-6s," Stitch replied while unzipping his G-suit. "One was tracking on me, but it detonated early. I saw flashes of light through the clouds, and the target area was saturated with AAA. The ZSU-23 looked like a fire hose of red tracers. We were out of their range, though. And since our lights were off, they never really came close to hitting any of us."

When the pilots finished debriefing maintenance on the status of their jets, we escorted them back to the squadron. Everyone was on an emotional high. We were expecting to lose two, maybe three pilots. But every one of them made it back safely.

We entered the squadron at the east end of the building near the sign-out desk. Posted on the squadron bulletin board was a letter from CENTCOM:

DESERT STORM MESSAGE TO OUR TROOPS

Soldiers, sailors, airmen, and marines of the United States Central Command: This morning at 03:00 we launched Operation Desert Storm, an offensive campaign that will enforce United Nations resolutions that Iraq must cease its rape and pillage of its weaker neighbor and withdraw its forces from Kuwait. The President, the Congress, the American people, and indeed the world stand united in their support for your actions. You are members of the most powerful force our country, in coalition with our allies, has ever assembled in a single theater to face such an aggressor. You have trained hard for this battle and you are ready. During my visits with you, I have seen in your eyes a fire of determination to get this job done and done quickly so that we may return to the shores of our great nation. My confidence in you is total. Our cause is just! Now you must be the thunder and lightning of Desert Storm. May God be with you, your loved ones at home, and our country.

H. Norman Schwarzkopf
Commander in Chief, U.S. Central Command

I went back to my room to take a nap, still beaming over the success of our first mission. I woke up around 11:00, wrote in my journal, then took a shower and headed over to the o'club to watch TV. CNN was replaying its coverage of the first attack.

The first voice we heard was that of Bernard Shaw: "This is . . . something is happening outside. Peter Arnett, join me here. Let's describe to your viewers what we're seeing. The skies over Baghdad have been illuminated. We're seeing bright flashes going all over the sky. Peter?"

"Well, there's antiaircraft gunfire going into the sky," Arnett said excitedly. "We hear the sound of planes. They're coming over our hotel. However, we have not yet heard the sound of bombs landing. But there's tremendous lightning in the sky, lightninglike effects. Bernie?"

"I have a sense, Peter," Shaw continued, "that people are shooting toward the sky, and they are not aware or cannot see what they're shooting at. This is extraordinary. The lights are still on. But as you look, you see trails of flashes of light going up into the air, obviously antiaircraft fire. We're getting starbursts, seeming starbursts, in the black sky. We have not heard any jet planes yet, Peter."

The scene cut to the Pentagon where CNN's Wolf Blitzer was standing by.

"David," Blitzer began, "there are strong indications here at the Pentagon that this war may . . . be beginning right now and that the president may be going on television later this evening to explain exactly what is going on."

The next scene was from the Al Rashid Hotel. As the air raids continued, John Holliman reported: "It would appear it's the real thing. There are some tracers going up in the air over this city of four million people. Baghdad is beginning to be blacked out now. I'm going to go back to the window and see what we can see."

He continued, "The sky is lighting up to the south with antiaircraft fire and flashes of yellow light."

Arnett said, "There's another attack coming in . . . it looks like the Fourth of July!"

Everyone in the lounge was on the edge of their seats. I couldn't imagine what it must have been like for those correspondents to sit in that hotel room as war descended upon them. Peter Arnett was trying to be calm, but I could sense the terror in his voice.

"The raids are continuing, wave after wave," Arnett reported. "Now it looks like missiles launched—four or five within seconds of each other—right into the sky."

There was a pause, and then he continued.

"We are crouched at the window, three miles from the center of the action. The antiaircraft! Four bomb flashes. Planes circling for more targets, I guess. The U.S. planes aren't trying to hit the antiaircraft fire. They have specific targets instead, it seems. . . . The skies are lit up. There is a terrible pounding going on. The air force is serious about its mission tonight."

"It's like the center of hell," said Holliman. "Every bomb we've seen land has hit something directly, like the refinery. We can continue to hear the sound of bombs. There's a tower of smoke over the city."

"We are seeing surgical bombing," Shaw said. "No bombs out of pattern. Specific areas, for the past three hours."

After the replay, a CNN reporter assessed the first night of the war. To sum things up, he quoted a statement Gen. Colin Powell made on his last visit to Saudi Arabia: "'When we launch it, we will launch it violently. We will launch it in a way that will make it decisive, so that we can get it over as quickly as possible, and there's no question who won when it's over. We're going to go deep using aerial assets, and challenge them in ways seen and unseen, in ways Saddam Hussein has never dreamed of.'"

23.
DEFINING MOMENT

Someone once said there are two types of people in the world: fighter pilots . . . and everyone else. Maybe. Certainly no one can argue with the fact that fighter pilots are a different breed. Flying sophisticated fighter planes is the most demanding job in the world. It requires a pilot who is aggressive and competitive, someone who can stare down danger without blinking. Other essential attributes include skill and a touch of arrogance. A fighter pilot's life is on the line every time he closes the canopy. If he isn't confident to the point of being cocky, he's doomed. Every squadron has a fighter pilot who's considered the unit's best. What defines the *attitude* of the squadron, however, is when every pilot in the unit claims *he's* that man. And believes it!

Everyone has a defining moment in his or her life. For me, that moment was about to arrive. War is full of unknowns. But on the eve of my first combat sortie, there were two things I was certain of: I flew the greatest fighter plane that man has ever built—the F-16 Fighting Falcon—and I represented the world's greatest country. It would be foolish of me to say I was not scared. I was terrified. But I knew that when the canopy closed and I crossed into Iraqi airspace for the very first time, I'd have but two objectives: Bombs on target. And survival.

18 JANUARY 1991
It seemed as though I'd just closed my eyes, and already, it was time to get up. I glanced at my watch: 02:30. Brief time was in thirty minutes. After a quick shower, I walked into my room and looked into my closet. I felt like a professional athlete who was about to suit up for the game of his life. All I'd ever done was practice. Now I would finally get to play.

Three flight suits hung neatly in front of me—all different in their own way. One fit a little looser than the other two. Another was slightly more worn. I grabbed one off the hanger and put each patch in its proper place. After I tightened the Velcro around my wrists, I reached for my scarf, which was neatly folded on top of my dresser. I wrapped it around my neck, tucked it in front of my shirt, then zipped up the green bag. As soon as I laced up my combat boots, I grabbed my hat and headed for the beer tent.

As 03:00 approached, pilots from all three squadrons began to filter in. This wasn't going to be another training mission with the master arm switch in Simulate. We were going downtown. Destination Iraq. Our target: the Latifya Scud missile production facility. The mission commander for the package of sixty-six aircraft was Lt. Col. Terry "Zappo" Adams, the 4th TFS operations officer.

"The chairs are set up in the order of your formation," Zappo announced. "Find your package and take a seat."

I spotted Grumpy and Wheel in the third row and walked over to join them. Sitting on my chair was an envelope. I opened it up and pulled out a lineup card, a tanker card, two maps, an attack card, and a satellite photo of the Scud facility. Col. Huddle arrived a few minutes later and sat beside me. Our call sign was Canine 71. We were a flight of four, mission number 1371F.

The briefing began at 03:00 sharp, with roll call and a time hack. After everyone synchronized their watches, an officer from the weather shop stepped up to the podium. He put a satellite photo of Iraq on the overhead projector, and, to our dismay, the northern half of the country—including Baghdad—was covered with a solid deck of clouds.

"There's a chance the clouds may burn off by the time you reach the target," the officer said. "But I wouldn't count on it."

I turned to Wheel and whispered: "There hasn't been a cloud in the sky for four months, and on our first combat mission, we're not even going to see the target." Looking disappointed, Wheel just shook his head.

Intel was up next. Pointing to a map that depicted our IP-to-target run and egress route, Major Marsh addressed the crowd.

"As you can see from this map, you'll cross Lake Buhayrat Ar Razzazah on a zero-one-nine-degree heading. As soon as you hit the IP, you'll pick up a new heading of zero-six-five and immediately enter this SA-2 envelope. Numerous SA-2 and SA-6 sites surround the target and the town of Al Iskandariyah, which is only seven miles to the southeast. We've identified a pair of SA-3 sites near Majarrah, but they shouldn't be a factor. Nor should the SA-8 sites north of Al Yusufiyah."

He continued, "If the weather clears, you'll see the Scud production facility as soon as you cross the Euphrates River. To avoid the heaviest concentrations of AAA, SA-2s, and SA-6s, I recommend coming off left after you drop your bombs."

He concluded, "If anyone is shot down, evade west toward the lake and wait for a pickup. The code word for today is Minnie, the number of the day is forty-nine, and the letter of the day is Y. If SAR forces need to identify you quickly, mention any one of these and they'll know you're an American pilot. Good luck!"

"Thank you, Major Marsh," Zappo said as he stepped back up to the podium. "Our objectives for today's mission are as follows: Destroy the target, meet delivery parameters, maintain mutual support, and survive. Step time is 02:20z. We'll start engines at 02:50z and taxi at 03:15z. Takeoff is scheduled for 03:40z."

"Engine start will be on uniform 1 and victor 2. I'll pass the mickey [Have Quick time-of-day (TOD) signal] on uniform 12 at exactly 03:10z."

As Zappo continued, I filled in my lineup card with the step, start, taxi, and takeoff times, the Have Quick frequencies, and our Mode 1, Mode 2, and Mode 3 squawks.

"Secure Voice will be Fill 1. Joker is 7.1 and bingo is 6.6."

Bingo fuel is the least amount of fuel we can have over the target and still make it back to one of our divert bases. Joker fuel is normally 500 pounds above bingo, and one should consider event termination when reaching it. For this mission, our planned fuel over the target was only a few hundred pounds above bingo. Fuel conservation was going to be important.

"Plan on single-ship afterburner takeoffs with twenty seconds of spacing between jets," Zappo continued. "Rejoin two-plus-two at 350 knots. I plan to level off at flight level 230 [23,000 feet]."

Zappo spent the rest of the briefing covering the air-refueling plan, target ingress, egress, and the weather backup plan.

"This is it, men," Zappo said. "We've waited a long time for this. Let's go out there and kick some ass! Bombs on target, and I'll see you back here for a cold one later on."

Before we were dismissed, Lt. Col. Scott addressed us.

"Right before the briefing, we learned that Iraq fired Scud missiles toward Israel and Saudi Arabia. Early reports indicate the Scuds landed in Tel Aviv and Haifa. The missile aimed at Dhahran was destroyed by an American Patriot missile before it hit the ground. We're not sure if the warheads contained chemical agents. If they did, I would expect the Israeli air force to respond quickly with an attack of their own. Make sure you have your chemical gear, and be sure to pick up your auto-injectors before you step. If you go down in an area exposed to chemical weapons, you're going to need them."

The war wasn't even two days old, and our worst fears had already materialized. Saddam Hussein had kept his vow to attack Israel, and it appeared as though he'd do anything to break up the coalition. I just hoped Saddam was smart enough to avoid the use of chemical weapons. If he launched a chemical attack on Israel, I would expect the Israelis to respond violently—perhaps with nuclear weapons.

No one likes to carry chemical gear in the cockpit. But the chances of diverting into Saudia Arabia were good, and exposure to mustard gas or nerve gas would mean almost certain death. Mustard agents HD and HT have a blistering effect on all parts of the body they come into contact with, both internally and externally. HT is a 60-percent mixture of HD mustard and 40-percent mixture of T. T is a compound similar to HD and is used to lower the freezing point. It's also used to increase the persistency/blistering effect of the mixture. Symptoms of mustard gas poisoning—redness of the eyes and redness of the skin—usually begin four to six hours after exposure. This is followed by blistering and inflammation of the skin, nose, throat, trachea, bronchi, and lung tissue. Systemic effects are malaise, vomiting, and fever. With amounts approaching the lethal dose, injury to bone marrow, lymph nodes, and spleen may result. Permanent blindness is also a possibility. HD and HT are considered carcinogenics, and long-term health effects may include chronic lung disease or cancer.

The nerve agents GB (sarin) and VX are even more lethal. These colorless, odorless nerve gases were invented in Nazi Germany. Both agents are quick-acting and affect one's system by inhibiting or deactivating cholinesterase, an enzyme found throughout the body. When cholinesterase is inhibited, hyperactivity of the glands and muscles results. Glands over-secrete, causing buildup of fluid in the lungs, and muscles uncontrollably fasciculate and convulse. This hyperactivity will continue until the muscles fatigue and go into a state of total relaxation. The agent VX was designed to present a liquid hazard (skin absorption). GB was designed mainly to present a vapor (respiratory) hazard; however, it can be absorbed through the skin or ingested in liquid form with lethal effect. Symptoms of exposure consist of pinpointed pupils, runny nose, difficulty in breathing, nausea, vomiting, urination, defecation, localized involuntary muscular movement, convulsions, and cessation of breathing.

To combat the effects of nerve-gas poisoning, each pilot carries three types of auto-injectors in his survival vest: atropine, 2-PAM (pralidoxime) chloride, and Valium. An injection of atropine improves respiration by decreasing bronchial secretions, and an injection of 2-PAM chloride reverses the binding of nerve agents with cholinesterase. If an exposed pilot is experiencing convulsions, an injection of Valium should be given. To administer any of the three antidotes, a pilot should simply stab himself in the thigh with the appropriate auto-injector.

Pyridostigmine Bromide (P-Bromide) is another antidote. It comes in the form of a pill. P-Bromide tablets are used to bind up reversibly a certain amount of cholinesterase so it can be available in the event of a nerve-agent attack. To ensure that enough cholinesterase enzymes are available, the pills must be taken a minimum of one day before exposure. A few days earlier, each pilot had been given a supply of P-Bromide pills. The flight surgeons warned us that the pills were considered experimental and could cause side effects. They recommended we take one a day, but each of us were allowed to decide for ourselves whether or not we wanted to take them. The word "experimental" didn't sit well with any of the pilots, so everyone decided to throw them away. The effects of Agent Orange on the soldiers who served in Vietnam made the decision an easy one. No one wanted to be a guinea pig.

As soon as Scotty finished, Zappo cleared us off to brief within our own formation. Grumpy told us there would be three crew vans outside to take everyone to the squadron, and he instructed Canine flight to meet in the briefing trailer across from the 421st life-support shop.

It was still dark outside, and I was a nervous wreck. I always have a few butterflies before a flight, but it had never been that bad. When I arrived at the squadron, I checked my watch and realized we had only twenty minutes to step time. Afraid I wouldn't have enough time to put on my flying gear, I rushed to the life-support shop and began to put on my G-suit. A few minutes later, Grumpy walked in and asked why I was getting dressed so early.

"We step in twenty minutes, and I need time to get ready."

"You need to relax, Rosey. Take your G-suit off and go over to the briefing trailer. We don't step for another *hour* and twenty minutes."

Feeling foolish, I walked over to the briefing trailer and joined the other members of the flight. Grumpy followed me in and spent the next forty-five minutes going over the specifics of the mission. He discussed tanker ops, formation discipline, the attack, and mutual support.

"This flight should be treated no differently than any other," Grumpy stressed. "'Fight like you train, and train like you fight.' It's the motto of every tactical fighter unit."

02:00:00z

I arrive at the life-support trailer and begin to prepare for the flight. I remove each patch and put them in a bag along with my scarf. The only thing I'll carry during the flight is a combat wallet, which includes my military ID, shot records, dog tags, and a twenty-dollar bill. After I zip up my G-suit, I put on my survival vest. It is equipped with a radio, compass, signaling devices, maps, and a first-aid kit. The mood in the room is somber. While others prepare, I walk over and check out my handgun, a 38-caliber revolver. I carefully load the weapon and place the extra rounds in my survival-vest pocket.

While I test my oxygen mask and comm system, MSgt. Rick Davidson, who runs the 421st life-support shop, walks over and hands me my auto-injectors and a blood chit. Blood chits can come in handy if a pilot is shot down and captured by ordinary citizens. The chit itself has a picture of the American flag and an inscription that reads:

> I am an American and do not speak your language. I will not harm you! I bear no malice toward your people. My friend, please provide me food, water, shelter, clothing and necessary medical attention. Also, please provide safe passage to the nearest friendly forces of any country supporting the Americans and their allies. You will be rewarded for assisting me when you present the number and my name to the American authorities.

The message is written in five different languages: English, Arabic, Turkish, Persian (Farsi), and Kurdish. The blood chit also has numbers on each corner that can be torn off and turned in for a monetary reward.

I stuff the injectors and the blood chit into my survival vest and place my helmet in my helmet bag. I grab my parachute harness and follow Col. Huddle, Grumpy, and Wheel back to the squadron. Sgt. Elizabeth Atisme and A1C Joe Grosfield are working the sign-out desk, and as soon as we sign out on the Form 10, they hand each of us our tapes and DTC cartridges. After I copy down everyone's tail numbers, I walk into the lounge and wait for the crew van.

02:25:00z

Few words are spoken on the way to the flight line. Everyone seems to be more comfortable keeping to themselves. When the crew van stops in front of tail number 357, I step out the back. My crew chief, a young airman, is there to greet me with a salute and a firm handshake. While I examine the aircraft forms, the crew chief takes my tape and places it in the jet.

"What's your Mode Two, sir?" he asks.

"One-three-seven-three," I reply.

While I climb up the ladder with my flight gear, the crew chief opens a small compartment in the nose section and programs the squawk. Sitting on top of the ladder, I check the switches in the cockpit, place my helmet on the canopy rail, and insert my DTC into its receptacle. When I finish, I step down and perform the aircraft preflight.

A 2,000 pound MK-84 is mounted under each wing and, with a piece of chalk, I write "Sweet Colette" on one and "Candice" and "Kristen" on the other. My three girls will be with me in spirit when I fly today.

Ten minutes before engine start, I climb into the cockpit. My crew chief follows me up the ladder and helps me strap in. Once I'm ready, we shake hands, and he wishes me luck. As soon as I put my helmet on and connect my oxygen hose, I sit back and wait. My mind is racing with emotion as I stare across the ramp. I've said everything I need to say to Colette, Candice, and Kristen. I've mailed the letters I needed to write to all my friends and family. If my time has come, I'm ready. I don't want to die. But, strangely, I'm not afraid of death.

02:49:30z

I switch my battery on and motor down the canopy.

"How do you read me, chief?" I ask.

"Got you loud and clear, sir. Chocks are in, fireguard's posted. You're cleared to start."

"Here comes start one."

I start on time with the rest of the Vipers on the ramp. Once the engine is up to speed, I complete my PRI/SEC and EPU checks. I turn on my systems and download my DTC information into the aircraft's computers. As soon as I finish punching in my INS coordinates, I load the Have Quick frequencies into my radio. While the INS aligns, I test my flight-control, brake, and air-refueling systems. Afterward, I clear my crew chief off the headset. While he stands at parade rest in front of the aircraft, I check each of the twenty-one steerpoints to ensure they're correct. The only point I have to input is my target. Reaching toward the up-front control, I call up steerpoint ten and enter the coordinates: N3300.483 E04413.083 with an elevation of 114 feet.

When I finish, I call up my air-to-ground bombing mode and check the bombing profiles. Profile one calls for a CCRP delivery. If I decide to switch to CCIP, all I have to do is hit the missile step button on the stick. The MK-84 fuse setting is Nose and the arming delay is 6.82 seconds. I'll be dropping singles versus pairs, so two release pulses are programmed. A check of the intervalometer setting shows .280 milliseconds, which will space the bombs seventy-five feet apart at impact. Profile two has the same numbers as profile one. But instead of CCRP, the profile two mode is set up to drop manually. In the event of a system malfunction, all I have to do is call up profile two, hit the pickle button, and the bombs will come off.

03:09:00z

My INS is fully aligned and the GPS status page shows high system accuracy. After one more check of the cockpit, I switch to uniform 12 and stand by to receive the TOD, which will synchronize my Have Quick radio frequencies. Without it, communicating with others on the jam-resistant radio will be impossible.

At exactly 03:10:00z, I hear the tone. My Have Quick radio is set. My checks are complete with five minutes to spare.

03:15:00z

Zappo begins the check-in and everyone answers in order. As soon as he's finished, we begin to taxi. When Grumpy and Wheel pass by, I twirl my finger in the air—a signal that I'm ready to go. My crew chief motions me forward, and, as I taxi by, he comes to attention and gives me a firm salute. I fire one back and follow it with the Juvat snake signal. My adrenaline's pumping.

On my way to the arming area, I complete a range-and-bearing check on each steerpoint. The most important points are steerpoints nine and ten: the IP and target. When I call up steerpoint nine, the bearing pointer swings to 309 degrees and the DME reads 766. Steerpoint ten bears 311 degrees for 755 nautical miles. The rest of the numbers match as well.

Passing the control tower, I turn on my VTR so I can title my tape. I wait a few seconds for the film start and then I begin:

"Captain Keith Rosenkranz . . . Mission number 1371 foxtrot . . . Two MK-84s . . . Takeoff time is 03:40z . . . Date is 18 January '91 . . . Tail number is 357."

As soon as I finish, I turn the camera off and continue toward the arming area. When I arrive, I set my brakes and wait for the arming crews to inspect my jet. While they work their way toward me, I adjust my kneeboard and make sure everything in the cockpit is stored properly. When the crew arrives, I release my parking brake and hold my hands in the air—a signal that the crew is clear to crawl under the jet. A few seconds pass, and then the lead crew chief signals me to roll forward so they can check my tires. Once they finish, he salutes and gives me a thumbs-up.

Five minutes prior to takeoff, I turn on my radar and my ECM pod. While they warm up, I check my fuel to verify the tanks are feeding properly. Zappo and the other members of Dane flight are already in position 1,000 feet down the runway. The next four-ship is set at the departure end.

03:40:00z

Zappo releases brakes at precisely 07:40 (03:40:00z). His wingman follows twenty seconds later, and the mission is under way. Grumpy makes his way toward the runway and Wheel follows closely behind. Prior to taking the runway, I arm my ejection seat, turn the pitot heat on, check that the master arm switch is in Simulate, and cool my missiles. Grumpy finally begins his takeoff roll, and a few seconds later, Wheel runs up his engine. As soon as he releases his brakes, I check my clock and start timing. With ten seconds to go, I run up my engine and check the instruments. Everything's looking good.

I release my brakes and smoothly select afterburner. The aircraft accelerates rapidly. I'm airborne in a matter of seconds, and as I climb away from the ground, I raise my gear. Relieved to be airborne, I call up my air-to-air radar and lock up Wheel. As my airspeed continues to increase, I complete my weapon-systems check. Crossing the eastern shores of the Persian Gulf, I pick up a visual on Grumpy and rejoin to his right wing. Once Col. Huddle is in position, the formation is complete.

We level off at 23,000 feet and proceed across the Gulf toward Saudi Arabia. Not a single word is spoken on the radios. It would be easy for the Iranians to eavesdrop and notify the Iraqis that a major package is airborne. The Iranian government vowed to remain neutral, but who knows what type of secret pact they may have made with Saddam Hussein.

As we continue east, I look around at the wave of F-16s. The air is calm, and morning fog rises from the Gulf below me. The scene is almost surreal. It reminds me of old World War II footage of American bombers on their way to Germany. A latter-day Hitler awaits us as well.

We reach the Lime air-refueling control point (ARCP) at approximately 05:21:00z— fifteen minutes ahead of schedule. Zappo planned the extra time in case anyone experienced problems on the ground. As we enter the track, I check my radar and spot four returns twenty degrees left for thirty miles. Using the radar cursors, I lock up the lead tanker to get an altitude readout. Before long, I spot the formation of KC-135s at my left ten o'clock. Each one is stacked 1,000 feet above the other.

It's Grumpy's responsibility to get us to the tanker, so I concentrate on maintaining good position. We begin a fighter turn on the second KC-135 and drop down to flight level 220. About a mile from the tanker, the KC-135 pilot begins a turn back to the west. Halfway through the turn, I look up in time to see a wave of F-16s pass directly over us. Startled by their proximity, I check my altitude. I don't want to break radio silence, but the last thing any of us needs is a midair collision—especially with live MK-84s on board.

As soon as Grumpy completes the rejoin, I proceed to the tanker's right wing. I open my air-refueling door and switch my radar to standby. After Grumpy's tanks are topped off, I drop down into position. I'm so nervous, I can barely stay on the boom. I keep reminding myself to wiggle my toes and stir the stick—techniques I used to teach my T-38 students when they were jittery.

My refueling complete, I climb back up and stabilize on Col. Huddle's right wing. Wheel drops down next and, after him, Col. Huddle. We remain with the tanker for twenty more minutes. Before we push, everyone tops off their tanks one more time. It's a long time to spend in formation, but other aircraft will be joining the package en route to the target, so timing is critical.

As the KC-135 turns to the south, Grumpy begins to drop back. Once our four-ship is clear of the tanker, he banks toward the north and clears me out to tactical. I float my aircraft to the right and stack high. Col. Huddle assumes a fighting wing position. As soon as we're stabilized, I check my fuel and call up steerpoint number six. Our new heading is 001 degrees, and a check of my DME shows the Iraqi border is less than two hundred miles away.

06:36:11z

Crossing steerpoint six, I accomplish my fence check. My heart is pounding and my muscles are tense. We've just entered Iraqi airspace.

"Canine 71, go strike primary," Grumpy calls out.

"Two!" "Three!" "Four!"

I reach toward my up-front control and program in 278.2—the AWACS strike frequency. Five E-3 AWACS aircraft are airborne, and each one is responsible for certain sectors of the KTO. Controllers on each aircraft provide clearance into the combat zone, warn pilots of Iraqi air threats, coordinate search-and-rescue efforts, and control air traffic.

"Choctaw, this is Dane 01," Zappo calls out.

"Dane 01, Choctaw has you loud and clear," the controller responds.

"Dane 01, authenticate alpha-mike!"

"Choctaw authenticates whiskey-delta."

Zappo checks in the package with our mission number, and the AWACS controller acknowledges: "All players are on board. Picture is clear!"

The other players include F-15 Eagles for air-to-air escort; F-4G Wild Weasels for suppression of enemy air defenses (SEAD); EF-111 Ravens for radar jamming; and F-111 Aardvarks for air-to-ground bombing. The F-15s are on the point, and they'll shoot down any Iraqi aircraft they come in contact with. The F-4Gs are next in line, each equipped with AGM-88 high-speed antiradiation missiles (HARMs), designed to destroy SAM radar guidance systems. A pair of EF-111s are flying in trail of the F-4Gs, followed by the F-16s and F-111s.

Each F-16 element is flying a fluid-four formation with one-minute spacing between elements. Numbers one and three fly a tactical spread 6,000 to 9,000 feet apart, while two and four maintain a "wedge" or fighting wing position. This puts them on the outside of one and three, fifteen degrees back, and 1,500 to 2,000 feet out. Fluid-four is a good offensive formation, especially at high altitude, because it provides a strong defense against enemy air threats and gives each F-16 pilot the freedom he needs to maneuver.

As the package continues north, the weather worsens. Solid clouds cover the southern deserts of Iraq, and the tops have forced us to climb above 30,000 feet. Maneuvering at this altitude is extremely difficult with MK-84s, but we have to stay at least 5,000 feet above the cloud layer to react against enemy SAMs. Another concern is the MiG-29 Fulcrum. According to intel, Iraq has thirty of these aircraft, and their best pilots are flying them.

06:52:20z

Passing over steerpoint seven, we pick up a new heading of 357 degrees. The Scud production facility is 146 miles away. My heart feels like its going to explode and my flight suit is drenched with sweat. I never knew the true meaning of fear until now. The sooner we drop these bombs, the better.

At 06:55:00z, I reach down and turn on my camera. I'm level at 32,000 feet, fourteen minutes from the target. The radios are full of static—probably Iraqi jamming. While maintaining a tactical position high and to the right of Canine 71, I continue to clear for SAMs and Iraqi fighters. My RWR scope is clean, but I expect it to come alive soon. The F-16 ALR-69 threat warning system reads radar signals and determines their frequency, power, and location. The information is fed into a computer and the data is compared to a threat table. If the system is recognized, the appropriate symbol is displayed on the pilot's RWR scope, which sits on the left side of the forward panel. Specific tones are also emitted in the pilot's headset when his aircraft is targeted or fired upon.

"Canine 71 . . . eight staff right two o'clock!" Grumpy calls out.

I check my RWR, then look toward two o'clock to see if I can pick up a visual. There's no way an SA-8 can reach us at this altitude, but Grumpy's RWR indication means the Iraqis have spotted us with their radars.

At 07:00:00z, I call up the IFF (Identify Friend or Foe) page on my up-front control and check the status of my Mode 1 squawk. We took off squawking transponder code 51, and it's supposed to change automatically to 43 at the top of the hour. Mode 1 is significant, because the F-15s will interrogate our IFFs during egress. If we aren't squawking, we could be shot down by our own forces.

To ensure other members of the flight are squawking, I click my mike and call out: "Canines . . . Timex!"

We cross over steerpoint eight at 07:00:47z and turn right to a heading of 013 degrees. The IP is 35 miles on our nose, and, to make sure I don't forget, I switch my master arm switch to Arm. Afterward, I check the GPS status page one last time. System accuracy reads "high." Since my INS is being updated by satellites every two seconds, my diamond should be right on top of the target.

Three minutes away from the IP, the radios erupt.

"Canine 73," Grumpy calls out. "You have flares at your seven o'clock!"

I turn to the left and spot them right away.

"Canine 73 . . . tally!" I reply.

The F-15s are capping over the IP, and if someone popped a flare, they've either engaged an Iraqi fighter or they're trying to avoid a heat-seeking missile. Choctaw never called out a bandit, so I'm puzzled by the situation. The radios are still full of static, and I haven't heard the Eagles or Wild Weasels call out any contacts either. To ensure we have complete radar coverage, Grumpy calls out: "Canine 71 flight. Wingmen, look cons down. Flight leads, look ground up!"

I tilt my radar down and sweep the skies at low altitude. The contrail level is 33,000 feet, so Wheel and Col. Huddle are responsible for the high-altitude sector.

As we approach the IP, Grumpy calls out SA-8 raw at his left ten o'clock. He tells the formation to begin a "level S," which is nothing more than a weaving maneuver forty-five degrees left or right of our heading. The combination of a level S, chaff, electronic noise from our ECM pods, and jamming from the EF-111s will confuse Iraqi SAMs fired toward the flight.

07:05:09z

It hits the fan just as soon as we cross the IP.

"Canine 71 has multiple missile launches!" Grumpy screams.

He pauses for a moment, then yells again: "Canines . . . SAMs at right three!"

I look to the right and spot two missiles coming up out of the clouds a mile to the east.

"Canine 73 is tally!" I reply.

A few seconds later, I spot another one.

"Canine 74 . . . SAM right three . . . high!" I scream.

I keep a close eye on the SAMs and check my HUD. We're twelve miles from the target. My chest is heaving as I attempt to catch my breath. The SAMs continue to rocket upward, trailing contrails of white smoke. Soon, though, they run out of momentum and begin to fall back toward earth. Still terrified, I call up my air-to-ground mode and prepare to drop my bombs.

A few seconds later, Grumpy calls out: "Canines . . . sky puke!"

The cloud layer has completely obscured the Scud production facility. Descending through the clouds to drop our bombs would be suicide, so Grumpy wants us to drop them from high altitude.

The CCRP steering line bisects my HUD, and the TD box is directly over the target. As the DME counts down, I correct left to put the flight-path marker over the steering line. At 7.8 DME from the target, the max-toss cue appears in the HUD. I clear outside for SAMs and, at 6.7 DME, I hit the pickle button, then wait for the bombs to release.

"Canine 71 is bombs away," Grumpy calls out.

My DME continues to count down, but I never get a solution cue. I check the DME, and it reads 2.3. Son of a bitch! Why aren't my bombs coming off?

"Canine 73 . . . hook left!" Grumpy yells.

"Canine 73 . . . my bombs aren't coming off!" I reply.

"Canine 73 . . . come left now!" Grumpy repeats.

Already past the target, I make a hard left turn and attempt to go over it again during the egress. I'm not sure what's wrong with the system, so I call up profile two and prepare to drop manually. I roll out of my turn approximately two miles north of the target. As soon as I hit the pickle button, the bombs come off.

"Canine 73 is bombs away," I radio.

At this point, I'm six miles in trail of my lead element. I check my right five o'clock, and Col. Huddle is right where he's supposed to be. I push the power up and catch up with Canine 71 over the egress point. For some reason, Wheel still has his bombs, and Grumpy leads the formation to the dump target so he can make another attempt to drop them. After he pickles, we proceed south toward the border. I feel relieved to be out of the target area, but I'm upset with myself for not getting my bombs off properly. I'll have plenty of time to figure it out during the debrief.

Reaching the Saudi border, we check out of Iraqi airspace with AWACS. We don't have enough fuel to make it back to Al Minhad, so Grumpy leads us to the Lime air-refueling track to post-strike refuel. When we arrive, three KC-135s are orbiting at 21,000 feet. After the rejoin, each of us takes on 5,000 pounds, enough to get us back to the base.

Six hours after taking off from Al Minhad, I roll out on final and spot the runway. After landing, I taxi clear of the runway and head for the de-arm area. The crew chiefs inspect my jet, and, when they finish, I taxi back to the ramp. Physically and mentally exhausted, I can't wait to crawl out of this thing. My crew chief motions me into my parking spot. As soon as he pins my EPU, he clears me to shut down.

My first combat mission is behind me, and even though I didn't hit my target, I am happy to be alive.

During the debrief, Grumpy reviewed our film and pointed out my mistake.

"We had a 125-knot tailwind over the target," Grumpy said. "If you didn't have your thumb on the pickle button early, you weren't going to get your bombs off."

I spotted the error right away. Immediately after the max-toss cue appeared, the solution cue passed through the flight-path marker. I wasn't on the pickle button yet, so my bombs never came off. Wheel and a number of other pilots in the package made the same mistake. All of us were extremely disappointed. We'd been training for months, and to screw up like we did on the very first mission was . . . unacceptable.

The sortie should have been a milk run. We didn't encounter a single Iraqi fighter, and the SAM threat at high altitude was insignificant. Unfortunately, the bad weather and our ineptness over the target meant the facility would have to be attacked again. We all wanted a chance to redeem ourselves.

After the debrief, everyone went to the o'club to relax and watch CNN. Some of the other pilots were in the lounge, anxious to hear about the mission. I described the poor weather, the mistakes some of us made, and how disappointed we were to not see the target. No one seemed to mind, though. They were just happy that we made it back safely.

I spent the rest of the afternoon in the lounge watching television. According to CNN, the American-led coalition had already gained air superiority in the skies above Iraq, and allied bombers had destroyed key Iraqi command and control centers. Nearly 1,500 sorties were flown the first day, and reports indicated ninety out of a hundred Tomahawk missiles had hit their targets.

CNN also confirmed that three Israeli cities had been hit earlier in the morning by Scud missiles fired from western Iraq. Dozens of people suffered minor injuries and four elderly people died while wearing their gas masks. A rumor went around that, after the attack, the Israelis launched a strike mission that was recalled when officials discovered the Scuds had conventional warheads instead of chemical.

A U.S. Marine pilot was reportedly shot down in his F-18 Hornet and was listed as missing in action. Two crewmen flying a British Tornado were also missing. Baghdad claimed its forces shot down fifty-five allied aircraft and twenty-three cruise missiles during the first day of fighting—a lie.

After dinner, CNN televised a briefing by Secretary of Defense Dick Cheney.

"To date, the operation is going very well," the secretary began. "I want, though, at the onset of my remarks this morning to emphasize the importance of being cautious in our comments. I don't mean to be critical of our friends in the press corps, but I think it's very, very important for people to remember a number of key things: that this is a very serious business, that we are in the very early stages of an operation that may run for a considerable period of time, that there have been casualties and there are likely to be more casualties. So while we feel very good about the progress to date, it is important, I think, for everyone to be careful about claiming victory or making assumptions about the ultimate cost of this operation in terms of casualties. So far so good, but I would urge all of you to be cautious in your reporting, just as we're trying very hard to be very cautious and very precise in terms of what we say about the status of the operation to date."

Cheney continued, "We've now flown over one thousand air sorties in the first fourteen hours of the operation. There have been over one hundred TLAMs—Tomahawk cruise missiles—launched as well. So far, as of 09:00 this morning, Washington time, there has been a single American aircraft lost and one British aircraft lost as well. . . ."

I walked back to my trailer to go to sleep. Grover walked back with me, asking if I'd seen the next day's schedule.

"I haven't seen it yet. What are we doing?"

"You're scheduled to fly on my wing. We're going to Baghdad."

24.
MISSION FROM HELL

ey, Rosey, time to wake up. Hey, Rosey." Standing in the doorway was Lt. Col. Rackley.

"What time is it, sir?"

"It's nine-thirty," Taz replied. "Which bed is Fist in?"

"He's in the far bed in the next room."

"You're flying this morning," Taz whispered. "Briefing starts in forty minutes in the beer tent."

"Okay, sir. I'll be there."

19 JANUARY 1991

"Here's the lineup for today's mission," Damien began. "I'll be the mission commander, and our target is the Iraqi nuclear research facility in Tawaitha, just south of downtown Baghdad. Everything you need—maps, satellite photos, lineup cards, tanker cards, and attack cards—is in your envelopes. The package will consist of seventy-eight aircraft. Pennzoil, a flight of four F-15s, will be on the point. They'll be followed by eight F-4Gs—call sign Schlitz and Löwenbräu. Wedge, a flight of two EF-111s, is next in line, followed by my flight, Basset 01 through 08."

Pilots from all three squadrons filled the makeshift beer tent, which reeked of stale cigar smoke and spilled beer. For many, that afternoon's mission would be their first in combat. Every commander in the wing, including Col. Navarro, was in attendance. By the looks on their faces, the sortie was going to be a tough one.

"Collar 11 through 18 will follow Basset," Damien continued. "Next will be Rover 21, a flight of four. They'll be followed by twelve pilots from the 69th—Dane 31, a flight of eight, and Ruff 41, a flight of four. Howler 51 and Pointer 61—a pair of eight-ships from the 4th—will complete the package from the 388th. Sixteen more Vipers assigned to the 401st TFW from Torrejon AB, Spain, will depart Doha, Qatar, and merge with us when we push across the Saudi border. Their call signs will be Clap 71 and Stroke 01."

The element I'd be flying in was about a third of the way into the package. Cliffy's call sign was Collar 11, and his flight included Raj, Harpo, and Martyr. Grover, sitting to the right of me, was scheduled to lead Collar 15 flight. I'd fly on his wing as Collar 16. Rounding out the rest of the formation were Capt. Jay "Mans" Moheit and Lt. Steve "Wheel" Ferris. While we copied down the lineup, Mans leaned over: "Thank God we're not at the end of this thing."

Damien spent the next hour covering every aspect of the mission. The weather over the target area was supposed to clear by the time we arrived, so everyone would get a good look at the facility as they rolled in. Unfortunately, clear weather also meant the Iraqi gunners would have a good view of us. Being shot at wasn't going to be fun.

As soon as Damien finished, Col. Navarro stood up to address the group. The Warden hadn't spoken to a room full of pilots in months, and everyone was surprised. Other than in the mess hall, I hadn't even seen him since Gen. Glosson was on base.

"Let me have your attention, if I could. Today's mission may very well be the most important mission of the war. For those of you who don't remember, on 7 June 1981, eight Israeli F-16s bombed the Osirak nuclear reactor in Tawaitha. The nuclear facility has since been rebuilt, and in a few hours you'll attempt to destroy it a second time."

Everyone listened intently. No one knew how close the Iraqis were to building a nuclear weapon, but if this mission was successful, Saddam Hussein's ability to build one would suffer another major setback.

"The 388th TFW is going to be in the spotlight today," Navarro continued. "President Bush and other coalition leaders will be watching closely to see how we do. You've trained all your lives for a mission like this, and a lot of people are depending on you. Make them proud. Make your country proud. Fly safe, put your bombs on target, and I'll see you at the bar after you land."

Since the nuclear research facility was so important to Saddam Hussein, we figured it would be Iraq's most heavily defended target. We expected to see a barrage of SA-2s, SA-3s, SA-6s, and SA-8s as we had encountered the day before. The AAA, ranging in size from 12.7 millimeters to 100 millimeters, should be thick as well. I also expected a confrontation with the Iraqi air force. Seventy-eight American fighters mixing it up with Iraqi MiGs would result in one hell of a fur ball.

10:00:00z

"Basset 01, check," Damien calls out.

"Basset 02, loud and clear." "Basset 03, loud and clear." "Basset 04, loud and clear." "Basset 05, loud and clear." "Basset 06, loud and clear." "Basset 07, loud and clear." "Basset 08, loud and clear." "Collar 11, loud and clear." "Collar 12, loud and clear." "Collar 13, loud and clear." "Collar 14, loud and clear."

All of a sudden, a pause.

Grover isn't answering. I hesitate a moment, then chime in: "Collar 16, loud and clear." The rest of the pilots continue the check-in. I look around to see where Grover is. I spot him across the ramp in the back of the line chief's pickup truck. He's on his way to a spare jet.

Son of a bitch! This is the mission of a lifetime, and my flight lead has a broken jet. There's no way he'll be ready to take off on time. If he can't go, there's a good chance I'll have to ground-abort with him. We need a four-ship flight lead to replace Grover, and we need him now. Mans and I are only two-ship flight leads, and Wheel is just a wing-

179

man. I'm disappointed, but I'm going to continue on until someone tells me otherwise. If the 388th TFW is going to make history, I want to be a part of it.

After the check-in, forty-seven Vipers begin to taxi. Only twenty minutes to takeoff, and Grover still doesn't have a jet. As I roll past the 69th ramp, Dane and Ruff flights complete their final preparations. All of a sudden, Lt. Col. Rackley calls out: "Collar 13, this is Taz."

"Collar 13, go ahead," Harpo replies.

"Are you ready to be a four-ship flight lead?" Taz asks.

"Yes, sir!" Harpo replies with gusto.

"Okay. Your new call sign is Collar 15, and Collar 11 will go as a three-ship."

"Collar 11 copies," replies Cliffy.

"Collar 15 copies," replies Harpo.

Harpo is only a two-ship flight lead, but he has plenty of experience in the F-16, and handling a four-ship shouldn't be difficult for him. I'm relieved. As soon as we reach the arming area, Harpo and I look at each other and throw our fists in the air.

Only five minutes to go before takeoff and I can feel the excitement on the flight line. Maintenance personnel standing along the taxiway cheer as the F-16s roll by. Dozens more wave from the balcony atop the 4th squadron.

As soon as I pull into the arming area, the crew chiefs rush over to arm my weapons. Once their inspection is complete, I turn on my VTR and title my tape.

"Captain Keith Rosenkranz . . . Collar 16 . . . 2211 foxtrot . . . Two MK-84s . . . TOT is 13:33 zulu . . . Takeoff time is 10:50 zulu . . . Date is 19 January '91 . . . Tail number is 452."

10:50:00z

Damien releases his brakes. Basset 02 and other members of the formation follow every twenty seconds. As each pilot begins his takeoff roll, another Viper taxies into position. Approaching the runway, I pass by Taz and give him the Juvat snake signal. Taz, a former Juvat himself, returns the signal and motions me on my way. I taxi into position alongside Harpo, set my brakes, and wait for my turn to take off. When Basset 08 releases his brakes, Harpo taxies forward to the 1,000-foot marker. By the time he arrives, Collar 11 begins his takeoff roll. I watch as the nozzle from Cliffy's engine expands. A burst of orange flame. The thrust rocks my wings. As he propels down the runway, I pull forward into position. One minute to go.

Before I run my engine up, I glance at the giant MK-84s sitting beneath my wing. The bomb on my right says "Candice and Kristen" on one side and "To Saddam from Phil and Charlee" on the other. The bomb on the left says "Sweet Colette" and "To Saddam from Dion." I know Skull would give anything to be a part of this. Unfortunately, most of the weapons-school instructors are back at Nellis AFB instead of where they should be—with us on this mission. If I can't fly on Skull's wing, the least I can do is let him fly on mine.

10:53:50z

With my feet firmly on the brake pedals, I push my throttle up to 80 percent RPM and check my engine instruments. After a quick salute to Mans, I'm on my way. Once airborne, I raise my gear and begin to search for Harpo. I spot him on radar passing through one thousand feet, and, within minutes, I complete the rejoin. Crossing the shoreline, I select steerpoint two—a tip of land at the southeastern edge of Qatar. Now that the mission is underway, I feel a lot more comfortable and confident. But anxiety still persists, and I know it will worsen as the mission progresses.

The "Railroad" ARCP is four hundred miles on our nose, and our ETA is 11:48:00z. As soon as we reach the track, we'll have roughly thirty-five minutes to refuel. Push time is 12:22:17z and we expect to cross into Iraqi territory at 12:49:12z. Our TOT is set for 13:33:00z, a little less than three hours from now. The plan isn't much different than what we did yesterday. Damien will check the entire package in with AWACS, and, to maintain the element of surprise, all air refueling will be accomplished using comm-out procedures.

12:49:12z

Passing steerpoint five, Harpo calls for a fence check, and the flight transitions to fluid-four. The afternoon sun is positioned above my right shoulder, and the clouds of yesterday have scattered. Below me, the brownish red tint of Iraq's desert landscape is plainly visible. Every muscle in my body is tense, but my mind is focused. The volume of my RWR is turned up, my air-to-air radar is scanning from 33,000 feet down, and my head is on a swivel, clearing for SAMs and bogeys. AWACS is calling "picture clear," but I have a feeling the Iraqis are nearby.

Passing steerpoint six, we veer left to a 335-degree heading. Our IP, an Iraqi airfield called Shayka Mazhar, is 253 miles on our nose. Tawaitha is only eighteen miles north of the airfield and sits on the eastern banks of the Tigris River. If everything goes as planned, we'll pick up a 337-degree heading after the IP and parallel the river. The sun should help disguise our roll-in and prevent Iraqi gunners from picking us up visually. In addition, transmissions from our ECM pods combined with radar-jamming from the EF-111s should flood Iraqi radar sites with dozens of false targets.

I know what it's like to be scared in the air. I can't begin to imagine how terrified the Iraqi soldiers must be on the ground. In less than thirty minutes, 128 MK-84s will begin to rain from the sky. Each bomb contains 945 pounds of tritonol explosive filler, encased in 1,000 pounds of steel. They're the largest weapons carried by an F-16 and are normally used to destroy buildings, bridges, runways, and concrete-reinforced bunkers. An instant before it explodes, the MK-84's steel casing swells to twice its normal size. The blast creates a fifty-foot-wide crater. It sends jagged pieces of steel half a mile in every direction. Within that half mile, death is instantaneous.

13:27:00z

I switch on my VTR and select HUD. Our element is 26 miles from the IP, at 27,000 feet. My RWR scope is clean. A check of my GPS page shows high system accuracy. My

INS diamond should be directly over the target when I roll in.

The closer I get to the facility, the faster my heart pounds. Again, a flight suit soaked in sweat. I'm waiting for the MiGs. They haven't shown themselves. Then an F-15 pilot calls out a visual on a missile at his left ten o'clock. As soon as he makes his call, another voice calls out: "That's Löwenbräu 3's HARM!" I check my RWR and air-to-air radar to be sure. They're both clean.

13:28:27z

"Basset 01 is in," Damien calls out.

Three seconds later, Basset 02 follows him down the chute. I check my master arm switch to ensure it's armed, and continue to clear for SAMs. The first bombs are about to hit the facility.

Twenty miles south of the IP, an SA-2 symbol appears in the upper-right quadrant of my RWR scope, and a steady buzz fills my headset. Before I can say anything, a series of seven beeps ring out. The SA-2 site has me targeted, and the missile is airborne.

"Collar 16, launch right two o'clock!" I radio frantically.

A death grip on my stick, I begin to weave while punching out bundles of chaff. A few seconds later, a second symbol appears on the scope, followed by another launch indication. I key my mike and call out again: "Collar 16, two launch on the nose!"

"Collar 18 is tally-ho!" Wheel answers.

Trying to stay calm, I continue my weave and search for the missile. Finally, I spot the contrail at my twelve o'clock.

"Collar 16, tally cons on the nose!" I radio.

Approaching the IP, my RWR is going ballistic. SA-2s, SA-3s, SA-6s, SA-8s—they're everywhere!

I roll left, then quickly to the right. Flashes of orange and yellow appear from both sides of the river below. Each flash is followed by another launch indication on my RWR scope. White smoke trails from behind each missile as it rockets skyward. One passes well to my left and another to my right. As if the SAMs aren't enough, antiaircraft shells begin to explode around me, sending popcorn-shaped cloudbursts of black flak in every direction. How long can I take this?

13:29:40z

Harpo is 2,000 feet away at my left eleven o'clock. As he turns in front of me, I pull to the right to maintain position. SAMs continue to appear off our left, but the radios are saturated, and it's hard to get a call out.

"Basset 01, SAM left eleven!" Damien screams.

I follow his call with three more of my own: "Collar 15, check your left ten!" "Collar 16, 17... check your left ten!" "Collar 18, check your left nine... cons left nine!"

A pair of enemy SAMs are tracking our formation, and if we don't do something about it fast, we're going to get spanked. All of a sudden, one of the missiles detonates at my left eight o'clock—too low to have an effect. The other missile is still tracking us, but it appears to be running out of energy. Frozen and unable to suck a breath, I watch as the dormant missile falls back toward the ground.

I check my HUD. The target is only thirteen miles away. I call up my air-to-ground mode and descend to gain airspeed. With one eye on the ground and another on Harpo, I prepare for the roll-in. Missile contrails fill the sky. The flak is thicker than soup. At 8.3 DME, I get a Hawk symbol on the left side of my RWR scope, along with another launch indication.

"Collar 16, Hawk launch left nine!" I yell.

Within seconds, my RWR scope fills up again. The Iraqi gunners know exactly where I'm at, and they have me locked. The launch indications are continuous. It finally reaches a point where I can no longer hear them. My mind is task-saturated. I *hear* radio calls and tones from my RWR, but I don't have the time to discern their meaning. Nor could I—not with all my energy focused on one thing: hitting the target. If I get shot down, then so be it. I am *not* going to miss this time.

I glance at the satellite photo, then outside again, looking for the bend in the Tigris River. The nuclear facility should be to the right of it and slightly south. Harpo is ahead and to my right. As soon as he rolls in, I pause for a moment, then follow. As I roll into ninety degrees of bank, the nose of my jet slices toward the ground. At this point, I'm oblivious to everything around me. Passing through 22,000 feet, I get the max-toss cue in my HUD. I still don't see the target. I increase my bank angle to 135 degrees, and, finally, my diamond appears. To my dismay, the entire facility is obscured by smoke. It has to be from the other bombs. My only option is to pickle on the diamond. I over-shoot slightly to the left, then roll back right. Passing 17,000 feet, I'm thirty-five degrees nose-low at 450 knots. I hit the missile step button and transition from CCRP to CCIP. I level my wings and place the bombfall line directly over the diamond. As the pipper tracks upward, my thumb sits on the pickle button. If I so much as blink, the pipper will pass long.

Not yet . . . just a little bit . . . now!

I hit the pickle button and start to pull off.

13:32:42z

Passing 14,700 feet, my aircraft shudders as the bombs release. I continue my five-G recovery until the nose of my F-16 reaches the horizon. I check right for Harpo, but he's nowhere to be found. With flak exploding in every direction, I plug in the afterburner and pull my nose up to thirty degrees. I'm in the heart of the SAM envelope. If I don't gain some altitude in a hurry, life as I know it will come to an end. I look to my right and see a bright red object streaking toward me. I pull back on the stick as hard as I can and scream into my mike: "Collar 16, SAM launch right nine!" I should have said "right three," but with so many missiles in the air, who cares?

I continue to climb and quickly realize that I've bled off too much energy. Passing 20,500 feet, my airspeed drops below 200 knots. If I'm going to outmaneuver this mis-sile, I have to decrease my drag and regain my energy. My only hope is to jettison my wing tanks. Reaching toward my left console, I hit the emergency jettison button. The aircraft shudders. I look out the left side of my canopy and see the tanks tumbling in slow motion toward earth. When I check back to the right, I see the missile pass at my six o'clock. It must have missed, because I'm still here.

13:33:48z

Passing 21,000 feet on a 130-degree heading, I see a missile explode a few thousand feet in front of me. It looks as though an aircraft may have been hit. To designate the position, I hit the Mark button on my up-front control. This stores the coordinates of my present position. If AWACS calls and needs a reference point, I can call up the coordinates and pass them along.

I accelerate to 300 knots and continue climbing. The radios are saturated, and I'm still getting launch indications on my RWR scope. Most pilots have lost sight of their wingmen, including me. I have no idea where Harpo is or if he's even alive. Passing 26,000 feet, though, I finally hear his voice.

"Collar 16, posit!" Harpo barks out.

"Collar 16 is blind," I reply. "I'm on the three-two-zero for one-four off of egress."

"Copy that," Harpo answers. "I'm three miles on your nose."

As I gain altitude, my fear begins to subside. I call up my air-to-air radar and begin to search for Harpo's jet. I call up steerpoint ten, the Gabriel exit point. According to the ROE, every fighter must pass over this point or risk being shot down by the Eagles.

Approximately 183 miles north of the Saudi border, I pick up a visual on Harpo and begin to rejoin. Seconds later, the radios erupt again: "Stroke 1 took a hit! Stroke 1 took a hit!"

"Stroke 1 took a hit!" I call out to Choctaw.

For a moment, the radios fall silent.

"Okay, I got a fire . . . standby . . . I'm just south of steerpoint number seven . . . I'm still flying . . . and I'm heading south. Okay, I took a pretty good hit, and I've got no engine."

I check my position from steerpoint seven. Stroke 1 is sixty miles behind me.

"I'm good!" Stroke 1 radios. "I'm an F-16 in a left-hand orbit just south of steerpoint ten. I've lost everything up here, guys."

I can't believe I'm hearing this. There's nothing any of us can do to help him. My heart is in my throat.

"I'm good," he calls out. "I'm good."

Thinking he said "I'm gone," I key my mike and radio: "He jumped out!" But a few seconds later, he starts talking again.

"Okay . . . Stroke 1 . . . I've still got an engine . . . it's still working. I'm angels 26! I don't know what steerpoint I'm at."

Angels 26 puts him at 26,000 feet. I'm only 175 miles from the border, so he must be just south of the IP.

"This is Stroke 1. I'm the wounded bird, and I got about three hundred fifty knots going two-eight-zero."

"Clap 7 is visual. I'm at your left eleven low!"

"Roger," Stroke one replies. "Unable to roll left very easily. I'm losing fuel like crazy up here. I've only got twenty-six hundred pounds worth of gas according to my totalizer. I'm going to take it as far as I can. How far are you from the border?"

I continue to close on Harpo, but all I can think about is Stroke 1. The border is too far. There's no way he's going to make it. Picturing myself in the same position reminds me of the movie *The Bridges at Toko-Ri*. William Holden plays a young fighter pilot whose jet is hit during a bombing run over Korea. His beautiful wife, played by Grace Kelly, and two young daughters are waiting for him to return to the United States. Unfortunately, he never makes it home. His jet can't make the border, and a search-and-rescue team is shot down trying to save him. He eventually dies at the hands of the communists in a muddy Korean ditch.

"Okay, Stroke 1 just sel-jetted his tanks. I'm going for the moon."

"Choctaw," AWACS calls out, "when able, posit on Stroke 1."

"Clap 7, Stroke 1. I got no heading indication up here, buddy. What should I do?"

"Turn left thirty degrees," Clap 7 responds.

"I don't know what thirty degrees is," Stroke 1 answers with frustration. "Does this look good?"

13:52:25z

"Clap 7, this is Stroke 1. How am I doing, buddy?"

"Looking good, bud," Clap 7 replies.

"How far to the border?" Stroke 1 asks.

"Two-oh-six!"

"Copy . . . two-oh-six."

The radios are silent for a moment, and then the conversation continues.

"Okay, Clap. Stroke 1 is not going to make it too much longer. Any idea where I'm at?"

"One hundred eighty miles to point ten," Clap responds.

"Okay," Stroke 1 replies. "I'm starting to lose oil pressure now."

Harpo and I continue heading south at 35,000 feet. Gabriel is one hundred miles on our nose and, as soon as we cross the border, we'll head for the Kiwi air-refueling track for post-strike refueling. In the meantime, I'm doing my best to keep it together.

"I've got a Raven right underneath me," Stroke 1 calls out. "I got a Raven underneath me."

"Roger," the EF-111 pilot replies. "We're watching you. We'll stay with you."

"Okay, Wedge," Stroke 1 answers. "I appreciate it. Please don't get hurt, buddy. You can go out in front of me, okay?"

"We're gonna stay with you, man," Wedge answers. "Just hang on."

"I'm hangin' on," Stroke 1 laughs nervously. "Don't worry about me. I'm just a little low on the fuel now."

13:55:00z

"Okay, Wedge, this is Stroke 1 . . . and we're about ready to lose it here. I'm okay right now. It ain't going to be much longer, though. The oil's just about zero. Hydraulics are good, though."

There's another pause and then Stroke 1 asks: "Hey, Wedge, how we doing? How far to the border?"

"One hundred sixty-four miles," Wedge responds.

"Okay. You get 'em out here for me in case I gotta go."

Before Wedge can respond, Stroke 1 calls out again: "Okay . . . Stroke 1 . . . I just lost my engine . . . I'm on EPU!"

The F-16 EPU is designed to operate automatically when an engine flames out. The unit is powered by hydrazine, a chemical mixture of nitrogen, hydrogen, ammonia, and water. When the EPU fires, the gaseous products spin a turbine gearbox, which powers the EPU generator and a hydraulic pump. Unfortunately, the system can only operate for about ten minutes. Once the hydrazine is depleted, the aircraft will go out of control.

"I'm doing my best Bogart here," Stroke 1 jokes.

14:00:00z

"Choctaw, Stroke 1."

"Stroke 1, go!" the controller replies.

"Roger. Stroke 1 is squawking emergency right now. I'm not sure of my position, but I'm about one hundred thirty miles north of Gabriel is my guess . . . heading one-nine-zero at this time."

"Stroke 1, Choctaw . . . good contact."

"Okay, I'm at angels 22 right now and I don't think I'm going to be with it much longer. We're hangin' on."

"Stroke 1, roger," Choctaw replies. "Good radar contact—good Mode C."

"Thank you," Stroke 1 responds quietly.

While Wedge continues to escort Stroke 1 south toward Gabriel, Clap 7 makes an emergency call for fuel.

"Choctaw, Clap 7."

"Clap 7, go," Choctaw responds.

"Got a three-ship of Vipers holding for fuel. Request snap to nearest tanker."

"Clap, say posit from Gabriel."

"Three-four-zero . . . one-eighteen," Clap answers.

The controller pauses for a moment, then barks: "Clap, snap two-two-five!"

"Copy, snap two-two-five."

"Tanker two-two-zero . . . one-eighteen," Choctaw radios.

"Two-two-zero . . . one-eighteen . . . Clap 7."

Without warning, Stroke 1 radios: "That's all I've got, guys. I'm outta here!"

There's a slight pause, and then I recognize Foot's voice on the radio.

186

"Good luck," he says.

It's a moment I'll remember as long as I live.

14:02:34z

As soon as we cross Gabriel and into Saudi airspace, Harpo turns toward the Kiwi air-refueling track. I'm getting low on fuel, and we need to find our tanker ASAP. As soon as we arrive at the ARCP, Harpo calls out contacts at our left ten o'clock for thirty miles. I check my radar and answer: "Two's same."

Harpo completes the rejoin and pulls to within a mile of the KC-10. The blue-and-white Extender is the only tanker available, and it already has three chicks in tow.

"F-16s on the Kiwi tanker, say call sign," Harpo radios.

"Collar 11, flight of three."

It's Cliffy!

"Collar 11, this is Collar 15. My wingman is low on fuel. Request permission to rejoin."

"Collar 15," Cliffy responds, "you're cleared to the right wing. As soon as Collar 18 is through, Collar 16 can refuel."

I open my air-refueling door as Harpo proceeds to the right wing of the tanker. When Wheel comes off the boom, I slide into position. I only need a few thousand pounds to make it back to Al Minhad, and, as soon as I have it, I disconnect and resume my position on the right wing of the KC-10. In the meantime, another flight reports the ARCP inbound. Cliffy tells me to head back to Al Minhad and puts Wheel on my wing for the flight home.

On our way back to the base, I level off and tell Wheel to take spacing. As soon as I call up steerpoint sixteen, I switch on my autopilot and proceed direct to Al Minhad. The sun has already set, and thousands of stars begin to flood the night sky. Looking back, I wonder how any of us made it out of the target area. If yesterday's flight was a milk run, today's sortie was the mission from hell.

Later that evening in the beer tent, pilots from all three squadrons met to congratulate each other on a job well done. Everyone had a war story to tell. It was hard to believe the 388th TFW didn't lose a single jet. The 401st TFW lost two F-16s during the sortie: Stroke 1 and Stroke 4. According to Col. Huddle, a SAM pierced Stroke 4's jet as he came off target. His aircraft came apart, and a chute was never spotted. The news about Stroke 1 wasn't good either. Search-and-rescue forces tried to recover the downed pilot—without success.

25.
MOTHER OF ALL BATTLES

There is no longer any room for delay because the great duel, the mother of all battles, has begun. Let the aggressors be set on fire and let them be hunted down wherever they may be in every corner of the world.

—Baghdad Radio
20 January 1991

Desert Storm began with a fury, and, according to CNN, allied air power was devastating the Iraqi military structure. Command-and-control centers, radar sites, ammunition depots, power plants, SAM sites, railroad yards, bridges, fuel depots, and Saddam Hussein's presidential palace had been hit. Major air bases at Irbil, H-2, H-3, Basrah, Habbaniyah, An Nasiriyah, Karkuk, and Mosul were destroyed. CNN reported other targets on the allied hit list: chemical and biological weapons plants in Akashat, Al Iskandariyah, Al Musayyib, Badush, Baghdad, Bayji, Samarra, and Salman Pak; rocket and ballistic missile plants in Fallujah, Hillah, Karbala, and Mosul; petroleum refineries in Karkuk, Baghdad, and Basrah; nuclear power plants in Basrah, Dibis, and Baghdad; the Scud missile production facility in Latifya; and nuclear weapons factories in Tawaitha, Mosul, and Irbil.

After Col. Navarro shut down the phones, CNN became our only link to the outside world. If a pilot wasn't sleeping, on MPC duty, or flying a sortie, he was on an o'club couch, watching CNN. Listening to Bernard Shaw, Peter Arnett, and John Holliman describe the beginning of the war was incredible. So too were videotapes of laser-guided "smart bombs" destroying military targets in Baghdad, and the infrared pictures of SAMs and AAA rocketing skyward toward allied aircraft. Flying through that barrage was terrifying. Seeing it on television a day later made the event seem even more horrific.

On 20 January, I was scheduled to be a spare in a package targeted against a division of Saddam Hussein's elite Republican Guard. The troops were located in southern Iraq, just north of the Kuwaiti border.

It was a short walk from the shuttle stop to the squadron, and I arrived in time to catch the tail end of a Pentagon briefing conducted by Lt. Gen. Thomas W. Kelly, director of operations for the Joint Chiefs of Staff. "Allied aircraft have flown approximately 4,700 sorties since the beginning of the air campaign," Kelly said, as I took a seat in the lounge. "In addition, two hundred sixteen Tomahawk missiles have been fired at targets throughout Iraq. Three U.S. aircraft were lost on Saturday, bringing the total to six, and

188

nine American airmen are listed as missing in action. Allied losses to date include two British Tornadoes, one Italian Tornado, and one Kuwaiti A-4. The pilots of these aircraft are also listed as missing in action."

Gen. Kelly continued by announcing that yesterday, U.S. and Kuwaiti forces captured twelve Iraqi soldiers on oil platforms near the coast of Kuwait. The platforms were being used to fire antiaircraft artillery at allied aircraft. Gen. Kelly said the Iraqis were taken to a holding area in Saudi Arabia where they were given food and medical treatment.

When asked about the status of the missing American airmen during the question-and-answer session, Gen. Kelly responded: "We know of no American prisoners of war at all."

Asked if there was any truth to the statement issued by Baghdad that 100 U.S. aircraft had been shot down, Kelly replied, "Those claims are ridiculous and without merit. The Iraqi air-defense system is no longer effective, and we have the capability to gain and maintain air superiority in any sector of Iraq which we wish to operate."

At the conclusion of Gen. Kelly's briefing, CNN shifted focus to Israel. For the second day in a row, a salvo of Scud missiles had struck the Jewish nation. A CNN military analyst said the attack was a desperate attempt by Saddam Hussein to draw the Israelis into the crisis, "to drive a wedge through the coalition, forcing Arab nations to abandon their alliance with the United States." President Bush praised the Israelis for their restraint in the face of aggression.

Recognizing the seriousness of the Scud situation, CENTAF headquarters tasked the 388th TFW to attack the Latifya Scud production facility for the second time in three days. At 07:05 local time that morning, forty Vipers departed Al Minhad AB and flew a five-and-a-half-hour mission to Baghdad and back. Sixteen Fightin' Fuujins led the way, followed by eleven Werewolves (one aborted due to a fire-control computer failure) and twelve Black Widows. The weather wasn't as bad as our first mission to Latifya, and most of the pilots put their bombs on target. Dozens of SAMs were fired, and the AAA flak was extremely intense. Fortunately, all pilots from the three squadrons survived the onslaught and returned to Al Minhad safely.

In addition to the attacks against the Latifya facility, the 388th TFW was tasked to aid in the search for fixed Scud missile sites and mobile Scud launchers. The night before, eight F-16 pilots from the 69th TFS began pulling Scud-alert duty at King Fahd AB in Saudi Arabia, approximately twenty miles to the northwest of Dhahran, close to the battle zone. Moving a portion of the 69th TFS to King Fahd AB gave CENTAF greater flexibility in dealing with the Scud threat.

To facilitate the search, two Scud "boxes" were established: one in western Iraq, where missiles had been launched toward Israel, and one in southern Iraq to combat attacks against Saudi Arabia. The western box was centered on the H-2/H-3 airfield complex near Ar Rutbah, a small town sixty-five miles east of the Jordanian border and fifty-six miles south of the Syrian border. The southern box was centered northeast of Tallil AB near An Nasiriyah, which is on the banks of the Euphrates River, 160 miles southeast of Baghdad and 119 miles north of the tri-border between Iraq, Kuwait, and Saudi Arabia.

Air force U-2, TR-1, RF-4C, F-15E, and A-10 aircraft flew reconnaissance missions in these areas to search for launch sites and transporter erector launcher (TEL) vehicles. Early warning satellites, capable of detecting Scud launches the moment they occur, also patrolled the skies. Locating fixed Scud sites was not very difficult, and many had already been destroyed. But finding mobile Scud launchers, especially at night, was a much greater challenge. Intel estimated Iraq had 150 to 200 mobile Scud launchers, which were hidden in residential neighborhoods during the day. Once the sun went down, Iraqi crews drove the TEL vehicles into the desert and launched the missiles toward Israel and Saudi Arabia.

For a Scud to be accurate, launching crews must know the exact coordinates of the launch site so they can program the Scud's inertial navigation system. The INS alignment, which takes forty-three minutes to an hour, begins as soon as the Scud is erected and coordinates for both the launch site and the target are programmed. During this period, the Scud has to be fueled, and the kerosene-based fuel has to be heated—a process that may take up to three hours, if done properly. Once the missile is launched, it takes about fifteen minutes for crews to dismantle the rig. At this point, the mobile launcher can be driven to another location, where the process can be repeated. During the night, Iraqi crews hid the mobile launchers underneath bridges and highway overpasses, in tunnels, caves, and warehouses. If U.S. pilots could force the Iraqis to use unsurveyed sites or launch the missiles before they were ready, missile accuracy, which was poor to begin with, would be degraded even further.

At 16:55, Capt. Curt "Cut" Jergensen and I, the two spares for the night's sortie, arrived at the briefing trailer. Damien was leading the package and he conducted the brief. Shortly after it began, SSgt. Rich Brown entered the room.

"Sorry to interrupt, sir. We just got a message from headquarters that your mission has been canceled. The weather in Saudi is real bad, and your tankers couldn't take off."

The mission was soon rescheduled for 03:30. Instead of being a spare, I'd be replacing Fist in the number eight position on Sweet Pea's wing. I watched the news until 22:00, then headed back to my room to take a nap. I set my alarm for midnight and fell asleep, thinking about Colette and the mission that awaited me.

21 JANUARY 1991

When I arrived at the squadron, Sudds and other members of his MPC team were putting the finishing touches on the day's strike packages. Our formation had increased from eight aircraft to twelve. By 01:00, everyone was assembled in the trailer across from life-support. Damien, the mission commander, started things off with a time hack. After setting my watch, I studied my map and lineup card while Damien reviewed the mission objectives. Our target was the Medina division of Saddam Hussein's Republican Guard, located northwest of Kuwait along Iraq's southern border. Out TOT was 02:10:00z, and each F-16 would carry four canisters of CBU-87/B combined effects munitions (CEM), a relatively new weapon, and extremely effective against both hard and soft targets—armored vehicles and personnel.

Each canister weighs 950 pounds and contains 202 BLU-97/B armor-piercing bomblets, which provide both fragmentation and incendiary effects. CBU-87/B is also equipped with a FZU-39 (Fuzzy-39) proximity sensor, which can be used as a radar fuse or a timer fuse. As soon as CBU-87/B munitions are pickled off the jet, lanyards are pulled. This activates either the timer or a thermal battery, which powers the Doppler radar. When the radar is turned on, it looks for the preselected height of function altitude. When this altitude is reached or when the time is up, a signal is sent to cant the tail fins, which causes the canister to spin. Spin rates can be programmed on the ground (settings range from 0 to 2,500 RPM in increments of 500) to produce different pattern sizes. Higher function altitudes and faster spin rates result in greater dispersion. For a denser bomb pattern, lower altitudes and slower spin rates are selected. When the programmed spin rate is reached, the canister opens, and the bomblets disperse. As soon as they're released, an air-inflatable retarder is deployed. When the bomblet senses a minimum of 6.5 Gs of deceleration, it arms. Average pattern sizes range from 150-by-150 feet for a 1,000 RPM spin rate, to 250-by-250 feet for a 2,000 RPM spin rate. Pickle four weapons on a single pass, and an awful lot of territory can be covered.

Damien gave us the standard briefing with one notable exception: "Beginning today, no strafing will be allowed, and the floor on every mission will be 5,000 feet. Taz and I were reviewing HUD film from yesterday's Latifya strike mission. A member of the 421st, whose name I won't mention, dropped down and strafed a SAM site. By doing so, he put himself in the heart of the Iraqi SAM and AAA envelope. He's lucky he wasn't shot down. Who was watching out for his wingman while he was doing this? The pilot has been grounded, and if anyone else pulls a stunt like that, they'll be grounded, too."

Many of us hadn't flown a night sortie in over a week, and everyone was anxious to test our medium-altitude tactics against the Republican Guard. Flying over Baghdad during the day was a treat, but the 421st was geared to fly at night.

23:30:00z

A Viper takes off every twenty seconds, and as soon as Sweet Pea releases his brakes, I begin my countdown. My eyes are focused on the clock on my data-entry display, which sits at eye level to the right of my up-front control. Finally, I drop my feet off the brakes and smoothly select afterburner. The jet accelerates rapidly. Airborne, I proceed west toward steerpoint one. I spot Sweet Pea on my radar screen and lock him up. It takes a few minutes to complete the rejoin, but before long, the entire package is level at 27,000 feet over the moonlit waters of the Persian Gulf.

We reach the ARCP on time and a KC-135 is in the holding track waiting for us. It takes about 4,000 pounds to top off my tanks, and as soon as I disconnect, Cliffy leads our formation toward the push point. When the formation is clear of the air-refueling track, Cliffy sends everyone to strike primary.

"Husky 11, go red one!" Cliffy radios. The call is made on Have Quick, so maintaining radio silence is unnecessary. Each of us answers: "Two!" "Three!" "Four!"

After we check in, Cliffy establishes contact with Choctaw, and our controller clears us into Iraqi airspace. Each aircraft is eight miles in trail of the other at an ingress altitude of 26,000 feet. The formation enters Iraqi airspace at 01:43:20z and proceeds north along Kuwait's western border. Within minutes, the radios come alive.

"Dane 01 has contacts, twenty right for thirty miles, high aspect."

"Contacts friendly," Choctaw responds.

Additional calls are made, and the answer is the same each time. I quickly realize the contacts heading south are other allied fighters who have just completed their missions. We're not the only ones dropping bombs this morning.

Sixty miles north of steerpoint five, I begin to pick up quite a bit of turbulence. The weather has been a hindrance since the beginning of the war, and it looks like it may be a factor again. The turbulence continues to get worse, and, before long, St. Elmo's fire begins to appear around the edge of my windscreen. A few seconds later, a bolt of lightning illuminates the sky around me. We're heading right into a line of thunderstorms.

"Dane 01 is descending to base plus five," Damien calls out.

The base altitude is a number that changes daily. Using the term "base" allows us to climb or descend without exposing our true altitude to the Iraqis. Today's base altitude is 13,000 feet, which means Dane 01 is descending to get below the clouds. The rest of us follow him down, but the weather continues to deteriorate. The turbulence is getting pretty bad, and a lightning strike with four live bombs is the last thing any of us needs.

Less than a minute later, Damien decides to abort the mission. He begins a right turn to the south and informs AWACS of his decision. The rest of us follow his lead. I'm disappointed we didn't get to drop. Forty-eight canisters of CBU-87 would have inflicted a lot of damage against the Republican Guard.

After a quick debrief, everyone returned to the o'club for breakfast. I hadn't slept much in the past twenty-four hours, and as soon as I finished eating, I walked back to my trailer to go to bed. Waking up around 17:00, I walked over to the o'club to watch Gen. Schwarzkopf give a briefing on CNN. Dressed in desert fatigues with his sleeves rolled up above his elbows, the CENTCOM commander stood in front of a small podium while addressing the throng of reporters. Schwarzkopf commanded attention every time he opened his mouth. He took no shit from young reporters who asked stupid questions. Everyone loved the way he brushed them off. When Gen. Schwarzkopf declared that allied forces had likely achieved one of their prime objectives—the destruction of Saddam Hussein's nuclear program—everyone in the room cheered. We knew he was referring to the mission we flew two days before.

During the question-and-answer period, a reporter asked Gen. Schwarzkopf whether or not Saddam Hussein was being targeted.

"We don't have a policy of trying to kill any particular individual," Schwarzkopf replied. "What we are trying to do is sever the leadership from the lower units. They are very much motivated by that leadership, and I think when that leadership is no longer available to them, it will seriously affect their motivation."

At the conclusion of the briefing, CNN broadcast a report on missing allied pilots. "Earlier today," the announcer began, "Iraqi television displayed footage of allied prisoners of war and announced the captured airmen would be placed at strategic sites to act as human shields against the ongoing air attack on Iraqi targets."

When the men appeared on the screen, a collective moan could be heard throughout the lounge. The pilots—three Americans, two Brits, one Italian, and one Kuwaiti— appeared to have been beaten. A British pilot, identified as Flt. Lt. John Peters, slumped in front of the camera with his eyes closed and his head down. His face was badly bruised. One by one, the other prisoners were also displayed in front of the camera.

"My name is Lieutenant Jeffrey Norton Zaun. I fly the A6-E Intruder. My mission was to attack the H-3 airfield in southwestern Iraq. I flew as part of a formation of four aircraft in order to commit this attack."

Zaun appeared dazed, his face cut and swollen. Another American pilot, whom CNN identified as Marine Corps Lieutenant Colonel Clifford M. Acree, said his mission was "observation and reconnaissance." Also dazed and battered, Acree said, "I would like to tell my wife and family I am alive and well."

CNN reported that the third American prisoner was Marine Corps Chief Warrant Officer Guy L. Hunter, Jr. Badly bruised under his left eye, Hunter said: "I think this war is crazy and should never have happened. It is an aggression against peaceful Iraq."

The men had obviously been coerced into making their statements. If Saddam thought he could win the war by abusing allied prisoners, he was sadly mistaken.

Later, in an interview on the White House lawn, President Bush reacted strongly. "America is angry about this," he said tersely. "If Saddam Hussein thought this brutal treatment of pilots is a way to muster world support, he is dead wrong. It is very clear that this is a direct violation of every convention that protects prisoners. This is not going to make a difference in the prosecution of the war against Saddam—it's not going to make a difference."

The U.S. military Code of Conduct once prohibited prisoners from giving their captors any information beyond name, rank, and serial number. The code was amended in 1977 to ease the terrible guilt that some POWs felt after they were tortured into talking. A sentence was added that states: "I will evade answering further questions to the utmost of my ability."

I've often wondered what my breaking point would be. The last thing I wanted was to be shot down over Iraq. But if it happened, would I be able to endure the pain and suffering? I don't know what Lt. Col. Acree, Lt. Zaun, and Chief Warrant Officer Hunter were subjected to, and I will never second-guess them for making the statements they made. But, I decided, if I had to make a choice between death or giving in to the Iraqis, my choice would be death.

26.
PHASE TWO

For the second time in three days, pilots from the 388th TFW, and the 401st TFW at Doha, Qatar, successfully bombed Iraq's nuclear research facility. More than one hundred MK-84s were dropped during the midmorning attack, raining terror and destruction along the eastern banks of the Tigris River. All of Iraq's high-value targets had been hit at least twice, and, according to Gen. Colin L. Powell, chairman of the Joint Chiefs of Staff, phase two of the air campaign was about to begin. In a couple of days, allied forces would shift their attention from strategic to tactical targets. The new focus would be on the destruction of Saddam Hussein's armored forces, primarily the Republican Guard.

During the afternoon's intel briefing, Maj. Marsh discussed Iraqi tactics and the methods they used to defend their territory. Decoy Scud missiles and cardboard launchers were set up to thwart allied attacks, and the cloud hovering over the nuclear research facility during the previous Saturday's bombing raid had been manufactured by smoke generators. The generators produced a cloud above the facility during the morning's raid, and, according to those who flew in the mission, a second cloud could be seen a few miles to the east. Some pilots were fooled by the dummy facility, but, for the most part, Iraq's attempt to camouflage the nuclear site did little to save it from destruction.

Visually identifying a target is important to a pilot, but not always necessary. The F-16's fire-control computer can accept latitudinal and longitudinal coordinates within one one-thousandth of a minute of a degree. This enables the system to pinpoint targets within six feet of each other, anywhere in the world. During Desert Shield, the coordinates we used were normally derived from maps supplied by the U.S. Defense Mapping Agency. But right after the 15 January deadline, computer tapes containing satellite imagery of Iraq and Kuwait were delivered to us from CENTCOM headquarters in Riyadh. Once the programs were loaded into our MSS computers, MPC planners were able to rely on recent satellite imagery instead of older maps, which weren't nearly as accurate. Placing a set of cross hairs on the computer screen over a specific target allows a mission planner to program accurate coordinates into each pilot's DTC. When a pilot plugs the DTC into his jet and downloads the coordinates into the F-16's fire-control computer, he can drop bombs accurately whether he sees the target or not.

After dinner, a group of us headed over to the beer tent to tell war stories. By that time everyone had been to Baghdad at least once, and there wasn't a pilot among us who would volunteer to go back again. A few of us had close calls, but nothing compared to what Capt. Tim "Booper" Boop experienced earlier in the day. According to Ark and Capt. Hal "H" Bird, who also participated in the mission, Zappo and Booper were a few miles south of their target when an SA-3 came up out of nowhere.

"We were flying along," Ark said, "and all of a sudden, Zappo started screaming: 'SA-3 coming up on Canine four-one! Four-two, it's guiding on you! Break! Break!' A few seconds later, Zappo called out again, 'Okay, it detonated in between us. Four-two, did you take a hit?' Everyone held their breath, and Booper answered, 'Four-two's hit!'"

"What happened next?" I asked.

"Someone told him to climb and head south," Ark continued. "Then Zappo started screaming again, 'Head two-two-zero! Head two-two-zero!' Booper acknowledged and said he was leaking gas bad. All of a sudden," Ark said laughing, "Zappo yells, 'Four-two's out! Four-two is in a chute . . . he's got a good chute!' There was a pause on the radios and then we heard Booper say, 'Four-two's still airborne!' I don't know what Zappo saw, but I started cracking up."

"Booper punched off his tanks," H interjected. "Zappo saw the tanks and thought it was Booper in a parachute."

"How high were you guys?" I asked.

"We were at thirty thousand feet!" Ark laughed. "You can't get a chute up there."

"They continued south and Booper eventually landed at King Fahd AB," H said. "He's supposed to come home on one of the C-130s in the morning."

23 JANUARY 1991

After dinner, I left for the squadron to prepare for my fourth combat mission. It was a dark, moonless night, and the air was cool. As I approached the entrance to our building, I was greeted by Sultan, one of the UAE helicopter pilots, sitting on the front steps, a cigarette wedged between his lips.

"How are you tonight, Rosey?"

"I'm tired, Sultan. I can't wait for this to end so we can go home."

"It will be over soon, my friend. Saddam will give up. You will see."

"I hope you're right. I miss my family. The past few months have been very difficult, especially for my wife."

"Have you spoken to her lately?"

"No. Col. Navarro shut the phones off more than a week ago. No one's been allowed to call off-base since."

All of a sudden, Sultan reached into his pocket and pulled out a set of keys. He took another drag off his cigarette, then turned to me: "Here are the keys to my car, Rosey. Go and use my cellular phone. Let your wife know you're okay. No one will know."

This was an offer I couldn't refuse. Sultan handed me the keys, and after I thanked him, I ran toward the parking lot. Once in Sultan's car, I started the engine and reclined the front seat. It was dark and I could barely see. I picked up the phone, dialed the local operator, and gave him my home-phone and calling-card numbers.

A minute later, the phone began to ring.

"Hello," Colette answered.

"Hi, baby!"

Colette burst into tears. "Oh, Keith, I've been so scared," she sobbed. "The past week has been a nightmare for me. Every time I turn on the TV, someone's talking about another jet being shot down. I have no idea if it's you or not. I can't stand it. I keep thinking Col. Fox will knock on my door. I can't sleep. I can't eat . . ."

"Calm down, honey," I interrupted. "I love you very much. I've had a couple of close calls, but I'm okay. How are Candice and Kristen?"

"They're fine," Colette replied. "They're such good girls."

"You need to take better care of yourself," I told her. "I know you're worried, but I'm okay. Promise me you'll start eating and don't sit in front of the TV all day."

"I know," Colette answered, "but it's hard not to watch."

"Have you heard from any of our friends?" I asked.

"The phone has been ringing off the hook ever since the war started. My mom calls every day . . . oh, and I even got a call from Bo Jackson."

In early December, my grandmother sent me a CARE package that included the book *Bo Knows Bo*. In it, Bo Jackson talked about his love for military aircraft—particularly the F-16. He referred to the Viper as "the sports car of military jets." "When I come back," he wrote, "I want to be reincarnated as a dolphin—or as an F-16." When I finished Bo's book, I asked Colette to send me the Los Angeles Raiders' address so I could write to him. The Raiders are my favorite team, and I'm one of Bo's biggest fans. I've always admired his athletic skill, and the idea that he wanted to be a fighter pilot intrigued me. I wrote him a long letter and told him about the F-16 and what our unit had been doing to prepare for war against the Iraqis. I promised to make him a copy of my HUD film if we ever went to war, and I asked him if I could stand on the sidelines one day and watch him play in a Raiders' game.

"I can't believe he called you! What did he say?" I asked excitedly.

"He called a couple of days after the war started, and when I answered the phone, he said 'This is Bo Jackson.' I paused for a second, then said: 'Oh, hi, Bo.' He said he never opens his fan mail, because he gets so much. But when he saw 'Operation Desert Shield' on your letter, he was curious and decided to open it. He told me: 'Your husband is doing something I've always wanted to do. I really admire him, and I wanted to call to let you know I was thinking about your family.' "

Colette continued, "We talked for about fifteen minutes. He asked if I needed anything, and he said he would be praying for us."

Bo couldn't have called at a better time. His thoughtfulness is something neither Colette nor I will ever forget.

Colette and I spent about twenty minutes on the phone. I couldn't discuss the missions we'd flown, but I promised to send her my journal notes so she could read about what things had been like for me. Before hanging up, I told her how much I loved her, and I promised to be home soon.

When I returned to the squadron, I walked down to the helicopter lounge to return Sultan's keys.

"Thank you so much," I told him. "This *really* meant a lot to me, and to Colette as well."

"You can call any time. Just let me know."

21:45:00z

"Tonka, say picture," Ruff 01 calls out.

"Tonka, picture is clean," AWACS replies.

My F-16 is level at 27,000 feet, thirty miles south of the Kuwait border. My airspeed is 380 knots. Damien—call sign Ruff 01—is the mission commander. Our formation consists of eight F-16s, and we've just entered Kuwaiti airspace. Flying on Damien's wing this morning is Capt. Randy "Spike" Roberts. Tater is number three, and Tonto is number four. Skippy—call sign Alpo 05—is leading the second element. His wingman is Jabba. I'm flying in the number three position, and at the end of the package is Cuda. Our target is a set of ammunition storage bunkers in southern Iraq, twenty-two miles north of the Iraq-Kuwait border and nineteen miles west of downtown Basrah.

It's nearly two o'clock in the morning. The void of night surrounds my aircraft. Down low off my right wing, bright orange flames flicker across the desert floor. "That's got to be the Al Wafrah oil field," I think to myself. The blaze looks huge, even from 27,000 feet. There's no telling how long it will be before the fires are extinguished; the effects on the environment will be devastating.

According to intel, the ammunition bunkers are located along a heavily traveled supply route west of Shaibah Air Base. Damien's element will concentrate on the bunkers south of the road, and our element will attack the bunkers to the north. Each F-16 is carrying two MK-84s, and, weather permitting, everyone will execute a forty-five-degree attack. After we drop our bombs, we'll egress east to the exit point, Bubiyan Island. Once we're over the Persian Gulf, everyone will fence out and continue direct to Al Minhad.

Ten miles from the IP, I turn on my VTR and check my air-to-air radar one last time. I've dropped back a little more than I would have liked. I push my throttle up and make a quick call to Damien.

"Ruff one, Alpo seven. Be advised I'm a little behind. I'm seven miles from the IP."

Continuing east, I call up steerpoint eight. The target is thirty-five miles on my nose. I roll the jet slightly left then back to the right, clearing for enemy SAMs. As the ground-map radar sweeps across the desert floor, a pair of bright returns appear to the north and south of the cursors.

"One's off," Damien calls out.

I hit the expand/field-of-view (pinky) switch on the lower part of my control stick, which sends my radar into the expand (EXP) mode. EXP provides 4:1 expansion of normal ground-map returns. Afterward, I press my left thumb against the cursor/enable switch on my throttle and slew the radar cursors north, directly over the bright returns.

"Three's off," Tater calls out.

I continue toward the target and begin to descend. The radios are fairly quiet. I'm surprised the Republican Guard hasn't been tracking us with their radars. Intel told us to expect heavy AAA and plenty of SAM activity, but my RWR scope has yet to make a sound.

"Four's off," Tonto radios.

Less than two minutes from the target, I key my mike to update Cuda on my radar work.

"Alpo eight," I radio, "seven's going to take the bright spot to the north."

"Alpo eight copies," Cuda answers. "Alpo eight has a bright spot just to the northeast of my cursors. I'll go for that."

As I approach the target, the returns continue to get brighter. To eliminate background clutter from the radar screen, I rotate the manual-gain control knob on my throttle, which darkens the area surrounding the target, allowing it to stand out better. To sharpen the resolution, I hit the pinky switch again, which shifts the radar from EXP to Doppler beam sharpening option 1 (DBS1). DBS1 provides 8:1 expansion of normal ground-map returns, and as soon as I refine my cursor position, I switch to DBS2, which provides 64:1 expansion.

21:48:23z

"Okay, let's go twenty-mile scope," I say to myself. "Gain down a bit." I'm only seventeen miles from the target. I check to make sure my master arm switch is in Arm. My airspeed is 420 knots, and I'm passing through 25,000 feet. As I continue to descend, I realize the entire area is covered with a solid deck of clouds. It looks like I'll have to pickle on my diamond again.

Five miles from the target, I roll inverted and begin my attack. As soon as I roll upright again, I reach down and switch my VTR from left MFD to HUD. Passing through 20,000 feet, I switch from CCRP to CCIP and place my bombfall line directly over the diamond. As the pipper tracks upward, I ready my thumb above the pickle button. I pull my throttle back just a little to keep my airspeed in check. My dive angle is a little shallower than I would like, but there's nothing I can do about it now. I hit the pickle button, passing 17,100 feet, and the aircraft shudders slightly as the MK-84s release. I pull back on my stick and begin to climb. As soon as the nose of my aircraft reaches the horizon, I roll into eighty degrees of bank and pull hard to the left. My RWR is still quiet, and there's no sign of any AAA.

"Alpo seven . . . bombs away . . . off left," I radio.

All of a sudden, the sky below me lights up with a burst of white light. The flash is gratifying. I continue to turn and eventually roll out on a 195-degree heading. As soon as I place my master arm switch to Simulate, I call up my air-to-air radar and begin to search for Jabba and Skippy. Passing through 23,000 feet, Cuda calls out: "Alpo eight's off . . . bombs away."

I reach toward my up-front control and call up the exit point. I know Cuda will be looking for me, so I key my mike and radio my position.

"Seven's on the zero-six-zero for twenty-six off of seven."

"Alpo eight copies."

Before long, the train of Vipers is back in line at 34,000 feet over the Persian Gulf. After we fence out, I engage my autopilot and relax the rest of the way home. This mission was a cakewalk compared to the nuke run. Unfortunately, clouds in the target area prevented us from seeing any secondary fires or explosions. But at least we didn't get shot at.

24 JANUARY 1991

The first week of Operation Desert Storm was completed. Allied aircraft flew more than 12,000 sorties, and phase two of the bombing campaign was about to begin. According to intel, forty-one Iraqi aircraft had been destroyed in the air or on the ground, and, of the sixty-six airfields used by the Iraqi military, aircraft had flown from only five in the previous twenty-four hours. In December, Saddam Hussein's air force averaged 235 sorties a day. During the first week of fighting, that average had dropped to somewhere between thirty and forty.

The second phase of the air campaign would focus on the destruction of the Republican Guard—the heart of Saddam Hussein's military capability and political power. Allied attacks subjecting Iraq's elite forces to intensive bombing would occur every fifteen minutes, twenty-four hours a day, seven days a week. During a Pentagon briefing the previous afternoon, Gen. Colin Powell described how the attacks would unfold.

"Our strategy for dealing with this army is very, very simple," Powell said. "First, we're going to cut it off, and then we're going to kill it."

The Joint Chiefs chairman also confirmed that considerable damage had been done to Iraq's chemical weapons facilities and to several biological warfare plants. When asked about the two operating nuclear reactors at Tawaitha that were thought to be capable of producing enriched uranium for nuclear weapons, Gen. Powell said: "They're both gone, they're down, they're finished."

The roar of an afterburner woke me from a deep sleep. It was almost three o'clock in the afternoon. I had the day off, so I got out of bed, gathered my dirty clothes, and headed over to the laundry tent. Later, I went to the o'club, just in time to see a videotape produced by the 388th Combat Camera team. The tape featured several members of the wing describing their experiences during the first few days of the war. Col. Navarro also offered his assessment, and began by reading a message sent to the wing by CENTAF commander Lt. Gen. Charles Horner:

> The first week of the war demonstrated a professional determination and competence unparalleled in air warfare. You should be proud as I know you are. However, there is much left to be accomplished and we must all maintain the same level of intensity and aggressiveness. Some taskings will get easier, but some may get harder.

As we react to high-priority targets—especially those that are perishable—you need to remain flexible and able to accept short-notice changes. Your individual efforts in leading this war effort have been singular. Godspeed.

When the tape was finished, we switched the television over to CNN. Peter Arnett, the only Western reporter still in Baghdad, was reporting that he had been taken to what Iraqi authorities described as a "baby-formula factory," that had been destroyed by allied bombing.

"It was the only source of infant-formula food for children one year and younger in Iraq," Arnett said during a telephone interview. "The steel girders that had been holding up the building were twisted and blackened, and the machinery inside was a molten pile. The intact signboard at the entrance to the factory read 'Baby Milk Factory' in English and Arabic."

According to White House Press Secretary Marlin Fitzwater, the building was being used to produce biological weapons. "It has a military garrison outside," Fitzwater said, "and numerous sources have indicated that the facility is associated with biological-warfare production. The Iraqis have hidden this facility behind a facade of baby-milk production as a form of disinformation. We've had information on this for a long time. I cannot share it with you, for intelligence reasons, but it certainly is our conclusion. We're confident of our information."

When asked about Peter Arnett's report, Fitzwater responded: "We must point out once again that any reports coming out of Baghdad are, in effect, coming from the Iraqi government. This is not a case of taking on the media. It's a case of correcting a public disclosure there that is erroneous, that is false, that hurts our government and plays into the hands of Saddam Hussein."

Watching the report, there was not a doubt in our minds that the building was a biological weapons plant. When CNN showed a poorly made sign with "Baby Milk Factory" printed on it—in English, no less—everyone laughed.

Most of us realized that Arnett's comments were censored by the Iraqis, but a few of the guys thought he was nothing more than a propaganda puppet for Saddam Hussein. I didn't have a problem with Arnett's reporting, because I took what he said with a grain of salt. Yet the tone of his reporting seemed to imply that the allies were deliberately targeting Iraqi civilian areas. This was simply not true. Iraq had more than 17 million people, which meant that civilian areas were going to be damaged. But Arnett never mentioned that most of the damage was the result of Iraq's own action. CNN showed dramatic footage of antiaircraft artillery, and of surface-to-air missiles being fired into the air. Those 100-millimeter shells, and missiles the size of telephone poles, fell back to earth. Where did Peter Arnett think they hit?

27.
THE MAILMAN DELIVERS

The outcome of Operation Desert Storm and, perhaps, the long-term stability of the Middle East, hinged on the coalition's ability to destroy Iraq's elite Republican Guard. This highly trained, highly privileged military corps, originally known as the Presidential Guard, was established primarily for the protection of Saddam Hussein. Most of the troops came from Saddam's home village near Tikrit. The soldiers lived in superior quarters and received higher pay than regular conscripts. A force of more than 150,000, the Republican Guard was led by Maj. Gen. Iyad Fathi Al Rawi, one of Iraq's top field commanders. The troops were Soviet-trained, and, according to intel, equipped with more than 1,000 Soviet-made T-72 tanks. The Republican Guard also had its own heavy artillery, antiaircraft batteries, medical units, intelligence specialists, and special-operation forces. They maintained their own air power and fought most of the major battles during the Iran-Iraq War.

25 JANUARY 1991
Postal deliveries dropped off significantly after the start of the war. I hadn't received a letter or package from Colette in two weeks, and it was really starting to aggravate me. Lt. Col. Rackley said that more than one hundred pallets of mail were sitting on the ramp in Dhahran, but delivering supplies and weapons to units throughout the KTO was a higher priority.

After I checked my mailbox—still empty—I walked into the scheduling office to see who I'd be flying with that night. I spotted my name next to the call sign Howler 04, but for some reason, the word *mailman* was written alongside.

Grover walked into the office. I asked him about "mailman."

"You're dropping M-129 leaflet bombs on the Republican Guard tonight, Rosey."

"Oh, great!" I replied. "The Iraqis get to fire SAMs and AAA at me, and all I have to defend myself with are bombs filled with paper."

With plenty of time before the briefing, I decided to visit the weapons shop for a quick lesson on the M-129. According to Duck, the M-129 is nothing more than a cluster bomb filled with leaflets instead of bomblets. Since accuracy isn't critical, Duck recommended dropping the weapons manually from high altitude. He said there was no reason to subject myself to enemy ground fire—an opinion I wholeheartedly agreed with.

The leaflets were part of a psychological-warfare program aimed at encouraging Iraqi soldiers to give themselves up. The invitation card showed a picture of an Iraqi soldier surrendering to a Saudi member of the coalition. The card also showed Iraqi soldiers in a Saudi camp, eating fruit and drinking tea. Printed in Arabic on the other side of the card was the following:

> This is the Central Military Command and Operation. You will be a guest of the allied forces. You are invited to join the allied force, and you will have the right of hospitality. You will be secure and treated medically. You will be able to return home as soon as the situation Saddam put us in is finished.
> My brother Iraqi soldiers, this invitation is open to you and your fellow soldiers. We wish you would accept it as soon as you can.
>
> Commander of Allied Forces and Operations Center

Additional leaflets warned Iraqi troops that they would die if they continued to fight. One leaflet showed an F-117 dropping bombs on Iraqi aircraft as they attempted to take off. Another showed an Iraqi skeleton lying in the sand next to his burning tank. A printed message on the front said: *Leave your equipment or defend your equipment until you die. You have the choice.* On the back, there was a picture of a large bomb with the following message:

> WARNING
> Your equipment is an easy target. This place will be attacked soon. Leave your equipment and save yourself.
> WARNING

As soon as Badger completed the mission briefing, the four of us walked over to life-support to prepare for the flight. Cliffy and Capt. Jim "Norge" Riess teased me about the mission as we zipped up our G-suits, but I really didn't mind. I was the only pilot in the squadron dropping leaflets, and, after talking with Duck, was looking forward to it. The view from 30,000 feet would be nice, and I would not have to worry much about being shot down.

16:31:22z
"Captain Keith Rosenkranz . . . Howler 04 . . . 3001 charlie . . . Two M-129s—I'm a mailman tonight. Takeoff time is 16:40z . . . TOT is 18:58:30z and date is 25 January '91. Tail number is 422."

18:52:40z
Flying east on a 090 heading, I look down to my left and spot a barrage of AAA erupting from the desert floor. The string of bright red tracers looks like a snake slithering upward. The Iraqi gunners can hear us, but our speed makes it difficult for them to know where we are. After checking to ensure my external lights are off, I key my mike and call out: "Howler four has AAA left eight . . . left eight! AAA up at about the mid-twenties." It continues to intensify and a few seconds later, I call out again: "Howler four, still heavy AAA, left eight . . . left eight!"

"Howler two . . . tally-ho AAA left ten o'clock."

My airspeed is 345 knots and I'm level at 30,500 feet. The clouds below me have scattered, and fires can be seen in every direction. Reaching up with my right hand, I hit the air-to-ground button on my up-front control. The ground-map radar begins to sweep and a good set of returns appears on the north side of my cursors. All of a sudden, a bright light appears ahead and to my left. It might be an SA-7, but I can't be sure. The SA-7 "Grail" is a man-portable, infrared-homing, light antiaircraft missile that can reach speeds up to Mach 1.5. It has a range of 2.6 nautical miles and a maximum altitude of 14,000 feet. It looks like it may be tracking toward Mans, so I make another call in case he isn't aware.

"Howler three, you've got a bright light off your left nine low," I radio.

"Three is no joy," Mans replies.

I continue searching for the missile, and, a few seconds later, Mans calls out: "Say status of the bright light."

"And it's gone away now," I reply. "Sorry."

I'm less than twenty-five miles from the target, and Badger's bombs have just exploded. A flash of light followed by a quick burst of orange fire illuminates the desert floor. We must be in the right area, because the AAA is coming at us from every direction.

"Howler three, check low, check low . . . your left . . . got heavy AAA left nine . . . low!" I'm so excited, I can barely get the call off.

"Three's tally!" Mans replies.

"Tonka . . . only friendlies airborne," AWACS calls out.

I observe the heavy ZSUs—the ZSU 23-4 Shikas, twenty-three-millimeter, four-barreled antiaircraft systems that sit on top of mobile carriers. Each gun is capable of firing 800 to 1000 rounds per minute. The system is extremely dangerous to aircraft flying below 6,600 feet.

As soon as I switch my radar to twenty-mile scope, Mans rolls inverted and executes his attack. The infrared image of his F-16 is visible in my HUD as it descends toward the desert floor. Jabba's bombs have just gone off, and secondary fires from Badger's bombs are burning out of control.

18:58:08z

I'm seven miles from the target, heading east at 30,300 feet and 345 knots. I press the pickle button. As soon as the weapons release, I call out: "Bombs away for Howler four." When I complete the call, I turn twenty degrees left and proceed toward steerpoint seven. Our egress point is directly overtop Bubiyan Island.

The four of us were back in the squadron by 01:30, eating MREs and watching CNN on television. According to military officials, a Saudi F-15 pilot shot down two Iraqi F-1 Mirage jets over the Persian Gulf just south of the Kuwaiti border. The two fighters, loaded with French-made Exocet missiles, were flying south along the Saudi coastline about two hundred feet above the water. The F-15 pilot rolled in behind them, fired two AIM-9 Sidewinders, and came away with a double kill.

CNN also reported that Saddam Hussein met with senior officers on the war front in southern Kuwait. In a speech broadcast by the official Iraqi News Agency, Hussein told the Iraqi people: "The American aggressors and their allies deluded themselves into believing they could carry out an overwhelming attack against Iraq, but they are disappointed. They will never defeat us, nor will they escape the punishment they deserve. They used all their means to achieve their purpose, including cruise missiles and a great number of airplanes. The forces of arrogance and evil even bombed us with lies and propaganda to cover their miscalculations and black wishful thinking."

"Hey, Rosey," Norge laughed, "looks like Saddam's already seen some of the mail you dropped tonight."

"The mailman delivered," I replied proudly.

Britain announced today that it would discontinue low-level air attacks against Iraqi airfields after losing its fifth Tornado in ten days. Even though the United States had lost twice as many aircraft, the RAF's casualty rate was alarmingly higher: one Tornado jet for every 80 sorties. In contrast, the United States was flying more than 750 missions for each downed aircraft.

Ever since hostilities broke out, RAF pilots flying Tornado GR-1 bombers had flown at altitudes below 200 feet. The attacks usually occurred at night. Each Tornado carried two 1,000-pound JP-233 dispensers mounted in tandem under the fuselage. The state-of-the-art JP-233, one of the most advanced weapons in the British arsenal, is equipped with thirty SG-357 cratering bomblets and 215 HB-276 delayed-action mines. To deliver the JP-233 effectively, Tornado pilots flew directly over Iraqi runways at low altitude. This method of attack exposed pilots to intense ground fire, which resulted in a higher attrition rate, compared to other allied nations. This was significant to me, because if Col. Navarro had had his way, the 421st would have been flying LANTIRN missions at low altitude the minute the war started.

26 JANUARY 1991

A steady downpour beat against the roof of our trailer, waking me out of a sound sleep. I'd been on base for nearly five months, and this was only the second time I'd seen rain in the desert. The deluge didn't last long, but it was enough to make me wish I were back home in front of the fireplace, snuggling with Colette. I had checked my mailbox one last time before leaving the squadron the night before and discovered a small package with my name on it. Inside were two letters Colette had written three weeks earlier, and a surprise videotape. Instead of going back to sleep, I got dressed and took the shuttle bus to Father Pierson's office to enjoy a private viewing of the tape. The tape began on Halloween night. Candice and Kristen were dressed like little geisha girls and were getting ready to go trick-or-treating. The videotape also included footage taken during Thanksgiving and Christmas. Being away from the family during the holidays was difficult, but seeing the turkey dinner Colette prepared, and watching the girls open their Christmas presents, made up for the lost time—in a bittersweet way. The tape ended with a short message from Colette. She told me how much she loved me and said the day I came home would be the happiest in her life. It would be the happiest day in my life as well.

I arrived at the squadron by 14:00 and spent the rest of the afternoon updating the weapons board. Since the unit was focusing on the Republican Guard, I decided CBU-52, CBU-58, and CBU-71 should be featured together as the "weapons of the week." CBU-52/58/71 cluster bombs are dispenser-type munitions. Slightly more than seven feet in length, a canister of CBU-52 weighs 785 pounds and contains 220 BLU-61A/B bomblets. Each softball-sized bomblet is 3.5 inches in diameter and is packed with .65 pound of explosives. The bomblets are spin-armed once they're released, and they explode on impact. Frag velocity is 5,000 feet per second, and the casing has a liner of zirconium tin, which provides incendiary effects.

CBU-58 and CBU-71 dispensers weigh 820 pounds and carry 650 baseball-sized bomblets, each containing four ounces of explosives. CBU-58 bomblets incorporate the M219 fuse for impact detonation, while CBU-71 bomblets are equipped with M224 fuses for random time-delay detonation after impact. Fragmentation is caused by the scored steel casing, which produces 260 fragments. The frag velocity is 4,900 feet per second, and incendiary effects can be produced by adding two five-gram titanium pellets to the bomblet.

After I finished updating the weapons board, I grabbed an MRE and relaxed in the squadron lounge in front of the television. According to CNN, a huge oil spill was spreading off the coast of Kuwait. The report said that Iraqi forces opened the valves on an oil-loading pipeline at the Sea Island terminal of the Al Ahmadi refinery. Crude oil was also being emptied from five large tankers, which had been moored off Kuwait City for the past three months. Hundreds of thousands of barrels of crude oil were spilling into the Persian Gulf. Environmentalists feared the spill would not only damage the Gulf's fragile ecosystem, but would damage the region's desalination plants, which provided most of the area's drinking water. The Bush administration called it "environmental terrorism of an immense and shocking magnitude."

27 JANUARY 1991

15:55:00z

"Capt. Keith Rosenkranz . . . Shepherd 21 . . . 3021 lima . . . Four CBU-87 . . . 16:05z takeoff time . . . TOT is 18:22:30 . . . 27 January '91 . . . Tail number is 357."

The target for tonight's mission is a POL facility located in southern Iraq near Basrah. According to intel, the site doubled as a major refueling depot for Republican Guard tank divisions. Sixteen Vipers from the 421st TFS had been fragged to destroy the facility, and, if we were successful, Saddam Hussein's elite forces would suffer a severe setback.

Stitch is the package commander. His formation, Howler 11, departed the airfield at 15:47z. Collar 11 flight, led by Tiny, followed three minutes later. Our element is the third in line, and, as soon as I'm in position on the runway, I turn off my taxi light. With my feet on the brakes, I run my engine up to 80 percent. Engine checks good. Flight controls are good. I pull my throttle back and turn my taxi light back on, signaling that I'm ready to go.

When all four taxi lights come on, Grumpy releases his brakes and begins his takeoff roll. Capt. Carlos "Jackal" Nejaime follows twenty seconds later. Grover is flying in the number three position. As soon as he releases his brakes, I begin my countdown. My hands grip the stick and throttle while my eyes focus on the data-entry display. "Eighteen . . . nineteen . . . twenty." I let off the brakes, drop my heels to the floor, and shove the throttle into afterburner.

Grumpy levels off at 24,000 feet on a 275-degree heading. As we approach the Saudi coastline, Grumpy turns toward the Railroad refueling track and switches the flight to pink six. After we check in, I push my throttle up and start a rejoin on Grover. Performing a fighter turn on the tanker with four aircraft at night is the last thing Grumpy wants to do, so Grover and I will hang back until he completes the rejoin. Once Grumpy is stabilized in the contact position below the fueling boom, Grover and I will execute our rejoin to the tanker's right wing.

18:15:00z

I'm level at 24,000 feet just inside the northwest border that separates Kuwait from Iraq. My airspeed is 375 knots, and I'm sixty miles southwest of the target, eight miles in trail of Grover. I roll left, checking for SAMs and AAA, but the only thing visible below me are dozens of small fires. It looks like the B-52s were here recently.

"Tonka, Collar 11," Tiny calls out.

"Collar 11, this is Tonka."

"Collar 11 is bed with all of us."

"Tonka copies."

"Bed" is tonight's egress code word. Tiny's element just completed its bombing run, and it sounds like everyone made it in and out of the target area safely.

"Tonka, Pointer 33," another pilot radios.

"Pointer 33, this is Tonka."

"Pointer 33 request snap to next nearest tanker."

"Tonka copies. We have a tanker in Pam."

"Pointer 33, I'll take that."

Before Tonka can answer, Grover interrupts: "Shepherd 23 has an SA-2 at ten o'clock!"

I check to my left and immediately spot the missile corkscrewing upward.

"Shepherd 24 has tally," I respond.

My heart begins to pound. I check my RWR for activity, but the scope is clean. The missile doesn't appear to be guiding on anyone. A few seconds later, it burns itself out and disappears. On the edge of my seat, I continue toward the target. As soon as I'm within forty miles of the POL site, I reach toward my up-front control panel and hit the air-to-ground button. After a few sweeps of the ground-map radar, a set of bright returns appears on the north side of the cursors.

"Shepherd 21, check cameras on, armed up," Grumpy radios.

My camera is already on, and I check one more time to make sure the master arm switch is in Arm. After I slew my cursors overtop the radar returns, I hit the pinky switch and call up the EXP mode. The picture looks great.

"Shepherd 23," I radio to Grover. "Shepherd 24 has bright contact returns north. Are you going to take those?"

"Shepherd 23, affirm," Grover answers.

"Copy. I'm going to take the southern side of those bright contacts."

"Shepherd 23's on the northern."

18:20:00z

I hit the pinky switch again, and the radar transitions to DBS1. A collection of oil tanks begins to appear on my MFD directly under my cursors. Since Grover plans to drop on the north side, I press my thumb against the cursor/enable switch and slew to the south. In less than three minutes I'll be over the target. Howler and Collar flights have already dropped their bombs and should be over Bubiyan Island by now. At my left eleven o'clock, I can see a large fire burning out of control. Bright orange flames billow toward the sky, illuminating the desert floor.

"Shepherd 21 has some contacts about two miles to the right of the cursors," Grumpy calls out.

"Shepherd 22 showing some tanks there," Jackal replies.

I switch to DBS2 to refine the target even further. The tanks Jackal referred to jump out at me. This is going to be good. I make one last correction with my cursors to ensure that my bombs cover the southern section of the facility. Suddenly a wall of tracers appears off my left wing. My head is on a swivel, and adrenaline is shooting through my veins.

"Shepherd 23, heavy AAA to the north!" I scream.

Grumpy should have a close-up view of the AAA, but his main concern is making sure the rest of us know where the target is.

"Shepherd 21's got a big bright return that's short of the cursors," Grumpy says calmly. "To the left and long of that I show some bright returns."

"Two same!" Jackal acknowledges.

I'm less than twenty miles from the target, and the AAA is getting worse. It's obvious that this a high-value target. The Republican Guard is working hard to defend it.

While descending toward the target, I reach down with my left hand and switch my VTR to the HUD position. My airspeed is 377 knots, and I'm passing through 24,300 feet.

"Tonka, picture for Sprite," someone calls out.

"Picture clear," the controller replies.

Iraqi guns are pouring everything they have into the air. I'm tempted to roll in on one of them, but I continue toward my target. As I descend through 21,500 feet, I notice a large explosion at my left ten o'clock. Grumpy's bombs must have just hit the facility. The AAA is getting worse. It's beginning to look like I'll have to fly through it to reach my target.

"Shepherd 22," Grumpy calls out. "If you've got my CBU in sight, there's AAA coming up about a half mile to the northeast."

All of a sudden, I get a missile launch indication in my headset. I check my RWR scope and quickly transition outside to see if I can pick up a visual. I rock to the left, then back to the right. Nothing! My chest is heaving, and my oxygen mask is filled with sweat. I'm less than ten miles from the target. I have to make a decision. Should I continue to descend or remain at medium altitude? I've completed my radar work, and the TD box is sitting on top of the burning tanks. I might as well use CCRP. CBU-87 is an area munition, and the bombs should go right through the TD box. Dropping at a higher altitude should also help me avoid some of the smaller-caliber AAA.

I quickly check my HUD. I'm only seven miles from the target. My airspeed is 475 knots and I'm twelve degrees nose low passing through 15,500 feet. While correcting toward the steering line, I get the max-toss cue indication. "Damn it!" I say to myself. "AAA on the nose." Red tracers shoot up in front of me. Every muscle tightens. One of these shells *has* to hit me. I can't jink, though. I have to stay on the steering line until my bombs come off.

"Altitude, altitude," a voice rings out. It's Bitchin' Betty, the F-16's Voice Message System, which "speaks" when certain conditions occur, such as flying too low. The voice is female—guaranteed to get a pilot's attention. Grumpy set the floor at 10,000 feet and I programmed my automatic low-altitude warning (ALOW) for 11,000 to make sure I don't go below it. My right thumb is holding down the pickle button while my eyes remain focused on the steering line. Finally, the solution cue appears and begins to descend toward my flight-path marker. The two meet as I pass through 10,800 feet, and all four canisters drop from beneath my wings.

I immediately pull back on my stick and push my throttle up to mil power. Red tracers whiz past me. I expect to feel a thump. But it never comes. I jink left, hold the position for a few seconds, then jink back to the right. The bombs should be hitting any second, so I roll the jet left and stare at the facility.

"Good fires down there," I say out loud. "Come on bombs, hit!"

Seconds later, the entire south side of the complex lights up. It looks like a giant fireworks show, and I've got the best seat in the house. The bright flashes of white and yellow last a few seconds. They're immediately followed by three secondary explosions. Flames burst into the air, lighting up the entire area.

"There they go," I yell. "Whooo-hooo!"

19:34:00z

I taxi off the runway and follow Grover to the de-arm area. Once the crew chiefs complete their inspections, we head for the hot pits to refuel. I feel a great sense of euphoria.

This is the most satisfying mission I've flown since the beginning of the war. The rest of the guys must feel the same way. We meet in the life-support shop and congratulate each other on a job well done. After the debrief, we walk over to the enlisted mess hall for a late-night spaghetti dinner.

The four of us finished eating by 01:45 and caught the shuttle bus back to the o'club. It was Super Bowl Sunday in the United States, and the game between the New York Giants and the Buffalo Bills was being televised—live—in the desert. The lounge was packed. President and Mrs. Bush paid special tribute to all of the troops in the desert. Fans wore yellow ribbons and waved small American flags. It felt good to know that people back home supported us.

The New York Giants dominated most of the second half, but Bills' quarterback Jim Kelly moved his team into field-goal position during the game's final minute. Trailing by one point, Bill's kicker Scott Norwood lined up a forty-seven-yard field goal that could give Buffalo its first Super Bowl victory. But with four seconds to go, the kick sailed wide right, and the closest game in Super Bowl history was won by the Giants, 20-19.

28.
PATRIOTISM

The biggest surprise of Operation Desert Storm had been the lack of activity by the Iraqi air force. Intel said the majority of Iraq's aircraft were hiding in concrete reinforced underground bunkers north of Baghdad. But CNN's Pentagon correspondent, Wolf Blitzer, reported that Saddam Hussein may have worked out a secret deal to shelter his aircraft in neighboring Iran. Blitzer said a high-level Iraqi delegation was in Tehran just before the Gulf War began. The group was led by Izzat Ibrahim, the number two official on the Revolutionary Command Council, and included Iraq's deputy prime minister, the minister of state for foreign affairs, the minister of transport and communications, the deputy oil minister, and several members of Parliament.

Shortly after the delegation returned to Baghdad, Iraqi civilian airliners—including 747s, 727s and 707s—took off and landed at commercial airports in Tehran and Mashad. This occurred *before* the start of the war. Yesterday, several of Iraq's top-line fighters took off out of northern Iraq and landed across the border in Iran. It's unclear why the aircraft left, and Blitzer said the Bush administration was concerned about renewed cooperation between Saddam Hussein and the Iranian government.

I wondered if Iraqi fighter pilots were defecting, or if Saddam Hussein was planning to use the aircraft against the coalition at a later date. According to CNN, Iran's National Security Council issued a statement saying: "The Islamic Republic of Iran will strongly prevent any action which breaches its neutrality." Gen. Schwarzkopf responded to the statement by telling reporters in Riyadh that the U.S. government "should take Iran at its word." Schwarzkopf quickly added that contingencies existed to take care of Iraqi aircraft that re-entered the conflict from Iranian bases.

Later in the briefing, Gen. Schwarzkopf told reporters that F-111 fighter-bombers swept into Kuwait late Saturday and dropped 2,000-pound GBU-15 data-linked bombs on two inland pipeline manifolds used to direct crude oil toward the offshore Sea Island loading station. The spill had been detected last Thursday, and oil had been surging into the Gulf at a rate of 1.2 million barrels a day. Gen. Schwarzkopf said it would take about twenty-four hours for the oil in the pipeline between the Sea Island facility and the inland manifolds to burn itself out.

When Gen. Schwarzkopf concluded his briefing, CNN military analysts began to discuss the impending ground war. One expert predicted that a full-scale ground offensive would begin in a matter of days. But Secretary of Defense Dick Cheney said that an allied attack against ground positions in Kuwait would not occur until the Bush administration was "absolutely certain that we have gained everything we can from the air campaign. There is no reason for us to rush into a ground conflict that would mean unnecessary American and allied casualties."

Another analyst predicted that allied ground forces would drive the Iraqis out of Kuwait and continue north to Baghdad in search of Saddam Hussein. Recent comments out of Washington suggested there would be a need to remove him from power and eliminate Iraq's offensive military ability. Arab members of the coalition privately hoped the war to free Kuwait would also end with Saddam Hussein's downfall. Publicly, however, there was concern that the focus of the war was shifting from the liberation of Kuwait to the systematic destruction of Iraq. Ali Hillal Dessouki, a political scientist from Cairo, Egypt, said: "The longer this goes on, the more restless all Arabs will get. No matter how many people think the invasion of Kuwait was wrong, there is an emotional dimension involved in watching an Arab people being bombed every day by American planes."

During an interview with reporters, Egypt's deputy foreign minister, Boutros Boutros Ghali, said his country did not want to see the Iraqi armed forces destroyed, and would support the allied effort only to obtain the liberation of Kuwait.

"Our position is not to change the regime inside Iraq or to interfere in the internal affairs of Iraq," Ghali said. "We cannot obtain the liberation of Kuwait without confronting Iraqi forces, but we are not interested in seeing the destruction of those forces. The aim of U.N. Security Council Resolution 678, which is the legal basis of the whole operation, is to liberate Kuwait, not to change the government in Iraq."

29 JANUARY 1991
On the previous night, two pilots from the 388th TFW were returned home to the United States. One was a member of the 421st TFS and the other belonged to the 4th. The pilot from my squadron was the same one who was grounded for strafing an enemy SAM site near Baghdad. He returned to the cockpit a few days later in a strike mission against the H-3 complex in western Iraq. But during this sortie, he lost track of his wingman and pointed the nose of his aircraft at various SAM sites located near the facility. According to Grumpy, he was heard on tape cursing the wing leadership for grounding him and not allowing him to strafe. The commanders reviewed our films, and when Col. Huddle listened to the tape, the pilot's fate was sealed.

I was shocked and disappointed. I knew he was upset the first time he was grounded, and we talked about the incident that night in the beer tent. I felt the wing leadership was overreacting. Later, however, Raj told me that Col. Huddle had called a special pilot meeting and showed everyone the film.

"If you saw the tape, Rosey," Raj said, "you'd understand why they sent him home. It wasn't the same guy you and I know. He was a wild man. He was out of control."

The pilot from the 4th TFS had inadvertently launched an AIM-9 Sidewinder missile for the second time in ten days. The first incident occurred during the bombing raid against the Tawaitha nuclear research facility. After dropping his bombs, the pilot transitioned to the air-combat mode (ACM) by positioning the dogfight/missile override switch on his throttle to the dogfight position. Unfortunately, the master arm switch was still in Arm, and his thumb was still on the pickle button. As soon as he selected dogfight, the missile came flying off the rail. Fortunately, no one was injured.

It would be easy to second-guess the pilot for having his thumb on the pickle button, but, in the heat of battle, when enemy soldiers are doing everything in their power to kill you, even the most experienced aviator can become task-saturated. Simple tasks, such as lifting your thumb off the pickle button, become difficult. And, in fact, Lt. Col. Welsh was able to overlook the first mistake. When it happened again, however, some of the pilots in the squadron began to complain. Fratricide is a major concern, and when a Sidewinder comes off the rail, it doesn't differentiate between an enemy pilot and a friendly one.

I hadn't flown in two days, and the time off was rejuvenating. I arrived at the o'club around 12:00 for lunch and sat with some of my friends from the 69th.

"This is our last meal at Al Minhad," Stal said glumly.

"What do you mean?" I asked.

"We found out this morning the rest of the squadron is being sent to King Fahd. If you think we have it bad here, you should see that place—it's a dump!"

"How long are you supposed to be there?"

"Col. Navarro says we're only going to be there for a week or two, but I don't trust anything he says."

For the last ten days, about a third of the Werewolves had flown dedicated Scud missions out of King Fahd AB in Saudi Arabia. The pilots were living in tents and operating out of one of the Myrtle Beach A-10 squadrons.

"Some of the A-10 pilots have been flying road reconnaissance missions during the day in search of Scuds," Maj. Mike "Cookie" Cook began. "Our unit generally flies at night. The F-15E Strike Eagles fly out of Al's garage [Al Kharj AB], and they've been flying at night also."

"Do you have to sit cockpit alert?" I asked.

"No," Cookie answered. "Guys usually stay in the squadron when they're on duty. If Scuds are located or a launch occurs, a scramble order is sent from CENTAF headquarters. As soon as we take off, we proceed to a tanker track and top off our tanks. Once we come off the tanker, we contact AWACS or ABCCC, and they send us to an area to search. Half the time it's to the western box, and the other half it's to the southern one.

"Finding Scud launchers at night is extremely difficult," Cookie continued. "A lot of times we don't find anything. Our time on station is limited to four hours, which includes four or five trips to the tanker. If we haven't found anything by then, we'll request a backup target from AWACS and hit it on the way back to King Fahd AB."

"Is there anything to do during the day?" I asked.

"Hell, no!" Stal snapped. "You can't walk around in shorts or go run, like you can here. We're required to wear flight suits, and we have to have our chem masks with us at all times in case there's a Scud alert."

"They have a phone tent there," Rock interjected.

"You gotta be kidding!" I replied. "I thought no one was allowed to call off base during the war."

"That's a Navarroism," Stal remarked. "You can call anywhere you want to at King Fahd."

The Werewolves left after lunch, and many of us were sorry to see them go. I spent the rest of the day at the club relaxing in front of the television. Later in the evening, I rode the shuttle to the air traffic control tower. I was the supervisor of flying (SOF) that night and I'd be on duty until 06:00.

30 JANUARY 1991

Opie relieved me in the control tower at 05:50. Twenty minutes later, I was in the mess hall eating breakfast. As soon as I finished, I walked into the lounge to watch President Bush deliver his State of the Union address:

> For two centuries, we've done the hard work of freedom. And tonight, we lead the world in facing down a threat to decency and humanity. Saddam Hussein's unprovoked invasion—his ruthless, systematic rape of a peaceful neighbor—violated everything the community of nations holds dear. The world has said this aggression would not stand—and it will not stand.

At this point, everyone in the chamber interrupted the president's speech with a standing ovation. I've never felt such a deep sense of patriotism in all my life. The president continued:

> There is no one more devoted, more committed to the hard work of freedom, than every soldier and sailor, every marine, airman, and coast guardsman—every man and woman now serving in the Persian Gulf. Each of them has volunteered to provide for this nation's defense—and now they bravely struggle to earn for America, for the world, and for future generations, a just and lasting peace. Our commitment to them must be equal of their commitment to their country. They are truly America's finest.

Once again, the president's address was interrupted with applause. I glanced at others in the lounge as the ovation continued. Everyone gleamed with pride.

> Our purpose in the Persian Gulf remains constant: to drive Iraq out of Kuwait, to restore Kuwait's legitimate government, and to ensure the stability and security of this critical region.
> Let me make clear what I mean by the region's stability and security. We do not seek the destruction of Iraq, its culture, or its people. Rather, we seek an Iraq that uses its great resources, not to destroy, not to serve the ambitions of a tyrant, but to build a better life for itself and its neighbors. We seek a Persian Gulf where conflict is no longer the rule, where the strong are neither tempted nor able to intimidate the weak.

As soon as President Bush completed his State of the Union address, I walked back to my room and went to bed. I fell asleep thinking about the president's speech, but, it seemed, no sooner did I close my eyes, than the alarm went off. I dragged myself out of bed around 15:00, ran down to the 4th and back, took a shower, had a bite, and then left for the squadron. I was scheduled to fly my eighth combat mission that night. By 21:00, Grumpy, Jackal, Ensign, and I were in the weapons shop reviewing our mission envelopes.

After Grumpy gave us a time hack, Maj. Marsh began the briefing with a stunning announcement: "Late last night, Iraqi forces crossed into Saudi Arabia and captured the deserted town of Khafji. The Iraqis advanced with fifteen hundred troops and fifty tanks in four separate attacks. Air strikes and ground fire destroyed twenty-four Iraqi tanks and thirteen other vehicles. Unfortunately, we just received confirmation that twelve marines were killed during the battle. If I hear any more before you step, I'll pass it on."

After Maj. Marsh completed his briefing, Lt. Col. Rackley walked in to tell us to take off as soon as possible. "Once you come off the tanker, contact ABCCC, and they'll tell you where to go. You may be dropping near allied forces, so make sure you have the right coordinates, and double-check them before you drop."

Thirty minutes after Grumpy's standard briefing, the four of us stepped to our jets. We cranked engines at 22:20 and taxied fifteen minutes later. As we approached the arming area, we were ordered to shut down. CENTAF headquarters had canceled the mission. Everyone was disappointed. We were looking forward to helping the U.S. Army take on the Iraqis.

31 JANUARY 1991

> Oh, Iraqis! Oh, Arabs! Oh, Muslims who believe in justice! Your faithful and courageous ground forces have moved to teach the aggressors the lessons they deserve. They have launched their lightning ground attack, bearing high the banner, saying God is great, and crushed the armies of atheism as they advance, routing those who could run away while cursing the infidels and heathens. Our units advanced on the battlefield approximately twenty kilometers into the battlefield where the enemy in the Saudi kingdom of evil is found.

This message was broadcast over Baghdad radio the previous day, as Iraqi tanks rolled into Khafji. Many of us thought the incursion was the beginning of the long-awaited ground war, but Iraq's bid to draw allied forces into a ground battle ended in death, retreat, and surrender. According to Gen. Schwarzkopf on television, Iraqi forces approached the border and signaled they were going to give up. "Their turrets were reversed and their main guns were locked," Schwarzkopf said. "Ten minutes later, they were engaging Saudi forces in combat. We have reports that the Iraqis did go into Khafji," Schwarzkopf continued. "Of course, as you know, Al Khafji has been abandoned and deserted since the very first day . . . so there was no one there."

When Iraqi troops crossed the border, they were engaged by a U.S. Marine light armored infantry battalion. It was during this battle that the twelve marines lost their lives.

After discussing the battle of Khafji, Gen. Schwarzkopf gave a detailed accounting of the first two weeks of war. The commanding general told reporters that more than 30,000 sorties had been flown and nineteen allied aircraft had been lost since the beginning of Operation Desert Storm. Schwarzkopf said allied aircraft attacked thirty-eight Iraqi airfields, some at least four times. He said that seventy underground aircraft shelters had been destroyed, and eighty-nine Iraqi aircraft had flown to Iran.

"Allied forces have gained absolute command of the air," Schwarzkopf announced. "The simple fact of the matter is that now every time an Iraqi airplane takes off the ground, it's running away."

Continuing with his summary, Gen. Schwarzkopf told the throng of reporters that thirty-one nuclear, chemical, or biological sites had been struck in more than 535 sorties. There were fifty-three Scud launches—twenty-seven against Saudi Arabia and twenty-six against Israel. There were thirty-five Scuds launched during the first week of fighting, and eighteen during the second. More than 1,500 sorties had been flown against the Scuds, and all major missile production facilities had been eliminated. Schwarzkopf also said that thirty-three of thirty-six targeted bridges had been hit, with more than 790 sorties, virtually cutting off supply lines to the south.

"Two days ago," Gen. Schwarzkopf declared, "we observed a supply convoy backed up for fifteen miles on the road from Baghdad to Basrah. It was backed up on the north side of the road right near the bridge that we had knocked out. Obviously, we attacked the convoy, and we observed countless secondary explosions when we attacked it."

During the briefing, Gen. Schwarzkopf showed dramatic footage of air attacks over Iraq, including the bombing of mobile Scud launchers, hardened aircraft shelters, and bridges. The reporters watched intensely, many clearly awed by the technological advantage we held over the Iraqis. On one occasion, Schwarzkopf bellowed: "I'm going to show you a picture of the luckiest man in Iraq on this particular day." A video came on, showing an Iraqi vehicle speeding across a bridge that was being targeted by an American pilot. "Keep your eye on the cross-hairs," he told the reporters. "Lookit here. And now through the rearview mirror . . ." All of a sudden, the bridge disintegrated. Fortunately for the driver of the vehicle, he had already sped across.

After the briefing, I left the club to attend Mass. I prayed for an end to the fighting. I liked to think that God was on our side, but deep inside, I knew He loved the people of Iraq just as He loved us. I hated the thought of killing people. I hated this war.

As soon as the Mass was over, I walked down to the squadron. I was scheduled to fly later in the evening, and, after I completed some paperwork in the weapons shop, I walked over to the pilot lounge. Having decided to skip dinner at the o'club, I ate an MRE instead. During the meal, SSgt. Hakeem Basheerud-Deen walked in with a large bag of mail, which he dumped on the table. Deliveries had been slow, so everyone rushed over to search through the pile. Some of the letters were from family and friends, but the majority were addressed to "any serviceman." I decided to open a few, and I was amazed at how supportive everyone was back home. Everyone in the lounge was touched by the show of support. One of the envelopes Norge opened included a check for ten dollars.

"Listen to this, guys," Norge declared, holding the check in the air. "The person writes: 'Keep up the good work. I know phone calls to the states are expensive, so enjoy the next one on me."

"Look what I got," Capt. Lex "Pappy" Brockington remarked. "Someone sent me a shirt."

"What's it look like?" Badger asked.

Pappy held the shirt up to his chest for everyone to see. It was black, with a large American flag on the front of it.

"Here's a letter from someone who isn't very supportive," Grover chuckled. "Listen to what this guy has to say:

"Dear Any Service Person,
 Do you believe in what you may be risking your fucking life for? Do you think we should be wasting our money and time over there playing a goddamn John Wayne movie? Jesus Christ, our stupid fucking moralistic fascist government is about to shut down for lack of funds. All the national parks are closing. And the museums on the mall are, too—just so George can parade around proclaiming that he has done the 'right' thing.
 Look, I don't care if you're a fucking patriot or a punk. But I get pissed off when I think that some asshole aristocrat can jeopardize your lives and my life, just because he wants oil or because he wants to be right.

"The next sentence is written in capital letters," Grover continued.

"NOT ALL THE FUCKING OIL IN THE GODDAMNED WORLD IS WORTH THE LIFE OF ONE OF YOU GUYS!
 I know this letter won't make your 135-degree day—I'm sorry. But I won't write some bull-shit I don't believe in. I also won't write 'kick ol' Saddam's ass for me, boy.' I don't believe in that either. So write me back. I'd like to know how you feel about this occupation.

"The letter is signed 'Mr. Fuck Your War,'" Grover concluded.

It upset me, and I asked Grover if he planned to write him back.

"Hell, no!" Grover snapped. "I have nothing to say to this guy."

"Let me have the letter," I asked. "I'll tell him what I think." I read the letter again, then grabbed a pad of paper:

Mr. Fuck Your War,
 In reply to your letter. The only time I feel remotely bad about being in the Middle East is when I realize I am fighting for the freedom of people like you. It's painfully obvious that some-where along the road of life, you forgot to get on the bus. It's easy to see that you have been walking uphill ever since.
 It was the will of God that allowed me to be born in the greatest country in the world, the

United States of America. While the country may have its problems, its overall intentions are good. The United States has always stood for freedom and human rights. Over the last century, many men and women have fought for that freedom and many have died doing so.

As a result, freedom has begun to spread throughout the rest of the world. Have you noticed lately the reforms in the Soviet Union? What about the reunification of Germany? Don't forget about the students in China, either. It may have taken fifty years, but communism is starting to take a backseat to freedom.

You should be happy you have a national park to go to. Would you prefer a wall and barbed wire on each of your state's borders? Be happy that you can watch a John Wayne movie instead of state-run propaganda. Be happy that you can vote for "some asshole aristocrat" instead of having your life dictated by the likes of people like Fidel Castro or your good friend Saddam Hussein.

As far as your life being jeopardized—give me a break! You obviously don't know what freedom is, let alone how to fight for it. Why don't you take a trip to South Africa, North Korea, or China? Spend some time there and then let me know what you think of the United States and people like me that volunteered to serve our country. If you don't like our "stupid fucking moralistic fascist government," then leave. Remember, it's a free country. You can leave if you want to!

The next time you put a little gas in your car or stand in front of a crowd and burn the American flag, remember that some "fucking patriot" like myself fought for you to have that right.

421st Tactical Fighter Squadron

As soon as I finished the letter, I put it in an envelope and asked SSgt. Basheerud-Dean to put it in the outgoing mail.

29.
FRIENDLY FIRE

It was hard to believe another week had passed. This night marked the third time I'd been on MPC duty since the beginning of the war. In a way, I was looking forward to the break. I'd flown six combat sorties in the past eight days, and it looked as though I'd be flying even more in the weeks ahead. The ground war could start at any time, and the 388th TFW would have an integral role once the campaign began.

3 FEBRUARY 1991

As soon as Raj and I finished dinner, we met Spike, Lips, and Stinger on the front steps of the o'club. The base shuttle pulled up a few minutes later, and the five of us stepped aboard.

"How's the flying going, Rosey?" Stinger asked.

"It's going good. I've flown ten combat missions so far."

"How many hours do you have?" Lips asked.

"A little over forty. We've been hitting Iraqi troops pretty hard the last few nights," I continued. "I flew with Taz, Jabba, and Ensign last night, and we hit a target about ten miles north of a small Kuwaiti town called Al Abdaliyah. The IP-to-target run took us right through the heart of Kuwait. It seemed like a normal mission until I began to descend. The night was dark and the FLIR picture was extremely poor. I completed my radar work and started down about thirty miles from the target. Passing 18,000 feet, I began to realize it wasn't a cloud layer I was flying through. It was smoke. I could see bright orange flashes filtering through the blackness. All of a sudden, I broke through the deck and the entire country appeared as though it were on fire. It was like flying into hell. Dozens of oil wells were burning out of control, their flames shooting hundreds of feet into the air. I pickled my bombs off around 8,700 feet, pushed the throttle to mil, and started jinking. There was AAA everywhere. The fires were so bright, I felt like I was flying a daytime sortie. I'm sure the Iraqi gunners saw me. I felt naked and vulnerable. As I continued to climb, the flames began to disappear. Before long, I was surrounded by blackness again. It was one of the eeriest experiences I've ever had."

As I completed the story, the shuttle came to a stop in front of the 421st. Raj and I walked into the squadron and immediately headed for the pilot lounge to check our mailboxes. Some of the Black Widows were getting ready to fly, while others relaxed in front of the television.

"You know those marines that died in the battle of Khafji yesterday?" Harpo asked as

Raj and I walked by. He had a grim look on his face.

"What about them?" Raj replied.

"Some of them were killed by friendly fire. CNN is gonna talk about it in a minute ... grab a seat."

"CNN has learned that seven of the eleven marines killed during the battle of Khafji died when an American-made missile struck the personnel carrier they were traveling in," the report began. "During this afternoon's military briefing from Riyadh, Marine Maj. Gen. Robert Johnston, chief of staff for the U.S. Central Command, told reporters the situation was still being investigated. But for the moment, it appears as though the seven marines who lost their lives were the victims of friendly fire."

"The missile that hit their transport entered the rear left-hand side during the fierce engagement with Iraqi tanks and armored personnel carriers," Johnston announced. Pausing, the Marine general continued: "What I'm describing for you is very intense, very close combat."

When asked what type of missile hit the vehicle, the general responded: "We have every reason to conclude that it was a Maverick missile that struck it."

Gen. Johnston was also asked about a second incident that left one Marine dead and two more injured when their convoy was hit by cluster bombs.

"That was a convoy well inside the border," Johnston replied. "And, again, because of the lack of proximity to enemy fire, it would appear reasonable to expect that that, too, could have been friendly fire."

I felt bad for the families of the Marines. I also felt bad for the two pilots who were responsible for their deaths. Flying low-altitude close air support missions at night is extremely demanding. The pilots involved in each incident were probably working with a forward air controller who may have been airborne or on the ground. Pilots flying CAS missions normally hold at a contact point until they are notified by their assigned FAC. When contacted, pilots will authenticate for security and provide the FAC with their call sign, mission number, number/type aircraft, number of ordnance/fusing, and play time. The FAC will then give the pilot a "nine-line brief": initial point; magnetic heading to the target; distance in nautical miles; target elevation; target description; target coordinates/location; target identification marks; location of friendlies in relation to the target; and the egress direction. Timing is critical, especially if the friendly forces are under attack. Once the pilot receives the nine-line briefing, he has very little time to load the coordinates, review his map, and commence the attack.

When a pilot leaves the contact point, he normally drops down to low altitude and accelerates to 540 knots. In all likelihood, the target area will be unfamiliar. Split-second decisions have to be made, and a pilot doesn't have time to distinguish between enemy and friendly forces. Pilots have to trust what the FAC gives them.

Incidents such as the one that occurred in Al Khafji are not unusual on the battlefield. During the Civil War, the Confederate Stonewall Jackson died when he and his staff were mistaken for Union cavalrymen near Chancellorsville, and fired upon by his own men. During World War II, just after the D-Day invasion, VII Corps soldiers advanced across Normandy beach and were hit by U.S. Army Air Force bombs.

After the report, Raj and I began work on the next day's packages. We'd been focusing on the Republican Guard for more than a week, and Gen. Schwarzkopf said the attacks were having a devastating effect. That may have been true, but most of the pilots in the wing believed we could be doing better. The ordnance we'd been dropping had been sitting in bomb dumps for years. Half the time, it didn't even work. CBU canisters were old and corroded. Fuses malfunctioned. In fact, one F-16 pilot from another wing was forced to eject from his aircraft when a fuse malfunction caused his bombs to detonate upon release. Fortunately, the pilot survived the explosion and was rescued by SAR forces off the coast of Kuwait.

The weapons we'd been fragged with may have had a psychological impact on Iraqi forces, but when it came to the destruction of Iraq's heavy armor, they were hardly effective. The older versions of CBU were unreliable, and dropping a string of MK-82s on revetted tanks from medium altitude was a waste of time. Everyone preferred to drop CBU-87, but the commanders insisted on saving them for the ground war. If our goal was to destroy as much armor as possible *before* the ground war, why not drop the most effective weapon from the start?

Another source of frustration was the lack of accurate target coordinates. CENTAF planners developed target lists based on intelligence information, data provided by E-8A J-STARS (Joint Surveillance Target Attack Radar System) aircraft, and data from reconnaissance platforms, including satellites, U-2/TR-1, and RF-4 aircraft. Once the information was verified, the targets would be incorporated into the ATO, which arrived on base each evening between 17:00 and 19:00. The mission planning cell would take the information and spend the rest of the night building the attack packages. The first launch would occur shortly after sunrise, and by the time pilots arrived over the target area, the coordinates they'd been given would already be twelve to fifteen hours old. Those of us who flew at night, when Iraqi ground forces liked to move, ended up using coordinates as old as thirty hours. AWACS and ABCCC were supposed to provide updates, but, more often than not, we were simply told to proceed to our primary target. A tremendous amount of planning went into each mission. When we would roll in on a target, and there was nothing there, it was disheartening, to say the least.

Lt. Col. Scott, promoted to assistant director of operations after Lt. Col. Welsh took over as squadron commander of the 4th, came in around 22:00 to say he was working on a project that would help alleviate the problem. The only question was whether or not Gen. Glosson and his staff would buy off on it. Over the next two hours, Scotty was in and out of the planning room at least a dozen times. Everyone was curious about the plan, but Scotty wasn't saying anything.

Shortly after midnight, Scotty hung up the secure phone and asked for everyone's attention. He told us to take one of the four-ships from the 4th and change its call sign to Pointer. Two of the aircraft would be loaded with four canisters of MK-20 Rockeye, and the other two would carry six MK-82s. Scotty planned to have the four-ship split into two separate elements as soon as it departed the tanker track. One element would hold over southern Iraq, and the other would orbit over central Kuwait. We were confused about the plan, but Scotty told us not to worry.

"I'll explain everything to the mission commander in the morning," Scotty said as he prepared to leave. "If this works, it will significantly change the way the 388th TFW operates during the day."

Later in the evening, Col. Casmier "Cash" Jaszczak paid a surprise visit to the planning room. Col. Jaszczak had been recently named the new vice commander of the 388th TFW (deployed). He had arrived a few days before from MacDill AFB in Tampa, Florida, where he had been the F-16 director of operations for the 56th Tactical Training Wing. Those of us who had had a chance to talk with Col. Jaszczak over the past few days had come to appreciate his leadership style. He attended briefings; he drove out on the flightline to see us off when we launched; and he was the first one to greet us after we shut down our engines. Col. Navarro, on the other hand, had yet to fly a single combat sortie with our unit. In fact, I couldn't even remember the last time he was in the squadron.

As soon as Cash walked into the room, he rolled up his sleeves and asked if he could help us mission-plan. Lips and I mentioned we were having trouble convincing CENTAF headquarters that the ordnance they'd fragged us with was unsuitable for the targets we'd be attacking later that day. Without any hesitation, Cash picked up the secure phone line and called Gen. Glosson. Ten minutes later, he hung up and announced the ordnance was being changed.

As the evening progressed, Col. Jaszczak visited with every member of the MPC team and thanked us personally for the hard work we'd been putting in. He asked if we were holding up okay, and he also asked about our family members back home.

"Your families have given up a lot," Cash said, "and I promise you'll be reunited with them soon. You're involved in something special here, and, as far as I'm concerned, you're all heroes. You will remember this experience for many years to come, and every one of you will be richer for it."

4 FEBRUARY 1991

According to CNN, six U.S. helicopter crewmen were killed the day before in two separate crashes. Four of the deaths were caused when a Marine UH-1 crashed on a noncombat mission in eastern Saudi Arabia. The other crew members died when the Cobra gunship they were flying crashed during an escort mission inside Saudi Arabia. CNN also reported that a B-52 Stratofortress crashed in the Indian Ocean near the island of Diego Garcia. Three crew members were rescued, and three more were considered missing. The missing airmen raised the total of Americans missing to twenty-six since the war began. The deaths of the six helicopter pilots increased the number of Americans killed to eighteen.

As of that night, the number of allied sorties had passed the 40,000 mark—10,000 more missions than were flown against Japan in the final fourteen months of World War II. Despite the incredible number of sorties, the coalition had only lost twenty-five aircraft. During the Korean War, the U.S. lost 1,466 air force and 1,248 navy and marine aircraft. In Vietnam, the U.S. Air Force alone lost 2,257 planes.

I arrived at the squadron around 22:00, scheduled to fly an early morning go with Capt. Lenny "Tiny" Dick, Capt. Tom "Swabby" Schaub, and Capt. Ed "Tonto" Christian. Takeoff time would be 03:20 local, and the four of us would attack the Hammurabi division of Iraq's Republican Guard. Tonto would be my wingman, and the two of us were looking over the contents of our mission envelope when Grumpy poked his head in. He asked to see me.

"How would you like to go back and be a member of the 4th again?" Grumpy asked.

"I don't understand," I answered hesitantly.

"The Fuujins are going to lose a couple of pilots soon," Grumpy continued. "I know how hard it was for you to leave the 4th."

Without giving it much thought, I told Grumpy that going back to the 4th would be fine.

"I'll talk to Damien and Taz about it," Grumpy said.

When I returned to the weapons shop, I sat next to Tonto, and the two of us continued to review for the night's mission. My mind wasn't on flying, however. The only thing I was thinking about was whether or not I really wanted to go back to the 4th again. The Black Widows had come a long way during the previous five months. Why leave, then? I was sure I'd enjoy working for Lt. Col. Welsh. I knew my friends would welcome me back. And, heaven knows, it sure would make Colette happy. Going back to the 4th sounded like a great opportunity. But I was really not sure I wanted to go.

My eleventh combat mission turned out to be extremely satisfying. Directly below me in the HUD field-of-view was the entire Hammurabi Republican Guard division. Tonto and I made two passes each, and there were plenty of secondary fires burning when we departed the area. We touched down at Al Minhad shortly before 07:00 and debriefed the mission over breakfast at the o'club. Iraqi soldiers may have thought they were safe under the cloak of darkness, but the truth of the matter was, they had no place to hide.

5 FEBRUARY 1991

On the previous morning, the 4th TFS had initiated a new program that would dramatically change the way airpower was used in the KTO. Since the focus of the air campaign had shifted to the destruction of Iraq's Republican Guard twelve days before, pilots in the 388th TFW became increasingly frustrated. Inaccurate coordinates and fewer targets resulted in a decrease in sortie effectiveness. Maj. Scott "Foot" Goodfellow, the 388th wing weapons officer, shared his concerns about the matter with Lt. Col. Scott, who agreed that a change in tactics was necessary. With Scotty's approval, Foot sent a message to CENTAF headquarters in Riyadh. He described the wing's problem and asked

Gen. Glosson's staff to consider three options: provide the wing with better intelligence and up-to-date target photos; designate aircraft—specifically the OA-10—that could spot targets and pass fresh coordinates to us; or give the wing bigger TOT windows, so we could spend more time in the target area and find our own targets.

Gen. Glosson, who had received similar complaints from other wings, said there weren't enough resources to provide fresh target photos. He also said that two OA-10s had been shot down recently, and he didn't want to take a chance on sending them deeper into Iraqi territory. The CENTAF director of campaign plans liked the idea of using airborne aircraft as spotters to pass up-to-date target coordinates to other units, though, so he fired a message back to Foot asking: "How would you guys like to do it?"

Foot met with some of the other weapons officers on base, and, together they developed a new tactic. Scotty liked the concept and secured Gen. Glosson's approval to implement it. When sixteen Vipers from the 4th TFS took off Monday morning on an attack against the Medina and Hammurabi Republican Guard divisions, each pilot's DTC was programmed with five sets of coordinates—one set for each of the four primary targets and one set for the dump target. The first four-ship—call sign Pointer 01—departed the tanker track thirty minutes ahead of the remaining three elements. As soon as they reached the target area, the Pointers investigated each set of coordinates. They identified the ones that were hot and those that were no longer viable. After the four pilots dropped their bombs, Pointer 01 passed the hot-target information over the secure radio to the remaining three elements. When Howler, Yorkie, and Rex flights arrived over the target area, they dropped their bombs on the hot targets and discarded the rest.

Scotty and Foot were extremely pleased with the results, and the experiment carried over to the afternoon go. As a result, every sortie flown by the Fightin' Fuujins that day was considered effective. This marked the beginning of the "Killer Scout" program.

I finished eating dinner at the o'club around 19:15 and departed for the squadron. Some of the pilots were in the lounge watching CNN when I arrived. Since I didn't have to brief until 22:50, I grabbed a seat next to Capt. Randy "Spike" Roberts, my wingman for that night's sortie. CNN was talking about the effect of the war on Iraqi civilians. The Iraqi government had said repeatedly that allied bombs were being used to destroy civilian neighborhoods in Iraq's major towns and cities. We knew this wasn't true, but seeing videotape of war-torn neighborhoods was hard to stomach.

"There is very little water to drink," the reporter said as he pointed toward a group of Iraqi children playing in what appeared to be a bomb crater. "And only intermittent power is available to those with portable generators."

Scenes of women and children with severe shrapnel wounds being attended to in hospital emergency rooms. Crumpled homes. Blanket-covered corpses lying in gutters. Limbs protruding from rubble. When the camera focused on the pain and suffering of Iraqi women and children, I could barely stand to look. How many kids' fathers, wives' husbands, or mothers' sons had *I* killed?

Spike and I walked into the weapons shop to review the contents of our mission envelope. According to the attack card, each of us would carry six MK-82s. Three of the 500-pound bombs were equipped with standard M904 nose fuses. The other three contained FMU-113 fuses. The FMU-113 gives the MK-82 an air-burst capability. Instead of making a crater, the MK-82 explodes approximately fifteen feet above the ground. Consequently, bomb fragments travel a much greater distance, making it an ideal weapon for soft targets such as troops in the open.

22:12:00z

My F-16 is level at 23,000 feet on a 285-degree heading. Spike is eight miles in trail, and our airspeed is 350 knots. My autopilot is engaged.

As we proceed toward Saudi Arabia, images of Iraqi women and children materialize before me. I see a woman sitting alone, thinking about the husband she hasn't seen since last July. Her children are asleep beside her, warmed by a single blanket. Their home has been without electricity since the first night of the war. Food is scarce and costly. What little money she has is spent on the children. The family has grown accustomed to the air-raid sirens and the blackouts, but the children still cry when they hear bombs explode nearby. They're confused by what is happening, and they miss the love of their father. They miss life as it once was.

I don't know what their father looks like. But I feel as though I've seen his face a hundred times. He grew up on the outskirts of Baghdad and was drafted into the army at eighteen. As a young conscript, he spent the last three years of the Iran-Iraq War fighting in the desert. When the war finally ended, he returned to Baghdad, married the daughter of a family friend, and fathered two children. He worked in the oil fields during the day and enjoyed his family at night.

Years have passed, and now the young soldier is fighting again. Tonight he sits behind the wheel of a fuel truck. On a dusty road seven miles west of the Kuwaiti border, he thinks about his family. Most of his friends are dead, and he knows the Iraqi military will soon be defeated. Still, he fights. The tanks and armored personnel carriers in his unit are in desperate need of fuel, and the depot is ninety minutes away. The soldier is one of four drivers who must fill up their trucks and return to camp before sunrise. Their commander is depending on them.

23:02:10z

I push the throttle up and ease my F-16 into position beneath the KC-10. Once the boomer plugs the fueling probe in, I focus my attention on the Extender's position lights.

"How are you doing tonight, sir?" the boomer asks.

"I'm doing all right. I'll feel better when this mission is over, though."

"What kind of weapons are you guys carrying?" the boomer asks as we begin a shallow turn to the left.

"I'm carrying six MK-82s," I answer. "Where are you guys from?"

"We're from Seymour-Johnson," the boomer replies.

"What are the pilots' names?"

"This is Capt. Tom Ferguson," a voice suddenly interrupts.

"The same Tom Ferguson who flew T-38s at Reese?" I ask.

"That's me."

"Hey, Fergie, this is Rosey. How the heck are you?"

"Hey, Rosey. I thought your voice sounded familiar. I'm doing okay. I work for Northwest Airlines and fly in the Seymour-Johnson reserve unit. We got called up a few months ago, and we've been flying out of a base in Saudi ever since."

"This is the last place I thought I'd run into you again," I answer. "My tanks are almost full, so take care of yourself."

"You be careful, too," Fergie replies.

23:43:11z

Forty-three miles southwest of Az Zubayr, in the heart of the Rumaila oil field, the Iraqi soldier forges ahead. The darkness that surrounds him is continually torn by flashes of jagged light as allied bombs rain down from the sky. He wonders how much longer the nightmare will continue. He hasn't eaten a solid meal in two weeks, and he can't remember the last time he had a bath. Two men in his unit found Saudi invitation cards during dawn patrol yesterday and asked if he would drive with them to the Saudi border tonight. He refused. Defecting is a no-win situation for him. If he were caught by his superiors, he would be executed. If he were lucky enough to make it into Saudi territory, his family would be tortured for his treason.

23:57:45z

I reach down to the left console and turn on my VTR. Our target is fifty miles ahead, but if Spike and I can lock up some movers on the highway below us, we'll drop three bombs early. After I access the air-to-ground master mode, I call up GMT. I program 40-mile scope and begin to sweep along the highway. Within seconds, four small lines appear near the top of my MFD screen. While descending, I slew my cursors over one of the targets and push the TMS switch forward with my right thumb. As soon as the target is locked, the ground-map video disappears, and a track diamond is displayed at the cursor intersection.

"Husky 17," I radio, "I've got some movers on the road about ten west of the steerpoint. I'm going to go for them with three, then to the steerpoint after that."

"Husky 18 copies," Spike replies. "I've got movers on the road also."

"Looks like the road moves from southwest to northeast," I continue.

Passing through 15,500 feet, I reach down and switch my VTR to HUD. The highway shows up well in the FLIR, and the TD box is directly overtop of it. The CCRP steering line is thirty degrees left of the flight-path marker, and my airspeed is 457 knots. Descending through 15,300 feet, I begin a turn to the left so I can intercept the CCRP line with my flight-path marker. I roll out of the turn heading 087, three degrees nose low. Everything is set. All I have to do is keep the flight-path marker on the steering line and wait for the solution cue to drop down.

23:59:08z

Using his knees to steer the truck, the Iraqi soldier reaches for a flashlight and shines it on his watch. It's nearly three in the morning. He's thirty minutes behind schedule. After he sets the flashlight down, he puts both hands back on the steering wheel. The fuel depot isn't much farther.

23:59:25z

I glance at the bottom-right corner of my HUD. The target is twelve miles in front of me. I pull the throttle back slightly and continue to descend. I have no idea what type of vehicle my radar has locked up or who is driving it. One thing I am sure of, though: He will be dead in less than a minute.

"Husky 18's locked on one about three miles east of the cursors," Spike radios.

"Copy," I reply. "I'm about five to ten west. They're on the road here. I've got about ten miles to go."

"Roger!" Spike answers. "I've got about eighteen miles to go and I'm sorted."

23:59:52z

Descending through 11,400 feet, the max-toss cue begins to flash in my HUD. The target is 7.1 miles ahead and my airspeed is 480 knots. Within seconds, the solution cue appears at the top of the CCRP steering line and begins to drop toward the flight-path marker. I pull back on the stick to break my descent and make a small correction to keep my flight-path marker on top of the steering line. When the solution cue intersects the flight-path marker, three MK-82s drop from beneath my wings.

"Husky 17 has dropped three off," I radio.

00:00:13z

The Iraqi soldier continues east. The sound of his engine is all he can hear. It reminds him of riding with his father through the . . .

Looking out the right side of my canopy, the flash from my weapons lights up the ground below me. A secondary explosion quickly follows, engulfing the vehicle. The bombs have hit their mark.

"Husky 18 is off right behind you," Spike calls out.

"Copy," I reply. "I'm proceeding to the steerpoint. Close side—the west one."

Level at 30,000 feet over Bubiyan Island, I engage my autopilot and call up the steer-point for Al Minhad AB. After I check out of the area with AWACS, I reach into my G-suit pocket and pull out a package of granola bars. While staring at the stars above, I think about the man who was driving the truck. On previous missions, I never knew for sure if my bombs had taken the life of another. Tonight was different. An Iraqi soldier lost his life doing what he believed in. I took his life away doing what I believe in. I doubt his family will forgive me.

30.
KILLER SCOUTS

While allied aircraft pounded Iraqi targets over a three-week period, U.S. ground forces maneuvered into battle positions for the start of the ground war. Six months had passed since President Bush ordered the first U.S. soldiers to Saudi Arabia, following Iraq's invasion of Kuwait. According to Lt. Gen. Thomas W. Kelly, director of operations for the Joint Chiefs of Staff, the 370,000 U.S. troops who would lead the ground offensive against Iraq were now "as ready as they reasonably could be."

6 FEBRUARY 1991

I crawled out of bed around 15:20, and as soon as I finished getting dressed, I left for the squadron. The night's first takeoff was scheduled for 19:00 and I was scheduled to fly in the first four-ship. Badger and Skippy were preparing for their missions in the weapons shop when I arrived. Neither of them looked very happy.

"What's going on?"

"Haven't you heard the bad news?" Skippy asked glumly.

"Don't tell me we lost a pilot."

"No, nothing like that," Badger offered. "We just found out Col. Navarro wants to send our squadron to King Fahd AB to replace the 69th."

"Where is the 69th going?" I asked in disbelief.

"Col. Navarro doesn't think the Werewolves are comfortable there. He told Taz the 69th would benefit the wing more if they flew out of Al Minhad."

"You gotta be shittin' me! We've been stuck here since August, and he wants *them* to be more comfortable? They haven't even been in theater a month yet."

"No kidding," Skippy added. "What the hell does Navarro think we were doing while the Werewolves were spending Thanksgiving and Christmas with their families?"

"We both fly the F-16 Block 40," I continued. "It doesn't make operational sense to swap the two squadrons just so the 69th can be more comfortable. The Werewolves are established at King Fahd AB. We're established here. Why make everyone move again?"

By 19:30, I'm cruising across the Persian Gulf at 23,000 feet. No time to think about King Fahd AB. Weasel is leading tonight's sortie, and our call sign is Canine 05. Flying in the number two position is Mans. I'm in charge of the second element, and my wingman is Jackal. As soon as AWACS clears us into Saudi airspace, Weasel locks up our

227

tanker on radar and begins to descend. During the rejoin, I notice something unusual. Directly below us, just a few miles south of the Kuwaiti border, a massive convoy of vehicles is proceeding west along tap-line road. The string of headlights stretches for miles. It looks like rush hour on the Santa Monica Freeway. American ground forces are on the move. The ground war might be starting sooner than I thought.

Our target tonight is the Medina Republican Guard division. According to the map I was given by last night's MPC team, the unit is situated forty miles west of Basrah on the north side of the Kuwaiti border. If everything goes as planned, we'll fly north along the Kuwaiti border until we reach the IP. The IP-to-target run is forty miles, and the run-in heading is 093 degrees. Weasel's plan is to have us roll in from the west, drop our six MK-82s, and egress east. It's a clear night, so weather shouldn't be a factor.

As soon as I reach the IP, I turn right to a heading of 093, program steerpoint seven, and call up the air-to-ground master mode. The ground-map radar begins to sweep. As soon as the radar breaks out a good set of returns, I slew my cursors on top of them. While using EXP, DBS1, and DBS2, I begin a gradual descent. I expect a flurry of SAMs and AAA, but, so far, Iraq's big guns are quiet. Approaching the target, I make one last check to ensure that my camera is on and that my master arm switch is in Arm. Everything's set. At precisely five DME, I roll inverted and commence the attack. Rocketing toward the desert floor at 475 knots, I call up my CCIP pipper. My HUD is full of target returns, and I pickle all six bombs on the first pass. As soon as the bombs come off, I push my throttle to mil power and begin to climb. My RWR is quiet. Still no sign of AAA. Passing 10,000 feet, I roll to the left and wait for the bombs to detonate. Within seconds, six consecutive flashes appear below me. I roll back to the right as I continue to climb, hoping for some secondaries. Unfortunately, there are none.

Passing 20,000 feet, I call up steerpoint eight and proceed toward the egress point. Before long, the entire formation passes over Bubiyan Island. After we fence out, Weasel calls for a fuel check and leads us back to Al Minhad. After I engage my autopilot, I reach into my G-suit pocket for a package of granola bars. Since late January, the after-attack snack has become a ritual for me. The stress of combat leaves me physically and mentally exhausted. Watching the stars from 39,000 feet with a granola bar in one hand and a cold bottle of water in the other is a great way to unwind.

We touched down at Al Minhad at 22:22 and, after Weasel completed the debrief, the four of us headed back to the beer tent. I grabbed a soda from the bar and joined Opie, Ark, and Senseless at one of the tables.

"How's that LANTIRN shit going, Rosey?" Ark asked sarcastically.

"It's a tough job, but somebody's got to do it."

"Do you like flying at night?" Senseless asked.

"You may think I'm nuts, but I really do. Flying combat at night has its benefits: Iraqi gunners are usually trying to sleep; those that are awake can't see us; we don't fly at low altitude; and I enjoy the challenge of flying with a FLIR."

"Did you get any kills?" Senseless asked.

"Who knows," I answered dejectedly. "We were carrying MK-82s, and no one reported any secondaries after they came off. Unless you score a direct hit, you aren't going to kill anything with a MK-82—especially from medium altitude. This war would be over a lot sooner if we could drop CBU-87, but Scotty says we need to save it for the ground war."

"He tells us the same thing," Opie said leaning back and rolling his eyes. "Dropping dumb bombs from medium altitude is a waste of time, as far as I'm concerned."

"Do you think the Killer Scout program will make a difference?" I asked.

"I flew my first ride today," Opie replied. "We're only using guys with FAC experience right now, and as soon as they're comfortable with the mission, we'll start upgrading the rest of the squadron. I flew with Spike this morning. Foot and Big O took off forty-five minutes before us and flew to a tanker track east of Kuwait City. As soon as they finished air refueling, AWACS assigned them to an area in northern Kuwait. While they searched for targets, Spike and I were in the refueling track, topping off our tanks. After we finished, we proceeded to the area and relieved Foot's formation. It takes twenty minutes to fly from the area to the tanker, five minutes to refuel, and another twenty minutes to fly back again. Each formation worked two forty-five-minute shifts in the area, which gave us three hours of coverage. As soon as we check out more pilots, we'll add more areas. Eventually, a two-ship will take off every forty-five minutes."

"Did you find many targets?" I asked.

"They were all over the place!" Opie said energetically. "We were passing coordinates to the F-111s, the A-10s, and the F-18s. AWACS gave them our frequency and told them to contact us if they didn't find anything under their primary target. I passed out eight different sets of coordinates and those guys hit every one of them."

"You guys had bombs too, though, didn't you?" I interrupted.

"Each of us had four canisters of CBU-58," Opie continued. "Once we found a good target, we set up a wheel and dropped on it. We spent the rest of the time marking targets for everyone else. It worked out great, and I really think the program will increase mission effectiveness—not just for our squadron, but for other units as well."

When Opie finished, I changed the subject and asked the guys how they would feel if I came back to the 4th again. Each of them seemed genuinely excited.

7 FEBRUARY 1991

I couldn't believe it. I hadn't received more than ten letters since the beginning of January, and as soon as I opened my mailbox, I found eleven. I was so excited, my hands shook. As I flipped through the envelopes, I found two from Colette, one from my parents, one from my sister, Denise. It was incredible! There was a letter from my brother, Darren, one from Ed and Lucile . . . Steve Oakley . . . Phil Cott . . . my aunt Janice . . . Mrs. Ziello . . . and one from Nana. After I put the letters from Colette in my pocket, I sat down and began reading. Most of the letters were written right after the war started, and each person described where they were when hostilities began. Some were on their way home from work. Others were watching the evening news. Everyone was concerned for my safety and told me Colette had been keeping them up to date.

After I finished reading, I grabbed a bottle of water and an MRE out of the supply room. I didn't have to brief until 16:45, so I turned on the squadron television and begin eating. CNN reported that two U.S. F-15 pilots shot down a pair of Soviet-made SU-25 Frogfoots as they attempted to escape to Iran. Marine Brig. Gen. Richard I. Neal, speaking to reporters in Riyadh, said the pilots spotted the aircraft on radar, chased them down, and destroyed them before they could reach Iranian territory. Gen. Neal reported that two MiG-21 Fishbeds may have also been shot down. CNN concluded the report by announcing that ten Iraqi jets had escaped during the previous two days, bringing the total number of Iraqi aircraft in Iran to 120.

The next report focused on the 850 Iraqi soldiers who had been captured since the war began. Many were in poor condition and told of getting only one meal per day. According to allied officials, the prisoners told American and Saudi interrogators that thousands more would love to surrender, but they were afraid of Iraqi intelligence officers, who were executing soldiers unwilling to fight. Of the 850 prisoners, CNN said fifty-one were Iraqi officers. One officer reportedly told his interrogators: "Kill Saddam Hussein and this will stop." CNN reported that most of the soldiers learned how to turn themselves in by reading leaflets dropped on their units by allied pilots.

Listening to the report, I began to believe the war might not last as long as some had predicted. If Iraq's front-line troops were in such poor condition, they wouldn't stand a chance against allied ground forces. In my heart, I felt compassion for these men. It was obvious they did not want to fight. I began to wonder if we weren't overdoing it, but my friends disagreed with me. Many of them thought we should kill every last one of the Iraqi soldiers. As far as I was concerned, however, the majority of Iraq's soldiers—with the exception of the Republican Guard, perhaps—had lost their will to fight. They couldn't even defend themselves! I knew these men had done tremendous harm to the people of Kuwait, but they were still human beings, and slaughtering them was something I would take no pleasure in.

After another mission, I returned to my room. I got undressed and read the letters Colette sent me. There was much fear in her words. More than anything, I wanted to comfort her. When I finished the letters, I decided to write one of my own:

7 February '91

Dear Colette,
  I landed a few hours ago, and right now I'm lying in bed thinking about you and the girls. It's 2:00 A.M. and as soon as I finish this letter, I'm going to sleep. I usually go to bed around 6:00 A.M., but I haven't slept as long as I would like lately. I'll catch up tonight.
  I flew my thirteenth combat mission earlier this evening. Cut Jergensen, Weebles Wiebener, Jackal Nejaime, and I bombed Iraqi Republican Guard troops along the northern border of

Kuwait. We found a lot of Iraqi vehicles parked near a road and each of us made two bombing passes. By the time we left, most of the vehicles were destroyed.

Today was Christmas for mail. I received eleven letters, including two from you. One letter was written on 17 January. The other was dated the 19th. I know how difficult it must have been for you to watch the beginning of the war. It was emotional for us, too. I wish I could have called you that night. I needed to hear your voice as much as you needed to hear mine.

As I mentioned in my last letter, I may be going back to the 4th. I know that makes you happy, but I've got to be honest with you, honey—I'm starting to have second thoughts about leaving the 421st. Lt. Col. Rackley has really turned the unit around since he took over as commander. I've made a lot of good friends in the squadron; I have a great job; and I love flying at night. Col. Navarro, Col. Huddle, and Lt. Col. Scott treat our unit like we're the black sheep of the wing, but I truly believe we're the best squadron on this base right now. Do you remember how depressed I was when I was transferred from the 4th last September? Well, I'm starting to experience those same feelings again. That was a very difficult time for me, and I don't think I can handle going through something like that again. I've got enough stress as it is.

Well, babe, it's time to go to sleep. I fly again tomorrow and I'm pretty tired. I love you and I'll write again soon. Tell everyone I appreciate their letters, and kiss the girls for me.

Love, Keith

9 FEBRUARY 1991

During a pilot meeting last night, Lt. Col. Rackley announced that the 69th TFS would remain at King Fahd AB for the duration of the war. Taz said Lt. Col. Harry "Laredo" Davis, commander of the 69th TFS, had spoken to Col. Navarro earlier in the day and told him the Werewolves were adjusting to their new location and preferred to stay. Taz also said the pilots in the 69th were averaging two sorties a night, and they enjoyed the challenge of finding Iraqi Scud missiles.

I woke up around 13:00 and exercised for about forty-five minutes. Having flown eight out of the last nine days, I was relieved finally to have a day off. The lounge wasn't as crowded as it had been at the beginning of the war. Many of the officers had grown tired of CNN's reporting, because the network spent more time telling the audience what a great job it was doing, instead of finding new things to talk about. A parade of military analysts consistently made incorrect predictions; reporters asked inane questions over and over again; and Peter Arnett made us feel like we were a bunch of serial killers. He continued to stir the pot by focusing on collateral damage in Iraq—the type of damage that the coalition tried desperately to minimize. Arnett seemed to have forgotten that during World War II, Allied bombs killed more than 300,000 German civilians and injured close to 800,000 others. The bombing of Tokyo in March 1945 killed approximately 84,000 civilians and injured another 41,000. More than 70,000 people were killed when the atomic bomb was dropped on Hiroshima, and 35,000 were killed at Nagasaki. The U.S.-led coalition would come nowhere close to these numbers.

Twenty-three days into Operation Desert Storm, allied pilots had passed the 52,000-sortie mark. Twenty-eight allied planes were lost, twenty-one in combat; thirty members of the coalition were killed in action, including twelve Americans; forty-three coalition members were now missing in action, including twenty-five Americans; and the Iraqis captured twelve prisoners of war, a number that included eight Americans.

Gen. Robert B. Johnston, chief of staff for U.S. Central Command, announced that 135 Iraqi aircraft had been destroyed, and a total of 147 had fled to Iran. Allied aircraft destroyed 600 out of 5,700 tanks, and 400 out of 3,200 artillery pieces. Approximately 885 Iraqi prisoners had been captured. The most impressive statistic had to do with the number of Scud launches initiated by Iraq. During the first week of fighting, thirty-five Scud missiles were launched toward Israel and Saudi Arabia. During the second week, after the Werewolves joined the A-10s and the F-15Es in the search for mobile launchers, the number of launches dropped to eighteen. Since the 69th TFS had been transferred permanently to King Fahd AB eleven days before, only six Scuds were fired.

After the briefing, CNN reported that in Amman, Jordan, on Thursday night, pro-Iraqi Palestinians auctioned off part of a wing from an American F-16, supposedly shot down over Iraq. A merchant was presented with the six-by-two-foot piece of camouflage-painted metal in front of a crowd of nearly 5,000 people who were shouting: "Death to Bush! Long live Saddam!" The auction resembled a telethon, and all of the bids were collected in a five-foot silver trophy cup. According to the report, the $20,700 Jordanian dinars ($33,100 U.S.) would be donated to the Iraqi children and their army.

"This auction is our contribution to the Mother of All Battles," one man shouted.

When CNN finally showed the piece of the "F-16 wing," all the pilots in the room erupted into laughter. Everyone immediately recognized that the shard of metal was nothing more than half of an empty canister of CBU that had landed in the desert. The yellow stripe against the green background was a dead giveaway. The Palestinians thought they were bidding thousands of dollars for a fragment of an American fighter. Instead, they were celebrating over the shell of a cluster bomb that probably destroyed a pair of Iraqi tanks and the soldiers who had been driving them.

After dinner, Raj and I joined the other members of our MPC team in the squadron planning room to discuss the Killer Scout program. In preparation for the ground war, CENTAF planners had developed a grid of "kill boxes" that covered the southern half of Iraq, Kuwait, and northeastern Saudi Arabia. Each kill box was 30 by 26 miles; six boxes covered an area from Kuwait City to the confluence of the Tigris and Euphrates rivers. The Pointers, as the paired Killer Scouts were called, worked the kill boxes together, flying between 15,000 and 20,000 feet to avoid SAMs and AAA. The missions lasted about four and a half hours and required as many as five air-refuelings. To help spot targets along the desert floor, each flight lead was equipped with binoculars. When a target was found, the pilots either bombed it or performed a "fix," in which the coordinates were passed along to other allied aircraft so they could drop their bombs on it.

When we finished, I walked downstairs to check the next night's schedule. Damien was in the scheduling office when I arrived. He asked me why I wanted to go back to the 4th. "I'm not really sure, sir," I replied.

"This is the best squadron on base, and you're an important part of the unit," Damien said. "I hate to lose you. Think about it, and if you change your mind, let me know."

31.
EDGE OF THE ENVELOPE

A knock on the weapons-shop door interrupted the mass briefing. In walked Maj. Marsh from intel. He approached Damien and handed him a pair of satellite photos.

"I'm sorry to interrupt, sir," Marsh said, "but these were taken this morning, and they just arrived from Riyadh. The targets are considered high priority, and CENTAF wants to know if we can take them out tonight."

"What are they?" Damien asked while studying the photos.

"This one is a picture of an Iraqi police station in downtown Basrah," Marsh said pointing at the picture. "According to CENTAF, an Iraqi execution squad is using the facility as their headquarters."

"And the other one?"

"The second photo was also taken over Basrah. The Iraqis are storing tanks and armored personnel carriers in what appears to be a park. I counted more than two hundred of them!"

"Call CENTAF and tell them we'll take both missions."

10 FEBRUARY 1991

As Maj. Marsh walked out, Damien set the satellite photos on the table in front of us. While everyone gathered around to look at the pictures, Damien told Capt. Mike Poggi, the 421st maintenance officer, to reconfigure two of the jets with MK-84s and the rest with CBU-87.

"Okay, guys, let me have your attention," Damien bellowed. "Stitch, I want you and Ensign to take out the police headquarters with MK-84s. The target coordinates are on the back of the satellite photo. Any questions?"

"No, sir," Stitch replied, picking up the photo.

"The rest of you will attack the storage area. You've got some planning to do, so let's get on it."

Sixteen Vipers, each loaded with four canisters of CBU-87, would attack the tank-filled park. To ensure maximum coverage with our weapons, we divided the target into four sections—one for each four-ship. Since the park was less than thirty miles from our original target, all we had to do was substitute a new set of target coordinates and reprogram the weapons data in our stores management system (SMS). Everything up to the IP, and from the egress point home, would remain the same.

233

While everyone updated their maps and lineup cards, Col. Jaszczak walked into the room and reviewed the satellite photo. The park was bordered by a pair of roads—one to the south and one to the west—and by a string of homes directly to the east. After studying the photograph, Col. Jaszczak asked for everyone's attention.

"Take a good look at the right side of this photo," Cash said while holding up the picture. "I don't want *any* bombs to come near these homes. Is that understood?"

"Yes, sir," everyone answered.

Saddam Hussein was keenly aware that we would never deliberately target Iraqi citizens. That's why the armored vehicles were being stored in a residential neighborhood. If the tanks and APCs were still there when we arrived, we'd destroy every one of them—except, of course, those on the east side of the park.

21:48:21z

"Captain Keith Rosenkranz . . . Howler 45 . . . 2245 foxtrot . . . Four CBU-87 . . . Takeoff time is 22:10 . . . TOT is 00:20:00 . . . Date is 11 February '91 . . . Tail number is 453."

After the crew chiefs complete their inspections, Jackal and I follow Capt. Eric "Grinder" Pell and Capt. Steve "Gabby" Lambert into position on the runway. After takeoff, the four of us proceed to the air-refueling track. When we depart the tanker, I roll out heading 355 and climb to 26,000 feet. After I level off, I turn off my lights and complete my fence check.

00:16:45z

Passing the IP, I call up steerpoint seven and turn on my VTR. As my ground-map radar sweeps the target area, I study the returns and compare them to the satellite photo strapped to my right leg.

"Bulldog, picture clear," AWACS radios.

While my radar transitions to DBS2, I clear outside. All of a sudden, a flash of light appears out the left side of my canopy.

"Something's exploding down at my left ten," I exclaim.

While checking my RWR scope, I roll to the left. The scope is clean, and I don't see any SAMs or AAA. Satisfied, I continue with my radar work.

"Okay, we've got some bright returns under the cursors," I comment to myself. "Let's cursor zero one more time."

I reach toward the right MFD and hit the cursor zero button. This removes any inadvertent slews to the ground-map cursors.

"Looks like there's some stuff burning down there," I comment. "Let's start down."

I push forward on my stick and begin to descend. I glance down at the satellite photo one more time to make sure I've identified the target properly. It looks like a match.

"Okay, painting out a good picture there," I comment to myself. "You can see the *L* on the left side."

As soon as I look up again, I see bright flashes and explosions on the ground up ahead. I know that Grinder must have already rolled in.

"There go 45's bombs—real nice," I say.

"Bulldog, Coors 43 checking in," a pilot radios.

"Coors 43, copy—searching," AWACS replies.

00:18:19z

I reach down and switch my VTR to HUD. I'm passing through 25,800 feet on a 010-degree heading. My airspeed is 375 knots. The target is at my right two o'clock, so I bank to the right and turn toward it. After I roll out, I check my distance to the target. At eight DME, I roll inverted and commence the attack. When the nose of my F-16 is twenty-five degrees below the horizon line, I roll upright again and focus on the target. I'm in a thirty-degree dive, passing through 22,500 feet. My airspeed is 410 knots and the TD box is in the HUD field-of-view. The northwest side of the park is burning brightly in the FLIR. There's a fire near the road on the south side of the park as well.

As I continue my descent, I hit the missile step button and the CCIP pipper comes into view. The TD box is replaced by a diamond. The string of residential homes that Col. Jaszczak wants us to avoid is clearly visible on the right side of the HUD. The pipper reaches the diamond as I approach 12,000 feet. As soon as I hit the pickle button, I pull back smoothly on my stick and push the throttle to mil. As the Gs increase, I feel the canisters of CBU drop from my wings. Once the nose of my F-16 is above the horizon, I bank to the right and turn to look back at the target. Within seconds, the south side of the park lights up. I continue my climbing right turn and roll out on a 100-degree heading. After Jackal calls off target, I place my master arm switch to Sim and call up my air-to-air radar. Grinder and Gabby are right where I expect them to be.

"Howler 47 tied," I radio.

"Howler 46 is buddy spike," Gabby replies.

Grinder leads the formation across the Gulf, and we touch down at Al Minhad right before dawn.

During the debrief, Grinder discussed the flight and reviewed our film. Everyone in the formation put their bombs exactly where they were supposed to. Unfortunately, the Iraqis must have moved the combat vehicles, because the park appeared to be empty. Everyone was disappointed until Stitch and Ensign walked in and showed us the film from their mission.

"We hammered the police headquarters building," Stitch said proudly as he rewound his tape.

"Wait until you see my film," Ensign interjected. "Stitch's bombs exploded right as I was rolling in. It was incredible!"

After we reviewed Stitch's film, Ensign put his tape into the machine and hit the rewind button.

"I was less than a minute behind Stitch," Ensign says. "As soon as I rolled in, this is what I saw."

The tape began to play, and Ensign's diamond was right on top of the police head-quarters. Stitch had already released his bombs, and Ensign was seconds away from dropping his. All of a sudden, the entire structure disintegrated. Stitch's bombs shacked the target, and all Ensign could say on the radio was: "Oh, shit!"

12 FEBRUARY 1991
I walked into the squadron the night before around 21:30 and cleaned out my desk in the weapons shop. Some of my friends stopped by and wished me luck. A few of them couldn't understand why I was leaving. I'm not sure I understood either.

My last flight as a Black Widow turns out to be a memorable one. The briefing begins at 23:00, and I am scheduled to fly with Damien, Rip, and Jackal. Damien plans to have us take off as a four-ship, but as soon as we reach the arming area, Jackal's FLIR system fails. Damien calls for maintenance assistance, but technicians are unable to repair the malfunction. Just when it looks like I'll have to abort my last flight as a Black Widow, Damien comes up on victor and tells me to give Jackal twenty more minutes. If Jackal isn't ready by 01:55, Damien wants me to take off as a single ship. He says he will wait for me in the tanker track.

After I acknowledge the radio call, Damien and Rip taxi onto the runway and take off. I continue to wait in the arming area while the maintenance crews try in vain to fix Jackal's FLIR. I finally take off at 01:54 and proceed directly to the Lime air-refueling track. Damien and Rip are orbiting with the KC-135 when I arrive. As soon as I top off my tanks, the three of us proceed north toward our target, an ammunition storage facility in southern Iraq. Each F-16 is carrying four canisters of CBU-58, and there are at least a dozen secondary explosions after we come off target. During the egress, I make a thirty-degree check turn to the right and look back toward the facility. The fires are burning brightly. I know the mission is a success.

The three of us touched down at Al Minhad shortly after 05:00 and taxied to the hot pits. After we refueled, we taxied back to the flight line and shut down our engines. As soon as I climbed out of my cockpit, Damien walked over, shook my hand, and thanked me for my contribution to the squadron.

"I wish you weren't leaving," Damien told me. "You've been an asset to the unit, and I appreciate all the work you've put in."

Flying on the "edge of the envelope" is a phrase often used among fighter pilots. In general, it means that an aircraft is being pushed to its structural limits. If a pilot flies outside the envelope, the aircraft will more than likely come apart.

My alarm went off at 10:00. While lying in bed, I glanced toward the table and focused on a picture of Colette and the girls. My mind raced with emotion, and the anxiety I felt about leaving the 421st made me realize that I might be approaching the edge of my own personal envelope. I thought returning to the 4th would be something I would enjoy. But over the previous few days, the emotions I had experienced in September began to surface again. I've always considered myself a strong person who could handle anything. Now I was not so sure.

I forced myself out of bed so I could begin adjusting to the daytime schedule. After a light breakfast, I walked into the lounge and spent the rest of the morning watching CNN. According to a news report, President Bush met with advisers to discuss the status of the war. After the meeting, President Bush spoke briefly to reporters about the anticipated ground war: "We are going to take whatever time is necessary to sort out when a next stage might begin. I'm very satisfied . . . with the progress in the war. The air campaign has been very, very effective and it will continue for a while."

Later in the afternoon, I lifted weights and ran to the other side of the base and back. As I passed by the 421st, I bumped into Ensign and Popeye.

"What's going on, guys?"

"We're on our way to work," Popeye said. "Both of us are in the first go tonight, and the briefing starts in an hour."

"I wish you were flying with us, Rosey," Ensign remarked.

"I wish I was, too," I replied as I continued down the dirt path.

As soon as I returned to my room, I took a shower and put on a clean flight suit. After I laced up my boots, I took my yellow Fuujin scarf out of my closet, wrapped it around my neck, and tucked it neatly inside the front of my flight suit. I replaced my Black Widow patch with the Fuujin patch I used to wear, grabbed my flight cap, and headed to the o'club for dinner. The mess hall was crowded. I felt awkward, trying to decide if I should sit with my friends in the 421st or my friends in the 4th, so I walked into the lounge and waited for everyone to finish. When the crowd began to thin, I prepared a plate and sat quietly by myself at an empty table toward the back of the mess hall.

After dinner, I returned to my room and read through the letters Colette had sent me over the past five months. I finally turned off the light around 22:00 and tried to go to sleep. My first combat sortie as a member of the 4th was scheduled for the next day. I'd be flying a Killer Scout mission with Maj. Jay "Momar" Lindell. As the night wore on without sleep, I agonized about my decision to leave the 421st. The more I thought about it, the more depressed I got. Finally, at two o'clock in the morning, I realized the only place for me was the 421st. I knew some people were going to be upset. I had to talk to Lt. Col. Rackley and tell him I'd changed my mind.

I crawled out of bed, got dressed, and walked back over to the o'club. I put a call in to the 421st, and when Lt. Col. Rackley came to the phone, I asked if the two of us could talk privately.

"I can't leave the squadron right now, Rosey. Can you come down to my office?"

"Yes, sir."

Lt. Col. Rackley's door was open, and he was sitting at his desk. Damien was also in the room. "Do you mind if Lt. Col. Nall joins us?" Taz asked.

"That's fine, sir."

"What's on your mind, Rosey?"

"Sir," I began, "I know it's pretty late to be saying this, but I don't want to go to the 4th. I want to stay in the 421st and remain a Black Widow."

"Why are you telling me this now, Rosey?" Taz asked calmly.

"When Lt. Col. Scott told me I was being sent to the 421st last September," I replied, "I was extremely disappointed. There was a lot of turmoil in the squadron, and *nobody* wanted to be here. But things began to change. LANTIRN became the wing's top priority, you took over as squadron commander, new pilots began to arrive, and a new spirit of camaraderie began to develop. We've come a long way and I sincerely feel that this squadron is the best one on base."

I continued, "When Grumpy asked if I would consider going back to the 4th, I told him I would do it. I thought it would be fun to go back to the 4th, but now that I've had time to think about it, I realize I made the wrong decision. Some of my friends have been asking me why I was leaving. We've accomplished a lot together, and many have encouraged me to stay."

"I never understood why you wanted to leave, either," Damien said. "You've been a key player in LANTIRN since the beginning."

"I love flying at night, sir," I continued. "If it's not too late, I'd like to remain a Black Widow."

"It's not a problem, Rosey," Taz replied. "I just want you to make up your mind about where you want to be."

"I want to stay in the 421st, sir."

"Okay, then," Taz answered. "I'll talk to Boomer as soon as he comes in this morning and work things out. In the meantime, I want you to do me a favor."

"Anything you'd like, sir."

"The 4th has you on their flying schedule this morning. It's too late to find a replacement, so I want you to fly the sortie as scheduled. By the time you land, I'll have spoken with Boomer and everything should be straightened out."

"Thank you very much, sir."

I took the shuttle bus back to the o'club, and, as soon as I returned to my room, I crawled back into bed and fell into a deep sleep.

13 FEBRUARY 1991

The shuttle bus dropped me off in front of the 4th TFS around 10:30. It was a gorgeous day, and I couldn't remember the last time I'd felt that good.

The briefing began with Momar's time hack and a review of the day's mission. "The 4th TFS is currently responsible for six different kill boxes," Momar declared. "Our objective is to find as many targets as possible within our assigned area. We'll drop our bombs and call in other assets to drop theirs. I would anticipate working in either AG-6, which is north of Kuwait City, or AG-7, which is south of Basrah. If we don't find anything, I'll ask AWACS if we can move into AF-5 or AF-6. I worked those two kill boxes yesterday and found plenty of targets."

Momar finished by discussing kill-box operations. "As soon as AWACS clears us to a kill box, I'll clear you to fighting wing and call for a fence check. My primary responsibility in the kill box will be to search the desert floor for targets. Your responsibility as my wingman is to maintain position and clear for the formation. Our altitude will fluctuate between the high teens and the low twenties, so keep an eye out for SAMs and AAA. If the Iraqis start shooting at us—and you can anticipate that they will—don't hesitate with a break call. I'll be using binoculars and writing down coordinates, so I probably won't see things as quickly as you will.

"Our ordnance is CBU-58, and each of us will carry four canisters. As soon as we find a legitimate target to attack, we'll set up a wheel pattern. I'll probably drop first, so plan on circling overhead while I roll in. As soon as I drop my bombs, I'll climb back up and reenter the wheel. Clear for ground fire and make sure you keep a tally. When I call off target, respond with your position in the wheel. If you lose sight for any reason, let me know, and we'll deconflict altitudes. I may drop four bombs on one pass or make two separate passes. It depends on what we find. In any case, let's try to get our bombs off during the first session. Carrying them back and forth to the tanker track wastes a lot of fuel. Any questions?"

"Let's do it!" I responded.

08:40:00z

I taxi into position on the right side of the runway. After I come to a stop, I give Momar a big head nod to signal that I'm ready. He gives me the engine run-up signal, and the two of us push our throttles up. I glance down at my instruments. Everything checks good. I look back at Momar and give him another head nod. He looks straight ahead, taps the side of his helmet, and leans his head back. He pauses for a moment, then snaps his head forward. As soon as his chin hits his chest, we release our brakes and begin to accelerate down the runway. As our airspeed increases, I vary my throttle to maintain position. My head is aligned with Momar's landing gear, and I'm waiting for his nose gear to lift off the runway. When it does, I smoothly pull back on my stick. Within seconds, the two of us are airborne.

As we continue to accelerate, Momar checks to see if I'm in position, then snaps his head back—a signal that he's about to raise the gear. I quickly place my left hand on the gear handle. As soon as Momar's gear comes up, I raise mine. Once the jets are cleaned up, Momar porpoises his aircraft. I clear right, then snap into a hard turn and maneuver toward the tactical position. The two of us continue climbing to the west and eventually level off at 24,000 feet. In all the time I've been here, I've never seen a day as clear as this one. The sandy deserts of Saudi Arabia and Qatar sit distinctly to my left, and the snow-capped mountains of Iran are clearly visible to the right. This is the first time I've seen the Iranian coastline. The view is breathtaking.

Thirty minutes into the flight, we pass over a large hospital ship. The vessel is completely white, and there's a large red cross painted on its deck. A few minutes later, I spot an aircraft carrier and several other U.S. warships. The deep blue waters of the Persian Gulf are extremely beautiful, but, as we approach the tanker track, I look down and see the huge oil slick that formed when Iraqi soldiers started dumping Kuwaiti oil into the Gulf. The spill is larger than I had imagined. How could anyone do such a thing?

Our formation reaches the tanker track, and Momar rejoins on the right wing of the blue-and-white KC-10. A pair of navy F/A-18 Hornets have just finished refueling. As soon as they depart, Momar drops down to take on fuel. Each of us spends a few minutes on the boom. Once our tanks are full, we proceed west toward Umm Qasr. Approaching the Kuwaiti coastline, I notice a large black cloud of smoke above the ravaged nation. The visibility worsens, so Momar begins to descend in an attempt to find clearer airspace. We level off at 18,000 feet and contact AWACS on strike primary.

"Bulldog, Pointer 11," Momar radios.

"Go ahead, Pointer 11," the controller replies. "Bulldog has you loud and clear."

"Pointer 11 authenticates charlie-lima."

"Bulldog authenticates kilo-alpha."

"Copy, Bulldog. Pointer 11 is mission number 1388 bravo. Request clearance to AG-7."

"Roger, Pointer 11. You're cleared to AG-7."

As we approach the kill box, Momar sends me to fighting wing and calls for a fence check. While maneuvering into position, I turn on my ECM pod, place my master arm switch in Arm, adjust the volume on my RWR, and call up steerpoint five: the center of AG-7. As we pass over Umm Qasr and into the area, I'm shocked by the magnitude of destruction. The desert floor looks like the landscape of the moon. Craters everywhere. I follow Momar to the northeast and continue to clear for SAMs and AAA. The highway that leads to Basrah is directly below us. Both sides of it are lined with hundreds of revetted bunkers—all empty.

As we approach the center of the area, we pass over a large electrical power station.

"Pointer 11, 12 on victor," I radio. "That power station looks like a good target. What do you think?"

"Let's hold off," Momar replies. "If we had MK-84s, I'd say yes. But our ordnance is better suited to armored vehicles. We'll probably find a convoy along the border, so let's wait.

"Pointer 12 copies."

While Momar circles above the power plant, I maneuver high and to the outside of the turn. This allows me to keep sight of his aircraft while clearing below for SAMs and AAA. All of a sudden I spot a muzzle flash, and a string of red tracers rocket skyward. The shells explode a few thousand feet below us, forming clouds of thick, black flak.

"Pointer 11," I radio. "AAA your left ten o'clock low."

"Pointer 11, tally-ho," Momar replies.

Momar continues to the north toward Basrah while I maneuver behind him. The Shatt al Arab waterway—the border that separates Iraq and Iran—is clearly visible off my right wing. I can also see the Iranian cities of Abadan and Khorramshahr.

"Pointer 12," Momar radios on victor, "I'm going to take a look at Shaibah Air Base and see if there's any activity on the airfield. If the Iraqis are doing any repair work, we'll hammer them."

"Sounds like a plan," I reply as Momar banks to the left.

The airfield is four miles northwest of Az Zubayr. I can't believe my eyes when we arrive overhead. The concrete runway is completely unusable. There are craters everywhere, and the hardened shelters once used to house Iraqi aircraft have been reduced to rubble. Those that remain standing have giant holes blown through their roofs. It would be great if we could destroy an Iraqi jet or two, but the airfield appears to be abandoned.

After we scout the area, Momar makes a turn to the south and proceeds toward Kuwait City. As we approach the border, I look down and notice cars traveling along the highway in both directions.

"Pointer 12 has vehicles on the highway," I radio.

"Pointer 11 copies. I'll drop down and take a look."

These guys are nuts. I can't imagine why anyone would travel along this highway, especially during the day. Don't they know there's a war going on?

"I don't see any armored vehicles," Momar radios. "They look like regular cars."

"Pointer 12 copies."

"I'm going to give AWACS a call and see if we can work AG-6," Momar continues. "Two!"

"Bulldog, Pointer 11," Momar calls out. "Is AG-6 available?"

"Pointer 11, affirmative. You're cleared in hot."

I punch in steerpoint six and check my HUD to see how far we are from the center of the area. The DME reads nineteen. As we continue south, I notice thick black clouds of smoke erupting from the desert floor at my left ten o'clock. I glance down at my kill-box map and try to identify the area. The smoke appears to be coming from the Sabiriyah oil field. As Momar circles overhead, bright orange flames billow into the air from a pair of burning tanks. A dozen others have already burned themselves out, and all that's left are blackened concrete slabs where the tanks once stood.

After we determine that AG-6 is uninhabited, we get clearance from AWACS to depart for the tanker track. It takes twenty minutes to reach the KC-10, another ten minutes to refuel, and twenty minutes to fly back again. AWACS clears us into AF-6. Within minutes, Momar spots a column of tanks heading east across the desert.

"Pointer 11 is going to make a dry pass," Momar radios. "If I think they're worth dropping on, I'll climb back up and set up for the attack."

"Pointer 12 copies."

While I circle above, Momar executes the dry attack.

"Pointer 11's in," Momar radios.

I watch from 16,000 feet as Momar dives toward the ground. As soon as he calls off target, I key my mike and radio: "Pointer 12 is in a left turn through south at base plus three."

"Pointer 11 is visual. I counted six tanks, and I'm going to make a second pass and drop all four."

"Pointer 12 copies. The area is clear."

I continue circling as Momar rolls in. I feel sorry for the Iraqi soldiers inside the tanks. They don't realize it yet, but they are about to die. As soon as Momar calls off target, I radio my position and stare at the ground. All of a sudden, a cloud of smoke engulfs the target area. Within seconds, I can see six tiny fires burning. Momar scored a direct hit.

After Momar levels off, I rejoin to the fighting-wing position, and the two of us continue to search for additional targets. We fly to the east. As we approach the eastern edge of the kill box, Momar spots something unusual.

"Pointer 12," Momar radios. "Check your nine o'clock low. Do you see those buildings down there? They look like hangars."

"Pointer 12, tally-ho."

"Why don't you hit those? The Iraqis might be storing supplies in them."

"Pointer 12 copies."

I call up the air-to-ground master mode and switch to CCIP. After I turn on my VTR, I check to make sure my master arm switch is in Arm. With the sun at my back, I roll into ninety degrees of bank and commence the attack.

"Pointer 12's in," I radio.

While diving toward the ground, I maneuver to put my bombfall line over the target. When the pipper reaches the middle building, I hit the pickle button. The aircraft shudders momentarily as the canisters of CBU-58 release from the TERs. As soon as I begin my recovery, I key my mike and radio: "Pointer 12 is off."

"Pointer 11 is visual," Momar replies. "I'm in a left turn through east at base plus four."

"Pointer 12 is tally."

"Copy. Rejoin fighting wing."

"Two!"

I continue to climb, waiting for the bombs to explode. All of a sudden, the hangars disappear under a cloud of smoke. I thought my pass was a little steep, but the bombs hit precisely where they needed to. I watch for a few more seconds, hoping to see a secondary explosion. Unfortunately, there isn't one.

As soon as I rejoin, Momar climbs to 26,000 feet and checks out of the area with AWACS. On our way to the tanker, we hear another two-ship from the 4th on the radios. Momar gives them a quick rundown of what we found, and they thank us for the update. After we refuel, Momar turns to the southeast and heads toward Al Minhad. I'm looking forward to returning to the 421st, but my lone sortie as a Killer Scout is one I will never forget.

32.
MAVERICK

O n the previous night, the month-old Gulf War turned deadly for hundreds of Iraqi civilians. According to CNN reports, an F-117 stealth fighter flew over Baghdad at approximately 04:00 and dropped a pair of 2,000-pound laser-guided bombs on what Iraq called a residential bomb shelter. Officials in Baghdad claimed that women and children from the middle-class suburb of Amariya had been using the shelter at night to avoid the continuous bombing that had rocked the area the past four weeks. Western journalists were brought in to film the ravaged facility. Charred and mutilated Iraqi bodies lay on the pavement as Iraqi men searched through the smoke and rubble for survivors. There was a gaping hole in the roof where one of the American bombs hit, and the film also managed to capture a sign that said Shelter in both English and Arabic.

14 FEBRUARY 1991

Marine Brig. Gen. Richard I. Neal said American intelligence sources identified the facility as a command-and-communications bunker.

"From a military point of view," Gen. Neal said, "nothing went wrong. The target was struck as designated. From a personal point of view, I'm outraged that civilians might have been placed in harm's way, and I blame the Iraqi government."

According to Capt. David Herrington, an intelligence officer for the Joint Chiefs of Staff, the roof was painted in camouflage, and the facility was surrounded by a barbed-wire fence.

"Intelligence sources have intercepted dozens of messages being sent from the center to front-line Iraqi forces stationed in Kuwait," Herrington said. "The facility was right across the street from a school and just a short distance from a mosque. Because it was located in the middle of a lot of civilian kinds of facilities, we chose four o'clock in the morning to strike the target. Had we known civilians were in the facility, U.S. warplanes would have never attacked it."

I felt for the families who lost their lives, and empathized, too, with the F-117 pilot who dropped the bombs. My friends and I trusted President Bush, his administration, and our military commanders. We had no reason to second-guess the targets they gave us, and despite the fact that hundreds of civilians might have been killed in the shelter, everyone continued to believe the facility was indeed a command-and-control bunker.

After the report, I rode the shuttle bus down to the 421st. I was scheduled to fly later

243

in the evening, and when I arrived at the squadron, everyone wanted to know about the Killer Scout sortie I flew. Standing in front of the large map of Iraq and Kuwait that hung on our weapons shop wall, I pointed out the areas I flew over and offered a detailed description of everything I saw. As I finished, SSgt. Brown walked in with an envelope.

"What's this?"

"Do you remember that letter the squadron received a couple of weeks ago from the guy who called himself 'Mr. Fuck Your War?'"

"He wrote back!" I replied with excitement. "He got my letter!"

"Wait until you read this one," SSgt. Brown laughed.

I began to read it:

Dear Mr. Tactical Squadron,

As you can probably tell, I was enraged when I wrote that letter. I was therefore overzealous in my remarks about our government. I used the letter to vent my frustration at the thought of you guys over there just because someone told you to go. I guess you want to. That's your right, maybe your responsibility (depends on how you see it). I don't trust this government enough to risk my life for it. I would if this country was in danger of being invaded, but it isn't. If it was being invaded, I'd be right alongside you guys, kickin' all their asses.

But I don't think the country is very free. If it were, wouldn't I be able, legally, to do whatever I want to—to or with myself? Wouldn't I be able to purchase drugs, have oral sex, or do whatever I wanted to do as long as it didn't hurt someone else? And another thing, do you think that our government doesn't use propaganda? Jesus, man, look at the commercials for the armed forces! Look at partnership-for-a-drug-free-America commercials. They don't let you think about the different facets of things. They make everything simple. America is good, drugs are bad. Saddam is bad, etc. . . . (I don't think Saddam is good or understand him, but the point is that no one gets a chance to.) Everyone's told *what* to think. And how to think it.

Anyway, I'm grateful to this country for a lot of things. It sure could be a hell of a lot worse; but what I'm saying is that it needs some work, from all of us. It's not always right, and it's not perfect. Watch your ass out there. I'd rather have you come back and kick my ass than have you not come back at all. Good luck.

Sincerely,
Me

I pinned the letter on the squadron bulletin board for everyone to read. I was hoping "Mr. Fuck Your War" would respond to my note, and he didn't let me down. I wish I could have seen the look on his face when he read my letter.

My first sortie back with the squadron was flown with Capt. Karl "Dr. K" Heinz. Dr. K was one of the pilots who went home back in October when the 421st TFS needed LANTIRN pilots. A few weeks after he returned to the States, Dr. K was sent to Luke AFB for LANTIRN training. He completed the course in December and returned to Al Minhad right before the war started.

Our call sign for the evening's flight was Ruff 15, and the two of us took off at 17:35. Dr. K and I were scheduled to attack Republican Guard forces along the southern border of Iraq, but after we came off the tanker, AWACS told us to contact J-STARS for a target update. The J-STARS commander sent us to a large assembly area in northern Kuwait, where there were dozens of armored vehicles. The coordinates he gave us turned out to be right on the mark. Since the armored vehicles were well spread out, we each made two separate passes. By the time we were finished, Dr. K and I had dropped eight 785-pound canisters containing a total of 1,760 BLU-61A/B softball-sized bomblets. We saw a number of secondary explosions, and the fires could be seen all the way to the egress point.

16 FEBRUARY 1991
While I was on MPC duty the previous night, a message from Gen. Buster Glosson arrived at the command post. According to Maj. Marsh, Gen. Glosson was sending a shipment of AGM-65D Maverick missiles to the 421st TFS, which he wanted us to employ against Iraqi armored vehicles as soon as possible. Firing Maverick missiles would be fun, although many of the pilots in the unit had been hoping we would receive the new Martin Marietta AAQ-14 targeting pod, an integral part of the LAN-TIRN system. A dozen units had arrived directly from the factory earlier in the week, but Gen. Glosson decided to give them to the F-15E Strike Eagles.

Flying with the AAQ-14 targeting pod would have certainly enhanced the effectiveness of our unit by increasing accuracy, but it made sense to give the few available pods to the Strike Eagles. The F-15E carries more bombs than the F-16, so the Strike Eagle was able to put the targeting pod to more effective use. The fact that the F-15E carries two crew members may have also influenced Gen. Glosson's decision. Learning how to implement a new system during combat would have been much more difficult in a single-seat fighter.

After Jackal and I finished lunch, we left for the squadron. A pilot meeting was scheduled to begin at 15:00, and afterward, Jackal and I would attack more Republican Guard units near the northern border of Kuwait. While waiting for the pilot meeting to begin, we watched more CNN reports on the "civilian shelter." In other news, we learned that Iraq had made an offer to withdraw its forces from Kuwait, on condition that land, sea, and air operations cease, and allied forces, weapons, and equipment withdraw. Other conditions included the abrogation of all boycott and embargo decisions against Iraq; Israeli withdrawal from occupied Palestine and other Arab territories; and the payment of allied war reparations to Iraq. President Bush called the offer "a cruel hoax, dashing the hopes of the people in Iraq, and indeed, around the world."

The pilot meeting began on time, and Damien started out with a discussion on Maverick missile tactics.

"According to intel," Damien began, "allied fighters have destroyed approximately 1,300 Iraqi tanks, 800 armored vehicles, and 1,100 artillery pieces since the beginning of the war. The Killer Scouts have done a tremendous job identifying targets during the day, but targeting and destroying Iraqi vehicles at night has been a different story. We know the Iraqis like to hide their armor in revetted bunkers, and many of you are aware of the difficulty we've had finding them. The FLIR system simply isn't powerful enough to distinguish between an empty bunker and one with a tank in it—especially from medium altitude.

"Having targeting pods would have been nice, but the Maverick missile will serve our needs just as well. You can expect to see more two-ships on the schedule, especially when the ground war starts. Maverick-qualified flight leads will carry a standard load of two missiles, and wingmen will continue carrying conventional munitions. CENTAF planners are going to assign us kill boxes to work in, and I expect the flight leads to use their Maverick video to search inside the revetments. Think of the missile as a poor man's targeting pod. If the bunkers contain armored vehicles, pass the information to your wingmen so they can bomb them. If the bunkers are empty, search in a different area. You might also consider using the GMTT radar to lock up movers. If you find something, by all means kill it. But don't feel like you have to fire the missiles on every mission. These things cost more than $100,000 apiece, and we don't want to waste them. Before I hand things over to Duck, let me see a show of hands from everyone who's Maverick-qualified."

I quickly raised my hand, even though I'd never been through a formal Maverick program. We had carried TGM-65 captive training missiles at Luke AFB when I went through LANTIRN school. Maverick was a low priority, and I never learned enough about the system to become proficient. Firing live Mavericks against real targets was a challenge I didn't want to miss out on. I also didn't want to be a wingman for the rest of the war. So I said I was qualified.

While Damien wrote down names, Duck handed out Maverick Operations Supplement manuals to everyone. The AGM-65D Maverick missile is a product of the Hughes Aircraft Company and was designed to be used against small targets such as tanks, armored vehicles, radar vans, bunkers, small buildings, and boats. Each missile weighs approximately 500 pounds and contains an internal-burning, boost-sustaining, solid-propellant rocket motor. The Maverick also contains a 125-pound warhead which can penetrate twenty-six inches of armor, thirty-two inches of steel, or ten feet of concrete.

After he handed out the manuals, Duck stepped to the front of the room and offered a more detailed look at the weapon: "The AGM-65D is an infrared (IR) Maverick, so let's start out by going over some basic concepts involving IR energy. Almost every object radiates energy and, therefore, has an IR signature. The seeker head in the Maverick missile looks for this signature and generates a video scene by displaying variations in temperature as variations in contrast. To understand contrast, picture a tank or APC traveling across the desert floor. The temperature of the armored vehicle may increase by absorbing direct solar radiation from the sun or from the heat generated by its engine. The IR signature of the vehicle will be greater than that of the desert floor—especially at night, when the ground has cooled. The resulting thermal contrast is referred to as Delta-T. The greater the Delta-T, the greater the video contrast in the cockpit."

Duck continued, "The AGM-65D guidance unit contains an IR detector that converts IR energy into electrical signals. An internal computer converts these signals into a TV-like picture, enabling a pilot to identify and lock onto objects within the seeker field-of-view. Our FLIR gives us a constant IR picture in the HUD, but the Maverick seeker gyro can move forty-two degrees left or right, thirty degrees up, or fifty-four degrees down. The Maverick seeker also incorporates a dual field-of-view lens that rotates to provide selectable magnification of the target. The wide field-of-view function provides increased target-area orientation, while narrow field-of-view provides maximum launch ranges and improved target identification."

Duck went on, "In addition to the field-of-view functions, two types of target contrast polarity may be selected in the cockpit: HOC—hot target against a cold background— or COH—cold target against a hot background. Objects that are hot appear white on the screen, and objects that are cool appear black."

Duck continued, "Let's talk about GMTT for a few minutes. In my opinion, using this system is the easiest way to employ the Maverick. Once you've tried it, I think you'll agree. The first thing you want to do is boresight your missiles so they'll be tied to your radar. A good time to do this is during the departure. Once you reach the target area, call up GMTT and use your radar cursors to lock up a mover. Next, call up the Maverick video. The target should appear on the wide field-of-view screen near the missile track-ing gates. At this point, all you have to do is slew the tracking gates over the target and lock it up."

Duck concluded, "Before you fire your Maverick, there are a few things you need to be aware of. First, the pointing cross must be within a keyhole-shaped area that doesn't appear on the video screen. The keyhole extends ten degrees around the missile tracking gates, all the way down to the fifteen-degree depression marker. Second, the pointing cross must be steady. Once a lock-on has been achieved, the 'good lock' algorithm ana-lyzes the target image for size and apparent Delta-T requirements. If the target meets the minimum requirements and the seeker look-angle is within the keyhole, the point-ing cross will remain steady. If it's flashing, the missile will break-lock after it's launched. Finally, you need to be in range when you fire the missile. Launch ranges are classified, so check the Dash 34 in the weapons safe before your first flight."

17 FEBRUARY 1991

Two American A-10s were shot down the day before as they attacked Republican Guard units along the southern border of Iraq. In addition, an F-16 from the 363rd TFW crashed during the night while executing an instrument approach to Al Dhafra AB. The pilot was returning from a combat mission, and, according to some of my friends who were airborne at the time, there was no attempt to eject. When word spread that the downed pilot was a former T-38 instructor pilot, I feared the worst. My good friend

Capt. Mike "Stapuff" Hudson had been flying out of Al Dhafra since August. We hadn't had a chance to speak to each other since arriving in the desert, but he and my other friends in the unit were in my thoughts. I arrived at the squadron at 19:00 and walked upstairs to Maj. Marsh's office.

"Maj. Marsh, do you have any info about last night's accident at Al Dhafra? I have a few friends in the wing, and I'm curious to know who the pilot was."

"I talked to a buddy in the unit earlier this afternoon," Marsh says. "The pilot was Capt. Dale Cormier, and he was a member of the 17th TFS Hooters. It'll be awhile before an official report comes out, but it sounds like he was spatially disoriented. It was dark, they were tired. He never made a radio call, and there was no attempt to eject. I bet he never even realized he was disoriented."

I felt bad for Dale and his family. It's one thing to be killed during combat, but hitting the ground during a routine approach . . . It just didn't seem fair. He was a fellow fighter pilot, but, in a way, I was glad I didn't know him. I didn't think I could handle losing another friend.

My twenty-first combat mission was scheduled for midnight, and I would be flying in the number three position of a four-ship. Cut and Weebles made up the first element, and I was paired with Jackal. Our call sign would be Alpo 55, and the four of us would attack the Tawakalna division of Iraq's Republican Guard. A few minutes before we began our briefing, some of the pilots who had just landed stopped by the weapons shop to warn us about the heavy AAA they encountered near our target.

"If the AAA is as bad as they say it is," Cut remarked, "we should probably split the formation into two two-ships. There's no reason to have four of us in the target area at the same time. The last guy through would be a sitting duck."

"I agree one hundred percent," Jackal laughed.

"As soon as we top off our tanks," Cut continued, "Weebles and I will proceed to the target area. Rosey, I want you and Jackal to stay with the tanker an extra ten minutes. When you push to the target, call me on victor, and I'll give you an update on the situation in the area."

19:37:04z

"Captain Keith Rosenkranz . . . Alpo 55 . . . 3255 alpha . . . We got two MK-84s on board . . . Takeoff is 20:00 . . . TOT is 21:56 . . . Date is 17 February '91 . . . Tail number is 509."

The four of us take off precisely at midnight and cruise across the Gulf to our refueling track. After Cut and Weebles push north, Jackal and I take turns on the boom. Ten minutes later, I make a climbing turn to the north and tell Jackal to take spacing. I level off at 24,000 feet and accelerate to 400 knots. Forty miles south of the IP, I hear Cut and Weebles on the radios as they prepare to roll in on the target.

"One's dropping on numerous vehicles on the left here," Cut radios.

"Copy," Weebles replies. "Understand just left of the road?"

"That's correct. There's a road going north-south intersecting an east-west road.

There's vehicles right by my bombs."

"Copy. . . . Looking," Weebles says nervously.

The radios are silent for a few seconds. All of a sudden, Weebles keys his mike and screams with excitement: "Okay, we got *lots* of AAA! Two's rolling in on the AAA!"

"AAA massive!" Cut shouts.

The radios fall silent. "Come on, Weebles," I think. "Say something."

Moments later, Weebles keys his mike and yells: "Okay, two's off on the AAA! Lots of AAA in the target area!"

Knowing I'm about to fly through the same gauntlet has me on the edge of my seat. My heart pounds as small beads of sweat roll down the sides of my face. I decide it might be better for Jackal and me to drop from a higher altitude. Flying through a wall of AAA would be suicide.

"Alpo 58, plan on high show," I radio.

"Lots of AAA!" Weebles screams again.

"Alpo 58, did you copy?" I repeat.

"Affirmative," Jackal responds.

"Awesome!" Weebles calls out.

21:52:21z

As I approach the IP, I turn on my VTR and ask Cut for a report on the target area.

"Just up the road," Cut begins, "there's some shooting from the right side of the road. There's vehicles all around the road. Most of the AAA seems to be blowing up at about nine to ten thousand feet."

"Copy," I reply. "Say again what time you broke out of the weather."

"The weather is not a factor coming in from the west. It starts . . . The bottoms are about 8,000. Over the target area is clear. I recommend coming in from south-southwest. There should be an opening just prior to the target area."

"Alpo 57 copies," I reply.

"Be advised they do have higher AAA also, blowing up around fourteen to fifteen," Cut adds.

"Copy. And where's the stuff in relation to the diamond?"

"Just look . . . To the north of the diamond is the majority of vehicles."

"Copy. I got a good paint-out return there."

"You'll have a north-south road intersecting an east-west road. Just to the northwest of the intersection is the majority of the vehicles."

"Alpo 57."

"Picture clear, Alpo 57," AWACS radios. "Five-five is zero-four-zero for forty."

The target is thirty miles on my nose, and a deck of scattered clouds sits below me. The road intersection Cut referred to shows up well in DBS2. I slew my cursors over the bright returns that sit to the north of the east-west highway and make a radio call to Jackal: "Alpo 57, I'm painting out good paints just to the north of the road."

"How far north are you looking?" Jackal replies.

"And Alpo 57, just about a quarter of a mile."

"Five-six is coming back to the point," Weebles calls out as he continues his egress. "I'm currently twenty miles west of the point."

"Copy that," Cut says. "I'm at eighteen and flight level two-six-zero."

"Okay," Weebles replies. "I'm at angels two-eight . . . And two's negative air-to-air TACAN."

21:55:50z

While Cut and Weebles try to find each other, I prepare to roll in on the target. I'm level at 24,500 feet at an airspeed of 400 knots. At nine DME, I roll inverted and pull toward the ground. The radios are quiet and so are the Iraqi guns. As soon as I roll upright, I key my mike and make my call: "Alpo 57's in."

I pause for a moment, then call out again: "Alpo 58, I've got a good hole here as I'm going in about nine miles."

"Eight." Jackal responds.

The north-south highway Cut mentioned is clearly visible. My TD box is right above it, and a pair of black holes are burning less than a mile from the intersection. That must be where Cut and Weebles hit, I think to myself, but where's all the AAA?

I switch to CCIP as I descend through 18,000 feet. I'm trying to decide where to drop, but there isn't anything significant near my diamond. As I continue toward the ground, I spot something just to the right of the road intersection. It looks like a AAA site. I quickly bank to the right and maneuver into position so I can drop on it. I hit the pickle button in a twenty-degree dive at 500 knots. I'm passing through 8,000 feet, and, as soon as the MK-84s release, I pull back hard on the stick. As the Gs increase, I begin my straining maneuver while clearing outside.

"Alpo 57's off," I radio.

I continue to jink until I get above 17,000 feet. Jackal should have called off target by now, but I haven't heard anything. I wait for a few more seconds and then I begin to worry.

"Alpo 58, call off target," I radio.

"Alpo 58's off."

Jackal pauses for a moment, then calls out again: "Five-eight's got AAA left seven!"

I check hard to the right and look back over my shoulder. I can see the red tracers rocketing skyward, and my only concern is for Jackal.

"Copy," I radio. "Move the jet!"

It's a stupid radio call, but I want to be sure Jackal is jinking.

"Thanks," Jackal replies sarcastically.

I laugh to myself and continue to climb. As soon as I reach the Gulf, I call up the steerpoint for Al Minhad AB and engage my autopilot. Jackal is eight miles in trail and the two of us are level at 36,000 feet. On the way back home, I munch on a couple of granola bars. It's a beautiful night. I'm surrounded by millions of stars, and I'm flying an F-16. What more could a fighter pilot ask for?

I touched down at 03:05, and, during the debrief, I found out why things were so calm over the target area. Weebles put his tape in the VCR to show us his attack.

"I've already dropped my bombs at this point," Cut said as we watched the video of Weebles rolling in. "There were tracers everywhere, and I thought for sure I was going to take a few hits."

While standing in front of the television, Weebles pointed toward the bottom of the screen.

"Look at these muzzle flashes. Watch what happens to the one on the right."

As Weebles continued with his attack, flashes of gunfire appeared at the bottom of the screen. All of a sudden, Cut's bombs hit directly on top of the southern AAA site. Seconds later, Weebles pickled his bombs on the northern site.

"These guys never knew what hit them," Weebles said. "Imagine what the guys at the northern site were thinking when Cut's bombs hit."

"They must have realized they were next," Jackal observed.

"They sure as hell did," Cut interjected. "And they got exactly what they deserved."

33.
PROPOSAL FOR PEACE

The previous morning, U.S. ground forces engaged an Iraqi armored column in a predawn attack, destroying three tanks, two bunkers, and a rocket launcher. Two American soldiers were killed and six were injured when their armored vehicles were hit by a pair of U.S. Hellfire missiles. It was the second friendly-fire incident since 29 January, when seven U.S. Marines were killed by an American Maverick missile during the battle of Khafji. Marine Brig. Gen. Richard I. Neal told reporters that the 17 February incident occurred "at night with moving vehicles. It was a very dangerous environment." He also said that forty-one Iraqi soldiers were captured by helicopters and infantrymen from the 101st Airborne Division. The soldiers had been firing small arms at one of the helicopters, which replied with a rocket attack. Within minutes, the Iraqis emerged from the bunker with hands in the air.

18 FEBRUARY 1991
A few hours after Gen. Neal completed his briefing, Jackal and I departed our tanker track and pushed into Kuwait. We attacked a convoy of Iraqi armor, and both of us scored direct hits. Three of the vehicles were burning when we departed the area.

Jackal and I touched down at 21:39, and as soon as we finished debriefing, the two of us joined some of our fellow Black Widows in the beer tent. The first month of fighting was behind us, and everyone celebrated until the wee hours of the morning. I left to go to bed around 04:00. On the way back to my trailer, I ran into Stitch, who had just completed a late-night sortie. I asked him if he would mind reviewing Maverick procedures with me. I'd read through the Maverick Operations Supplement, but I needed someone with experience to review the boresight process with me.

The two of us stood alone beneath a sea of stars in the dark, cold desert for more than an hour discussing Maverick techniques. Stitch walked me through the firing process. A lot of pilots say firing the Maverick is a switchology nightmare, but Stitch made it sound easy. I walked away feeling extremely confident, and I was looking forward to getting my first Maverick missile kill.

19 FEBRUARY 1991
I woke up around 13:00 and, after a quick shower, walked over to the o'club to watch CNN. The lounge was packed, with everyone anxious to hear what President Bush had to say about the Soviet Union's latest effort to mediate a peaceful withdrawal of Saddam

Hussein's troops from Kuwait. But Soviet presidential spokesman Vitaly N. Ignatenko refused to provide details of the peace initiative, and he concluded the news conference with the following statement: "Bearing in mind the necessity of avoiding a further escalation of war in the Persian Gulf, and being mindful of the Iraqi statement of February 15, Mikhail Sergeyevich Gorbachev has proposed a concrete plan of action to resolve the conflict in the Persian Gulf area through peaceful means."

According to CNN, the morning edition of the German newspaper *Bild* listed the points contained in Gorbachev's proposal: that Iraq should withdraw from Kuwait unconditionally to make a "quick peace" possible; that the Soviet Union would commit itself to maintaining Iraq's state structure and borders; that the Soviet Union opposed all sanctions against Iraq, and any punishment against Saddam Hussein personally; and that all further issues, including the Palestinian question, should be debated.

My initial reaction to Gorbachev's proposal was enthusiastic. Allied forces had been systematically destroying the Iraqi military for more than a month, and I was ready for the war to end. No one wanted to see President Bush give in to the demands of Saddam Hussein, but if the Iraqi dictator was willing to accept the Soviet initiative and withdraw his forces from Kuwait, then many of us felt President Bush should put an end to the fighting. It was a fact that Iraqi troops had committed atrocities against the people of Kuwait, but dropping bombs on soldiers incapable of defending themselves was becoming difficult for me to handle. These men were huddled together in bunkers beneath the desert floor like frightened animals, waiting to be slaughtered.

While we waited for an announcement from President Bush, CNN televised footage of an interview with Gen. Schwarzkopf. The general said, "Iraq's military is hurting and hurting very badly. Our assessment of them is that they are on the verge of collapse. The Iraqi military has suffered so much damage that even if everything stopped today and Saddam Hussein walked out the door, Iraq would have a very dramatic setback in its military. And if they leave Kuwait quickly, they may have to leave a lot of stuff behind, because, like some of the T-72 tanks that are sitting there buried in the sand, some things just aren't going to run."

When asked if he would consider his military mission successful if Iraq withdrew unconditionally from Kuwait, even though Saddam Hussein might remain in power with part of his military intact, Gen. Schwarzkopf replied: "Absolutely. The president has said all along that we weren't out to destroy the country of Iraq."

After the interview, CNN switched to the White House, where President Bush had been meeting with congressional leaders and members of his cabinet. Hoping for positive news, everyone in the o'club lounge leaned forward, listening intently. But President Bush revealed to reporters that the Soviet proposal "falls well short of what would be required" to put an end to the war. Everyone in the lounge let out a collective groan.

"As far as I'm concerned," President Bush continued, "there are no negotiations. The goals have been set out. There will be no concessions—not going to give."

President Bush's statement was extremely disappointing to me. I thought the war was going to end that day, and I couldn't understand why his stance had to be so harsh. But as the afternoon wore on, I realized President Bush made the right decision. The United States and the rest of the world could not afford to give in to the demands of Saddam Hussein. If we allowed him the opportunity to save face, the Arab world would consider him a hero for standing up to the West and gaining something for it.

I left for the squadron to prepare for my next mission. I was flying with Lt. Col. Rackley that night and we were scheduled to take off at 18:00. The first thing I did when I walked into the squadron was check my mail. A package from Colette was sitting in the lounge. I opened it right away and found two letters, laundry soap, air fresheners for my room, and another box of granola bars. The letters were written in late January, and reading them was a tremendous boost to my morale. When I finished, I put the letters back in the box and walked down to the weapons shop to review my strike package.

Our briefing began at 15:45 with an update from wing intel. According to Maj. Marsh, Iraqi mines damaged two American warships operating in the northern Persian Gulf the day before. The *Tripoli*, an amphibious assault carrier, was hit in the early morning hours during mine-sweeping operations. Several compartments were flooded, and a 16-by-20-foot hole was opened approximately ten feet below the water line. Three hours later, the guided-missile cruiser *Princeton* was struck by a mine while responding to a call for help from the *Tripoli*. Maj. Marsh also said that another F-16 from the 363rd TFW went down yesterday in Kuwait, fifty miles north of the Saudi border. The pilot ejected, and SAR forces were immediately dispatched to rescue him. Allied fighters in the area were called in to provide cover. Before Iraqi soldiers could reach the downed pilot, he was rescued by an American helicopter. It was a chilling story, and everyone in the room was happy the pilot made it back safely.

The evening's mission turned out to be another uneventful sortie as Taz led us into northern Kuwait, where we bombed another Republican Guard division. There was more AAA than usual, but the Iraqi gunners never came close to us. One thing I did notice was that the AAA stopped as soon as we started dropping our bombs. The Iraqis were finally beginning to realize that we could see them better than they could see us.

20 FEBRUARY 1991

I walked into the weapons shop shortly after 15:00 and began work on a Maverick checklist. I'd now read everything there was to read about the weapon, but I figured it would take a few sorties to get comfortable employing it. In the meantime, I wanted a checklist in front of me, in case I forgot anything. While I looked through the Maverick Operations Supplement, Duck walked in.

"Hey, Rosey. What's going on?"

"I'm trying to make a Maverick checklist that I can carry on my kneeboard while I'm flying. I told Damien I was Maverick-qualified at the meeting the other day, but, between you and me, the only time I've ever worked with a Maverick missile was during LANTIRN training."

"The LANTIRN handout has a section in the back on the Maverick," Duck said. "I'm almost positive there's a Maverick checklist in it."

The two of us spent the next twenty minutes going over employment procedures. "Firing a Maverick isn't as hard as some guys make it out to be," Duck said. "As long as you take your time and go through each step properly, you won't have any trouble."

After we finished, Damien walked in and asked to see me. He told me I was being upgraded to four-ship flight lead.

"Congratulations, Rosey. You've earned it."

Later in the evening, I flew another sortie near the northern border of Kuwait. Grumpy was the four-ship flight lead, and his F-16 was equipped with two Maverick missiles. This sortie marked my twenty-fourth combat mission and the seventeenth I'd flown in the past twenty-one days. I was looking forward to MPC duty the next night, which would give me a chance to catch up on my sleep and complete a few chores.

21 FEBRUARY 1991

After eleven hours of sleep, I awoke feeling great. It was a beautiful day. I spent the afternoon doing laundry, cleaning my room, and writing letters. Colette's last letter mentioned how tired she was of shoveling snow from our driveway. I don't like the cold, but at that point, I would have given anything to see the snowcapped mountains of Utah.

At the o'club, everyone was in an upbeat mood. We'd been receiving a steady stream of mail lately, and, according to Grumpy, Col. Navarro had decided to open the phone lines again. The war had become routine as we waited for the ground war to begin.

Raj and I waited for the frag, relaxing in the lounge with cookies and hot tea. CNN was on the big-screen TV. According to sources in Washington, Baghdad radio was claiming that Iraq's Revolutionary Command Council had considered Soviet president Mikhail Gorbachev's peace proposal and sent foreign minister Tariq Aziz back to Moscow with the leadership's reply. Officials in the Bush administration feared the Gorbachev initiative would complicate allied efforts to drive Iraqi forces from Kuwait.

After a group of analysts discussed the Soviet peace proposal, CNN recapped the previous day's events in the Gulf. According to Pentagon correspondent Wolf Blitzer, American warplanes flew more than 2,900 sorties, bringing the total number to approximately 86,000. Blitzer said U.S. aircraft bombed an Iraqi armor concentration, destroying twenty-eight tanks, twenty-six other vehicles, three artillery pieces, and three ammunition dumps. Blitzer also reported that American Apache and Kiowa helicopters swarmed across the border and destroyed a number of Iraqi bunkers.

"According to Marine Brig. Gen. Richard I. Neal," Blitzer said, "the Iraqis were stunned. As soon as fighting began, between 450 and 500 Iraqi soldiers immediately surrendered. It seemed as though they had little, if any, will to fight."

Gen. Neal reported no estimate of how many Iraqis had been killed, but he said that the number of Americans killed in battle remained at seventeen. Thirty Americans were still listed as missing in action, and nine were known to be prisoners of war. "Amazing as it may sound," Gen. Neal remarked, "more Americans have died as a result of traffic accidents in the desert. Since U.S. forces deployed to the Gulf last August, one hundred thirty-five Americans have been listed as noncombat deaths. Of those, thirty-three have died in accidents involving motor vehicles."

After the report, Sweet Pea gave Raj and me a ride to the squadron, where the rest of our MPC team had assembled. We walked upstairs to the planning room. Shortly after 22:00, Maj. Marsh walked in excitedly.

"Hey, guys, come take a look at this Maverick video. Stitch just finished debriefing his sortie, and you'll be amazed at what he did."

Everyone stopped what they were doing and walked over to the intel shop. A crowd of people, including Sweet Pea, was gathered around the television.

"What's going on?" Lips asked.

"Watch this tape, and you'll see," Sweet Pea replied.

He pushed the play button and a picture of Stitch's right MFD appeared on the screen. After a few sweeps of the GMT radar, a small line appeared on the scope. Stitch slewed his cursors over the target and locked it up. A few seconds later, he switched the VTR from the right MFD to the HUD. The desert floor was clearly visible in the FLIR, and there was a road on the right side of the screen that ran to the northwest. As Stitch descended through 24,000 feet, I noticed the TD box near the bottom of the HUD, just to the left of the road.

"I'm locked on a mover just west of the steerpoint," Stitch radioed.

While he continued to descend, I glanced at the instrument readings in his HUD. The nose of his jet was fifteen degrees below the horizon, and his airspeed approached 375 knots. In the bottom right-hand corner, the distance to the target read thirteen miles.

"I've got a single mover moving west in the desert," Stitch radioed again. "I'm gonna plan on firing on this one two."

"Two will support," Ensign replied.

"Okay," Stitch continued. "He's got tracks behind him, so it's probably an APC or a tank, and he's heading to the west toward a bunch of revetments."

Everyone in the room stared at the television, waiting for something to happen. All of a sudden, a flash of light appeared on the left side of the screen. Stitch had just fired his first missile. The target was only 4.5 miles away, and sparks from the Maverick's exhaust lit up the FLIR. Moments later, Stitch called up the video to his second Maverick and switched his VTR back to the right MFD. Everyone gasped as a close-up view of the target appeared on the screen. It was an armored personnel carrier, and the infrared picture was extraordinary. The bright, white image of the APC made it stand out against the cool, black desert background. The infrared detail was so precise that even the track marks (the heat generated by the friction of the wheels against the sand) stood out. It suddenly dawned on me that this APC was going to explode right before our eyes. The first Maverick would reach the target within seconds, and we were watching a close-up view of the same target, courtesy of Stitch's second Maverick.

"The Iraqis in that APC are about to be toast," Stinger said glumly.

A bright white object appeared on the left side of the screen. The Maverick missile struck the left rear of the APC, which disintegrated. A fireball of white light filled the screen as molten pieces of hot metal rocketed skyward. This was the first time any of us had seen such a vivid picture of death.

"Splash the mover," Stitch radioed calmly.

A few minutes later, Stitch walked in to retrieve his tape. Everyone began to applaud, but while Stitch described the missile shot, Damien walked in and barked: "Knock it off! Everyone get back to work! Stitch, I want you in my office. Now!" He grabbed the tape out of Stitch's hand and headed for the door.

"Are you going to let us make copies of the tape, sir?" I asked.

"Nobody's making copies of anything," Damien bellowed.

"Why not?" I asked politely.

"Because I said so. That's why," he screamed in return.

A few hours later, Grumpy walked into the planning room. Everyone wanted to know what happened to Stitch and why Damien flew off the handle. Grumpy explained that Lt. Col. Scott watched the tape and was upset by the tactics Stitch used to film his pass. Scotty felt that Stitch endangered himself, his wingman, and his aircraft by not coming off target immediately after firing the missile. After viewing the tape, Scotty walked into Damien's office and chewed him out, suggesting that Stitch be grounded. He said there was a chance that he might be sent home.

"I thought Damien was just being Damien," Raj remarked sarcastically.

"From a tactics point of view, Lt. Col. Scott is probably right," Grumpy said. "But I told Damien that Scotty was overreacting a little, and, after a while, he calmed down."

"What's going to happen to the tape?" Raj asked.

"Col. Jaszczak came over to the squadron a little while ago and watched the film," Grumpy continued. "When he found out Scotty wanted to ground Stitch, he told him that Stitch was following his instructions by filming the pass. Col. Jaszczak said members of Gen. Schwarzkopf's staff have been critical of the F-16's performance during the war, and he wanted Gen. Schwarzkopf to see what the 421st is capable of accomplishing with the Mavericks we've recently received. The tape is being sent to CENTAF headquarters tomorrow morning, so if you want to make copies, I suggest you do it tonight."

"Will Damien let us?" I asked.

"Stitch and Ensign are copying it right now, and they said you can make copies when they're finished."

Once again, Col. Jaszczak proved to be the only leader in the wing who seemed to have the big picture. Everyone appreciated that he stood up for Stitch, and I hoped Gen. Schwarzkopf would enjoy the tape as much as we did. It would be great to sit in the club one afternoon and watch it again on CNN.

34.
PLAY TIME

T he next morning, after a two-hour meeting at the Kremlin between Soviet president Mikhail Gorbachev and Iraqi foreign minister Tariq Aziz, the Soviet Union announced that Iraq had agreed to withdraw its troops from Kuwait. According to CNN, Secretary of State James Baker arrived at the White House shortly after Soviet presidential spokesman Vitaly N. Ignatenko began his televised statement in Moscow. U.S. presidential spokesman Marlin Fitzwater met with reporters in the White House press room: "President Bush thanked President Gorbachev for his intensive and useful efforts. President Bush did state the concerns that he felt the coalition would have on the matter, both in terms of points that are in the plan that we have problems with, as well as issues that are not included." When asked about the status of the war and the possibility of a ground assault, Fitzwater said: "There is no change at this point in our schedule for prosecution of the war."

I could tell by the tone of Fitzwater's statement that President Bush had problems with the Soviet Union's peace proposal. Some of my friends were thinking the war was about to end, but as far as I was concerned, it was too early to celebrate. Saddam Hussein had proven time and time again that he couldn't be trusted. So why should anyone have trusted him then?

22 FEBRUARY 1991

I arrived at the squadron shortly before 15:00. Jackal and I were scheduled to take off at 17:40. This would be my first combat sortie with Maverick missiles. Before the briefing started, Jackal and I reviewed our mission envelope. Included in the package was a kill-box map, which covered Kuwait and a good portion of southern Iraq. According to the SPINS, our flight would be one of eight two-ships scheduled to work kill box AG-6, ten miles north of Kuwait City. The box contained a stretch of highway connecting the Kuwaiti capital with the Iraqi city of Basrah. Flight leads in each formation would carry two Maverick missiles, and wingmen would carry four canisters of CBU-87. AWACS controllers would monitor the different kill boxes, and each element would have twenty minutes of play time in their assigned area.

After reviewing the map, I decided the best way to work AG-6 was north-south along the highway. The length of the kill box was thirty miles, so Jackal and I plotted two sets of coordinates: N2933.00 E4739.50, which marked a point on the highway near the southern boundary; and N2957.00 E4739.50, which marked a point near the northern boundary. Once AWACS cleared us into the area, Jackal and I would work between the two points, using the same tactics Duck and I had developed back in December. Jackal would maintain a position eight miles in trail of my aircraft and clear for SAMs and AAA while I searched for targets. After I fired my missile and we reached the northern boundary, I'd call for an in-place 180-degree turn. I'd pass the tactical lead to Jackal and our roles would be reversed. During his pass, Jackal would have the option of dropping two canisters of CBU-87 or all four. He'd make that decision based on the size of the convoy he locked up. When he dropped his bombs, I'd call for another in-place turn, so I could fire my second missile. Twenty minutes would give us plenty of time to complete our work. When we finished, I'd give AWACS an in-flight report, and the two of us would return to Al Minhad.

During the briefing, I discussed the mission objectives, ground operations, Maverick boresight procedures, tanker ops, operations within the kill box, egress, and the recovery. One of the most important aspects of the brief would be altitude deconfliction within the kill box. Since I was planning to operate closer to the 5,000-foot floor, I briefed Jackal that I'd remain at or below 11,000 feet. Jackal should have no problem dropping from medium altitude, and since CBU-87 was considered an area munition, I told him to remain at or above 12,000 feet—the effective range of the ZSU-23-4.

After the briefing, Jackal and I proceeded to the life-support trailer. Duck and Tater were to work AG-6 before us, and we ran into them on their way to flightline. I asked Duck if he would mind giving me a pirep when he departed the area, and he agreed to do so. After the two of us exchanged victor frequencies, Jackal and I stepped into the trailer to put on our flying gear.

13:32:09z

"Rover 51 . . . 3251 alpha . . . Captain Keith Rosenkranz . . . We got two AGM-65 Delta Mavericks on board . . . Takeoff time is 13:40z . . . TOT is 15:40z . . . Date is 22 February '91 . . . Tail number is 435."

As soon as I finish titling my tape, I reach down and turn off my VTR. Ten minutes later, Jackal and I are climbing through 7,000 feet on the departure. After we complete our chaff/flare and climb checks, I pass the lead to Jackal. While he continues to the west, I drop back and begin to boresight my Maverick missiles. I follow each step in my checklist, and everything works just as advertised. When I finish, I resume the lead and continue toward the eastern coast of Saudi Arabia.

It's a beautiful night. The view from 24,000 feet is magnificent—a sky full of stars, and the Saudi coastline visible ahead. After checking in with AWACS, Jackal and I receive clearance to our assigned tanker track. Twenty minutes later, the two of us are flying formation with a KC-135 Stratotanker. We complete our refueling ahead of schedule, so I decide to hold with the tanker until it's time to push north. While we orbit in the holding pattern, I talk myself through the Maverick procedures one last time.

15:23:00z

As the KC-135 begins another turn to the south, Jackal and I climb away and push to the north toward Kuwait's southern border. As soon as I tell Jackal to take spacing, I reach toward my up-front control and call up steerpoint six. I'm level at 21,000 feet. My airspeed is 350 knots. If everything goes as planned, we should reach the southern point of AG-6 one minute after our scheduled TOT. As we cross the border into Kuwait, I call for a fence check and power up my Maverick missiles. Passing over the top of AG-4— each kill box has a ceiling of 20,000 feet—I glance down to see if I can spot any activity in the area. All of a sudden, multiple flashes of light appear below me. From what I can tell, allied ground forces appear to be firing rockets across the border into southern Kuwait. One by one, in quick succession, the rockets light up the desert floor.

"Rover 54," I radio. "Check your right wing low."

"Rover 54," Jackal replies. "It's pretty amazing."

In addition to the multiple rocket launches, I notice dozens of fires burning on the Kuwaiti side of the border. From 21,000 feet, the flames look like flickering candles. As I continue north, I reach into my G-suit pocket and pull out my map. It looks like the fires are coming from the Al Wafrah and Umm Gudair oil fields. Saddam Hussein had threatened to destroy Kuwait's ability to produce oil. It looks as though the destruction has begun.

15:34:00z

"Rover 54, go victor 7," I radio.

"Two!"

After I switch frequencies, I key my mike a second time.

"Rover 54, check."

"Two!"

I pause for a moment to see if Duck and Tater are still working in the area. After a few seconds of silence, I call out: "Howler 45, this is Rover 53."

"Rover 53, this is Howler 45. Go ahead, Rosey," Duck replies.

"I'm five minutes south of AG-6. Any words?"

"Copy that," Duck answers. "The weather is clear, and the threat is minimal. There's a lot of activity in the area. GMT is a real player, Rosey, and easy to use. So I recommend that. Look around steerpoint seven for us."

While Duck gives me his report, I continue to clear for SAMs and AAA. Suddenly a flash of light appears below and to my right. It's a SAM, and it's heading right for me. My heart begins to race and my muscles tighten. I make a twenty-degree check turn to the right, so I can place the missile directly on the beam. In the middle of Duck's pirep, I fire off a flare and scream out: "Rover 53's got a SAM launch right nine!" Before I can correct myself and say right three, Duck responds: "Yeah . . . I'm tally-ho, Rosey. Is it on you?"

My eyes remain fixed on the missile. All of a sudden, it disappears behind me and to my right.

"Okay . . . It's burned out," I radio. "It's gone off my right wing. It was an IR SAM!"

"Is it on you, Rosey?" Duck responds.

"Yeah . . . He's a . . . it must have gone behind me."

Anticipating a second missile, I continue clearing off my right wing. After pausing for a moment, I key my mike and radio: "Okay . . . copy your words. Thanks!"

"You bet," Duck replies.

A few seconds later, I get a call from an F-4G Wild Weasel pilot who's operating in the area.

"Rover 53, Löwenbräu 31," the pilot calls out.

"Go ahead, Löwenbräu," I answer.

"Okay . . . we've got no signals. It's unguided in that area. Also, your target area is clear."

"Copy. Thanks a lot!"

15:40:00z

I reach the southern boundary of AG-6 and continue north toward steerpoint seven. While passing over the kill box, I key my mike and call out on strike primary: "This is Rover 53 in the blind. We are over top of AG-6 and we will be working this area for the next twenty minutes." After the call, I begin to descend. As soon as I reach the northern steerpoint, I make a turn back to the south and select steerpoint six. Halfway through the turn, I program GMT in my left MFD. The radar begins to sweep, and as soon as I roll out, four contacts appear on the screen. After a few sweeps, I program snowplow on the radar and TMS forward to ground-stabilize the radar cursors. Next, I slew the radar cursors over one of the returns and TMS forward.

"Rover 53 is locked on a mover, twenty miles on my nose," I radio.

After I check that my master arm switch is in Arm, I depress the uncage switch on my throttle. The Maverick missile on station three comes to life and the video appears in my right MFD. I quickly check the HUD, and the TD box is where I expect it to be—on top of the highway. The target is visible in the right MFD. I can see the vehicles as they proceed south toward Al Jahrah, a small town roughly five miles west of Kuwait City. With my right thumb, I push the display management switch (DMS) aft to put the sensor of interest (SOI) in the weapon (WPN). Afterward, I hit the pinky switch and the Maverick shifts from wide field-of-view (WFOV) to narrow field-of-view (NFOV). Using my right thumb again, I push the TMS switch forward and hold. Then, with my left thumb, I use the cursor/enable switch on my throttle to slew the Maverick tracking gates overtop the target. As soon as I release the TMS switch, the target is locked. I quickly check the position of the Maverick pointing cross. It's steady at the five-degree depression mark. I push forward on the stick to increase my rate of descent. The target is only six miles away. I'm ready to fire. I put my finger on the pickle button and make one last check to ensure the master arm switch is in the correct position. After I confirm that it is, I push the pickle button. With a ferocious roar, the missile shoots out from under my left wing. The Maverick missile's internal-burning, boost-sustaining, solid-propellant rocket motor uses 10,000 pounds of thrust for 0.5 seconds, followed by 2,000 pounds of thrust for 3.5 seconds. The flight controls begin to function 0.5 seconds after ignition and the autopilot takes over 0.5 seconds after launch.

"Rover 53. Missile's off!" I radio.

I pull hard to the right and clear for enemy fire. It looks clear below. A few seconds later, I check back toward the target. I roll to the left and stare into the darkness below, waiting for the missile to reach its mark. For a moment, I think about the soldiers in the vehicle. Their deaths will be quick. And painless? I also think about the soldiers driving the other vehicles in the convoy. I wonder what their reaction will be when the missile hits. A bright flash lights up the desert floor below me. I've scored my first Maverick kill.

"Rover 53, that's a kill!" I radio excitedly.

While climbing, I check my HUD to confirm our position in the kill box. If I call for the in-place turn too soon, Jackal won't have enough time to make a legitimate target run. I level off at 11,000 feet, and as soon as I reach steerpoint six, I key my mike and radio: "Rover 53, in-place one-eighty left . . . now."

"Two!"

I snap my F-16 into ninety degrees of bank and initiate a four-G turn to the left. I roll out on a 355-degree heading, call up my air-to-air radar, and pass the tactical lead to Jackal.

Less than a minute later, Jackal radios on victor: "Rover 54 is locked a mover fifteen miles on my nose. I've only got three hits, so I'm only going to drop two bombs on this pass."

"Rover 53 copies," I reply.

As we continue north, I clear outside for SAMs and AAA. My RWR has been quiet the entire sortie. The last thing I expect to see is an Iraqi jet, but I check my radar just in case.

"Rover 54, bombs off!" Jackal radios.

"Rover 53 copies. Wait until you reach steerpoint seven to call for the turn."

"Two!"

During the next thirty seconds, I focus my attention outside. Jackal's bombs explode directly below my aircraft, and the fireworks are spectacular.

"Rover 54, it looks like you got two of them," I radio. "I can see two separate fires burning below me."

"Rover 54 copies. Let's come one-eighty left . . . now!"

As soon as we roll out, I make a call on victor and resume the lead. I've got the entire area to work with, and the highway is crawling with targets. I call up the air-to-ground mode and prepare to fire my second missile. Jackal and I have already made two great passes. We've destroyed three armored vehicles, and there's no reason why we shouldn't destroy three more. While my GMT radar sweeps across the ground, Grover makes a courtesy call to let me know his two-ship will reach the area soon. After I fire my second Maverick, Jackal and I will head north for his last pass, then egress to the east.

"Rover 51 is twenty miles out," Grover radios.

"Copy. I'm heading south for one more run."

"Rover 53, say range off your target."

"I'm about ten miles heading south."

"Say angels."

"Twelve."

A few seconds later, my RWR scope lights up. The familiar chirping noise in my head-set is from the radar of an F-16. Grover has me locked.

"Four is angels one-seven . . . ten miles south," Jackal radios.

"Copy that," Grover replies. "Continue heading south. Rover 51 and 52 will be going over the top of you."

"Copy," I respond. "I've got a lock. I'll be firing in a minute." As soon as I take my fin-ger off the mike switch, I slew the Maverick tracking gates over my target and lock it up. A second vehicle trails my target by six car lengths, and there's another heading north in the opposite direction. Passing 9,500 feet at 450 knots on a 190-degree heading, I hit my pickle button. The Maverick flies out from under my right wing and streaks toward the target.

"Rover 53, shot's off!" I radio.

"Five-three," Jackal replies, "five-four is twenty south ready to turn back north."

"Copy," I respond. "Go to point six—the IP!"

"Roger."

I continue south on a 180-degree heading, waiting for the missile to explode. There's no sign of Iraqi AAA, but I can see dozens of oil wells burning in the distance. The high-way is right below me, and, seconds later, the missile explodes.

"Got another kill," I radio.

"Two's got AAA my six . . . fifteen south!" Jackal interrupts.

This is the first time any of us have been fired upon. I want to call for an in-place turn so Jackal can make his last pass, but our time is up, and Grover is waiting to get in the kill box. I decide to ask Grover if we can have five more minutes.

"Rover 51, 53."

"Go ahead," Grover replies.

"Can I circle here and make one more pass? There's a lot of GMT stuff down there."

"That's affirm. Let me know when you're done."

"Copy. I'll let you know when I'm in."

"Stay fifteen miles away from the north part of the area," Grover says.

"Copy. I'll stay fifteen miles away."

I call for an in-place turn and remind Jackal to stay in the bottom half of the area. He acknowledges the call and turns to the north. While I clear for the formation, Jackal drops the remaining two canisters of CBU-87. As soon as he calls off, I instruct him to make a right turn to south and climb to 20,000 feet. Once we reach steerpoint six, I call Grover and advise him that we're departing the kill box. During the egress, I pass an in-flight report to AWACS and climb to 35,000 feet. Jackal rejoins to a trail position, and the two of us proceed direct to Al Minhad. Jackal and I touch down at 21:16 and taxi to the hot pits. After our tanks are full, we taxi to the ramp and shut down our engines.

During the debrief, I critiqued our film and discussed the things Jackal and I could have done better. Afterward, we returned to the squadron, grabbed an MRE out of the supply room, and relaxed by the television in the squadron lounge. The Soviet peace proposal continued to be the focus of everyone's attention, and shortly after we sat down, CNN went live to Washington, where President Bush addressed reporters.

"The United States and its coalition allies are committed to enforcing the United Nations resolutions that call for Saddam Hussein to immediately and unconditionally leave Kuwait," the President began.

"In view of the Soviet initiative, which very frankly we appreciate, we want to set forth this morning the specific criteria that will ensure Saddam Hussein complies with the United Nations mandate. Within the last twenty-four hours alone, we have heard a defiant, uncompromising address by Saddam Hussein, followed less than ten hours later by a statement in Moscow that, on the face of it, appears more reasonable. I say 'on the face of it' because the statement promised unconditional Iraqi withdrawal from Kuwait, only to set forth a number of conditions; and needless to say, any conditions would be unacceptable to the international coalition, and would not be in compliance with the United Nations Security Council Resolution 660's demand for immediate and unconditional withdrawal.

"More importantly and more urgently, we learned this morning that Saddam has now launched a scorched-earth policy against Kuwait, anticipating, perhaps, that he will now be forced to leave. He is wantonly setting fires to, and destroying, the oil wells, the oil tanks, the export terminals, and other installations of that small country. Indeed, they are destroying the entire oil-production system in Kuwait. And at the same time that that Moscow press conference was going on and Iraq's foreign minister was talking peace, Saddam Hussein was launching Scud missiles.

"After examining the Moscow statement and discussing it with my senior advisers here late last evening and this morning, and after extensive consultation with our coalition partners, I have decided that the time has come to make public with specificity just exactly what is required of Iraq if a ground war is to be avoided. Most important, the coalition will give Saddam Hussein until noon Saturday to do what he must do—begin his immediate and unconditional withdrawal from Kuwait. We must hear publicly and authoritatively his acceptance of these terms."

I was disappointed that President Bush rejected the Soviet proposal, but I respected his judgment.

23 FEBRUARY 1991

The sons of Iraq have prepared for them what they deserve—God's burning fire, which will devour the evil and the despicable traitors who have sold themselves cheaply to the foreigner. They wanted a ground war. The soldiers of Iraq, the soldiers of the leader, Saddam Hussein, supported by God and the people, welcome it with hearts full of faith . . .

—Baghdad Radio
23 February 1991

The shuttle bus dropped me off in front of the 421st shortly after 15:00. I would fly my first sortie as a four-ship flight lead, with Jackal, Stitch, and Ensign. Stitch would act as my instructor during the flight, and the two of us met in the weapons shop to formulate a game plan for the evening's mission. I'd carry Maverick missiles. The rest of the pilots would carry two MK-84s with FMU-113 fuses set to function at fifteen feet AGL. Our objective: destroy as many of Iraq's armored vehicles as we can.

The briefing began at 15:55 with an update from wing intel.

"Earlier today," Maj. Marsh began, "the Killer Scouts flew twenty-four combat missions in the skies above Kuwait. The pilots in the 4th TFS worked sixty aircraft in kill boxes AF/AG—5/6/7, and fifty-eight aircraft in kill boxes AD/AE—5/6/7. According to Maj. Goodfellow, it was a target-rich environment. Dozens of armored vehicles were destroyed, and some of the pilots reported that a massive Iraqi repositioning is under way. I would expect to see even more movement tonight, now that President Bush has issued an ultimatum. For those of you who aren't aware, the deadline for Iraq to begin its withdrawal is 21:00 this evening." Major Marsh continued, "If the ground war begins while you're airborne, contact Warmonger, the 7th ASOC [Air Support Operations Center], or Nutcracker, the 18th ASOC. These are air force people at the army corps level. They will provide information concerning the position of allied ground forces. Tell them your call sign, mission number, and the kill box you're assigned to. They'll keep you out of trouble. It shouldn't be a factor tonight, but if and when the ground war does start, you'll receive information concerning allied troop positions in briefings like this one. Fratricide is a major concern, so pilots flying at night will be required to stay at least fifteen miles away from the forward edge of the troop advancement. We'll update you on troop positions before you take off. AWACS and ABCCC will provide additional updates when you depart your assigned tanker track. Be flexible. They may restrict you from working certain quadrants of your kill box. If you aren't doing it already, I suggest you get in the habit of contacting them."

14:35:00z

Captain Keith Rosenkranz . . . Husky 55 . . . 3255 alpha . . . Ordnance is two Mavericks . . . Takeoff time is 14:40 . . . TOT is 16:30 to 17:00 . . . Date is 23 February '91 . . . Tail number is 453 . . . Four-ship flight-lead upgrade.

Approaching the eastern coast of Saudi Arabia, I check in with AWACS and receive clearance to the Lime air-refueling track. Within twenty minutes, I'm executing a fighter turn-on rejoin with a KC-135 full of JP-4. I'm the first F-16 on the boom and it takes less than five minutes to top off my tanks. When I finish, I maneuver to the outside of Jackal on the left wing of the Stratotanker. While the others refuel, I put in a call to AWACS, ABCCC, and J-STARS to see if they have any target updates for me. They don't, which means we'll be proceeding to AG-6 as briefed.

As soon as Ensign disconnects from the boom and rejoins on Stitch's right wing, Jackal and I push north. We have only thirty minutes of play time in the kill box tonight, so Stitch and Ensign will orbit with the KC-135 for fifteen minutes before they come to replace us. After Jackal and I switch to strike primary, I power up my Maverick missiles. As we cross into Kuwaiti territory, I look down at the war zone below. A steady stream of artillery shells and rockets shoots across the border. There are twice as many oil-well fires as last night, and it looks like the Iraqis have finally ignited the oil trench that separates them from allied ground troops. The line of bright orange fire extends for miles. It must be hell down there.

As soon as we enter AG-6, I call up steerpoint sixteen and begin to descend. Intel gave us coordinates for an Iraqi Republican Guard camp in the southern part of the area, so I spend a few minutes using my Maverick video to search for tanks. The first thing I do is call up my ground-map radar and zero in on a set of returns slightly east of the steer-point. After I slew my cursors over the contacts, I hit the uncage switch on my throttle, which activates the Maverick video in my right MFD. The missile is slaved to the radar, so I use it to look inside the revetments. I can see a trench in the video display and it looks like there are a few tanks sitting in bunkers nearby. There aren't very many, though, so I tell Jackal to save his bombs for other targets in the area. Stitch and Ensign will be along in ten to fifteen minutes. I'll pass the information on to them, and they can decide whether or not they want to bomb them.

With Jackal in eight-mile trail, I turn toward the town of Al Jahra so I can set up for a run to the north. While maneuvering, I switch from visual (VIS) to preplanned (PRE) and call up my GMT radar. I roll out heading north and begin my target search. The highway is crawling with movers. I lock up a vehicle in the northern half of the box. As soon as the radar goes into fixed-target track, I key my mike and radio: "Husky 55 is locked a mover, twenty-six miles on my nose." The airspace is crowded tonight, and the radios are hectic.

"Bulldog, Black 71 authenticate two-golf," a pilot calls out.

"Bulldog authenticates echo-echo."

"Ram, Bengal, Buck, let's go cherry four," says another pilot.

"Black 71, push cherry four."

As I descend toward the target, Cut calls out on victor: "And Husky, Rover 51's up."

"Go ahead, Rover," I respond.

"I'm at the very north tip of the box. I'd like to make a run from north to south on the highway if I could, to get one more Maverick off."

"Okay, go ahead and do that. I'm on the one-nine-five for ten off of steerpoint six, and I'm heading north. I've got a mover locked right now about nineteen miles in front of me, so stay on the east side of the road if you would."

"Copy that."

Continuing north, I hit the uncage switch and reactivate my Maverick. The WFOV video display appears in my right MFD and I can almost make out the highway. As I descend through 9,000 feet, Jackal reminds me to turn on my air-to-air TACAN so he can keep track of the distance between our aircraft. I reach toward my up-front control and call up the TACAN page. After I turn the system on, I key my mike and radio: "Got the air-to-air TACAN up now . . . Sorry! I'm on the left side of the area heading north."

Turning my attention back to the target, I hit the uncage switch, and the Maverick field-of-view changes to NFOV. The tiny white vehicle and the highway are clearly visible. After I DMS aft to select WPN as the SOI, I move my right thumb to the TMS switch and push it forward. While it's depressed, I slew the missile tracking gates over the target. Once they're in place, I release the TMS switch, and the missile locks onto the vehicle. When I'm in range and the pointing cross stops flashing, I'll be ready to fire.

"Missile's away!" Cut radios.

"Husky 55 is locked a mover now on my nose eleven miles," I reply. "I'll be firing in a couple minutes."

"Copy. Rover 51 is out of your hair now."

16:33:11z

I reach down toward my left console and switch my VTR to HUD. The nose of my F-16 is seven degrees below the horizon and I'm descending through 8,000 feet. My airspeed is 400 knots and I'm currently on a 355-degree heading. The Maverick circle and the TD box in the HUD are superimposed over each other, and the pointing cross is steady. I place my right thumb on the pickle button, and, passing through 6,500 feet, I hit the switch. There's a loud *whoosh* as the missile flies off the rail. The Maverick streaks toward its target while Bitchin' Betty calls out "altitude, altitude" to remind me that I'm approaching the 5,000 foot floor.

"Husky 55, missile's off!" I radio excitedly. "I'm coming off to the right!"

I make a climbing right turn to 060 and check below for SAMs and AAA. A few seconds later, I check back toward the target and roll to the left. When the vehicle explodes, I call out: "Husky 55, got a kill on that one!" I make a hard turn to the right and begin to climb. After leveling off at 11,000 feet, I turn off my VTR and call up steerpoint six. I'm on a 200-degree heading and I'm going to use my other Maverick to check out a few bunkers in the southeast corner of the kill box.

"Husky 55 is base plus nine heading south," I radio. "I'm going to check quadrant four with my other missile. I'll let you know if I find anything."

"Husky 56 copies. I'm five east of steerpoint seven . . . base plus thirteen."

I continue south and activate the video from my other Maverick. After I program VIS on the SMS page, I reach down and turn my VTR back on.

"Bulldog, Oiler 05 is derby at this time, climbing to base plus one-nine-zero," someone radios.

"Oiler 5, Buckeye—correction—Bulldog copies."

After I switch from WFOV to NFOV, I notice a small bright return. I slew the Maverick tracking gates overtop of it and radio: "And Husky 56, I slewed just to the left in quadrant four. There's one small bright return. Looking down here, it looks like there's a little road Y just to the left of the bright returns. I'm locked on something now. I'll take a look for you."

"Roger," Jackal replies.

"Bulldog, Firebird 67."

"Firebird 67, Bulldog posit ID. Picture clear."

"Firebird 67."

I descend as low as I can without going through the 5,000-foot floor. There appears to be something in the bunker, but I can't say for sure what it is. When the missile reaches the seeker-head gimbal limit, I pull to the right and begin to climb.

"Husky 55 is off to the right climbing up," I radio. "Couldn't tell for sure what's down in there. You'll have to take a look for yourself."

"Roger, 56 is in."

All of a sudden, a burst of AAA shoots into the sky off my right wing. I quickly call out: "If you look, there's a black cloud area down there off my right. And there's AAA on this side of it and on the southern side of it too."

"Looking," Jackal replies.

"Some coming up right out of the middle of it now!"

"Tally! Say range, bearing from the steerpoint!"

"Zero-four-five for six. I'm heading north. You're cleared in on that if you want."

"Roger."

After Jackal acknowledges my call, Stitch comes up on victor: "Husky 55, 57."

"Go ahead," I respond.

"Could you see if there were tanks in the southern area?"

"The steerpoint I came up on earlier?"

"Affirm."

"Yeah. There were some bright spots in it on the weapon page there. You may want to drop just one. Just to the right of the cursors there was a trench in there. Looked like some bright returns. I had one of them locked up just to the right of the trench."

"Roger that."

"Confirm angels seventeen?" Jackal radios.

I glance at my altitude in the HUD and respond: "I'm climbing up through fourteen."

"Roger. I'm north for ten now, turning southbound towards the target."

"Copy. You're cleared in. I'm gonna head back up to the north, then I'm gonna come back for another run along the road."

"Roger. And I've got AAA about ten north of the target too."

I check thirty degrees to the right and spot the stream of red tracers over my shoulder.

"Copy," I radio. "I'm tally that. If you can find some way to roll in on them, that would be great."

"Right," Jackal responds.

I circle back to the west and call up my GMT radar. There's no danger of running into Jackal, so I decide to remain at 14,000 feet. The AAA is a lot heavier than it was last night, and I don't want to take a chance on getting hit. As soon as my radar begins to sweep, I spot a target on my nose less than twenty miles away. I transition to the EXP mode and slew my cursors over the contact.

"Husky 58," Stitch radios. "Five-seven will look at steerpoint sixteen. If I can find that bright return, I'll go ahead and look at it and see if I can drop."

"Husky 56 is off," Jackal announces.

"Copy."

"And I've got AAA low."

"Copy. Come off to the right. I'm heading west now. I've got a mover locked up fifteen miles on my nose."

"Roger."

I'm descending through 11,000 feet, and my airspeed is 400 knots. The target is fourteen miles on my nose, and the highway is running left to right across the video display in my right MFD. I hit the uncage switch and the video changes to NFOV. The vehicle is right in the middle of the screen. While I slew the Maverick tracking gates over the target, I hear a chirping noise in my headset. I quickly glance at my RWR scope. There's a symbol at my deep six and before I can say anything, Jackal calls out: "Check buddy lock."

"Crickets," I respond. "I've got a mover locked up. I'll be firing in a minute."

16:44:10z

While descending through 10,000 feet, I reach down and switch my VTR to HUD. I'm thirteen degrees nose low flying at 435 knots. The vehicle is less than five miles away, and it looks like a semi truck. Unfortunately for the driver, the missile is locked on the cab. Passing 7,000 feet, I hit the pickle button. I check to the right, key my mike and radio: "Husky 55, missile's away!" I roll out on a 300-degree heading and stare into the darkness below. As soon as I see the fireball, I call out: "And Husky 55, second kill! I'm in a right-hand turn climbing up. Let's egress steerpoint seven."

"Husky 56," Jackal responds.

Within minutes, Jackal and I are feet-wet over the Gulf, climbing through 24,000 feet. After I give my in-flight report to AWACS, I call for an ops check and fence out. I level off at 37,000 feet, and, while staring into the blackness of the night, I think about the young American soldiers who have spent the last five months preparing for tonight. The deadline for Iraq to begin its troop withdrawal has finally passed. Now the real war begins.

35.
"ALTITUDE ... ALTITUDE"

Good evening. Yesterday, after conferring with my senior national security advisers, and following extensive consultations with our coalition partners, Saddam Hussein was given one last chance, set forth in very explicit terms, to do what he should have done more than six months ago: withdraw from Kuwait without condition or further delay, and comply fully with the resolutions passed by the United Nations Security Council.

Regrettably, the noon deadline passed without the agreement of the government of Iraq to meet demands of United Nations Security Council Resolution 660, as set forth in specific terms spelled out by the coalition, to withdraw unconditionally from Kuwait. To the contrary, what we have seen is a redoubling of Saddam Hussein's efforts to destroy completely Kuwait and its people.

I have therefore directed Gen. Norman Schwarzkopf, in conjunction with coalition forces, to use all forces available, including ground forces, to eject the Iraqi army from Kuwait. Once again, this was a decision made only after extensive consultations within our coalition partnership.

The liberation of Kuwait has now entered a final phase. I have complete confidence in the ability of the coalition forces swiftly and decisively to accomplish their mission. Tonight, as this coalition of countries seeks to do that which is right and just, I ask only that all of you stop what you are doing and say a prayer for all the coalition forces, and especially for our men and women in uniform who, this very moment, are risking their lives for their country and for all of us.

May God bless and protect each and every one of them, and may God bless the United States of America.

—President George Bush

The greatest bombing campaign in military history had begun thirty-eight days earlier, when President Bush announced the beginning of Operation Desert Storm. Since then, the United States and its allies had flown more than 94,000 sorties and dropped thousands of tons of munitions. In the early days of the war, laser-guided smart bombs and Tomahawk missiles devastated Iraq's command-and-control network. Additional bombing raids destroyed Scud-missile and nuclear-production facilities, as well as chemical and biological weapons sites. Airfields throughout Iraq had been cratered, and aircraft that had taken off either fled to Iran or were shot down by allied fighters.

Airpower had also had a devastating effect on Iraq's field army. Coalition aircraft averaged more than 2,300 sorties a day since fighting began, subjecting Saddam Hussein's army to around-the-clock bombing. Every major supply line leading into southern Iraq and Kuwait had been cut off, depriving Iraqi soldiers of food and water, fuel, spare parts, and ammunition. More than 3,500 Iraqis had laid down their arms and surrendered. Tens of thousands more had died. Despite the fury of the allied air attack, Saddam

Hussein had remained defiant. He told the Iraqi people that his army awaited the beginning of the ground war. Well, the time had finally arrived. At 04:00 Baghdad time, the 1st Marine Expeditionary Force drove across the southern border of Kuwait toward Ahmed Al Jaber AB. Additional allied ground forces, supported by Cobra and Apache attack helicopters, unleashed some of the heaviest artillery bombardment yet on Iraq's front-line troops.

24 FEBRUARY 1991

I arrived in the o'club lounge shortly after 15:00 and took a seat in front of the television. According to CNN reports, Iraqi forces had sabotaged more than 300 Kuwaiti oil wells during the previous few days and had arrested between 2,000 and 10,000 civilians. Eyewitnesses in Kuwait reported that prisoners were being raped, tortured, and executed. Brig. Gen. Richard I. Neal called it "terrorism at its finest hour."

"They are executing people on a routine basis," Neal said, "people not connected with the resistance. They may think the game is up, and they are trying to destroy the evidence, and that evidence is the people."

Prince Bandar ibn Sultan, Saudi Arabia's ambassador to the United States, reported: "As many as eight thousand Kuwaitis have been killed since the Iraqi invasion last August, and another eleven thousand have been reported missing. We believe between five thousand and eight thousand—it's very hard to confirm until we get there—were killed, mostly by mass execution or punishment or interrogation."

The people of Kuwait had suffered tremendously. But at that point, my only concern was for the safety of American ground forces fighting in the desert. I had the utmost confidence in their ability to win, but in the back of my mind, I couldn't help but wonder if this was what Saddam Hussein had been waiting for. Would he use his remaining combat aircraft to launch kamikaze air strikes? What role, if any, would be played by the aircraft that had fled to Iran? Would Saddam Hussein saturate the battlefield with chemical and biological weapons, as he had threatened so many times in the past? Will Scud missiles filled with chemical agents be launched into Saudi Arabia, or even worse, Israel?

After dinner, Jackal and I walked outside and waited for the shuttle bus. The two of us were scheduled to take off at 22:00, and this would be the eleventh time we had flown together since the start of the war. Jackal and I worked extremely well with each other. There wasn't another pilot in the squadron I would rather be paired with. Both of us had been in the air force since 1983. While I was in pilot training at Reese AFB, Jackal was attending the Euro-NATO Joint Jet Pilot Training (ENJJPT) program at Sheppard AFB in Wichita Falls, Texas. After he earned his wings, Jackal became a forward air controller in the O-2A at Shaw AFB, South Carolina. He later transitioned to the OA-37 and flew with the 21st Tactical Air Support Squadron, also at Shaw AFB. He was eventually selected to fly the F-16, and attended RTU training at MacDill AFB, Florida. Upon graduation, Jackal was assigned to the 421st TFS at Hill AFB. He deployed with the squadron to Al Minhad last August, but returned to the United States in October. He attended LANTIRN training at Luke AFB as a member of the 34th TFS, and returned to the Gulf five days before the war started.

As Jackal and I walked toward the squadron, we discussed the ground war and some of the objectives we wanted to achieve later in the evening. When I told him I was looking forward to getting my fifth and sixth Maverick kills, his demeanor turned serious: "How do you feel when you see a Maverick missile destroy an Iraqi armored vehicle filled with troops?"

It was a tough question. I hesitated, then turned to him and replied: "Do you remember how you felt the first time you dropped your bombs and realized you had killed someone? It happened to me a couple of weeks ago, and a day doesn't go by that I don't think about the person I killed. While we speak, there's a group of Iraqi soldiers in Kuwait who will die tonight because of me. I have no idea who they are, where they come from, or if they have families waiting for them back home. They could be raping and torturing innocent civilians or simply loading up their vehicle with Kuwaiti goods to take back home. In any case, they'll soon be heading north along the highway to Basrah. By then, it will be dark, and I will be stalking them in my F-16. Approximately forty miles out at fifteen thousand feet, I'll call up my GMT radar. Their vehicle will be nothing more than a blip on my left MFD. I'll lock them up with a Maverick, and, as soon as I'm in range, I'll fire the missile. Thirty seconds later, their lives on earth will end. I wish I wasn't the one hitting the pickle button, but it's God's will . . . and I can live with that."

After entering the squadron, I walked down the hall and signed in for my mission. On a clipboard next to the Form 10 sign-out sheet was a letter from Gen. Buster Glosson. It was addressed to every pilot in theater, and, according to SSgt. Brown, everyone in the squadron was supposed to read it before they flew that night. The letter read:

Personal from BGen Glosson, 24 February 91, 16:00z
1. Please brief the contents of this message to every aircrew member before their next flight.
2. The accomplishments of each and every one of you have been awesome, and that is probably an understatement. You have added a new dimension to the phrase: "kicking ass and taking names." The record will show you have accomplished more in less time than any air campaign in history. Your individual efforts have made it happen.
3. We have now entered a totally new phase of the war, one requiring that each flight lead have the flexibility to support American and allied troops on the ground without being encumbered by well-meaning, but unnecessary, restrictions. Therefore, effective immediately there will be no altitude restrictions or weapons-delivery parameters dictated to the flight leads. Depending on the criticality of each situation, flight leads will make those decisions consistent with the risk to American and allied troops. Flight lead decisions have always been, and will continue to be, the key to the greatness of U.S. airpower.
4. I have total confidence in your tremendous flying abilities and your innate capabilities to make the right decision for each situation. Good hunting and Godspeed.
—Buster C. Glosson, BGEN, 14AD/CC

As soon as I read the letter, I walked down to the weapons shop and began to prepare for my mission. Jackal sat down next to me, and, as time passed, other pilots began to filter in. The briefing began at 19:00 with a prayer from Father Willie, our squadron chaplain. When he finished, we received a weather update from the wing meteorologist. According to the forecast, cloudy skies and heavy rain showers were expected in Kuwait and southern Iraq during the next few days. If the forecast was correct, it couldn't have come at a worse time. Allied ground forces were depending on our support, and if the weather was bad, it would hinder our ability to engage the enemy. We owned the skies, but for airpower to be effective, we needed good weather—especially at low altitude. For those of us who were carrying Maverick missiles, clear skies were even more important. Dust, haze, and smoke in dry air have little effect upon IR energy. If water vapor is present, though, it can combine with haze particles and form a "moist" haze, which can attenuate IR energy and reduce the maximum-range capability of the Maverick's IR seeker.

The briefing continued with an update from Maj. Marsh. Notes in hand, he walked to the end of the table and stood next to the large map of Kuwait that hung on the weapons-shop wall.

"The ground offensive began before sunrise this morning when thousands of American forces surged across the border," Marsh began, while pointing at the lower half of the map. "Arab forces consisting of troops from Saudi Arabia, Egypt, Syria, and Kuwait advanced to the north along the Kuwaiti coastline. Stretching to the west of Kuwait's eastern border with Iraq, the U.S. Army's 1st Mechanized Infantry Division, 2nd and 3rd Armored Cavalry Divisions, and the 101st Airborne led a charge into Iraqi territory in what is being described as a large flanking maneuver designed to encircle the Republican Guard. Other forces involved in the initial assault include the British 1st Armored Division and the French 6th Light Armored Division. According to my sources in Riyadh, the resistance along the border has been extremely light. There have been skirmishes, but reports indicate that Iraqi troops have been surrendering in mass numbers.

"Allied ground forces have already advanced as far north as the dividing line between AG-4 and AG-5, bringing them to within thirty miles of Kuwait City. Looking to the west, ground forces have also advanced halfway into AF-5, AE-5, and AD-5. The deepest penetrations into Iraqi territory occurred as far north and west as AC-7, AB-7, and AA-7. The western flank of the attack consists of the French 6th Light Armored Division and troops from the army's 82nd Airborne. They're currently approaching the Iraqi town of As Salman, which sits along the northern boundary of AA-7. As Salman is approximately 73 miles north of the Saudi border and 134 miles northwest of the tri-border area."

As Maj. Marsh described the advancement, I looked down at my kill-box map to see where the allies were in relation to AE-6, the kill box Jackal and I had been assigned to work. When I realized allied ground forces had closed to within fifteen miles of our box,

I pulled out my lineup card and wrote down the frequencies for AWACS, ABCCC, and J-STARS. "We're going to have to contact every one of these before we enter our area to make sure we know where the leading edge of the advancement is," I whispered to Jackal. "The last thing either of us needs is a friendly-fire incident."

After Maj. Marsh concluded his brief, Lt. Col. Rackley addressed the group.

"Did everyone read Gen. Glosson's letter?" Taz asked. Everyone nodded, and then he continued. "I agree with what the general says, but I still want you to adhere to the five-thousand-foot floor. We haven't lost a pilot yet, and, as far as I'm concerned, there's no reason to change the way we've been doing things. It's going to be a few hours before you reach your kill boxes, and a lot can happen between now and then. Make sure you know exactly where the friendly forces are before you fire a single missile or drop one bomb. If there's any doubt whatsoever, come off dry. Does everyone understand?"

"Yes, sir," we answered in unison.

"That's all I've got."

Jackal and I take off at 22:00 and proceed across the Gulf toward northern Saudi Arabia. The tanker rejoin is uneventful, and as soon as I top off my tanks, I call AWACS, ABCCC, and J-STARS. Each controller gives me unrestricted clearance to work AE-6. We arrive in our kill box one minute into our window and begin searching for targets. For the next twenty minutes, Jackal and I comb every square mile of the area, but never find a single target. We use our ground map and GMTT radars, and we still come up empty. I put in a call to J-STARS, but they don't have anything in the area either. Two more passes produce negative results, so I send Jackal over to strike primary and try AWACS. I ask if we can work another box, but the controller says everything is full and he has more formations inbound. When our play time is up, Jackal and I depart the area and head back to Al Minhad with a full complement of weapons beneath our wings. The flight home is disappointing, to say the least. I know there are plenty of Iraqi tanks to hit, and I'm frustrated that none of them were in our kill box. We touch down at 01:30 and head for the beer tent.

"I guess a few Iraqi soldiers got lucky tonight," Jackal remarks.

"Yeah, but we'll be back again tomorrow."

25 FEBRUARY 1991

Fight them, oh brave, splendid men. Oh men of the Mother of All Battles . . . Fight them with your faith in God. Fight them in defense of every free and honorable woman and every innocent child, and in defense of the values of manhood and the military honor which you shoulder. Fight them because with their defeat you will be at the last entrance of the victory of victories.

—Saddam Hussein,
24 February 1991

After sleeping nearly all day, I arrived at the squadron and joined a few of my fellow

Black Widows in the lounge. Some of the guys reviewed their strike packages. Others read mail or ate MREs. The television was broadcasting Gen. Schwarzkopf's news conference from Riyadh, where the CENTCOM commander summed up the opening stages of the ground war: "Friendly casualties have been extremely light—as a matter of fact, remarkably light."

The burly commander announced that 5,500 Iraqi prisoners were captured during the first ten hours of fighting, and reports indicated there were hundreds more to the north with white surrender flags. While Schwarzkopf described the plight of Saddam Hussein's troops, CNN showed footage of captured men being escorted across the desert. They looked dirty, tired, and hungry. Most stared at the ground, humiliated. The mass surrender proved that airpower had had a devastating effect on the spirit of the Iraqi soldiers. I felt bad for the men, and I thought it was disgraceful to parade them on television. They'd been humiliated enough already.

After the news conference, I went back to the weapons shop to get my strike package from the safe. That night's mission would be similar to the previous day's with two exceptions: Grover would fly on my wing instead of Jackal, and our assigned kill box would be AG-6. While Fleetwood Mac's greatest hits played softly in the background, Grover and I filled out our lineup cards and discussed our objectives for the mission. We had thirty minutes of play time in the area, and if the highway between Kuwait City and Basrah was as saturated as I thought it would be, we wouldn't have a problem finding targets. Our biggest challenge would be the weather. Low ceilings and heavy rain were impeding the allied advancement, and the poor weather wasn't expected to let up until later in the week.

The mass briefing began at 17:00 with a short prayer from Father Willie. After a weather update, Maj. Marsh stepped to the front of the room: "Despite harsh winds and heavy rain, allied forces continue to advance along a three-hundred-mile front. Resistance has been minimal, and the U.S.-led offensive was able to achieve every one of its first-day objectives in just twelve hours. I had a chance to speak with some of the pilots in the 4th earlier this afternoon. They spent most of the day operating in kill boxes AF-6, AF-7, AG-6 and AG-7. Lt. Col. Welsh said the visibility was extremely poor in the region, and his men only worked twenty-four aircraft into the area. He said the clouds are layered up into the thirties and nearly half of the Pointers returned with their ordnance."

Marsh continued, turning toward the map of Kuwait: "As far as the ground forces are concerned, the French 6th Light Armored Division is currently fifteen miles inside of AA-8. That puts them roughly forty-five miles south of the Euphrates River. The 101st Airborne is here, about fifteen miles into AB-8. They're less than thirty miles from the Euphrates and the city of As Samawah. The 24th Mechanized Infantry Division has advanced halfway into AC-8, which, as you can see, puts them less than thirty miles from the city of An Nasiriyah. Once these units reach the Euphrates valley, they will sweep to the east in an effort to enclose the Republican Guard. The rest of the allied forces are proceeding in more of a northeasterly fashion to confront the Republican Guard head-on. The 1st Armored Division is five miles into AD-7; the 3rd Armored Division is here—twenty miles inside of AD-6; the British 1st Armored Division Desert Rats are five miles into AE-6; and the remaining units are spread across AE-5, AF-5, and AG-5.

"The allied advance continues as we speak, so remember to contact AWACS, ABCCC, and J-STARS before you push across the border. If there aren't any questions, good luck and fly safe."

16:55:00z

"Husky 07, check!"

"Two!"

As soon as Grover answers, I reach down to my right console and switch my KY-58 radio to C/RAD 2, so we can check the secure voice operation of our victor radios.

"Husky 07, check victor secure."

"Husky 08, loud and clear."

"Husky 07, come up channel three . . . victor eleven . . . plain."

"Two!"

I signal my crew chief to remove the chocks, and less than a minute later, Grover and I begin to taxi. After my crew chief and I exchange salutes, I give him the Juvat snake signal and proceed toward the main taxiway. It takes about five minutes to reach the arming area. When I come to a stop, the arming crews crawl beneath my jet. With my arms in the air, I look at my cockpit setup one last time to ensure every switch is in the proper position. After the arming chief gives me a thumbs-up, the crews run to Grover's jet. While they go through their checks, I reach down and turn on my VTR to title my tape.

"Captain Keith Rosenkranz . . . Husky 07 . . . 3207 alpha . . . Two Maverick missiles on board . . . Takeoff time is 17:15 . . . TOT timeframe 19:00 to 19:30 . . . Tail number 465."

Exactly three minutes prior to our scheduled takeoff time, I taxi onto the runway. Grover follows and comes to a stop off my right wing. As soon as he turns off his taxi light, I switch my position lights to steady, and the two of us run up our engines. When my clock reads 17:15:00, I release my brakes.

An hour into the flight, I switch us over to cherry four—the primary check-in frequency for AWACS in the eastern sector of Saudi Arabia. I'm currently level at 24,000 feet, and Grover is eight miles in trail. We had climbed into the weather after I boresighted my Maverick missiles, and we've been in the soup ever since.

"Bulldog, Husky 07," I radio.

"Husky 07, Bulldog has you loud and clear."

"Husky 07 is checking in at base plus eleven, mission number 3207 alpha. Authenticate bravo-victor."

"Bulldog has radar contact. Authenticate mike-lima."

The authentication matches and the controller clears us to our assigned tanker track.

I send Grover to tanker common, and we proceed to our rendezvous point. We're still in the weather. If things don't improve quickly, we're going to be in for a long night. I continue west and call up my air-to-air radar. Before long, I lock up the tanker and call out: "Husky 07 has radar contact twenty right for thirty miles angels two-one."

"Two same," Grover replies.

"Husky 08, rejoin one-mile trail."

"Two!"

The tanker is at my right one o'clock heading south at 21,000 feet. While easing into a left-hand turn, I pull my throttle back and begin to descend. Rejoining on a tanker at night is extremely difficult. Performing the maneuver in the weather will make it even more challenging. I level off at 20,500 feet and accelerate to 340 knots. The tanker is three miles in front of me, and I have thirty knots of overtake. Thank God for the FLIR. Without it, Grover and I would be on our way back to Al Minhad.

I call the tanker to report my position and the pilot advises that they still have two chicks in tow. He says they will clear me to join as soon as they finish refueling. After acknowledging his call, I pull my throttle back, open my air-refueling door, and switch my ECM pod to standby. A few minutes later, the tanker pilot clears me to rejoin. I push my throttle forward again and accelerate to 340 knots. The clouds are thick. I'm 500 feet below the tanker. With one eye on my airspeed and another on the distance between us, I continue toward the tanker. As I close to within a few hundred feet, the outline of the aircraft begins to appear in my FLIR. It's a KC-10, and I've got the boom in sight. As soon as I put my radar in standby, I push my throttle up and ease into the contact position. The boomer eventually plugs in, and the fuel begins to flow.

While Grover waits patiently on the left wing, my eyes remain fixed on the refueling-position lights. I'm afraid to blink for fear of falling off the boom. Stir the stick. Wiggle your toes, I think to myself as the turbulence bounces my jet around. My muscles are tight, and I can feel beads of sweat dripping down the back of my neck. The boomer hasn't said a word over the intercom, which is fine with me. I'm working too hard right now. The last thing I need is idle conversation.

When my tanks are full, the boom disconnects from the receptacle behind my canopy and an amber DISC light appears on the air-refueling status indicator. I pull my throttle back ever so slightly and begin to fall back. As soon as I'm clear of the boom, I maneuver into position on the tanker's right wing. While Grover drops into position, I call him on victor and advise him that I'll be off freq for a few minutes so I can contact AWACS. At this point, things begin to get tricky. I can barely read the frequencies on my kneeboard, and if I look away from the tanker too long, I may lose sight. The last thing I can afford to do is go lost wingman with the tanker, especially while Grover's on the boom. With my right hand on the stick, I punch in the strike primary frequency and contact AWACS.

"Bulldog, Husky 07," I radio.

"Go ahead, Husky 07."

"Husky 07 checking in with two, mission number 3207 alpha. We're carrying Mavericks and CBU-87, and we've been assigned to AG-6. Any words?"

"Negative, Husky 07. The area is clear. Advise when you're ready to proceed north."

I continue to orbit with the KC-10 and switch over to J-STARS. I make the same call as before, and the controller gives me the same response as AWACS. The next call I make is to ABCCC, and the controller tells me to contact a marine commander who checked in a few minutes earlier looking for air support. The controller gives me two different frequencies and wishes me luck. By now, Grover has finished refueling and is in the process of rejoining on my right wing.

"Husky 08, take the left wing," I radio.

"Two!"

It would be impossible for me to give Grover a smooth platform to fly off while copying down information. I'm having enough trouble keeping sight as it is. While Grover maneuvers to the left wing of the KC-10, I punch in one of the frequencies and make a call to the marines. To my relief, the commander responds quickly: "Go ahead, Husky 07."

"Husky 07 is a pair of F-16s carrying Mavericks and CBU-87. ABCCC told me you might be able to use us."

"Copy that, Husky 07. Let me tell you what we've got. We're getting ready to take an airfield called Ali Al Salim. The base is located just north of a highway, ten miles west of Al Jahrah in AG-5 quadrant one. I'm anticipating some resistance from Iraqi forces located east of the field. If possible, I'd like you to come in and work along the stretch of highway between the base and Al Jahrah. You can destroy anything you want. Remain east of the airfield and give me a call when you come off."

"Husky 07 copies. We'll work the highway, and I confirm your instructions to remain east of the airfield. We're about ready to depart our tanker track and we should be in the area by 19:00z."

I switch back to the tanker frequency and tell Grover to rejoin on my right wing. As soon as he's in position, I check out with the KC-10 crew and begin to climb. Once we're clear of the tanker, I call Grover again and tell him to come up victor secure. I reach down and switch to C/RAD 2 and radio: "Husky 07, check victor secure."

"Husky 08 has you loud and clear."

"I talked to a marine commander, and he wants us to do some work for him in AG-5 quadrant one. They're getting ready to take Ali Al Salim air base. I want you to take spacing while I pull out my map and plot some coordinates. As soon as I'm through, I'll cross-check them with you to make sure we match. We have to remain east of the airfield, so one of the points will be the base and the other will be along the highway fifteen miles to the east."

"Husky 08 copies."

I level off at 24,000 feet and engage my autopilot. As I continue north, I plot the coordinates and program them into steerpoints 15 and 16.

"Husky 08, Husky 07."

"Husky 07, go ahead."

"Okay. Stand by to copy new steerpoint fifteen."

"Husky 08 is ready to copy."

"New steerpoint fifteen is north 2921.000 and east 4732.000. New steerpoint sixteen is north 2918.000 and east 4747.000. How copy?"

"Husky 08 copies steerpoint fifteen is north 2921.000 and east 4732.000. Steerpoint sixteen is north 2918.000 and east 4747.000."

After Grover loads the coordinates, I call for a bearing and range check. There's no room for error on this one. Dropping bombs or firing missiles anywhere west of the airfield may result in a friendly-fire incident. The check is good, and within minutes, the two of us are crossing Kuwait's southern border. I call up AWACS on strike primary and tell them we will need to work AG-5 from 19:00z to 19:30z.

"AG-5 is empty," Bulldog responds. "I'll advise when the next formation is five minutes out."

"Tell them to take AG-6," I radio. "That's the kill box we were originally scheduled to work."

"Bulldog copies."

I tell Grover our weather plan remains the same and that he can work 14,000 feet and above. I'll remain at or below 13,000 feet, and the two of us will work the highway between steerpoints fifteen and sixteen. As soon as Grover responds, I turn to a 010-degree heading and proceed directly to steerpoint sixteen. While descending, I power up my Mavericks and complete my fence check. I have no idea what the bottom of the cloud deck is, so I check to make sure my ALOW is set at 9,000 and 6,000 feet. If I'm still in the weather, Bitchin' Betty will let me know I'm approaching the 5,000-foot floor.

I fly to a point ten miles east of steerpoint sixteen and make a hard turn to the northwest. I put steerpoint fifteen on my nose and call up my GMT radar. After a few sweeps, I lock up my first vehicle. The contact is twenty miles on my nose, five miles east of the airfield. I begin to descend, hoping to find clear airspace below the cloud layer. My airspeed is 360 knots and I'm on a 335-degree heading. Passing 9,000 feet, Bitchin' Betty calls out: "altitude, altitude." Seconds later, Grover radios: "08 is unable to lock any movers." I continue to descend, and, as I pass through 7,000 feet, the weather begins to clear.

"Copy. I've got a mover locked . . . he's moving in the dirt!" As I pass through 6,000 feet, Bitchin' Betty calls out again: "altitude, altitude." While leveling off, I hit the uncage switch, and the Maverick video appears in my right MFD. The vehicle I locked up is close to the Maverick tracking gates. I push the TMS switch forward and slew the tracking gates over the vehicle. The infrared picture is perfect, and the pointing cross is holding steady. Approximately five miles from the target, I hit the pickle button. With a loud roar, the missile flies off the rail.

"Husky 07, missile's away," I radio. "I'm climbing back up!" I pull hard to the right and spot a stream of red tracers at my right four o'clock. I jink a couple of times, then check back to the left.

"Copy that," Grover responds. "I'm thirteen miles in trail. Say heading, and tell me when you're coming off left."

I roll to my left and stare into the blackness below. While I wait for the missile to reach its mark, I key my mike and radio: "I'm in a left-hand turn now through three-two-zero . . . Splash the target! He's burning! It's a tank!"

What an incredible sight! The armored hulk blew up directly underneath me, and I can see it rolling off the highway. I'm so excited, I can barely catch my breath. My heart feels like it's about to explode, and I quickly radio: "He's in a left turn, rolling off the side of the road." While Bitchin' Betty reminds me of my altitude, Grover calls back and says: "Say your heading and reference off steerpoint five."

"Okay . . . stand by," I reply. I realize Grover made reference to the wrong steerpoint and, after pausing a moment, I call him back and say: "Understand steerpoint fifteen?"

While waiting for a reply, I glance inside the cockpit at my instrument panel. After confirming that I have the correct steerpoint in, I perform a range and bearing check so I can relay my position to Grover. In the middle of my calculations, my instincts tell me something isn't right. The flight controls are extremely sensitive, and the wind blast against the canopy is deafening. The situation reminds me of the supersonic flights I used to fly with my students when I was a T-38 instructor at Reese AFB. Every student breaks the sound barrier during their first flight, and they come away with two distinct impressions: It's extremely noisy in the cockpit, and, because of the increase in air flow over the wings, the flight controls are much more sensitive.

When I realize what's happening, I look directly at my main attitude director indicator (ADI). I'm thirty degrees nose low, diving straight toward the ground. I quickly check my HUD and notice my altitude decreasing through 1,600 feet. Without hesitation, I pull back on the stick as hard as I can. The rapid onset of Gs causes me to lose my vision. Straining with all my might, I key my mike and radio: "Oh man . . . Hold on!" As soon as I feel myself climbing, I relax back pressure against the stick. As my vision returns, I take a deep breath and check my attitude. I'm forty degrees nose high. My airspeed is quickly decreasing, so I roll inverted and pull the nose back down to the horizon line in my HUD. Once I regain my situational awareness and level off, I key the mike and radio: "Okay, say your altitude right now."

"Two-three-zero in a left-hand turn over steerpoint fifteen," Grover replies.

"Copy. Stand by . . . I was just a little nose high . . . hold on a second."

With my left thumb, I switch the dogfight/missile override switch to dogfight, so I can recage the seeker head of my remaining Maverick missile. My preoccupation with Grover's position and the excitement of achieving another Maverick kill nearly cost me my life.

"Okay," I continue. "I'm on the zero-five-zero for fourteen off of fifteen."

"Check buddy lock," Grover responds.

"And I'm clean."

"I've got a high aspect contact here. . . . Five miles on my nose. Say angels."

"I'm at thirteen."

"Copy. We've got someone working in our area."

"Copy that, I'll talk."

Realizing there might be another aircraft in our area, I make the following call on strike primary: "Any aircraft in AG-5. This is Husky 07. We're in the area."

"They're angels nineteen," Grover radios. "Five east of steerpoint fifteen."

"Say again."

"They were five east of steerpoint fifteen."

The intruding aircraft never responds, so I turn back toward steerpoint sixteen and begin to prepare for my second pass. I'm in the weather at 13,000 on a 270-degree heading. My flight suit is soaked, and I've got to make a conscious effort to slow my breathing rate. When I'm thirty miles east of Ali Al Salim AB, I roll into forty-five degrees of bank and execute a hard turn to the left. After I call up my GMT radar, I reach down and turn on my VTR. In no time at all, another contact appears on my radar scope. I slew my cursors over the target and lock it up.

"Husky 08 is over east steerpoint angels one-six," Grover radios.

"Copy. I've locked a mover twenty-four miles on my nose and I'm heading east."

"Copy!"

As I begin to descend, I call up the LANTIRN page and program the SCP for 1,000 feet. I don't want to make the same mistake as last time, but if I do, at least I'll have fly-up protection. As soon as I activate the TFR system, I get a break-X signal in the HUD and a fly-up command. I immediately hit the paddle switch on my stick and retake control of the aircraft. I don't have time to investigate, so I abandon the plan and continue toward my target. As I pass through 9,000 feet—still in the weather—Bitchin' Betty calls out: "altitude, altitude."

"Husky 07, say status," Grover radios.

"Stand by."

I break out of the weather at 7,000 feet and switch the Maverick to NFOV. The target is in the middle of the video display, so I hit the slew button and place the tracking gates overtop of it. Once the target is locked, I place my thumb on the pickle button and stare at the pointing cross.

"Come on, stop flashing," I yell into my mask.

Within seconds, the cross goes steady. I hit the pickle button, and the exhaust from my missile lights up the sky.

"Husky 07, missile's off!" I radio excitedly.

"Husky 08 copies."

As soon as the Maverick destroys the target, I climb away from the desert floor and make a hard turn to the northeast. Grover is twelve miles ahead of me, so I tell him to continue toward the egress point. After I give the marine commander an in-flight report, I switch back to strike primary and check out of the area with AWACS. While Grover heads toward Bubiyan Island, I put the steerpoint in for Al Minhad and proceed direct. A few minutes later, I tell Grover to check his right two o'clock, and he locks me up with his radar. He eventually rejoins and the two of us level off at 35,000 feet.

During the flight home, I eat my granola bars and reflect back on the mission. A part of me wonders if I'm even alive. I squeeze my arms and pinch my legs. Maybe I hit the ground, and I just don't know it yet. I close my eyes and think about my love for Colette. Candice and Kristen don't even know me, but Colette and I have shared a life together. I can picture Col. Fox in his dress blues standing on my porch with the chaplain and the flight surgeon. Please don't open the door, Colette. This isn't the way I want things to end. When I open my eyes again, the cockpit is dark. As I stare toward the sky, I thank God for watching over me. The only thing I've asked of Him during the last five months is to see my family again. Tonight, He kept that dream alive.

36.
HIGHWAY OF DEATH

I woke up shortly before noon, refreshed and optimistic. Allied forces had been on the offensive for nearly fifty-four hours, and the speed at which they moved led me to believe that this might be the last day of the war. I hustled over to the o'club to catch the latest from CNN. The lounge was full of pilots, and when CNN announced that Iraq had agreed to withdraw its forces from Kuwait, everyone applauded. But it proved to be another trick on the part of Saddam Hussein. A few hours after Baghdad announced it was pulling out of Kuwait, White House Press Secretary Marlin Fitzwater met with reporters and said: "We continue to prosecute the war. We have heard no reason to change that.... We have no evidence to suggest the Iraqi army is withdrawing. In fact, Iraqi units are continuing to fight..."

26 FEBRUARY 1991
After replaying the White House press conference, CNN showed footage of a demolished building in Saudi Arabia, struck the night before by an Iraqi Scud missile. The attack occurred just outside the port city of Dhahran, approximately 160 miles south of Kuwait. According to military sources in Riyadh, the converted warehouse was being used to house troops from the 475th Quartermaster Group, a reserve water-supply unit out of Farrel, Pennsylvania. CNN said twenty-seven Americans died in the fiery blast, and ninety-eight more were injured. The soldiers were the first Americans killed by Iraqi Scud missiles, which had already claimed one life in Saudi Arabia and two in Israel.

After lunch, my friends and I returned to the lounge and watched the daily military briefing from Riyadh. "Where we're meeting the enemy, we are defeating the enemy," Gen. Neal began. "We continue to achieve tremendous success. During the past thirty-six hours, allied aircraft have destroyed more than 270 Iraqi tanks, including thirty-five of Iraq's top-line T-72s. Overall, more than 97,000 allied sorties have been flown and only forty-five allied aircraft have been lost. Of that total, thirty-six were combat-related, including twenty-seven U.S. aircraft and one U.S. helicopter. Iraq has lost 135 aircraft and six helicopters. Seventy-nine have died since fighting began; fifty-five U.S. and twenty-four allies. There have also been fifty U.S. noncombat deaths, and of the fifty-one considered missing, thirty are American. The number of prisoners still stands at thirty, including nine from the U.S.

"More than 20,100 Iraqi soldiers have surrendered or been captured since the beginning of the ground war. In some cases, entire battalions at a time have surrendered."

After the briefing, I walked outside to wait for the shuttle to arrive. Fifteen minutes later, I was at the 421st. Jackal and I were scheduled to fly together later that evening, and the mass briefing began at 16:45. When I arrived in the weapons shop, Skippy, Biff, Duck, and Grover were going through their strike packages.

"Which kill box did they give us?" I asked, pulling my envelope out of the safe.

"AG-6," Skippy replied. "If the Iraqis are on the run, it'll be a turkey shoot up there."

The briefing began on time, and, according to Maj. Marsh, Iraqi troops had begun to pull back. "The Medina and Hammurabi Republican Guard divisions are in rapid retreat," Marsh announced. "They're heading toward Basrah, and CENTAF wants you to destroy as much of their armor as possible before they escape to the north. The 1st and 2nd Marine Divisions are approaching Kuwait City, and allied forces should have control of the capital by tomorrow.

"If you take a look at your kill-box maps, I'll show you the areas that remain open and the ones that are currently occupied by allied troops. U.S. forces reached the Euphrates valley a few hours ago, and the only kill boxes still open are as follows: AE-6/7/8; AF-6/7/8; and AG-6/7/8. Allied forces occupy every kill box west of alpha-echo, and the ones that are numbered five and below. The guys on the ground are moving extremely fast, so remember to contact AWACS, ABCCC, and J-STARS before you push. The controllers will let you know if there have been any changes. Does anyone have any questions? Oh, just one more thing. I spoke with Ozone this morning. He's working in the command center at Riyadh, and he told me Gen. Schwarzkopf and his staff watched Stitch's Maverick film. Ozone said everyone raved about it. Gen. Schwarzkopf thought it was one of the best pieces of combat footage he'd seen, but he decided not to release it to the media pool. According to Ozone, the general felt the American public would realize human beings were in the armored vehicle and it might be too graphic. That's all I've got."

When Maj. Marsh finished, Damien reminded everyone to fly safe and take no unnecessary chances. "Use your best judgment out there, guys. We're coming down to the wire. We all want to help the troops on the ground, but it's more important that all of you make it back safely. You're doing an outstanding job, and I appreciate the hard work you've been putting in. Just don't get complacent."

16:08:37z

"Captain Keith Rosenkranz ... Mastiff 03 ... 3203 alpha ... Two maverick missiles on board ... Take-off time 16:15 ... TOT timeframe 18:00 to 18:30 ... The date today is 26 February '91 ... Tail number 465."

Jackal and I take off a few minutes early and reach the tanker track in northern Saudi Arabia at approximately 17:20z. Once again, the weather is extremely poor. Fortunately, the tanker pilot found a layer of clear airspace from 23,000 to 25,000 feet. The rejoin is a piece of cake, and it doesn't take long for me to top off my tanks. As soon as I disconnect from the boom, I maneuver to the right wing of the tanker. While Jackal drops down into the contact position, I call AWACS to get an update on our kill box. According to the controller, AG-6 is still wide open, and we're cleared to proceed north when ready. After a similar call to ABCCC, I punch in the frequency for J-STARS and radio: "Mastiff 03 is a pair of Vipers with Mavericks and CBU-87. Our mission number is 3203 alpha and we're scheduled to work AG-6 from 18:00z to 18:30z. Is the area still open?"

"That's affirm, Mastiff 03," the controller responds. "Stand by one."

I maintain my position on the right wing of the tanker, and a few seconds later the controller comes back and says: "Mastiff 03, AG-6 is open, and we have two convoys in the area heading north out of Kuwait City. One is fourteen kilometers long and the other appears to be sixteen kilometers long. Be advised you may have to hold before AWACS clears you into the area. We closed AE-6 a short time ago, and the fighters were diverted to your kill box. When AWACS gives you the green light, you're cleared in hot on the convoys. How copy?"

"Mastiff 03 copies all."

By the time I finish, Jackal cycles off the boom and rejoins on my right wing. Before we depart the track, I call AWACS one more time. The controller confirms that AE-6 has been closed, and he pushes my TOT window back to 18:20z. Since Stitch and Ensign aren't due on the tanker for another thirty minutes, I decide to remain in the track with the KC-10. I send Jackal back to the left wing and advise him of the TOT change. After two more trips around the racetrack pattern, the two of us top our tanks off one last time. When Jackal disconnects, I tell him to take the right wing. I begin a slow climb and proceed to steerpoint five, which marks the Saudi/Kuwaiti border. While Jackal takes spacing, I call for a fuel check and follow it up with a fence check. After I turn my lights off, I call up the air-to-ground mode and power up my Maverick missiles. I'm level at 21,000 feet and as I approach the southern boundary of AG-6, I call Skippy on victor and ask him for a pirep on the area.

"The highway is loaded with tanks and APCs, Rosey," Skippy responds. "They're heading north toward Basrah. We got seven kills, and I just checked out of the area with AWACS. You should be cleared in hot."

"Good job," I reply. "How's the weather?"

"It's fine. The bottoms of the clouds are from twelve to thirteen, so you shouldn't have any trouble getting your Mavericks off."

"Copy. Thanks for the report."

18:21:55z

AWACS clears us into the kill box. By the time I reach steerpoint six—the southern point in AG-6—my GMT radar screen is full of contacts. I pick a target, lock it up with my cursors, and begin descending. Breaking out of the weather around 12,000 feet, I spot the target next to the Maverick tracking gates.

"Okay, got a good mover," I radio.

As I close in on the target, I begin to realize that I may have locked a mover that has already been hit. The infrared display is extremely bright, compared to the other vehicles on the highway, and my target is the only one that doesn't appear to be moving. "It might be a mover that's already been bombed," I radio to Jackal. "We'll see here." I switch to NFOV and, sure enough, I can see flames radiating from the wreckage.

"It looks like it's smokin'!" I call out again. "Yeah, it's a bomb . . . It's smokin'!"

I quickly break lock and climb back up to 11,000 feet. I'm only ten miles from the northern point, so I call for an in-place 180 so Jackal can make his first pass. I roll out of the turn, heading 180. Jackal is six miles ahead of me, and, as we proceed along the highway, I clear below for SAMs and AAA. The highway is full of Iraqi armored vehicles, and Jackal doesn't waste any time locking up part of the convoy. Within seconds, he calls in and drops his bombs. I check ten degrees to the right and stare out the left side of my canopy, hoping to catch a glimpse of the fireworks.

"Mastiff 04 is off," Jackal radios.

"Copy. Continue south to steerpoint six, then call for the in-place turn."

"Roger."

As soon as I let go of the mike, Jackal's bombs explode at my left eleven low. The CBU looks like fireflies dancing on the ground. I drop down for a closer look and see two separate fires burning. "Mastiff 04, you got two kills! I see two of them burning down there!"

"Mastiff 4 copies. Tally two fires."

As soon as I roll out of the in-place turn, I put steerpoint seven on my nose and proceed direct. I'm on a 350-degree heading at 11,000 feet. It's a moist, hazy night, and my GMT radar is painting dozens of targets on the highway below. While concentrating on the radar display, I slew my cursors over one of the targets and TMS forward. The target is locked. In less than a minute, another group of Iraqi soldiers will be dead.

I inch my throttle forward and begin to descend. Passing 9,000 feet, Bitchin' Betty sounds off: "Altitude, altitude." I call up my Maverick video and spot three vehicles moving north along the highway. I slew the tracking gates over the vehicle nearest to me—the one at the end of the line.

"Altitude, altitude." I glance quickly at the HUD as I pass through 6,000 feet. After switching my VTR from the right MFD to the HUD, I place my thumb on top of the pickle button. My airspeed is 370 knots, and I'm on a 352-degree heading. I continue through 5,000 feet, then 4,000. The target is 3.2 miles away. As soon as I hit the pickle button, the missile shoots out from beneath my wing. I key my mike and call out: "And missile's off! I'm coming off to the right . . . to the east. Go ahead and start your pass in."

"Two!" Jackal replies.

I make a climbing right turn, then check back to the north. I can see a number of fires burning below me. The 421st is having a field day, and the Iraqis are paying a heavy price. While I wait for the missile to strike, Jackal calls me on victor and says: "Say angels."

"Passing through seven," I reply.

"Roger, I'm seventeen . . . five east."

All of a sudden, there's a large explosion below me. "Okay, the missile's hit . . . look for the fire . . . they're heading north!" I begin a climbing right turn and ask: "Do you see it?"

"I'm gonna come off to the north and come back down the road and drop on them," Jackal responds.

"Copy. Is he on fire?"

"I see one fire slightly north. I don't see your fire."

"Well, that one is slightly north because I slewed up there."

"I see your fire."

Jackal pauses for a moment, then calls out again: "Tally fire. It's burnin' down there."

"Copy that. I'm heading south. Let me know when I'm cleared back in."

"Roger."

I turn south while Jackal sets up for his second pass. We're approaching the end of our TOT window and I'm anxious for Jackal to call off. I need to get one more pass in before Stitch and Ensign arrive. I level off below the cloud deck and continue to fly toward steerpoint six.

"Mastiff 04's in," Jackal radios.

Thirty seconds later, Jackal calls off and tells me I'm cleared to make my last pass. I haven't quite reached the steerpoint, so I make a 270-degree left turn and roll out on a 245-degree heading. It doesn't take long for me to lock another mover. As soon as I activate my Maverick, I key my mike and radio: "Okay, I've got a lock. Be ready to go to steerpoint eight."

"Copy," Jackal replies.

Steerpoint eight is our egress point, and I want Jackal pointed in the right direction as soon as I complete this pass. We only have two minutes left in the area, and I don't want to impose on Stitch's play time. As I descend toward the highway, I hit the uncage button, call up the Maverick video, and lock the target. The pointing cross flashes for a moment, then turns steady. I hit the pickle button, and the missile explodes off the rail, leaving a trail of fire in its wake.

"And missile's away!" I radio excitedly.

"Roger," Jackal replies. "Four's proceeding to steerpoint eight."

"Copy, steerpoint eight."

I pause for a moment and stare into the darkness below. A few seconds later, the armored vehicle explodes.

"And kill second target!" I shout into my mask. "I'm in a right turn to steerpoint eight. I'm on the two-five-zero for forty-nine off of eight!"

"Two-five-five for thirty-eight," Jackal replies.

"Copy, proceed direct steerpoint eight."

"Roger."

I climb into the weather and give an in-flight report to AWACS. "We destroyed five armored vehicles, and the highway is still saturated with targets," I tell the controller.

Reaching Bubiyan Island, I turn toward Al Minhad and the two of us touch down a few minutes before midnight. After we refuel in the hot pits, we taxi back to the ramp and shut down our engines. When I climb out of my jet, I walk over and shake Jackal's hand. I'm extremely proud of what we accomplished together—not just tonight, but during the other missions we've flown together as well.

As soon as we finished debriefing maintenance and intel, we walked back to life-support and stowed our flying gear. Afterward, we walked over to one of the trailers and reviewed the mission. Duck, Grover, Skippy, and Biff had just finished debriefing, and they were getting ready to watch one of Tiny's Maverick passes.

"How'd you guys do tonight, Rosey?" Duck asked.

"Jackal and I got five kills," I replied. "How about you?"

"We took out five as well. Skippy and Biff hit the jackpot. They got seven kills."

"Wait until you guys see my tape," Tiny chuckled.

He turned on the television and hit the VCR play button. The beginning of the tape looked like a normal Maverick pass. But as Tiny closed in on his target, a different picture began to appear. Everyone in the room was amazed when a dozen infrared figures began to run from the armored personnel carrier Tiny had locked up.

"There's a lot of guys walking out of it!" Tiny said on the tape. "See if you can hit that thing."

"Imagine what those guys were thinking about when they heard Tiny fly over," Biff laughed.

"They probably saw a Maverick take out a group of their friends, and they decided it might be safer to walk home instead," Skippy interjected.

As soon as we finished, we turned in our tapes and headed for the beer tent. The trailer was crowded with pilots and everyone was ready to start celebrating. Allied forces would arrive in Kuwait City by dawn, and there was a good chance the war would be over this time tomorrow. Fine with me. I had twenty-nine combat missions under my belt and eight Maverick missile kills. I had taken the lives of a lot of men, and, as far as I was concerned, it was time for the fighting to stop.

27 FEBRUARY 1991

As soon as my alarm sounded, I rolled out of bed and hit the shower. When I left the squadron ten hours before, allied forces were approaching the outskirts of Kuwait City. As I fell asleep, I was thinking the war might end, and I couldn't wait to find out if I was correct. When I arrived at the squadron, a handful of pilots were in the lounge watching CNN. Allied forces had entered Kuwait City early in the morning, and the Kuwaiti capital was expected to be liberated at any time. "The Iraqi army is in full retreat, although there is some fighting going on," said Lt. Gen. Thomas W. Kelly, chief of operations for the Joint Chiefs of Staff. "Through the night and into the day tomorrow, we will continue to press the battle. We are still engaged in combat, and we will not let up."

After Gen. Kelly's briefing, I walked into the scheduler's office to see if I was on the board for that night. Sure enough, I was one of eight pilots scheduled for the evening's first go. But I hated the thought of killing soldiers in the process of retreating. Six weeks of relentless bombing had not only destroyed Iraq's military equipment, it had broken the Iraqi army's will to fight. The only goal left for these men was to return home safely to their families. That was my goal, too.

After a time hack and a prayer from Father Willie, Taz announced that allied aircraft accidentally fired on a pair of British armored vehicles the previous night, resulting in more allied casualties. "Situational awareness is a must out there," Taz cautioned. "Make sure you know which kill box you're supposed to be in, and double-check your coordinates before you commence your target runs. We're flying at night; the weather is poor; and in the heat of battle, mistakes are going to happen. Just make sure you know where you're at before you fire your missiles or drop your bombs. As I've said before, come off dry if there's any doubt."

Next, Maj. Marsh stepped forward to give us the latest from intel.

"Twenty-seven of Iraq's forty-two divisions have been overrun or destroyed. We've captured 38,000 prisoners, and allied casualties number twenty-eight dead, eighty-nine wounded, and five missing. As of right now, it appears as though AG-7 and AG-8 are the only two kill boxes that remain workable. But don't be surprised if that changes by the time you get up there."

"Have you heard anything about a cease-fire?" Spike asked.

"There's a rumor that it may come sometime tonight. Until you hear an announcement on guard, though, continue to attack. There's an awful lot of Iraqi armor on the highway to Basrah, and CENTAF wants us to destroy as much of it as possible before the cease-fire is declared."

"If you hear a cease-fire announcement," Taz interjected, "do not fire another missile or drop another bomb. Be heads-up on the radios. If we're lucky, this will be over by tomorrow morning."

After the formal briefing, Jackal and I walked out to one of the briefing trailers and went over the details of the mission. As soon as we finished, we walked next door to life-support and changed into our flying gear. As I took off my patches and scarf, I removed myself from the emotional issue of killing Iraqi soldiers. I knew what was expected of me, and my attention was now focused on completing my mission effectively. My objectives were the same as they had been since my first combat mission: destroy target, meet delivery parameters, maintain mutual support, and survive!

When I arrive at the aircraft, my crew chief snaps to attention, greets me with a firm salute, and says: "This Viper is ready to fly, sir!"

"This could very well be my last mission, chief."

"How many have you flown, sir?"

"This will be number thirty."

"I hope it's a good one for you, sir. I'll look forward to seeing you when you get back."

"I'll look forward to seeing you, too, chief."

16:25:00z

"Captain Keith Rosenkranz . . . Dane 05 . . . 3205 alpha . . . Two AGM-65 Delta Mavericks . . . Takeoff time 16:35 . . . TOT range 18:30 to 19:00 . . . 27 February '91 . . . And tail number 416. Hopefully, this will be the last day."

As soon as I title my tape, I look toward Jackal to see if he's ready to go. When he gives me a thumbs-up, I give him the signal to come up channel one. We're not due to take off for another five minutes, but I want to get airborne early in case the command post announces the cease-fire has occurred. I still want to fly, even if it means burning down fuel. As soon as we receive clearance from tower, Jackal and I run up our engines and take off. I hit the UAE coastline at 350 knots and eventually level off at 16,000 feet. After we complete our climb checks, I pass the lead to Jackal so I can drop back and boresight my Maverick missiles. When I finish, I reclaim the lead and climb to 22,000 feet. An hour later, I'm approaching the Saudi coastline. After I check in with AWACS, I turn to a 295-degree heading and proceed directly to the Lime ARCP. After refueling, I make my calls to AWACS, ABCCC, and J-STARS. Last night's ATO had us scheduled to work AG-6, but AWACS tells me the only area still open is the northwest quadrant of AG-8. When I contact J-STARS, the controller says there are numerous armored vehicles backed up along the highway that leads north out of Basrah. He also says there are a number of formations in front of us waiting to take their turn in the box. Our original push time—18:10z—is less than ten minutes from now. It sounds like Jackal and I will have to hold, so we remain with the tanker. Spike and Tonto are still twenty minutes out, so I inform Jackal that we'll remain in the track until 18:30z.

After four trips around the refueling track, Jackal and I climb away from the tanker and push north. Since our kill box has changed, I'm going to need to figure out a new set of coordinates to work between when we reach the area. I level off at 21,000 feet, call for a fence check, and tell Jackal to take spacing. After the fuel and fence checks, I engage my autopilot, pull out a flashlight, and do some map study. Basrah is located on the southern boundary of AG-8, and the highway that leads to the northwest parallels the Euphrates River. After I plot the coordinates, I key my mike and tell Jackal to come up on victor secure.

"Dane 05, check."

"Dane 06 reads you loud and clear."

"Copy, Dane 06. According to J-STARS, the only area left open is AG-8 quadrant one. Do you have your kill-box map out?"

"Dane 06, affirm."

"The highway is full of Iraqi armor, and they're trying to escape to the north. We'll plan on working a ten-mile stretch of the highway that runs through the quadrant. Let me know when you're ready, and I'll pass you the coordinates."

"Dane 06, standby."

"Okay, Dane 06 is ready to copy."

"The following set of coordinates will be the new steerpoint six: north 3045.000 and east 4740.000. This point marks the gas/oil separator plant located six miles south of Shahban. Steerpoint seven will be the northeast point. The coordinates are north 3056.000 and east 4730.000. This marks the boundary line between AG-8 and AF-8, one mile south of the town of Duwa. How copy?"

After Jackal confirms the coordinates, I call up my Maverick missiles, so they'll be timed out by the time we arrive. AWACS informs us that the only area open is the northwest section of AG-8. "Right now it's being worked by Mastiff 03," the controller radios, "and I've got two pairs of navy A-6s waiting in line."

"Dane 05 copies. I'm going to set up a holding pattern on the boundary between AG and AF-7. I'll remain at my present altitude, and I'd like you to notify me when it's our turn for the area."

"Bulldog copies."

"And Bulldog, is everyone working the area on Blue two?"

"That's affirm."

I continue north until I reach the holding point. Before I enter the pattern, I tell Jackal to slow to max endurance so we can conserve fuel. I also inform him that we'll be flying ten-mile legs with left-hand turns. A quick check of my fuel gauge shows we have enough to hold for forty minutes and work thirty minutes in the area. I just hope the ground forces stay far enough away so we'll have a chance to spank some Iraqi tanks. Two more kills will give me a total of ten, and I don't want to go back to Al Minhad with ordnance on what may very well be the last night of the war.

After one turn in holding, I hear Mans and Wheel check out of the area with AWACS. The controller acknowledges the call and clears the next two-ship into the kill box. Ten minutes pass. Then twenty. Jackal and I continue to hold and, finally, the next formation is cleared in hot. Ten minutes later, the A-6 flight lead tells AWACS he is egressing east. As soon as the controller clears me in, I make a turn to the left and immediately switch to steerpoint six. The point is less than twenty miles away. As soon as I call up my air-to-ground radar, I begin sweeping the highway for movers. To my delight, the left MFD is flooded with contacts. I slew the cursors a few miles north of the steerpoint and lock my first target. While descending, I hit the uncage button and the Maverick video comes alive.

"Dane 05, locked a mover now . . . fourteen miles on my nose."

I break through the clouds at 8,000 feet and switch the Maverick video to WFOV. The weather is extremely poor, though, and a heavy amount of moisture in the air prevents me from acquiring the target. By the time the vehicle appears, I'm too close to get a shot off. As soon as I break off the attack, I make a turn to the south and tell Jackal he's cleared to make his first pass. Airspace is tight, so I continue south along the western

291

edge of the kill box to avoid interfering with Jackal's target run. After twenty seconds of silence, Jackal keys his mike and radios: "Dane 06 is locked a convoy just north of steerpoint six. It looks big enough for me to drop all four bombs on it."

"Dane 05 copies. You're cleared in."

As soon as Jackal drops his bombs, he calls off target and says he's climbing to base plus 14,000 feet. I instruct him to hold above the area until I get my missiles off.

"There's lots of movers on the road just below you," Jackal replies.

"Copy that. Lot of fires down there. I'm gonna head a little further to the north."

After I lock my second target and begin to descend for the kill, AWACS calls and says: "Dane 05, Bulldog."

"Go ahead," I reply.

"Roger, can you go green?"

"Not right now, I'm kind of busy." The tone of my voice isn't very pleasant. I'm right in the middle of an attack, and the last thing I want to do right now is talk to AWACS.

"Roger, we've got another target for you if you can."

"Okay, stand by one," I reply disgustedly. I break off the attack and radio again: "Okay, are you ready to go green?"

"I'm gonna need you to push to red one to go green," the controller answers.

"Copy, going to red one."

I switch uniform frequencies and call out: "Bulldog, Dane 05."

"Roger Dane, go green."

I reach down to my right and switch my KY-58 radio to C/RAD 1.

"Bulldog, Dane 05 . . . how copy?" I radio.

The only response I get is static. I pause for a moment, but I still don't hear anything.

"Dane, say angels," Jackal radios on victor.

"I'm passing through eight."

"Roger, I'm at ten."

I don't understand why Jackal is flying so low, so I look down at my bearing pointer and quickly calculate my position in the area. Jackal's supposed to be above 13,000 feet. We don't need a midair. As soon as I know where I'm at in relation to steerpoint six, I key my mike and radio: "I'm in a left turn on the three-two-zero for twenty-one."

"Roger."

Jackal seems to be satisfied, so I make another call to AWACS: "And Bulldog, I'm not copying you on green. Do you copy me?" Once again, the only thing I hear is static. This is costing me valuable time in the area, and I'm beginning to get frustrated. Why can't AWACS just say what they have to say in the clear? At this point in the war, I doubt if the Iraqis are listening in on our conversations.

"Come up plain," I radio in the blind. As soon as I switch back to plain, I call out: "Bulldog, Dane 05, how copy?"

"Bulldog has you weak but readable."

"Okay, I don't hear you at all. Go ahead and give them to me in the clear."

"And Dane 06 can hear them," Jackal interjects.

"Bulldog, roger. Push Blue two."

"Copy!"

"Bulldog, Dane 05 go ahead." There's no answer. "Bulldog, Dane 05 on Blue two!" I repeat again.

"And Dane 05, is your ordnance good for bridges?"

"Not really. We've got CBU for movers and Mavericks for movers. If you've got movers in that area, we can hit 'em."

"Okay, we've got a bridge that they want taken out."

"Okay, we're unable to do that with our ordnance. We can stay in this area and hit a lot of movers in here."

"Roger, understand."

I can't believe what I've just been through. All the controller had to do was ask me in the clear if I had ordnance to take out a bridge. I would have told him no, and that would have been the end of it. While I maneuver into position for my next attack, I check my position in the area and radio: "Dane 05 is at 9,000. I'm on the two-nine-zero for fifteen heading back to the southeast." I drop back down below the wispy clouds and call up my GMT radar. Once again, my radar scope is full of contacts. In no time at all, I lock up a target fifteen miles on my nose.

"Altitude, altitude," Bitchin' Betty calls out as I begin to descend.

As soon as I break through the clouds, I switch to WFOV and slew the Maverick tracking gates overtop the infrared return. The armored vehicle is less than five miles away, but the pointing cross won't stop flashing. There's too much moisture in the air, and the Maverick seeker is having more trouble than I thought. Passing 6,000 feet, I radio: "Okay, I've got a good convoy on my nose. I'm locked one . . . I'll be firing in a second if I can stop flashing."

"Roger," Jackal replies.

I level off as soon as I reach 5,000 feet. There are one, two, three—eight vehicles heading north along the highway! The only thing saving these poor bastards is the weather. The target is less than three miles away and it's a tank. The turret and gun are clearly visible, but the damn pointing cross won't stop flashing. Finally, the missile reaches its gimbal limit and breaks lock. While climbing through 6,000 feet, I call out: "Okay, I'm off . . . I'm gonna mark." I hit the mark button on my up-front control so I can circle back and hit the same area. There are a lot of tanks down there, and I'm determined to get one. I continue west for ten miles, then circle back for another pass. As soon as I lock another target, I hit the uncage button and call up my Maverick video. Like the pass before, the weather is terrible. I slew the missile tracking gates over the target and lock it up. For the second pass in a row, I've locked up an Iraqi tank. Unfortunately, the pointing cross is still flashing. If I hit the pickle button, the missile will go straight into the ground. I continue toward the tank until the missile breaks lock.

"Dane 05, this is Dane 07," Spike calls out on victor.

"How much longer will you be in the area?"

I continue west and climb back up to 9,000 feet. Extremely frustrated, I key my mike and reply: "I've got two Mavericks left. My other guy is already done. I'm having trouble, though. They keep flashing!"

"Roger that. Any AAA?"

"Negative."

"And what box are you working?"

"AG northwest."

"AG-8?"

"That's affirm."

"Dane 05, traffic one-nine-zero for ten, northbound friendly," AWACS interrupts. "Altitude unknown."

The traffic is well south and of no concern to me, so I turn back and begin my fifth pass. My radar scope is still full of contacts, and it doesn't take long to lock one. I drop below the weather and call up my Maverick video.

"And, Dane 05," Spike radios, "Dane 07 will be there in about ten minutes."

"Copy that. There's plenty of tanks. You can tell they're tanks."

"Say again, Dane 05?"

"There's plenty of tanks moving. You can tell they're tanks!"

"Okay. And, Dane 05, give me a heads-up call when you leave on victor nine."

I slew the tracking gates over the target and immediately realize the tank is on fire. There's another vehicle near it on the screen, so I TMS forward and slew the tracking gates over it instead. Passing 6,000 feet, Bitchin' Betty reminds me that I'm near the floor. My thumb is a quarter of an inch above the pickle button, and if I can just get the pointing cross to go steady, this guy will be toast. Inside of three miles, the missile breaks lock.

"Darn it!" I shout into the radio. "They won't stop flashing! I'm coming off again!"

"Dane 06 copies. And be advised I'm approaching joker."

"Roger. I'll make two more passes, and then we'll egress. Be ready to go, and if we have to, we'll bootleg fuel on the way home."

"Two!"

I can't believe this is happening to me. I've never seen such a target-rich environment, and I can't get my damn missiles to lock. If a miracle doesn't happen on these next two passes, it looks like I'll have to take them back to Al Minhad. I roll out heading 140 and lock another target on my radar scope. With my left thumb, I slew the Maverick tracking gates along the highway, searching for another tank to lock. The weather is still poor, but there's a large truck in the Maverick field-of-view, and it looks like it's pulling a flatbed trailer. It could be a Scud launcher! I continue toward the vehicle, but the missile won't lock. There's another vehicle right behind it, so I slew the Maverick over it instead. It looks like a large recreation vehicle. The pointing cross goes steady. But just as I'm about to hit the pickle button, it begins to flash again.

"Dane 05, say status," Jackal radios.

"Stand by!"

"God, they're all over the place! I'm gonna make another run."

I circle back and make another pass to the northwest. I'm near bingo fuel, but I know I can hit a tanker if I need to. I'll make one more run to the northwest and another to the south. If I have to take the missiles home, then so be it.

"Dane 05, are you out of the area?" Spike radios.

"I'll be out in two minutes."

"Okay. I'm about twenty miles out from my target."

I roll out heading 320 and lock another vehicle fifteen miles on my nose. Inside of six miles, the target appears in the Maverick video, and I quickly lock it up. The pointing cross begins to flash. All of a sudden, it stops. I can't believe it. I pause for a moment to make sure it's a good lock, then I mash down the pickle button. With a loud roar, the missile flies off the rail.

"Dane, one's off! Missile's . . . one off!"

I can barely get the words out, I'm so excited. While I circle back for my last pass, Jackal calls out: "Dane 05, say status."

"I'm heading south for egress . . . last pass."

My adrenaline is pumping, and as soon as I roll out, I lock another target with my radar. I call up my Maverick video and within seconds of locking the target, the pointing cross goes steady. I hit the pickle button and immediately pull back on my stick. I push my throttle to mil power and call up steerpoint eight. I key my mike and radio: "Missile's off! I'm heading out!" After I tell Jackal to proceed to steerpoint eight, I call Spike on victor nine and tell him I'm departing the area. I pass my in-flight report to AWACS and continue to climb. My fuel is low, but it looks as though I'll have enough to make it back to Al Minhad. It takes about fifteen minutes to catch Jackal, and as soon as I do, he passes me the lead. An hour later, the two of us are on final approach to runway 27 at Al Minhad. I touch down at 00:28 and taxi clear of the runway.

That was one of the most frustrating missions of the war. It was also one of the most satisfying. Quadrant one of AG-8 was the only area in the KTO where fighters were allowed to attack that night, and, for nearly twenty minutes, I owned it. What a way to end the war.

37.
WELCOME HOME

Kuwait is liberated. Iraq's army is defeated. Our military objectives are met. Kuwait is once more in the hands of Kuwaitis in control of their own destiny. We share in their joy, a joy tempered only by our compassion for their ordeal.

Seven months ago, America and the world drew a line in the sand. We declared that the aggression against Kuwait would not stand, and tonight America and the world have kept their word. No one country can claim this victory as its own. It was not only a victory for Kuwait, but a victory for all the coalition partners. This is a victory for the United Nations, for all mankind, for the rule of law, and for what is right.

After consulting with Secretary of Defense Cheney, the chairman of the Joint Chiefs of Staff, Gen. Powell, and our coalition partners, I am pleased to announce that at midnight tonight, Eastern Standard Time, exactly 100 hours since ground operations commenced, and six weeks since the start of Operation Desert Storm, all United States and coalition forces will suspend offensive combat operations.

This suspension of offensive combat operations is contingent upon Iraq's not firing upon any coalition forces and not launching Scud missiles against any other country. If Iraq violates these terms, coalition forces will be free to resume military operations.

At every opportunity I have said to the people of Iraq that our quarrel was not with them, but instead with their leadership, and above all with Saddam Hussein. This remains the case. You, the people of Iraq, are not our enemy. We do not seek your destruction. We have treated your POWs with kindness. Coalition forces fought this war only as a last resort, and look forward to the day when Iraq is led by people prepared to live in peace with their neighbors.

This war is now behind us. Ahead of us is the difficult task of securing a potentially historic peace. Tonight, though, let us be proud of what we have accomplished. Let us give thanks to those who risked their lives. Let us never forget those who gave their lives. May God bless our valiant military forces and their families, and let us all remember them in our prayers. Good night and may God bless the United States of America.

—President George Bush

As the president ended his emotional speech, I wiped the tears from my eyes and reflected on our accomplishments. I could hardly believe it: Kuwait was free. In less than three hours, the guns would fall silent, ending six weeks of ferocious allied attacks against an army that was outclassed and outmanned on every front.

After breakfast, everyone returned to the lounge to watch a replay of the military briefing Gen. Schwarzkopf conducted in Riyadh the night before. With charts at his side and a pointer in his hand, the commander of Operation Desert Storm stood in front of a crowd of reporters and detailed the strategy of the allied forces. When asked about the role of airpower, the general said: "What we did, of course, was start an extensive air campaign. One of the purposes of that extensive air campaign was to isolate the Kuwaiti theater of operations by taking out all the bridges and supply lines that ran between the north and the southern part of Iraq. We also conducted a very heavy bombing campaign. It was necessary to reduce these forces down to a strength that . . . made them weaker, particularly on the front-line barrier that we had to go through."

Schwarzkopf continued, "There's a lot of people who are still saying that the objective of the United States of America was to capture Iraq and cause a downfall of the entire country of Iraq. Ladies and gentlemen . . . we were 150 miles away from Baghdad, and there was nobody between us and Baghdad. If it had been our intention to take Iraq, if it had been our intention to destroy the country, we could have done it unopposed, for all intents and purposes."

Gen. Schwarzkopf also talked about Iraqi casualties, the absence of chemical warfare, battles against the Republican Guard, the lack of Iraqi air support, and the quality of the Iraqi army. Schwarzkopf said that rating an army is a tough thing to do, and he attributed a great deal of the Iraqi army's failure to their own leadership. "They committed them to a cause that they did not believe in," Schwarzkopf said. "They are all saying that they didn't want to be there, they didn't want to fight their fellow Arab, they were lied to, they were deceived, and when they went into Kuwait, they didn't believe in the cause. And then after they got there, they had a leadership that was so uncaring for them, that they didn't properly feed them, they didn't properly give them water, and in the end, they kept them there only at the point of a gun."

The funniest moment of the briefing occurred when the general was asked if he considered Saddam Hussein to be a great military strategist. "Ha!" Schwarzkopf laughed. "As far as Saddam Hussein being a great military strategist, he is neither a strategist, nor is he schooled in the operational art, nor is he a tactician, nor is he a general, nor is he a soldier. Other than that, he's a great military man, I want you to know that."

Exhausted, I finally headed back to my room to go to sleep. Rip woke me up around 16:00 and said the wing was throwing a big party for everyone on base in one hour. After a quick shower, I threw on a clean flight suit and headed for the soccer field. Hundreds of pizzas were brought in from the downtown Pizza Hut. For dessert, a truckload of 31 Flavors ice cream was delivered. The music was loud and the food was great. The party continued well into the night, and when it finally ended, most of the pilots headed for the beer tent to continue the celebration. When I returned to my room, I sat on the edge of my bed and stared at pictures of Colette, Candice, and Kristen.

The next afternoon, Brig. Gen. Buster C. Glosson arrived on base to debrief the pilots and answer questions about the war. As director of campaign plans, Gen. Glosson was in charge of the Black Hole special planning and operational action group. Working out of the Royal Saudi air force building in Riyadh, Glosson and his staff spent five months developing what became known as the "master attack plan." Every pilot on base was seated in the o'club lounge. As Gen. Glosson walked in, we all snapped to attention.

"Take your seats, men. Before I begin, I'd like to congratulate each and every one of you on a job well done. Airpower won this war, and every one of you in the F-16 community should be proud of what you accomplished. I'm sure Col. Navarro has already told you this, but let me say it again anyway: I'm extremely proud of each and every pilot in this room. The president recognizes you as heroes; I recognize you as heroes; and most important, your country recognizes you as heroes.

"Under the direction of Gen. Horner, my staff and I created an air campaign with five basic objectives: Isolate and incapacitate Saddam Hussein and his regime; quickly gain and maintain air superiority; destroy Iraq's weapons of mass destruction, including nuclear weapons, Scud missiles, chemical weapons, biological weapons, and the production facilities that produce them; eliminate Iraq's ability to maintain any type of offensive operation; and render the army in the KTO ineffective. I'm pleased to tell you that we achieved every one of those objectives.

"I have some interesting statistics I'd like to go over with you. During Operation Desert Storm, we had more F-16s in theater—249 of them—than any other aircraft. Viper pilots flew more sorties—approximately 13,500—than any other aircraft in theater, and you also dropped more bombs than any other aircraft. Of all the fighter wings, I have to say that the 388th was probably the most successful. As soon as the war started, Gen. Horner and I realized the biggest threat from Iraq would be the Scud missile. The war lasted forty-two days and the Iraqis launched eighty-six Scud missiles: forty-nine against Israel and thirty-seven against Saudi Arabia. Most of the Scuds were launched at night, and we knew we had to have an aircraft with night-strike capability if we were going to stop them. We decided to send the 69th Werewolves to King Fahd AB, and we told them their top priority was to destroy the Scuds. In the first nine days of the war, the Iraqis launched forty-nine Scuds. After the 69th arrived in Saudi Arabia, the number of launches decreased dramatically. During the last thirty-three days of the war, Iraq launched a total of thirty-seven Scuds. The F-16s from the 69th, combined with F-15Es, A-10s, navy A-6Es, and the British Tornadoes, flew 2,493 sorties against the Scuds. The Werewolves flew a total of 1,509 combat sorties: fifty-eight over western Iraq; fifty over Baghdad; and 1,401 inside the KTO—842 of which were dedicated Scud missions.

"I would also like to recognize the Fightin' Fuujins from the 4th TFS. At various times throughout the war, extremely poor weather prevented our satellites and reconnaissance aircraft from detecting an Iraqi war machine that was often on the run. Allied bombers flew thousands of sorties in search of that machine, and in the early going, a good percentage of the missions were ineffective. The pilots in the 4th were quick to recognize the problem, and the solution they came up with dramatically changed the way the war was fought. When the 4th took on the Killer Scout role, sortie effectiveness doubled overnight. During the later stages of the war, allied bombers were destroying more than one hundred Iraqi tanks a day—a direct tribute to the work of the Killer Scouts. All together, the 4th TFS flew 1,078 combat sorties: twenty-six over western Iraq; 198 over Baghdad; and 854 inside the KTO—494 of which were Killer Scout sorties.

"Finally, I'd like to recognize the 421st Black Widows. The 388th Tactical Fighter Wing was one of the few wings in theater to conduct around-the-clock operations. Most pilots hate to fly at night—and I'm one of them! Seriously, men, you took a brand new system—LANTIRN—and changed the course of the war. You developed some great tactics that will be used for many years to come. This war was won at night, and the role you played was instrumental. Gen. Horner and I were worried about the Republican Guard and the effect they might have against our ground troops. We knew things would deteriorate quickly on the home front if the American people started seeing their husbands and sons come home in body bags. Thank God it never happened. The 421st TFS flew 1,292 combat sorties: 104 over western Iraq; fifty-four over Baghdad; and 1,134 inside the KTO against Iraq's Republican Guard and other front-line units. The Black Widows also flew 124 Maverick missions, most of which were flown during the ground war. I've seen pictures of the highway to Basrah, and let me tell you something, the damage you helped inflict was beyond anything I had ever imagined.

"Altogether, the 388th flew 3,879 combat sorties, the most of any wing in the Middle East Theater. What amazes me more than anything is that you never lost a single pilot.

"I know all of you are ready to go home. We may have to bring a C-5 or two through here, but we'll do what we can to get you out of here before the army takes all of the transports. I know you have some questions and hopefully I can answer them all."

Foot was one of the first to raise his hand. He asked the general his opinion of the media and, in particular, CNN correspondent Peter Arnett. Gen. Glosson paused for a moment, then began: "Let me start by saying it would be wrong to speak against one of the things the United States stands for—that is, free speech. I think the media handled itself as well as can be expected under extreme circumstances. Some members of the press were upset with us because we limited their access to information. But in almost every one of those cases, allowing media access might very well have endangered the lives of not just Americans, but other coalition members as well. As for my feelings on Peter Arnett? I realize he is highly respected in his field, but as far as I am concerned, the man was duped. The CIA approached him halfway through the war and told him the Iraqi military was operating a high-level communication network from the basement of the Al Rashid Hotel, which is where he and a few others from CNN were staying. The CIA wanted him out so we could bomb the place, but Mr. Arnett refused. He said he had been given a tour of the hotel and denied that there was such a facility. History will decide whether or not he was a good reporter. As for me, I have no respect for the man."

"How close did we come to killing Saddam Hussein, sir?" I asked.

"We tried to get him, and we were almost successful on two occasions. A few weeks ago, we received intelligence information that Saddam was in a particular building near downtown Baghdad. We sent a pair of F-117s in to bomb the facility. Unfortunately, one of the fighters had a malfunction with its bomb-bay doors and couldn't drop. The other jet hit the building but didn't destroy it. Saddam was shaken up a little, but his injuries were minor. The other incident occurred when Saddam was in Kuwait visiting his troops. His convoy was on its way back to Baghdad when an F-16, either from the 421st or from Shaw, fired a Maverick missile that took out one of the vehicles. Twelve of his bodyguards were reportedly killed, but Saddam escaped unscathed."

"What about the Iraqi air force, sir?" Lt. Col. Scott asked.

"They never had a chance. We used to eavesdrop on them electronically—don't ask me how. I knew exactly when they were starting their engines and turning on their radars. When they started running to Iran, we moved our F-15 caps farther to the north. I'd send the Eagles in when it looked like someone was going to take off. On one occasion, I heard the pilots call for taxi. By the time they were in position to take off, the F-15s were circling overhead. The Eagles shot down two of the jets as they were bringing their gear up. After that," Glosson laughed, "I heard the others call back and say they were having problems with their engines, and they were taxiing back in. The Iraqi pilots finally got smart and started taking off without saying anything on the radios or turning on their radars. They flew low in full afterburner until reaching Iranian territory."

"What about the so-called 'baby-milk factory' and the civilian bunker that was destroyed?" another pilot asked.

"The baby-milk factory was a biological weapons plant," Glosson replied without hesitation. "There were a number of chemical and biological weapons plants that were targeted for destruction, and that specific facility was one of them. Some of the chemical and biological agents have to be refrigerated. Infrared satellite imagery made facility identification easy. It's also important to point out that a few of our coalition partners helped build these facilities. We knew a lot more than the Iraqis thought we did. As far as the shelter is concerned, we watched that place for three straight days. We watched high-level Iraqi officials enter and exit the building, and we also intercepted numerous messages that emanated from the facility. The facility was a command-and-control center during the day. At night, it was used as a shelter for the Iraqi officials and their families. We bombed it in the middle of the night because we thought it was empty. Had I known there were civilians in the building, I would have never ordered the attack."

The briefing lasted for more than an hour, and I could tell that Gen. Glosson was extremely tired. The fire and enthusiasm evident during our first meeting in January was missing, and the dark circles under his eyes betrayed long hours. Everyone made it a point to shake hands with the general before he left for Al Dhafra to meet with the F-16 pilots of the 363rd TFW.

3 MARCH 1991

Shortly before noon, at the abandoned Safwan airfield in southern Iraq, Gen. H. Norman Schwarzkopf and Lt. Gen. Prince Khalid Bin Sultan al-Saud, commander of Saudi Arabia's air-defense forces, met with Lt. Gen. Sultan Hashim Ahmad, Iraq's deputy chief of staff of the Ministry of Defense, and Lt. Gen. Salah Abud Mahmud, commander of Iraq's III Corps. The Iraqi generals agreed to an immediate exchange of all prisoners of war, and agreed to help locate their mines and booby traps in Kuwait and the Persian Gulf. A few hours after the meeting ended, the U.N. Security Council received a letter from the Iraqi government announcing acceptance of Resolution 686, which required Baghdad to return all POWs and Kuwaiti hostages, to stop hostile or provocative acts, formally to rescind its annexation of Kuwait, to pay war reparations, and to disclose the location of its mines and booby traps, among other conditions.

Later in the afternoon, Lt. Col. Nall approached Skippy and me and asked if we'd like to go home in the next couple of days. "Some of the pilots who flew jets over on the initial deployment are going to have to take transports home," Damien said. "We've got more pilots than jets, and some of the guys have never had an ocean crossing before. The squadron may be here a few more weeks, but Col. Navarro has given approval to send six pilots home as soon as they're ready to leave."

Jabba, Batman, Raj, and Norge were also asked, and the six of us quickly accepted Damien's offer. Part of me wanted to stay and return with the rest of the unit, but I missed Colette and the girls. Over dinner at the club, the six of us mapped out a strategy for getting home. Six pilots in the 4th were also given permission to leave, and we found out they'd already had their orders cut. According to Ark, they were already packed, and planned to catch a C-130 flight to Dhahran the next morning. We would need at least a day to pack and outprocess, so Jabba suggested we leave on Tuesday, 5 March.

Col. Jaszczak came by the beer tent later in the evening and congratulated each of us.

"Make sure you have 'aircrew members' typed on your orders," Cash said. "There's going to be a lot of people trying to get home, and if your orders are done right, you can bypass most of the ground troops and sit up front with the pilots that fly you home. I want you to wear your flight suits all the way home, too—even in civilian airports. You guys are heroes, and I want all the people back home to recognize you."

"Thanks for the advice, sir," Raj said. "We wish you were going back to Hill with us."

Each of us shook hands with Col. Jaszczak, and we thanked him for his leadership as vice commander. We'd been disappointed in the lack of leadership from Col. Navarro since we arrived on base six months before. He hadn't said a word to anyone since the cease-fire was announced, and he avoided the 421st throughout the entire war.

When I woke up the next morning, I called Colette to tell her the news. By the end of the day, the six of us were packed and ready to go. We met at the club for one more plate of "bones and rice," and then we headed over to the beer tent to tell our friends goodbye. I hit the sack around midnight and woke up the following morning at 07:00. After a quick shower, I threw on a clean flight suit and carried my things over to the club for breakfast. As we passed by the port-a-cabins, I looked at the place I'd called home the past few months. I was already beginning to sense the loss of camaraderie. In the coming weeks, some of us would transfer to other bases, and a few would even leave the air force. I sensed I might never fly with these guys again, and I knew I would miss that.

As we walked toward the C-130, Col. Jaszczak drove up.

"I wanted to come out and see you guys off. I want you to know it was an honor to fly with you, and I'm very proud to have served with you here. You've sacrificed more than your country could ever ask, and I hope you receive a hero's welcome."

Col. Jaszczak was the only commander who came out to see us.

A few minutes after we strapped in, the back door closed and the engines began to spool up. As we taxied toward the runway, I looked out a tiny window and gazed at the flightline. I'll never forget the shock when I opened my canopy that hot, humid first day.

We finally began our takeoff roll, and I made it a point to hack my watch so I could see how long it would take us to get home. The C-130 is no F-16, so it took a couple of hours to reach Doha, Qatar, our first stop. The aircraft parked on the main ramp in front of a dozen F-16s of the 401st TFW, Torrejon AB, Spain. We had flown a few missions with the unit during the beginning of the war, and we were now anxious to meet some of the guys.

Our C-130 arrived in Dhahran shortly after noon. We took our bags over to the main hangar so we could check in and get our names on a flight manifest. It didn't look good. There had to be at least five hundred soldiers from the U.S. Army camped out in the giant hangar adjacent to the flightline, where an air force C-5 Galaxy was parked alongside a Federal Express 747. They wanted to go home as bad as we did. Once we got settled, Raj and I walked over and asked how long it would take to catch a hop back to the States. The air force sergeant keeping track of the manifests replied, "That could take anywhere from two to twenty-four hours. These guys have been here since early this morning, sir," he said. "You might as well relax and make yourselves comfortable."

"We're aircrew members, sergeant, and we have that on our orders," I replied. "That should allow us to ride up front with other flight-crew members, shouldn't it?"

"That's correct, sir. But it's up to the aircraft commander whether you can come."

"Are any of these aircraft scheduled to depart this afternoon?"

"We've got aircraft coming and going all day long. I suggest you find the pilots and ask them, or wait out front when the planes come in."

"Thanks a lot, sergeant," Raj answered.

Raj and I walked back to let the others know what was going on. All we had to do was find an aircraft heading back to the States. I decided to take a walk out to the flightline to check things out. Norge joined me, and the two of us climbed on board the Fed Ex 747 and made our way up to the flight deck. The ship's captain was sitting in the cockpit. After we introduced ourselves, I told him there were six of us trying to catch a hop back to the states.

"I'd love to take you guys, but we're only allowed to take cargo. I'm sorry."

After a quick tour of the cockpit, Norge and I moved next door to the C-5. We climbed inside the mammoth jet, and the first person we ran into was the loadmaster. I asked if we could catch a ride home, but he said they had just arrived from the U.S. an hour before, and they'd be making a few stops around the Middle East before heading home later in the week. Disappointed, we were not about to give up. More aircraft would be coming in, so we decided to go back to the hangar to have lunch. The six of us spent the next several hours in the hangar, waiting impatiently for the transports to arrive. When an aircraft would taxi in, I was the first one on the flightline to greet the crew members. Unfortunately, every pilot I talked to was either continuing on to another base in theater or had a full load. Finally, around 16:30, another C-5 Galaxy pulled up in front of the hangar. Before the pilot had a chance to shut down his engines, I was standing near the front of the jet. Shortly after the enormous engines unwound, the front door opened and the aircraft commander stepped down off the ladder.

"How's it going today, sir?" I asked.

"Doin' great. What's up?"

"Are you going back to the United States today?"

"We're gonna be here for a couple of hours, and then we're leaving for Torrejon AB in Spain. After we refuel and load up some more cargo, we'll continue on to Dover AFB."

"Can you fit six extra pilots on board? We all have orders with 'aircrew members' typed on them."

"We've got plenty of room on the crew deck. Tell your friends to put their gear on board. We're going to get something to eat and we should be back in about an hour."

"Thanks a lot!" I shook the major's hand and ran back to the hangar. "We're going home, boys!"

As the sun began to set across the Saudi desert, the six of us settled in for the long trip home. The flight to Spain took approximately eight hours, and we passed the time playing cards and telling war stories to the C-5 crew. We tried to catch a few hours of sleep, hoping it would make the time go by faster, but most of us were too excited. We touched down around 02:00 in a driving rain, taxied to the ramp, and came to a stop in front of a large hangar. As soon as the pilot shut down the engines, we descended from the flight deck and climbed off the jet. It was a cold, windy night, and everyone ran to the hangar to avoid getting drenched. Once inside, we were greeted by a representative from the base. The young lieutenant said we could take showers or naps, and he pointed toward a dining hall that would serve us breakfast. Hundreds of cots were spread across the hangar floor. According to the lieutenant, Torrejon AB would be used as a staging area for troops returning home from the desert.

By 05:00, we were back on board, and thirty minutes later we took off for the United States. Skippy handed out no-go pills supplied by Doc McGunigal to help us sleep on the way home. I took my pill, grabbed a pillow and a blanket, then settled into my seat for the long flight home.

I wished I could fall asleep, but I would only nod off for a little while, wake up stiff and uncomfortable, switch positions, then doze off again. Awake, I thought about Colette, Candice, and Kristen, and tried to imagine what our reunion would be like. I'd dreamed about the day many times.

The sun rose over the Atlantic. The sky was clear, and, according to the INS, we would be touching down at Dover AFB within three hours. When the east coast finally appeared, everyone crowded into the cockpit to catch a glimpse. There it was, the United States of America. What a sight.

Once we were established on final approach, the landing gear came down. I watched from the cockpit jumpseat as the aircraft commander set the lumbering jet down on the runway. We thanked the crew for bringing us home, and, as soon as we came to a stop, we grabbed our gear and made our way downstairs. When the door opened, the base Public Affairs officer welcomed us home and escorted us to base operations.

"We notified the local media as soon as we learned you were coming," he told us. "News teams from ABC, CBS, and NBC are on their way from Philadelphia, and they're anxious to interview you. I'll show you where you can shower and get cleaned up, if you want. We're going to have a barbecue for you, and, later this afternoon, someone will drive you to Philadelphia International Airport so you can catch a flight back to Utah."

We walked across the street and took showers at the base gymnasium. Afterward, we walked back to base operations and met with members of the media, who treated us like celebrities. Photographers took our pictures, and everyone congratulated us on the victory over Iraq. Next, we feasted on burgers, hot dogs, baked beans, and potato salad.

The view along the way to the Philadelphia airport was magnificent. I never thought I would miss seeing trees and flowers, the sound of a horn honking, or children playing. When we arrived at the airport, the driver dropped us off in front of the American Airlines terminal. We still had our flight suits on, and it didn't take long for people to recognize that we'd been fighting in the Gulf. Applause greeted us as we walked by. Some made it a point to shake our hands. Women gave us hugs and parents introduced us to their children. We were embarrassed—but it sure felt good.

We arrived at the gate, and Jabba asked the agent if we could upgrade to first class.

"First class is already full," she said. "Don't worry, though. I'll put all of you together in the back."

Thirty minutes later, an American Airlines representative took us on board and introduced us to the flight crew. The pilots and flight attendants greeted us at the doorway and asked if they could have their picture taken with us. Afterward, we headed to the back of the aircraft and took our seats.

As we taxied toward the runway, the captain came on the public address system: "Ladies and gentlemen, American Airlines is pleased to announce we have six United States Air Force fighter pilots on board with us this afternoon. The pilots have been in the Persian Gulf for six months, and this is their first day back in the United States. On behalf of the entire flight crew, I want to say thank you and welcome home."

After the announcement, all of the passengers turned around and applauded. The six of us stood and waved while the cheers continued. As if that weren't enough, as soon as we leveled off and the captain turned off the seatbelt light, everyone on board walked to the back of the plane to shake our hands and personally welcome us home. We told a few war stories and posed for pictures. During the hoopla, Raj pulled out his Arab head-dress, and one of the flight attendants wore it while serving the passengers.

Before long, we taxied into the gate at Dallas/Ft. Worth International. Arriving in the terminal, we realized we had less than ten minutes to make our connection. When we arrived at the gate, the agent greeted us with a big smile: "I knew you guys were coming. We wouldn't think of leaving without you."

Thirty minutes later, we were on our way to Salt Lake City. I was not sure what to expect when we arrived. I was terribly nervous. Somehow, I knew Colette was probably feeling the same way.

The sun set as we crossed over the Rocky Mountains. Forty-five minutes later, we began to descend. As we passed over the Wasatch mountains, I could see the lights of Salt Lake City in the distance. Batman's face was glued to the window in front of me, and I asked him if he was as nervous as I was. His wife gave birth back in December, and this would be the first time he saw his newborn child. The passengers around us seemed just as excited as we were. Most of the women were crying, and everyone wanted to know if our families would be there to greet us.

A few minutes after the captain shut down the engines, an American Airlines representative came on the address system and asked us to remain on board the aircraft: "We have about two hundred people in the concourse, and the local news wants to capture the reunion on film."

After the other passengers deplaned, the flight attendants gave each of us a hug. The agent was standing in the jetway, and told us they were ready for us to come out. We said goodbye to the pilots and began to make our way toward the concourse. I was so nervous, I could barely walk. As we approached the end of the jetway, bright lights appeared.

"Oh, man," Jabba muttered. "There's gonna be a bunch of cameras up there."

Batman and Norge were ten feet in front of us. As they entered the concourse, every-one started to scream. I followed the two of them out. Seconds later, I spotted Colette running toward me. We embraced and the tears began to flow. We kissed and hugged, and then I reached down to pick up Candice and Kristen. The girls were so beautiful.

Our neighbors Dan and Sue Runyan were there, along with hundreds of others who came out from Hill AFB to welcome us home. While I was holding Kristen, a reporter from one of the local stations walked up and asked me how my family looked to me.

"They're beautiful. Everyone's beautiful!"

"Is there anything you want to say to the people watching at home?"

"Thank you for supporting us, and everything you did the past six months."

"Anything else?"

I looked at Colette, Candice, and Kristen.

"It's great to be a family again."

AFTERTHOUGHTS

I completed my last flight in the F-16 Fighting Falcon on 28 February 1991—the last night of the war. Shortly after I returned to the United States, I decided to leave the air force. I had accomplished everything I wanted as a fighter pilot, and the fact that I had spent twenty-one of the past twenty-four months away from my family convinced me that it was time to move in a new direction. Leaving the air force was difficult, and at times I've regretted it. Nothing will ever replace the camaraderie of a fighter squadron or the exhilaration of flying the F-16. I miss the challenge of flying upside-down in the middle of the night, a few hundred feet above the ground at 600 miles per hour. I miss nine-G turns, the thrill of shacking a target, and the never-ending pursuit of the perfect sortie.

When my friends and I touched down at Al Minhad Air Base on 29 August 1990, we thought we were ready for war. But when members of Congress proposed economic sanctions that might have lasted a year or more, our morale was crushed. None of us was ready for a protracted stay in the UAE desert. We wanted to fight or come home—period! In retrospect, it is clear that initiating sanctions and pursuing diplomacy was the correct course of action. President Bush needed time to assemble the international coalition, and our military needed time to reposition its forces in the Middle East.

While American troops prepared to deploy, a stopgap was needed to prevent Saddam Hussein's military from capturing the eastern province of Saudi Arabia. If Saddam had wanted his army to cross the border and advance south, American ground forces would have been hard pressed to stop them. Casualties would have been extremely high, and the Iraqi leader would have likely gained control of Saudi Arabia's strategic oil fields. As it turned out, airpower became the deterrent that kept Iraqi forces from advancing further. A few days after the invasion of Kuwait, Secretary of Defense Dick Cheney met with King Fahd and convinced the Saudi ruler to allow American forces into his kingdom. In the days that followed, the role of airpower began to take shape. Fighter units from Langley and Shaw air force bases departed for the Middle East, and the largest airlift in military history was under way. Over the next six months, Military Airlift Command (MAC) aircraft flew more than 15,000 strategic airlift missions, transporting more than 483,000 passengers and 521,000 tons of cargo. In addition to the C-5s and C-141s, 151 MAC C-130s provided tactical airlift within the Kuwait Theater of Operations. These aircraft flew approximately 47,000 sorties, delivering more than 209,000 troops and 300,000 tons of cargo.

The role of airlift was extremely important. Even more critical, though, was the performance of the tanker community. During the war, every F-16 sortie originating from Al Minhad AB required pre-strike refueling. In some cases, post-strike refueling was also necessary. Without the tankers, our wing and a number of others would have virtually been grounded. The fighters and bombers received most of the glory, but the contribution of the tanker community cannot be overlooked.

America's success in the air is also a tribute to the effort put forth by the men and women who worked on the ground. During Operation Desert Storm, the U.S.-led coalition flew approximately 110,000 sorties. Of that number, 4,052 were flown by the F-16s assigned to the 388th TFW. Only 71 sorties were aborted for maintenance reasons during the war, giving the wing an incredible sortie effectiveness rate of 98.2 percent. We demanded a great deal from our maintenance personnel and they came through for us with flying colors. I'm proud to say that of the thirty combat missions I flew, I never once had to abort a single jet.

Years have passed since the end of the Persian Gulf War, and a day doesn't go by that I'm not reminded of the experience. When I hear the commanding voice of James Earl Jones announce, "This is CNN," my mind immediately flashes back to the o'club lounge at Al Minhad. When I fly into Salt Lake City and pass over Hill AFB, I look down at the end of the runway and still see Colette waving. Looking back, I would have been extremely disappointed if our unit had been left behind during the initial deployment. On the other hand, the war stole a part of my life that can never be replaced, and left me with a burden of guilt that will remain in my heart forever. I felt compassion for the people of Kuwait and everything they went through. I also felt compassion for the people of Iraq. Many of them were innocent victims of Saddam Hussein's brutality, and I feel bad for any additional suffering that I personally may have caused them. Time has a wonderful way of healing wounds, and I hope I have an opportunity to visit with the people of Iraq some day, under circumstances different than my last visit.

During the past few years, many people have criticized President Bush and his administration for failing to remove Saddam Hussein from power. Some have even suggested that the war ended too soon. On 8 August 1990, when President Bush announced that troops were being deployed to Saudi Arabia, he looked the American people in the eye and said: "Four simple principles guide our policy: The immediate unconditional withdrawal of Iraqi forces from Kuwait, the restoration of Kuwait's legitimate government, the restoration of security and stability in the Persian Gulf region, and the protection of the lives of Americans abroad." President Bush reiterated these goals in the months preceding the war, and during the war itself. He assured the American people, our coalition partners, and, most importantly, the people of Iraq, that we had no intention of seizing Baghdad and installing a new government. On 27 February 1991, President Bush sat in the Oval Office with his advisers and asked each of them if these objectives had been achieved. Everyone in the room answered yes, and at that point, the decision was made to end the war.

During Operation Desert Storm, 148 Americans were killed in action and 467 more were wounded. In addition, forty-four Americans were listed as missing in action and nine were captured as prisoners of war. A total of 157 Americans were killed in non-combat related incidents, including 105 casualties during Operation Desert Shield. While any American death is unacceptable, it must be pointed out that casualties were extremely light compared to previous conflicts. If President Bush had ordered American forces into Baghdad, he would have contradicted everything he had said during the previous six months, the coalition would have come apart, and many more Americans would have been killed. If that had happened, the same people who now criticize President Bush for not going to Baghdad would instead be criticizing him for having lied to the American people.

Another issue that has gained a lot of attention during the past few years is Gulf War syndrome. To date, my health has not been affected, and, to my knowledge, everyone I flew with in the Gulf is also in good health. Al Minhad AB was 497 miles away from the southern tip of Kuwait, so we never worried about an Iraqi chemical attack. Were trace amounts of chemical agents released into the air? I believe they were, because allied pilots bombed the manufacturing facilities, as well as ammunition dumps that probably contained chemical weapons. Consideration should also be given to the large amount of toxic chemicals that were released into the air when Iraqi forces torched hundreds of Kuwaiti oil wells. Some scientists suggest that P-Bromide tablets—intended to combat chemical weapons—might have caused Gulf War syndrome. I won't speculate on this because, like most of the pilots at Al Minhad, I threw away my P-Bromide tablets. But regardless of what the cause might be, the United States should step forward and take care of the men and women who are suffering from Gulf War syndrome. These people gave America a reason to be proud of its military again. To quote President Bush, "Our commitment to them must be equal of their commitment to their country. They are truly America's finest."

ACKNOWLEDGMENTS

The inspiration for this book began, appropriately, in the cockpit. I left the air force a few months after returning from the Gulf, and began a flying career with Delta Air Lines. In July 1992, I flew with Delta Captain Tim Eby, and over the course of the month, we spoke at length about our past military experiences. Tim was an OV-10 FAC during the Vietnam War, and he suggested I write a book chronicling my six-month deployment to the Middle East. I have to admit I was hesitant at first. I was trying to put the war behind me, and the last thing I wanted to do was relive the experience. Tim was persistent, though, and he convinced me that writing would heal the emotional scars I'd received. Looking back, I think he was right.

Once I decided to write, I knew it would be necessary to include a historical perspective of the Middle East—most importantly, Iraq and Kuwait. The region has been a cauldron of instability for centuries, and I knew very little about it while I was stationed in the Gulf. During my research, I was introduced to Dr. Steven Yetiv, one of the U.S.'s leading authorities on the Middle East. Steven understood what I was trying to achieve, and offered expert advice throughout the writing. His contribution to the book is deeply appreciated.

I am also indebted to Jay Miller, a man who knows more about aviation than anyone I have ever met. Jay, an accomplished writer in his own right, has been my mentor and adviser for the past three years. Despite a hectic schedule, he always takes the time to answer my questions or point me toward someone who can. Without his guidance and encouragement, I would have probably given up on this project shortly after I started. Another person I'd like to thank is Eric Hehs, managing editor of Lockheed Martin's *Code One* magazine. Jay introduced me to Eric while I was researching the history of the F-16. Eric helped me obtain the information I needed, and was more than willing to read the manuscript. He sometimes told me things I didn't want to hear, but his writing experience and editorial advice proved invaluable.

My sincerest appreciation goes to my editor, Alan Axelrod. Over the years, I've learned that to be successful—both in publishing and in life—you have to navigate your way through minefields of individuals who don't believe in you, and who think your ideas will never work. Alan Axelrod believed in this project from the outset, and I'm deeply thankful for the opportunity he gave me.

This is a book about flying, and I would be remiss if I didn't recognize the individuals who taught me the art. Drew Riolo was an early role model who instructed me on the fundamentals of flight. He convinced me that I should join the United States Air Force, and it was the best advice I have ever been given. My T-37 instructor pilot, Jerry Corbett, and my T-38 instructor pilot, David Cohn, were selfless individuals who always demanded perfection. Two of the best, Jerry and David helped lay the foundation for my flying career. Without them, I would never have realized my full potential.

During Operation Desert Storm, Carlos "Jackal" Nejaime and I were paired together for nearly half of our combat missions. He was always there for me, both as a pilot and a friend. Mark "Skippy" Lankford and Dion "Skull" Thorpe, two of the best "Viper drivers" in the world, read the manuscript in whole or in part and verified my explanations of F-16 weapons, systems, and tactics. Others that deserve recognition include Tim "Doc" Hursh, Mark "Stitch" Miller, Mike "Grumpy" Daniels, Randy "Roebuck" Siers, Mike "Cookie" Cook, and Marc "Stal" Stalnaker. Their contributions helped immensely and I will always be grateful.

It would be impossible to acknowledge every individual I flew with over the years. Instead, I salute the following groups: The instructors and students stationed at Reese AFB from April 1983 to February 1988; my instructors and classmates in the 433rd TFTS at Holloman AFB during March and April 1988; my instructors and classmates in the 310th TFTS at Luke AFB from May 1988 to January 1989; and the "Juvats" with whom I served in the 80th TFS at Kunsan AB, Republic of Korea, from February 1989 to February 1990. Whether you were a general or a young lieutenant, I want you to know that I learned something every time we flew together.

Finally, and most important of all, I would like to recognize the pilots I served with at Al Minhad Air Base in the United Arab Emirates from August 1990 to March 1991. To the Black Widows, Fightin' Fuujins, and Werewolves, never forget what we accomplished together. Though years have passed, look with pride upon each other, for there was a time when we were the best fighter pilots in the world. And no one can ever take that away from us.

GLOSSARY

A/A: Air to Air
A/G: Air to Ground
A/I: Air Intercept
A/S: Air to Surface
AAA: Antiaircraft Artillery
ABCCC: Airborne Battlefield Command and Control Center
Abort: Directive to cease action, attack, event, or mission.
AB: Air Base
ACM: Air Combat Mode
Action: Directive to initiate a briefed attack sequence or maneuver.
ADI: Attitude Director Indicator
AFB: Air Force Base
AFOQT: Air Force Officer Qualifying Test
AFOTEC: Air Force Operational Test and Evaluation Command
AGL: Above Ground Level
ALOW: Automatic Low Altitude Warning
Angels: Height of friendly aircraft in thousands of feet.
ANG: Air National Guard
APC: Armored Personnel Carrier
ARCP (Air Refueling Control Point): The planned geographic point over which the receiver(s) arrive in the observation or pre-contact position, with respect to the assigned tanker.
ARCT (Air Refueling Control Time): The planned time that the receiver and tanker will arrive over the ARCP.
AREFS: Air Refueling Squadron
ARIP (Air Refueling Initial Point): The planned point to enter the refueling track.
Arm/Armed (Safe/Hot): Select armament (safe/hot) or armament is safe/hot.
ASAP: As Soon As Possible
As Fragged: Fighter, FAC, mission package, or agency will be performing exactly as stated by the air tasking order.
ASOC: Air Support Operations Center
Aspect: Request or comment regarding target aspect information.
ATO (Air Tasking Order [Frag]): Assigns A/A and A/S targets, TOTs, and mission support information.
Attack/Attacking: Indicates A/S attack on a specific ground target.

311

ATWATS: Academic Training for Weapons and Tactics

Authenticate: To request or provide a response for a coded challenge.

AWACS: Airborne Warning and Control System

Bandit (Radar/Heat/Striker): A positively identified enemy aircraft (and type ordnance capability, if known). The term is a function of identification and does not necessarily imply direction or authority to engage.

Base (Number): Reference number used to indicate information (e.g., headings, altitudes, fuels).

BFM: Basic Fighter Maneuvers; training designed to apply aircraft handling skills to gain proficiency in recognizing and solving range, closure, aspect, angle off, and turning room problems in relation to another aircraft to either attain a position from which weapons may be employed, deny the adversary a position from which weapons may be launched, or defeat weapons employed by an adversary.

Bingo: Prebriefed fuel state which is needed for recovery using prebriefed parameters.

Bogey: A radar or visual contact whose identity is unknown.

Box: Groups, contacts, or formations in a square or offset square.

Break (Up/Down/Right/Left): Directive to perform an immediate maximum-performance turn in the indicated direction. Assumes a defensive situation.

BSGT or BORE: Boresight

Buddy Lock: Locked to a known friendly aircraft. Normally a response to a "spiked" or "buddy spiked" call and accompanied with "angels."

Buddy Spike (Position/Azimuth/Altitude): Receiving friendly A/I RWR.

CAP (Combat Air Patrol): Refers to either a specific phase of an A/A mission or the geographic location of the fighter's surveillance orbit during an A/A mission prior to committing against a threat.

CAS: Close Air Support

CBU: Cluster Bomb Unit

CCIP: Continuously Computed Impact Point

CCRP: Continuously Computed Release Point

CEM: Combined-Effects Munitions

CENTAF: Central Air Forces

CENTCOM: Central Command

Chaff: A passive form of electronic countermeasure used to deceive airborne or ground-based radar.

Check (Left to Right): Turn ( ) degrees left or right and maintain new heading.

Clean: No radar contacts on bandits, bogeys, or aircraft of interest. Also used to confirm a good battle-damage check (i.e., no A/S ordnance remaining on the wingman's aircraft).

Cleared Hot: Ordnance release is authorized.

Cleared: Requested action is authorized (no engaged or support roles are assumed).

Clock Position: Description of position using the aircraft as a reference: the nose is twelve o'clock; the tail is six o'clock.

COH: Cold On Hot

Come off (Left/Right/High/Low/Dry): A directive to maneuver as indicated to either regain mutual support or to deconflict flight paths for an exchange of engaged and supporting roles. Implies both "visual" and "tally" (A/A). Directive to maneuver or execute a specific instruction (A/G), (i.e., "Come off dry").

Contact: Radar/IR contact at the stated position; should be in bearing, range, altitude (BRA), bullseye, or geographic position format.

DBS: Doppler Beam Sharpening

Deploy: Directive for the flight to maneuver to briefed positioning.

DGFT: Dogfight

DISC: Disconnect

Divert: Proceed to alternate mission or base.

DME: Distance Measuring Equipment

DMS: Display Management Switch

DO: Director of Operations

DTC: Data Transfer Cartridge

ECCM: Electronic Counter Countermeasures

ECM: Electronic Countermeasures

Element: A flight of two aircraft.

Engaged: Maneuvering with the intent of achieving a kill. If no additional information is provided (bearing, range, etc.), engaged implies visual/radar acquisition of target.

ENJJPT: Euro-NATO Joint Jet Pilot Training

EPU: Emergency Power Unit

ETA: Estimated Time of Arrival

EXP: Expand

FAC: Forward Air Controller

FAIP: First Assignment Instructor Pilot

FCC: Fire Control Computer

FEBA (Forward Edge of the Battle Area): The foremost limits of an area where ground combat units are deployed. Designated to coordinate fire support, position forces or maneuver of units.

Feet Wet/Dry: Flying over water/land.

Fence Check: Set cockpit switches as appropriate prior to combat area.

Fence: Boundary separating hostile and friendly area.

Flares: Flares have been detected or directive to deploy flares.

FLIR: Forward Looking Infrared Radar

FOD: Foreign Object Damage

Fox Two: Simulated or actual launch of IR-guided missile.

Frag: Fragmentary Order (ATO). Fragmentation pattern of a weapon.

Fratricide: Destruction of friendly forces when destruction of enemy forces is intended.

Friendly: A positively identified friendly aircraft. Amplifying data should be used if known (e.g., friendly helicopter).

Furball: A turning fight involving multiple aircraft.

GLO: Ground Liaison Officer

GMTT: Ground Moving Target Track

GMT: Ground Moving Target

Go Active: Go to briefed Have Quick net.

Go Secure: Activate secure voice communications.

GPS: Global Positioning System

HARM: High Speed Antiradiation Missile

Have Quick: A UHF jam-resistant radio.

HOB: Height of Burst

HOC: Hot On Cold

Hostile: Operational command ROE definition of an enemy aircraft or action.

HUD: Head-Up Display

IFF: Identification, Friend or Foe

In Place (Left, Right): Perform indicated maneuver simultaneously.

INS: Inertial Navigation System

Intercept: A phase of an A/A mission between the commit and engagement.

IP: Initial Point or Instructor Pilot

IR: Infrared

J-STARS: Joint Surveillance Target Attack Radar System

Jink: Unpredictable aircraft maneuvers to negate a gun-tracking solution.

Joker: Fuel state above Bingo at which separation/bugout/event termination should begin.

Killer Scout: Aircraft that locates and controls attack of targets in a specific operating area. Usually performed beyond the fire-support coordination line and not operating in the FAC-A role.

Kill: A destroyed target. Directive to commit on target with clearance to fire. In training, a fighter call to indicate kill criteria have been fulfilled.

KTO: Kuwait Theater of Operations

LANTIRN: Low-Altitude Navigation and Targeting Infrared for Night

LDGP: Low-Drag General Purpose

Lead/Trail: Tactical formation of two aircraft or groups separated in range or following one another.

LFE: Large Force Employment

LGB: Laser Guided Bomb

LIFT: Lead-In Fighter Training

Line Abreast: Two groups, contacts, formations, or aircraft side by side.

MAC: Military Airlift Command

Magnum: Launch of AGM-88 HARM.

MEA: Minimum En-route Altitude

MFD: Multifunction Display

MIA: Missing In Action

Mickey: Have Quick time-of-day (TOD) signal.

MOA: Military Operating Area

MPC: Mission Planning Cell

MRE: Meal Ready to Eat

MSIP: Multinational Staged Improvement Program

MSS: Mission Support System

MUD (Direction-Type): Indicates unknown RWR ground threat displayed; followed normally by clock position/azimuth.

Mutual Support: The coordinated efforts of two or more aircraft to provide combined firepower and survivability.

MWR: Morale Welfare and Recreation

NATO: North Atlantic Treaty Organization

NFOV: Narrow Field-Of-View

No Joy: Aircrew does not have visual contact with the target/bandit/landmark; opposite of term "tally."

NORM: Normal

Off (Direction): Informative call indicating attack is terminated and maneuvering to the indicated direction.

OPEC: Organization of Petroleum Exporting Countries

Ops Check: Periodic check of aircraft systems performed by the aircrew (including fuel) for safety of flight.

OSD: Office of the Secretary of Defense

PACAF: Pacific Air Forces

Play Time: Amount of time aircraft can remain on station.

POL: Petroleum Oil Lubricant

Pop: Starting climb for A/S attack.

Posit: Request for position; response normally in terms of a geographic landmark or off a common reference point.

POW: Prisoner Of War

PRE: Preplanned

PRI: Primary

RAF: Royal Air Force

RFP: Request For Proposals

ROE: Rules Of Engagement

Roger: Indicates aircrew understands the radio transmission; does not indicate compliance or reaction.

ROTC: Reserve Officer Training Corps

RTU: Replacement Training Unit

RWR: Radar Warning Receiver

Saddled: Informative call from wingman or element indicating the return to briefed formation position.

SAM: Surface-to-Air Missile

SAM (Direction): Visual acquisition of a SAM or SAM launch, should include position.

SAR: Search And Rescue

SCP: Set Clearance Plane

SEAD: Suppression of Enemy Air Defenses

SEC: Secondary

Separate: Leaving a specific engagement; may or may not reenter.

SMS: Stores Management System

SOF: Supervisor Of Flying

SOI: Sensor Of Interest

Spike: RWR indication of an A/I threat in track, launch, or unknown mode. Include bearing/clock position/azimuth and threat type if able.

SPINS: Special Instructions

Squawk ( ): Operate IFF as indicated or IFF is operating as indicated.

Status: Request for an individual's tactical situation or position.

STBY: Standby

TACAN: Tactical Air Navigation

TAC: Tactical Air Command

Tally: Sighting of a target, bandit, or enemy position; opposite of "no joy."

TD: Target Designator

TEL: Transporter Erector Launcher

TER: Triple Ejector Rack

TES: Test and Evaluation Squadron

TFR: Terrain Following Radar

TFS: Tactical Fighter Squadron

TFTS: Tactical Fighter Training Squadron

TFTW: Tactical Fighter Training Wing

TFW: Tactical Fighter Wing

TF: Terrain Following

Tied: Positive radar contact with element or aircraft.

TLAM: Tomahawk Land Attack Missile

TMS: Target Management System

TOD: Time Of Day

TOT: Time Over Target

UAE: United Arab Emirates

UHF: Ultra High Frequency

Uniform: UHF/AM radio.

UN: United Nations

UPT: Undergraduate Pilot Training

USAFE: United States Air Forces in Europe

USAF: United States Air Force

VHF: Very High Frequency

Victor: VHF/AM radio.

Visual: Sighting friendly aircraft or ground position; opposite of "blind."

VIS: Visual

VTR: Video Tape Recorder

WFOV: Wide Field-Of-View

WPN: Weapon

WX: Weather

SOURCES

1. *U.S. News and World Report:* 15 January 1979, "Iran: Carter's Biggest Crisis."

2. *U.S. News and World Report:* 29 January 1979, "Iran's Crisis: No End to Turmoil in Sight."

3. *U.S. News and World Report:* 12 February 1979, "With Khomeini's Return, Crisis Deepens in Iran."

4. *U.S. News and World Report:* 19 February 1979, "Iran: On Road to Civil War."

5. *U.S. News and World Report:* 12 March 1979, "How Far Will U.S. Go To Protect Mideast Oil?" and "Saudis No Longer Have Confidence in U.S."

6. *U.S. News and World Report:* 3 August 1987, "Coping with Khomeini" and "Kuwait Rolls the Dice for High Stakes."

7. *U.S. News and World Report:* 13 August 1990, "The Man Who Would Be King" and "The New Order of Things."

8. *U.S. News and World Report:* 20 August 1990, "The Guns of August."

9. *Newsweek:* 13 August 1990, "Baghdad's Bully"; "The Anchor and Hope of the Weak and Meek"; "Requiem for an Oil Kingdom"; and "And Now: The War of the Future."

10. *Newsweek:* 3 September 1990, "Special Report."

11. *Newsweek:* 3 September 1990, "What To Expect in a War."

12. *Newsweek:* 3 September 1990, "Advice from a Desert Warrior."

13. *Newsweek:* 1 October 1990, "The Price of Success"; "For the Air Force, It's the Big One"; and "The Search for Scapegoats."

14. *Newsweek:* 8 October 1990, "Inside Iraq" and "Talking Peace and Moving Toward War."

15. *Time:* 6 August 1990, "The Crude Enforcer."

16. *Time:* 13 August 1990, "Iraq's Power Grab"; "Can the U.S. Turn Off Iraq's Oil?" and "Master of His Universe."

17. *Time:* 20 August 1990, "Read My Ships"; "The World Closes In"; and "Planes Against Brawn."

18. *Time:* 3 September 1990, "In the Heat of the Desert"; "The Center Holds—For Now"; "Sitzkrieg in the Sand"; "Gathering Storm"; "A New Test of Resolve"; "Where Shadows Are Dark"; and "What Price Glory?"

19. *Time:* 10 September 1990, "Pausing at the Rim of the Abyss."

20. *Time:* 17 September 1990, "A New World."

21. *Time*: 24 September 1990, "Call to Arms."

22. *Army News* service: September 1990, "Arabs Sensitive About Customs."

23. *The Washington Post*: 10–16 September 1990, "How Lines in the Sand in 1922 Sketched the Invasion of 1990." Glenn Frankel.

24. *U.S. Air Force Fact Sheet*: August 1992, "388th Fighter Wing"; 388th Public Affairs Division, 388th Fighter Wing, Hill AFB, UT; SSGT Byron Beers, 388th FW Historian.

25. *U.S. Air Force Fact Sheet*: August 1992, "4th Fighter Wing"; 388th Public Affairs Division, 388th Fighter Wing, Hill AFB, UT; SSGT Byron Beers, 388th FW Historian.

26. *U.S. Air Force Fact Sheet*: August 1992, "421st Fighter Wing"; 388th Public Affairs Division, 388th Fighter Wing, Hill AFB, UT; SSGT Byron Beers, 388th FW Historian.

27. *U.S. Air Force Fact Sheet*: October 1994, "Hill Air Force Base"; Ogden Air Logistics Center, Hill AFB, UT; Donald W. Klinko, Ogden Air Logistics Center Historian.

28. *Brotherhood of Arms*: 1985, Times Books, Jacob Goodwin.

29. *The Pentagon Paradox*: 1993, Naval Institute Press, James P. Stevenson.

30. "Report on the F-14 and F-15 Tactical Fighters." Washington, D.C.: Members of Congress for Peace Through Law.

31. *The History of the U.S. Air Force*: 1984, Bison Books Corp., Bill Yenne.

32. *The Vietnam Experience: Thunder from Above*: 1984, Boston Publishing Company, John Morrocco.

33. *Fighter Wing*: 1995, Berkley Books, Tom Clancy.

34. *The Gulf War Reader: History, Documents, Opinions*: 1991, Times Books—Random House, "Give Sanctions A Chance" (Testimony Before the Senate Armed Services Committee, 28 November 1990) Admiral William J. Crowe, Jr.

35. *The Gulf War Reader: History, Documents, Opinions*: 1991, Times Books—Random House, "How To Cut Iraq Down To Size" (Testimony Before the Senate Armed Services Committee, 28 November 1990) Henry A. Kissinger.

36. *The Gulf War Reader: History, Documents, Opinions*: 1991, Times Books—Random House, "In Defense Of Saudi Arabia" (Speech of 8 August 1990) President George Bush.

37. *Pine Bluff Chemical Activity Fact Sheet*. Distributed by Pine Bluff Arsenal, Pine Bluff, Arkansas 71602-9500. Sheets provided by Brig. Gen. David A. Nydam (U.S. Army Ret.).

38. *Los Angeles Times*: A Times Mirror Newspaper, 16 January 1991–28 February 1991.

39. *The Gulf News*: Al Nisr Publishing; United Arab Emirates, September 1990–February 1991.

40. *Khaleej Times*: United Arab Emirates, September 1990–February 1991.

AAA, *see* Antiaircraft artillery
Abu Dhabi, 66
Accidents while training, fatal,
    98, 140–44, 153
Acree, Lt. Col. Clifford M., 193
Adam, Capt. Robin "Batman,"
    85, 117, 131–34
    Operation Desert Storm and,
    160
    returns home, 301–305
Adams, Capt. Mark "Stinger,"
    121–22, 141
    Operation Desert Storm and,
    218, 257
Adams, Lt. Col. Terry "Zappo,"
    43
    Operation Desert Storm and,
    166–68, 171, 173
"Aerial Attack Study," 14
Afghanistan, 8
Ahmad, Lt. Gen. Sultan
    Hashim, 300
Ahmed Al Jaber AB, Kuwait, 152
Aipoalani, Capt. Dundy "Skids,"
    151
Airborne Warning and Control
    System (AWACS), *see* AWACS
    (Airborne Warning and
    Control System)
Air Force Officer Qualifying Test
    (AFOQT), 74
Al Dhafra Air Base, 66
Ali Al Salim AB, Kuwait, 152, 278
Al Kharj AB, 212
Al Minhad AB, United Arab
    Emirates, 36, 44
    flight to, 45–56
    Operation Desert Storm and,
    151–300
    preparation for war with Iraq,
    57–72, 83–90, 96–157
Al Rashid Hotel, 299
Al Wafrah oil field, 197
Amoebic dysentery, 64, 72, 83, 85
Antiaircraft artillery, 5, 91, 100,
    110, 200
    encountered by coalition pilots,
    163, 179, 182, 188, 203,
    207–208, 218, 228, 240, 248,
    249, 254, 263, 268–69
Arab culture, understanding, 59
Arab League, 10, 32

Arkell, Capt. Jeff "Ark," 13, 60, 69,
    86, 113, 114, 118, 138, 142,
    228
    Operation Desert Storm and,
    160, 195
Arlington National Cemetery,
    viii
Arnett, Peter, 163–64, 188, 200,
    231, 299
Ashley, Capt. Ron, 76–77
Associated Press, 135
Atisme, Sgt. Elizabeth, 169
AWACS (Airborne Warning and
    Control System), 9, 97, 116,
    123, 136, 152, 173, 175, 184,
    192, 197, 203, 212, 226, 227,
    229, 234, 235, 239–42, 245, 249,
    258, 259, 264, 265–66, 269, 274,
    276, 277, 282, 285, 287–88, 291,
    292
Aziz, Tariq, 11, 94, 118, 121, 135,
    138, 140, 145–46, 148, 154, 255,
    258

Baath Party, Iraq, 9, 26
Bahrain, 63, 95
Baker, James, 27, 28, 95, 110, 118,
    121, 126, 135, 138, 140, 145,
    146, 148, 258
Bakr, Maj. Gen. Ahmad Hasan
    al-, 26
Bartels, Lt. Brad "Martyr," 119,
    178
Basheerud-Deen, SSgt. Hakeem,
    215, 217
Belgium, 16, 17, 19
Bender, Maj. Glenn "Ahkbar,"
    138
Beste, Sgt. Craig, 122
Bild, 253
Biological weapons, *see* Chemical
    and biological weapons and
    warfare
Bird, Capt. Hal H., 195
Bishop, Capt. Brian "Lassie," 42
Blitzer, Wolf, 164, 255
Blood chit, 169
Boeing Corporation, 15
Bopp, Capt. Tim "Bopper," 1–4,
    137, 195
Boyd, John, 14–15
Bridgeton (tanker), 9

Britain:
    history of Middle East and, 25,
    26
    Persian Gulf War and, 27, 204
Britton, Lt. Col. Delford, 75
Brockington, Capt. Lex "Pappy,"
    216
Brown, SSgt. Rich, 190, 244, 272
Bubiyan island, 10, 11, 94
Bush, George, 26, 144
    building of international coali-
    tion, 65, 95, 109, 112, 306
    negotiations to avoid war and,
    94, 118, 138, 145, 146, 148
    text of letter to Saddam
    Hussein, 156–57
    Operation Desert Storm and,
    193
    end of, 296, 307
    ground war, 237, 265
    Israeli restraint, 189
    Soviet peace initiative,
    252–54, 258, 264
    speeches, 162, 213–14, 270,
    296
    tributes to the troops, 209,
    308
    response to Iraqi aggression,
    26–29, 32, 33, 35, 94
    troop buildup in the Gulf and,
    112

Call signs, fighter pilots', 158
CCIP, *see* Continuously comput-
    ed impact point (CCIP)
CENTAF (CENTCOM's air
    force component), 113, 114,
    189, 199, 212, 214, 222–23, 233,
    246, 257, 284, 289
CENTCOM, 84, 90, 120, 122, 130,
    219, 275
    messages to the troops, 163
Central Intelligence Agency
    (CIA), 299
Chambers, Lt. Col. John, 81
Chemical and biological
    weapons and warfare, 67,
    167–68, 271, 297, 300, 308
    preparation for, 46, 67–68, 213
    production facilities, bombing
    of, 152, 188, 199, 200, 215, 270

319

About the Author

Captain Keith Rosenkranz was a top-rated flight instructor and, subsequently, Top Gun in F-16 fighter training. He served in South Korea and then flew 30 combat missions—the bulk of them at night—during the Gulf War. Rosenkranz scored ten Maverick missile kills on the infamous "Highway of Death." He was awarded four Air Medals and two Aerial Achievement Medals. He is currently a pilot for a major airline and lives with his family in Texas. His e-mail address is **ROSEYF16@IBM.NET**. For more information about the book, visit our web site at www.Vipersinthestorm.com.